Critical Psychophysical Passages in the Life of a Woman

A Psychodynamic Perspective

Critical Psychophysical Passages in the Life of a Woman

A Psychodynamic Perspective

EDITED BY

JOAN OFFERMAN-ZUCKERBERG

The Psychoanalytic Society of the Postdoctoral Program
  in Psychotherapy and Psychoanalysis
New York, New York
and Founding Board Member
Faculty and Supervisor
Brooklyn Institute for Psychotherapy
Brooklyn, New York

PLENUM MEDICAL BOOK COMPANY
NEW YORK AND LONDON

Library of Congress Cataloging in Publication Data

Critical psychophysical passages in the life of a woman: a psychodynamic perspective /
    edited by Joan Offerman-Zuckerberg.
        p.   cm.
    Includes bibliographical references and index.
    ISBN 0-306-42639-0
    1. Women—United States—Psychology. 2. Women—Health and hygiene—United
States. 3. Maturation (Psychology). I. Offerman-Zuckerberg, Joan.
HQ1206.C74   1988   88-12615
155.6'33—dc19

The quotation from Doris Lessing's *The Golden Notebook*, which appears on pages 71-72
of this volume, is reproduced by permission of Simon & Schuster, copyright 1962.

© 1988 Plenum Publishing Corporation
233 Spring Street, New York, N.Y. 10013

Plenum Medical Book Company is an imprint of Plenum Publishing Corporation

Printed in the United States of America

To Alice Korobow
Analyst
Colleague
Devoted friend

Contributors

Bonnie Robin Aronowitz • Ph.D. Clinical Psychology Candidate, Ferkauf Graduate School, Yeshiva University-Einstein College of Medicine, Bronx, New York; Neuropsychology Intern, Neurological Institute, Columbia Presbyterian Medical Center, New York City; Psychology Intern, Postgraduate Center for Mental Health, New York City; Psychologist in Training, New York City Police Department, New York City.

Naomi Berne, Ph.D. • Consulting Psychologist, Alcott Montessori School, Scarsdale, New York; Psychologist, Pleasantville Cottage School, Pleasantville, New York; private practice.

Roni O. Cohen, Ph.D. • Clinical Instructor of Psychology, Department of Psychiatry, Cornell Medical Center; Supervisor, Payne Whitney Clinic; Seminar Faculty, The Psychoanalytic Society of the Postdoctoral Program; private practice.

Mary Beth M. Cresci, Ph.D. • Faculty, Senior Supervisor, and Assistant Director of Training, The Psychoanalytic Institute, Postgraduate Center for Mental Health, New York City; Supervisor, National Institute for the Psychotherapies; Board Member, Faculty, Supervisor, Brooklyn Institute for Psychotherapy; private practice.

Leanne Domash, Ph.D. • Consulting Psychologist, Beth Israel Medical Center, New York City; Adjunct Assistant Professor of Psychiatry, Mount Sinai School of Medicine; private practice.

Alice Eichholz, Ph.D. • Associate Professor, Vermont College of Norwich University, Montpelier, Vermont; Contributing Editor to *Journal of Psychohistory*.

Ruth Formanek, Ph.D. • Professor of Education, Hofstra University, Hempstead, New York; Chief Psychologist, Jewish Community Services, Rego Park, Long Island; private practice.

Melinda Gellman, Ph.D. • Director, Division of Eating Disorders, Fifth Avenue Center for Counseling and Psychotherapy, New York City; private practice.

Susan Adler Kavaler, Ph.D. • Faculty and Supervisor, National Institute for the Psychotherapies, New York; Psychoanalytic Faculty, Postgraduate Center for Mental Health, Psychoanalytic Institute; Board of Directors and Supervisor, Brooklyn Institute for Psychotherapy; Senior Supervisor and Training Analyst, International School of Mental Health Practitioners.

David Kliot, M.D. • Clinical Associate Professor of Obstetrics and Gynecology at the State University of New York Health Science Center at Brooklyn; Attending at Obstetrics, Methodist Hospital; private practice.

Susan S. Lichtendorf • Medical Science Writer, Journalist, and Author; Member, National Association of Science Writers; Women in Communications.

Dale Mendell, Ph.D. • Faculty and Supervisor, The Psychoanalytic Institute, Postgraduate Center for Mental Health, New York City; Senior Supervisor, Training Analyst, and Faculty, Training Institute for Mental Health; Senior Supervisor, National Institute for the Psychotherapies; private practice.

Sue A. Shapiro, Ph.D. • Clinical Supervisor, New York University, Doctoral Program in Clinical Psychology; Clinical Instructor of Psychiatry, New York University Medical School; Faculty, Manhattan Institute for Psychoanalysis; private practice.

Joan Offerman-Zuckerberg, Ph.D. • Founding Board Member and Supervisor-Faculty, Brooklyn Institute for Psychotherapy, New York; Supervisor, National Institute for the Psychotherapies, Yeshiva University; private practice.

Preface

After the birth of my second son some 11 years ago, I was painfully torn by the timing of my reentry to work—my wish to return to a prestigious and stimulating position as chief psychologist of a large agency, or my equally powerful wish to enjoy fully my beautiful new son's infancy, undivided and untorn.

At the time I had a dream that my body was cut in half at the waist—my head leaned to the books neatly contained on the library shelves; my belly went to the crib, all sweet-smelling and soft. Not having had the opportunity to be "undivided" with my first son (now 17 years old), I chose to resign my agency position and stay home as long as I wished and then develop my private practice. It was a decision that at the time entailed much loss—cerebral, collegial, social, prestigious—and generated some self-doubt, but in retrospect it is not regretted and was perhaps wise. This son's infancy will always be remembered as a time in which I experienced mothering with ease and grace.

Ten years later, I dreamed again, this time of "breaking new waters." Having had a number of years to resolve a good part of the ambivalence regarding a possible third child (actually a wish for a daughter), I do not believe the dream signaled birth in the literal sense. Instead, what it means to me is the birth of a creative self—breaking new ground—perhaps the shaping and editing of a book.

Thank you to my husband Richard and sons Joshua and Benjamin, who as always "are" the very stuff of my dreams—the flesh-and-blood embodiments of my deepest wishes.

JOAN OFFERMAN-ZUCKERBERG

Contents

Introduction

JOAN OFFERMAN-ZUCKERBERG

This book is intended to make a beginning in carving out some critical passages in a woman's life—passages that involve both body and psyche. Though there has been recent literature on these developmental stages, they are typically presented as unitary, discrete phenomena, with a focus on the psychological or the physiological. Here we offer a perspective, a life continuum, and a backdrop against which we can measure and understand these transitions as thematically related—as cyclical, interconnected, and interdependent.

Our vision is rich. We are psychoanalysts, psychologists, educators, obstetricians, and journalists; we are women and men, mothers and daughters, fathers and sons. As human beings we integrate all of this, and in responding to our patients, we are moved by the texture and weight of these psychophysical passages. We were brought together by our experience as individuals living out these passages and by an intellectual conviction fueled, by and large, by psychoanalytic understanding. It was both a conviction that female psychophysical passages are powerful events that have been superficially understood and a belief that the psychodynamic approach and inquiry has something substantial, creative, and good to offer. As the book grew and as we grew, thoughts solidified and themes emerged. At first, I cautioned myself that such commonalities might be figments of my wish-fulfilling imagination, but data from different sources kept accumulating and connections became clear.

A synthetic thread appeared, and I will try to weave it integratively: throughout passages of the body-self, there is attachment and loss. Central to the concept of transition is the giving up of old bonds and moving to the new: menstruation, pregnancy, birth, and menopause alike signal growth, birth, mourning, and loss. Throughout passages of the body-self, the unconscious is provoked. There is in every phase of growth an opportunity for regression and pathology or reintegration and further emotional maturity. Throughout passages of the body-self, there is the uniqueness of female body–self boundaries with attendant qualities of permeability, diffuseness, and flexibility. These qualities can act as an obstacle to individuation or can facilitate and enhance the growth of empathy, creativity, mothering, and sensitivity in relationships. A new positive psychology of female development emerges, one born out of innerness, empathy, emotional complexity, and richness.

1

Women go through many births, many developmental crises, each one marked by changes of body and changes to self. Kaplan (1984) describes adolescence as an inner emotional upheaval, as "a struggle between the eternal human wish to cling to the past and the equally powerful wish to get on with the future" (p. 19). She likens the adolescent to a mourner who, in saying farewell to childhood, must give up passionate attachments to parents and equally passionate idealizations.

In like manner, women learn to mourn many times over. Separation and loss are integral parts of their psychology from birth. Concretely reminded of aging through clear bodily signs such as breast development, menstruation, pregnancy, nursing, and menopause, they are throughout the life cycle grieving past infantile attachments and are being given opportunity to work through unconscious issues regarding femininity, womanhood, and ultimately personhood. A woman's puberty rites are repeated through her life and are typically and inexorably linked to actual physiological events.

Female passage continues throughout the life cycle. Femininity is expressed in organic events and this fact inescapably underscores identity. The quality of female development rests on the abilities to both possess and empty out. Fullness and loss, attachment and separateness are dynamically recurring themes in a woman's life. In the course of preparing this book, we have all experienced these themes, learned from them, and fully expect that they will continue.

REFERENCE

Kaplan, L. J. (1984). *Adolescence: The farewell to childhood.* New York: Simon & Schuster.

Early Developmental Themes
The Emotional Birth of the Female

Part I of this book deals with early developmental themes: genetic, developmental, and psychohistorical roots of female psychophysical passages are explored. Alice Eichholz traces the changes of body image in our culture over time, with a focus on child-rearing practices as a determinant in the development of self–body individuation. Dale Mendell shifts our vantage point to the richly intrapsychic world of the little girl. In reviewing contemporary psychoanalytic theories about early female development, she outlines and then develops in depth the emergence of a uniquely feminine track of evolution. Joan Offerman-Zuckerberg underscores the uniqueness of the mother–daughter relationship by pointing to an early, intricate network of mutual projective identifications—projections that lay the foundation for body–self boundary permeability, vulnerability, and creativity. Susan Kavaler systematically and developmentally reminds us of the critical role of the father in the self-development of the daughter—a father who seduces, admires, who is at once a transitional object during the Oedipal period, an inspiration, a romancer, an audience, and then a colleague and teacher. Both Offerman-Zuckerberg and Kavaler point to pathological repercussions when the mother and father fall short of being "good enough."

Chapter 1

Psychohistorical Reflections on Changing Body Images for Women

ALICE EICHHOLZ

Bodies haven't changed much in our evolutionary development, but body image probably has not been quite as stable. Certainly one might observe this to be the case in the last 200 years in the United States, as a representative of Western culture. Pictures of women today portray very different messages from those drawn or photographed in the past. In trying to understand the effects of psychophysical passages on women, it is appropriate to try to draw some observations about changes in body image.

"Women's bodies have a history of their own," begins Shorter (1982, p. xi) in his extensive exploration of that subject. Indeed they do. How could they not, given that women's major source of identification has been related to an intimacy with their bodies. A woman's body is the stage upon which psychophysical passages take place. All periods of transformation, by definition, include change. As boys become men, new roles are added on to the demands made on their bodies, but with some exceptions their bodies change basically only in size. A girl has to readjust to her body and, as we shall soon see, to her sense of self, which becomes quite different, not only in size, but in shape and in internal processes. Roles are added on as well, but to different body structures with new bodily processes.

Given that, it would not be surprising to discover that a woman's body may be more vulnerable to cultural and internal messages, many of which are predominantly unconscious. Bodies do "remember" on an unconscious level. How much they remember we don't yet know. But since our understanding of the unconscious, anatomy, and biology certainly has changed, it is possible that some interesting observations can be made about the way women have had to deal with the psychophysical passages through historical changes in their body image.

The reflections which follow are rooted in the history of the West. While they will end with the last 200 years in the United States, the historical and cultural changes that occurred here necessarily find roots in earlier times and cultures.

To begin with, the concept of "body image" itself is a late-20th century devel-

ALICE EICHHOLZ • Associate Professor, Vermont College of Norwich University, Montpelier, Vermont; Contributing Editor to *Journal of Psychohistory*.

opment which grew out of psychiatric research on self image (Fisher, 1970, 1973, 1986). Body image is a large, amorphous category which refers to perceptual behavior—the values, attitudes, perceptions, and expectations a person has concerning her body. The body is seen as a point of junction between the psychological and physiological self. Some of the techniques for determining body image have included projective tests, questionnaires rating feelings about one's body, and therapeutic techniques, such as biofeedback and rolfing. Needless to say, none of such material is available in this form from people who lived in the past. Instead, reflections about changing body image remain in the sphere of just that—reflections—based on observations for what little the ordinary woman or those who interacted with her have left in writing, pictures, and demographic materials.

While it is possible to chart when it was first discovered that the fetus actually "develops" in the uterus instead of existing in it as a miniature adult, waiting to be hatched, or when the uterus did not "float" inside the body, supposedly causing numerous "female" problems, it is much harder to determine when women in general understood those "discoveries" and what effect that understanding had on them. Regardless, nearly all of what we know now to be the basic physiological occurrences within a woman's body has only been available knowledge the last 200 years. Many of the specifics have become known only within the last half of the 20th century.

Women have been reaching menarche, giving birth, and becoming menopausal for thousands of years with no real knowledge of what was happening to them. Life imposed many limits on them because of these psychophysical passages. In addition to being just plain difficult to reach adulthood at all, the hurdles to it required women to survive body challenges that were exclusively theirs.

During the last two years, I have observed women in a brief residency bachelor's degree program for adults struggle with their self-esteem at a point in their lives when they are making major changes. The issues they constantly articulate concerning their attempt to raise their low self-esteem involve three "costs" among a list of many costs described by Sanford and Donovan (1984): (a) the search for completion through motherhood, romance, and work; (b) poor body image; and (c) inability to stop playing "critical tapes" defined as "negative statements about the self or equally powerful and negative visual images" (p. 294) which run constantly. No external event need start this tape, but it appears to be deeply embedded messages which have existed so long that their validity is never questioned. Is there something that is inherently connected between the three issues of search for completion, poor body image, and critical tapes?

The image of "self" begins to be formed out of the individuation process which is literally, as well as figuratively, separating one body from another. It is certainly well established that boys go through this process differently from girls. The challenge brought by changes to self-images for girls *is* a challenge to body image at the point of the psychophysical passage. Perhaps the connection of self-image and body image is more loaded for women because of the intensive reservoirs of memories in both. This might explain the intensity of the struggle women have in developing high self-esteem as it is related to body issues. Perhaps by looking at critical tapes and the need for completion from the point of view of changing body image we can see a more dynamic explanation of why women struggle with acquiring a more affirming sense of self.

Before 1900, femininity for women was a negative concept, a burden from God because Eve talked Adam into being nourished by the tree of knowledge, despite God's warning (Shorter, 1982). Femininity certainly did not mean the positive acceptance of changing psychophysical roles and the ability to act both receptively and penetratingly in the culture, which might be one way of describing it as a positive concept. Femininity as punishment from God is clearly a powerful critical tape.

Fisher (1973) suggests an extension of this critical tape; although he describes it for both men and women, we can see already that such a tape would have more effect on women.

> Negative feeling about one's body derives from the negative attitude toward body events in most religious and moralistic systems. . . . For centuries . . . [woman] has been made to feel that [her] body is not only dirty and bad but also powerless and useless (pp. 4–5).

CHALLENGES TO SURVIVAL

A Western historical review of the challenges women's bodies faced is appropriate here. Five major challenges seem to be operating: infanticide, abandonment, ambivalence, intrusion, and socialization. Since there appears to be a relationship between those five challenges and the periodization of modes of parent–child relations, as described by deMause (1982), it is presented here in that format.

Infanticidal Mode

First, women had to survive. The evidence is overwhelming, now, once we begin to look at it without the blinders of the romance of the past. Girl babies were killed as a regular occurrence, a way of "child rearing," at least from antiquity to the fourth century (deMause, 1982; Pomeroy, 1975). There was little value to having another girl in the household. If she did make it past infancy, she was likely to be the victim of parental projections and "urges to mutilate, burn, freeze, drown, shake and throw [her] violently about" (deMause, 1982, p. 33). The ratio of men to women in the reproductive years may have been as high as two to one (Pomeroy, p. 227). The practice of infanticide has diminished considerably, but the effects of it may, today, still be part of the critical tapes, the experience of worthlessness, passed on from one generation to the next.

DeMause (1982) describes three possible interpersonal relationships between parent and child in history: (a) projection, or using the child as a container for parental unconscious feelings; (b) reversal of roles so that the child is used as a substitute for adult figures prominent in the parent's childhood, and (c) empathic reactions, ability for parent to regress enough to help the child reach her individual goals and in the process re-parent him- or herself without loading the child with the parent's adult projections. In the infanticidal mode, projection and reversal are the means by which parents interact with children. Historically and psychologically, it is a long way from empathy. Those who have been witness to physical or sexual abuse of children or who have dealt with patients struggling to control their internal compulsions to brutalize women and children will notice the difficulty with which people can move past projective and reversal interactions. It is also not hard to accept the possibility that even present attempts to estimate the widespread use of such mistreatment in the past have been severely underestimated (Russell, 1986).

How does a girl, growing up in a culture with a clearly pervasive message of worthlessness to the point of nonexistence (death) and brutality, feel about herself, and the psychophysical changes she faces if she reaches adulthood? Her body/self has value as a dead or mutilated body, but little more.

This is the toughest stage to reflect about because it is only the survivors who are capable of reflecting. Women today are survivors of survivors of survivors (not that men aren't either, but the message to them is clearly different). What reservoir of memories or critical tapes come attached to that "privilege?" What fears are locked away so deeply in the struggle to succeed lest it be for naught? What magic will help keep them alive or not mutilated?

Threats of infanticide and mutilation, especially to girls, still exist on some level today, although there are more "progressive" ways of responding to children now, making the fear of death and sexual molestation somewhat less of an omnipresent force than it must have been for girls in the past. Is there any wonder why children fear that their "bad" behavior might bring serious retribution from the more powerful adults? Beside being a developmental issue, there was objective evidence in the culture to suspect the worst. She might need to be rescued even if she was good.

Abandonment Mode

The rescue theme finds itself firmly entrenched in the second stage through which women's bodies/selves have passed historically to reach adulthood. They had to be fed, nourished. But women were hungry, not only from being at a disadvantage in gathering food, but from how the food was shared within the household.

Institutionalized abandonment and extensive swaddling were the prevalent child-rearing practices in the 4th through 13th centuries as a developing alternative to the infanticidal mode. Projection was still extensively operative and apparently reversal reactions were diminishing since there seems to have been a reduction in using children for sexual purposes. Restricting early movements severely was nearly universal under the belief that a baby

> if left free . . . would scratch its eyes out, tear its ears off, break its legs, distort
> its bones, be terrified by the sight of its own limbs, and even crawl about on all
> fours like an animal (deMause, 1982, p. 41).

In actuality, the practice of swaddling was probably instrumental in perpetuating rickets, a ravaging disease among children which affected women profoundly (Shorter, 1982).

Nourishment and care came from outside the home. Needless to say, this form of abandonment was both literal and beginning to be emotional. Not enough progress in child-rearing practices had been made for adults to even consider that the child would have any feelings of abandonment. The abandonment was for the sake of the parent who, by then, had begun to suspect that children did have souls (not feelings). "The only way a parent could escape the dangers of their own projections was by abandonment" (deMause, 1982, p. 61).

The abandoned female body is a hungry and, still, molested body, one available for the use of others. Hunger produces desperation, little ability to have "conscious" thoughts, an easy target or victim for the projections of stronger others, needing the protection of others. As will be seen shortly, in the past, women fared much worse in the attempts for nourishment than men. We may see remnants of this critical tape today when women are afraid to leave their husbands for fear they and the children will starve. It would probably be hard to find a man with the same fear.

What if it is very hard to give up fairy tales because they were *literally* stories of survival from the projection and reversal reactions of parents (or the stepparent who existed extensively because of mortality of women), and not just stories of psychological death until the "completion" of a prince's kiss?

Ambivalent Mode

Third, a woman had to develop a healthier body. She had to continue to ward off sexual molestation and to survive a series of debilitating diseases exclusively her own and those, because of her femaleness, that effected her more profoundly than men. All this just to make it to adulthood, and she was still less likely to do that than men.

Shorter (1982) describes several problems within the architectural body of women and diseases of sexual significance that have affected women's ability to survive. Although in the distant historical past, women and men were about the same size, between the 14th and 18th centuries, with a downturn in the economy in the West, women got much less to eat and began getting increasingly shorter than men. This period described by Shorter corresponds with deMause's Ambivalent Mode of parenting during the same time period. By the late 18th century, women began growing again (although they were consistently behind men) up to the 20th century.

What everyone ate was a minimally adequate diet with grave deficiencies. Women fared worse than men under the notion that men did the harder physical labor and should consequently get the best of the food. Why didn't women simply eat what they wanted, since they apparently had control over the dispersement of food in the household? One answer may lie in the fact that women consistently had to contend with debilitating effects of diseases peculiar to women. It may have produced the kind of debilitation which encourages self-depredation and interferes with the desire to eat.

While many children had rickets, women fared worse because of the extra stress that childbearing placed on their skeletal structure. The use of swaddling during this period, even though it was less than in the previous period, exacerbated the preconditions for this disease. Rickets results basically from insufficient exposure to sunlight which makes it impossible for calcium to be absorbed into the bone. When children are not given appropriate sunlight (or cod liver oil, we now know), they are more susceptible to this disease.

For women, the dangers of pregnancy and childbirth (which continued to tax the lives of women because of the conjugal rights of men) were worsened since their pelvic structures were likely to have been severely damaged in childhood. Shorter calls this the "scourge of adult women" (p. 22).

As if the damage and bodily stress from rickets, and successive childbirth were not enough for women, it seemed not possible to overcome, as Shorter (1982) so appropriately describes, "diseases of sexual significance" (p. 255) until the 20th century. Among these chronic problems with which women were struggling to be healthy were vaginal discharge (including menstruation), venereal disease, and the long-term effects of damage from childbirth.

Apparently, according to Shorter's (1982) extensive use of primary source material, women had continual problems with vaginal discharge of all kinds, most of which are easily treatable today with the advent of gentian violet (in the 1920s); sulfa drugs (1936); and metronedazole, or Flagyl (1955). But before then, discharge "represented a terrible affliction for women . . . a constant reminder of the special sexual burden of womanhood" (p. 256). Discharge ran the gamut from being clear white and relatively innocuous to yellow-green with offensive smell and painful intercourse.

Menstrual flows, something the late 20th century woman takes relatively in stride since the development of first the sanitary napkins and then tampons, were another constant reminder of the burden of womanhood. And a burden it was, no matter how much we would like to see it otherwise. The evidence suggests that women simply let the menstrual discharge flow into their clothes. Doing so again taxed the immune system by setting up preconditions for constant infection and pain.

Eating seemed, then, to be the least of women's problems. The abandonment period of parent–child relations is symbolized by the lessening of swaddling but the physical molding and shaping of the infant's body and using enemas to rid it of waste. An increase in the number of child instruction manuals occurred near the end of the 17th century. There was "no image more popular than that of the physical molding of children, who were seen as soft wax, plaster or clay to be beaten into shape" (deMause, 1982, p. 62).

Numerous devices for molding and shaping the body became prevalent during this time period, of which the remnants are still with us today. There are some conflicting views about the corsets—what good they were as well as who wore them. While holding a women in may not have had a deleterious effect on women's health in general, as many believed, they were clearly a psychological message that the molding and shaping of the body was desirous. And physiologically, any women who has worn constricting clothing can attest to the fact that it is harder to eat and digest food, and, when pregnant, particularly harder to breathe, and may increase pain in pregnancy and childbirth since constriction makes pain worse.

Shorter (1982) suggests that the use of corsets never filtered down to the middle and lower classes. An examination of the Sears catalogues in the last 100 years and the buying habits of women might disprove this. It certainly cannot be considered as "suddenly swept . . . away forever" (Shorter, 1982, p. 29) by the 20th century.

This theme of molding one's body remains prevalent in the culture today, even without considering restricting body apparatus, as well, particularly when applied to women. There are enough 20th-century popular songs and advertisements to attest to this influence on women's bodies. Maybe the reason this approach still "works" in the love lives and body images of women today is that it is part of the critical tape of needing to be molded and shaped, again, in order to survive, a message from the ambivalent mode of child rearing. All such forms of "help" are hard to give up because they have been literally aids for survival.

Intrusive Mode

A major change in the lives of children and women seemed apparent by the 18th century. Bodies were not to be just molded, but controlled.

> The child was no longer full of dangerous projections, and rather than just examine its insides with an enema, the parents approached even closer and attempted to conquer its mind, in order to control its insides, its anger, its needs, its masturbation, its very will. The child raised by intrusive parents was nursed by the mother, not swaddled, not given regular enemas, toilet trained early, prayed with but not played with, hit but not regularly whipped, punished for masturbation, and made to obey promptly with threats of guilt as often as other methods of punishment (deMause, 1982, p. 62)

This is a child-rearing practice that is clearly recognizable today and is sometimes the subject of much ethnic humor. Since its inception seems so prevalent in the American colonies, it may have been aided by *some* "freedom" allowed white women from the conjugal rights, since men in the colonies were slightly distracted by the problems of becoming colonizers, first of native Americans and then of black slaves. Perhaps it represented to women enough time to "listen" to their children so that the beginning of true empathy was possible.

Although general health was improving some, diet for the general population, and particularly for frontier families, was still deficient. Women's own diseases found only some relief during this period although major changes were in the making with regard to family life (Shorter, 1975; Stone, 1977; Cox and Quitt, 1980). Pediatrics was born and resulted in general improvement in child care which reduced infant mortality.

Changes were occurring during the intrusive period in the birthing process as well. In the upper and middle classes, male attendants were called in to deliver babies. Childbirth, although a universal experience, has always been potentially dangerous to women's lives. To call it a natural, normal event is to make it seem that all births are alike, and that to women in the past, it was painless and easy, with little danger. With all the literature available on birth today, in the culture we still lack a general understanding about the historical, psychological, and physiological effects of birth on both women and babies, although some extremely admirable attempts have been made to correct the misconceptions of birth in the present and the past (see particularly LeBoyer, 1975; Shorter, 1982; Odent, 1984; Macfarland, 1977). Women in the 18th century began using men (Donnison, 1977), first as midwives and then as surgeons, to the point where that practice became extensive.

What anyone knew about childbirth before 1800 was filled with "a whole armada of threats from supernatural, from those dark forces which, most of our ancestors believed, hovered constantly at the threshold" (Shorter, 1982, p. 49). Although the percentage of death from childbirth was still small, it was probably larger in colonial America and on the frontier than in Europe. But word gets around. Fear is harder to contend with when one is facing a new or unknown experience. And if for generations women have been taught and believed the worst about their internal processes, it is understandable why they would identify with the small portion of their population for whom the worst happened. It remains to be determined how much expectation of pain and suffering is inherently an unconscious part of feminine identity and how much has been incorporated in the psyche over generations.

If women turned to male attendants during the 18th century, although in the long run this may have had some contradictory effects, it may have been because the men had had some training in the more advanced understanding of the birth process. Women were not allowed to be so trained. Again, women may have been simply trying to survive, trying to find a way through the array of critical tapes to live on the other side of that body of experience so endemic to their physiology and, perhaps, psychology.

And for all of their attempts to do so, it worked to some extent. With more knowledge and less interference from both devastating critical tapes and physiological maneuvers, by the end of the 18th century more women were apparently living past the birth experience. Nonetheless, it is likely that physiological damage from birth experience had not improved much. In many ways, then, women had more control of their bodies and were freer to be conscious of "feeling," since they were not just desperate for food or survival.

Socialization

Beginning in the 19th century, progress moved critically forward in the lives of women. So many things we take for granted now are products and discoveries of the children who were raised, not to be conquered, but to be trained and guided. In some ways this mode of child rearing has become the enthnocentric point of view of 20th-century America, as if none other ever did or will exist.

Woman's socialized body is one which is allowed sexuality, as long as it is guided into socially acceptable roles, asked to be as nearly close to the cultural ideal as possible, and has been, at least, likely to be tended to by her father as well as raised nearly exclusively, at least up to the mid-20th century, by her mother.

Those changes that affected women the most were control of childhood diseases; recognition of childhood sexuality; solutions to the problems of contraception, sexually significant diseases, and safe childbirth; and development of sanitary pads and tampons. That is a lot for approximately 150 years. Is it any wonder why the roles with which women have been struggling are in such upheaval? Within the space of a few generations, problems endemic to the nature of being a woman, with which women have been attempting to survive for centuries, have been effectively eliminated. "What now?" she asks.

Many women are caught in the remainders of the effects of older modes of child rearing, trying to shed the critical tapes that have been part of them for generations. Of course, it isn't that everyone is raised in the socializing mode. When a woman who is freed enough from the constrictions of her own psyche and past looks around to find models of "what now," there are plenty of nagging reminders visible in others of what she has come through.

What could account for such a dramatic change in the quality of life of women? Needless to say there might be many points of view about such a shift. A psychohistorical view would clearly note that parents became progressively more psychologically available to interact with the lives of their children in empathic ways, making it possible to regress to their own childhood experience (in the service of the ego) and hear the needs of children in better ways. It isn't that any *one* quality or condition of childhood directly produces a quality or condition in the culture. This view of psychohistory is not reductionistic. It is simply that psychologically more available parents make it possible for children to be freer from the psychological restraints of the past, thereby setting up preconditions for a change to occur. It is the "quantum leap from impersonal to personal and affective sources—the sense that it is the feeling individual and not the inanimate institution or inorganic custom which is the source of change" as described by Davis (1976, p. 19) when reflecting on Calvin Hall's notion of fantasy in invention.

Any advertising agency knows that something can't be sold for which the public isn't ready. Their business is helping people regress to the level at which such anxiety is created that it will be resolved in the purchase or use of the product they are advertising. Women's rights can't be sold to people who are stuck in the clutches of projecting their own bad feelings on others and brutalizing them to get rid of the feelings. A woman who is daily struggling to simply survive the next day is not likely to be interested in the vote for women. Progress comes because the preconditions are set in childhood.

Tampons were available for 20 years before they "caught on" and, to many women, it still is not an appropriate way of dealing with menstruation. It would be fascinating to know what the market is for sanitary pads and tampons in different parts of the country and different communities. Shorter (1982) even suggests that the advent of cheap cotton underpants may have been closely related to the lessening of vaginal infections. Not that one caused the other, but the preconditions for the use of undergarments were set in the psyche for it to be possible to see the connection between their use and lessening infections.

By the 19th century, child-rearing practices for at least a large enough part of the population had allowed room for the psyche of a new generation to develop to stretch its limits of what was possible and to imagine, fantasize, and try those things out in productive ways rather than have to struggle for substinence survival.

An alive, healthy person who is less consumed by the demons and critical tapes of the past, whose validity hasn't been accepted without questioning, and who is not the victim of battering and sexual molestation from family is more likely to make use of new developments that would be even more liberating. Women have been doing the best they can for generations. Their best is getting better.

Helping Mode

There is a newer approach to child rearing which began to find roots in the mid-20th century. The helping mode, as deMause (1982) decribes it, is the approach of helping children to meet *their* daily goals rather than to mold, train, or guide them into the parent's daily goals. A recent ad on television for tampons starts with an attractive, gray-haired woman talking to the viewer, as if she were her daughter. "You're becoming a woman, and a lot of wonderful and new experiences are going to be happening to you!" This is a very different message than one passed around the schoolyards just 30 years ago about the "curse" and having to make one's own "rags" and wash them out only one generation ago. A student remarked in the women and self-esteem seminar mentioned in the beginning of this chapter that the next stage was to say, "I have my friend."

Value, sometimes too much, is placed on women's bodies now. Women are attempting to view their bodies in more positive ways. Hopefully, we have more and more young girls who are being psychologically helped to learn about their own bodies, and their value and limits.

I can't avoid a personal note as a final point. It is really the reason I was ready to look at changing body images for women. I was 8 years old when my mother decided to have a discussion with her three children about sexual differences in the best way she knew how. The three of us had been fooling around with the *Sears* catalog looking at girdles and bras for pregnant women and in the creative and not all to accurate minds of latent children, designing apparatuses for holding sanitary napkins. My mother was visibly concerned about such behavior. Her explanation started with "girls and women have three holes. . . . " My sister was young enough to want to look and see where hers were. I, being only 2 years older, was mortified that my mother or any adult would even have found out I was thinking about such things. All I heard was the word "holes." Holes were empty, and I had three emptinesses in me. It took years of growing and several years of analysis before I had any clear notion about what was really inside me.

My daughter was 3 years old when she came home from day care one day and announced, "I don't have a penis." I didn't even have to stop and think; I said, "No, you have a vagina." I knew she and I had made a quantum leap, one which will continue to play positive critical tapes for both of us and make it at least possible to not look for completion outside of ourselves. That interaction between parent and child is what the roots of psychohistory are all about.

References

Cox, V. C., & Quitt, M. (1980). *Loving, parenting and dying.* New York: Psychohistory Press.

Davis, G. (1976). *Childhood and history in America.* New York: Psychohistory Press.

deMause, L. (1982). *Foundations of psychohistory.* New York: Creative Roots. [deMause, L. (1975), "Evolution of Childhood," can also be found in deMause, L. (Ed.) (1975). *The history of childhood.* New York: Psychohistory Press.]

Donnison, J. (1977). *Midwives and medical men: A history of inter-professional rivalries and women's rights.* New York: Schocken Books.

Fisher, S. (1970). *Body experience in fantasy and behavior.* New York: Appleton-Century Crofts.

Fisher, S. (1973). *Body consciousness: You are what you feel.* Englewood Cliffs, NJ: Prentice-Hall.

Fisher, S. (1986). *Development and structure of the body image,* (Vols. 1 and 2). Hillsdale, NJ: Lawrence Erlbaum Associates Press.

LeBoyer, F. (1975). *Birth without violence.* New York: Alfred A. Knopf.

Macfarland, A. (1977). *Psychology of childbirth.* Cambridge, MA: Harvard University Press.

Odent, M. (1984). *Birth reborn.* New York: Pantheon.

Pomeroy, Sarah B. (1975). *Goddesses, whores, wives, and slaves: Women in classical antiquity*. New York: Schocken Books.

Russell, D. (1986). *The secret trauma*. New York: Basic Books.

Sanford, L.T., & Donovan, M. E. (1984). *Women and self esteem: Understanding and improving the way we think and feel about ourselves*. New York: Penguin.

Shorter, E. (1975). *Making of the modern family*. New York: Basic Books.

Shorter, E. (1982). *The history of women's bodies*. New York: Basic Books.

Stone, L. (1977). *The family, sex and marriage in England, 1500–1800*. New York: Harper & Row.

Chapter 2

Early Female Development
From Birth through Latency

DALE MENDELL

The physiological maturational steps in a woman's life are accompanied by a series of psychological changes. How does a young girl become a person who anticipates, greets, and encompasses within the scope of her intrapsychic being those uniquely female events, from menarche to menopause, which she will encounter, many of them totally without volition? How does she develop the capacity for adjusting to her ever-changing body and reintegrating her perception of herself after each psychophysical event? This chapter describes some of the precursors of these integrative capacities by discussing the little girl's developing relation to her body and the meanings that body assumes.

The foundations of the gendered self are shaped by integrating bodily experiences and mental representations of self and others. Greenacre (1948) refers to anatomy as our "primary environment" and in conjunction with our earliest relational self, it does indeed have a major formative role in determining later psyche and character.

> Every event in the sexual life of a woman—the onset of puberty, the growth of her breasts, her menstruation, the loss of virginity, pregnancy, giving birth—each of these events uncompromisingly marks her corporal being, stirring up archaic feelings, and the earliest fantasied fears regarding the inside of her body. Femininity is experienced in flesh and blood and inescapably underscores the identification to the woman-as-mother. . . . (Montgrain, 1983, p. 173).

As the child progresses through the psychosexual phases of development, the particular qualities and tasks of each phase overlap with what has come before and with succeeding phases. In addition, there is the necessity to rework preceding phases into a consistent set of representations of the self with each progressive developmental task. Thus, it is possible to discern lifelong themes specific to female

DALE MENDELL, PH.D. • Faculty and Supervisor, The Psychoanalytic Institute, Postgraduate Center for Mental Health, New York City; Senior Supervisor, Training Analyst and Faculty, Training Institute for Mental Health; Senior Supervisor, National Institute for the Psychotherapies; private practice.

development which are expressed differently and progressively more coherently throughout psychosexual development. These themes include identifying with, separating from, and bonding with the mother, and the concommitant progressive differentiation between inside and outside, open and closed, as they relate to female genitalia and their attendant functions.

The current psychoanalytic climate is particularly conducive to the investigation, elaboration, and revision of earlier theories of female development. Much of the relevant literature concerns the relationship of ego capacities, object relations, and narcissistic development with emerging bodily experiences. Therefore, it is possible to present a current view of early female development that draws on recent theoretical, clinical, and observational findings.[1] Of necessity, this will be a personal view, as I have selected from a range of contemporary theories those which seem to me to make the most sense both in terms of their internal coherence and methodology and of their usefulness in my own clinical practice and that of my students, supervisees, and colleagues.

This chapter emphasizes contemporary theories of early female development and presents only a brief summary of the major concepts of Freud and some of his contemporaries. (See Chasseguet-Smirgel, 1970; Fliegel, 1982; and Kleeman, 1976, for more comprehensive reviews.) Next, some of the literature on core gender identity and observational research on infants and infant–parent interaction is briefly reviewed. The bulk of this chapter is devoted to a revised version of the epigenetic psychosexual phases of development, emphasizing aspects that prepare a woman to anticipate and cope with the unique psychophysiological changes she will encounter.

Freud's theory of female development (1925, 1931, 1933) is noteworthy for its phallocentrism; it is a "one body" theory which maintains that libido, sexuality, and excitement are masculine. Freud appears to have had rigid resistances to imaginative identifying with woman's internal sexuality (Fliegel, 1985; McDougall, 1985). According to Freud, "the little girl is a little man" when she enters the phallic phase; until then her mother is her sole love object, she is unaware of the existence of her vagina, and her masturbation is clitoral.

At the beginning of the phallic phase, the little girl wishes to make a baby with her mother and considers her father to be her rival—a position frequently referred to as negative Oedipal. However, when she becomes aware that she does not possess a penis, "she sees it, knows that she is without it and wants to have it" (Freud, 1925, p. 252). In recognition of the inferiority of her clitoris, the small girl stops masturbating and develops an envy of the penis. This constellation leads her to hate and turn away from her mother, as she blames the mother for not having given her a penis, recognizes that she cannot give the mother the penis that the

---

[1]There have been a number of voices claiming that observational data on young children have no relevance for psychoanalytic thinking, as they do not provide access to the child's inner world; there are also those who claim that retrospective reports from the analytic couch are of no value in confirming analytic developmental theory, as they are merely anecdotal and speculative. I do not agree with either of these positions, as I think that theory can only benefit from the conjunction of as many observational modes as we are able to obtain. Therefore, the material in this chapter is based on the literature from child observation and from the treatment of both children and adults.

mother also wants, and despises the mother for being castrated, like herself. She then turns to the father in hopes of receiving first a penis and later, its attainable replacement, a baby. As the little girl already believes that she has been castrated, she has little reason to leave the Oedipal position or to develop a strong superego. The three tasks of female development involve changing from activity to passivity, from mother to father as love object, and from clitoris to vagina as erogenous zone.

As the vagina is unknown until puberty and clitoral masturbation is renounced upon the girl's discovery of her castration, she essentially spends much of her childhood without a sexual organ. Women's narcissism and masochism were seen as logical outgrowths of the little girl's passivity in the face of relinquishing clitoral masturbation and phallic activity and turning toward her father in an attempt to hide and compensate for her "genital deficiency" (Freud, 1931, 1933).

While Freud admitted that he did not understand the "riddle" of femininity and, in collaboration with Ruth Mack Brunswick (1940), became aware of the importance of the little girl's pre-Oedipal relationship with the omnipotently perceived mother, he neglected its importance in forming a "developmental continuity" (Schafer, 1974), out of which further feminine growth evolves, and to the end insisted on the centrality of penis envy and the castration complex as major determinants of femininity. Helena Deutsch (1930), an adherent of this premise, perceived the normal adult female as both narcissistic and masochistic in her sexuality. Feminine masochism was seen as stemming from the Oedipal stage, when the girl's desire to have a penis is supplanted by the desire to be castrated and raped by her father. Parturition as masochistic sexual gratification is a logical outcome of this position.

Opponents of the Freudian view of femininity as a secondary and compensatory formation include Karen Horney, who maintained that "the undiscovered vagina is a vagina denied" (1933). Horney's pediatric observation of little girls led to her realization that vaginal masturbation begins at an early age. For Horney, vaginal excitations become repressed both because of specifically feminine fears of being damaged by the father's huge penis and because castration wishes toward the father, due to Oedipal frustration, lead her to fear his revenge. Knowledge of menstruation, defloration, and parturition reinforce the girl's bodily fears.

Melanie Klein (1957) perceived the little girl as having "dominant feminine instinctual components." For Klein, penis envy originates in the infant's envy of the feeding breast and of the contents of the mother's body, which the little girl wants to attack to obtain its phantasied contents, which include babies and the father's penis. The infant girl turns from the frustrating breast to an oral desire for the paternal penis, which becomes the prototype of the vaginal desire for the penis. Oral frustration, based upon envy, can result in adult genital sexuality too colored by oral grievances and anxieties. As the little girl does not possess a visible genital, she has difficulty reassuring herself that she has not incurred damage during the phantasied retaliatory attacks by her mother on the inside of her body. She therefore envies the penis as it is external and its wholeness can be verified. Ernest Jones (1933) agrees with Horney and Klein that, from the beginning, the girl is more feminine than masculine and more concerned with the inside than the outside of her body; that her desire for a child is not a compensation for the lack of a penis but a basically feminine wish; and that penis envy and indeed the entire phallic phase is a secondary, defensive formation for girls.

In their belief in a primary femininity that is neither secondary to nor compensatory for male sexuality, Freudian contemporaries such as Klein, Horney, and Jones anticipated basic current conceptualizations. For the most part, modern theorists consider feminine development to begin at birth and to stem from a confluence of constitutional, environmental, identificatory, and cognitive factors.

Stoller (1976) has coined the term "core gender identity" for "the sense we have of our sex . . . a conviction about one's self and one's role" (p. 61), and postulates it to be the result of genetic patterning, resulting in the neurophysiological organizing of the fetal brain; sex assignment at birth, which in most cases is forever unquestioned by parents, child, and all others; parental attitudes about a child of the female sex; early postnatal effects similar to imprinting; and the developing body ego, formed from the sensations which help define the physical and thereby the psychic dimensions of the self. Core gender identity is seen as possibly irreversible by 18 months of age and firmly secure by age 4 or 5 (Kleeman, 1976).

Observational studies on sex differences in infancy reveal little in the way of very early differences in areas such as exploration or aggressivity (see Formanek, 1982, for a review). However, an examination of "state systems," a number of clustered stable constellations, for example, the calm-to-crying continuum (see D. K. Silverman, 1987a, 1987b, for a review) demonstrate smoother and more stabilized functioning in the female infant. This is evidenced in her greater alertness, calmness, and lack of irritability, and in the greater length of time she spends gazing at, or vocalizing to, a caretaker. (Infant females are born 4 to 6 weeks more mature than are males in terms of skeletal development. Their neurological status is also more advanced and may account for at least a portion of the "state system" findings.) Silverman hypothesizes that the female infant's smoother functioning and heightened ability to interact facilitates earlier connectedness with the mother and, reinforced by the mother's greater expectations of bonding with her daughter than with her son, becomes a major factor in producing the relatively more emotionally responsive female adult.

Parental responses differ depending on the sex of the child. For example, observational studies show mothers vocalizing more to their 3-month-old daughters than to their sons (Lewis & Freedle, 1973) and parents of both sexes spend more time trying to obtain smiles from their baby daughters (Moss, 1982). These observations only scratch the surface of manifold and pervasive unconscious parental attitudes and expectations about femininity, which are fed both by the larger culture and by individual expectations and fantasies. They range in nature from specific attitudes toward female genitalia, expressed in the quality and quantity of care during bathing and dressing and in degree of discussion or labeling of female genitalia, to general attitudes about differences between a "good girl" and a "good boy," particularly in the areas of dependency and aggression.

Conscious imitation of important people, primarily mother, add to the baby girl's underlying, primary identifications, which include the as yet relatively undifferentiated sensing of mother's female smell, sound, touch, and rhythms as well as the beginning reception of mother's range of feelings about the infant's gender. During the first year of life, genital fingering emerges as the infant explores the boundaries of her physical world. More focused masturbatory activity does not emerge until the second half of the second year (Galenson & Roiphe, 1976; Klee-man, 1975), when the little girl becomes more mobile and self-aware, and her attention shifts to her perianal area.

The child's ability, from as early as 15 months of age, to label herself a girl is particularly important for gender-identity formation, as it serves as a cognitive organizer for earlier, less differentiated perceptions of her bodily self (Kleeman, 1976; Kohlberg, 1966), as well as a guide for her identification with maternal qualities and her complementary behavior toward her father.

In short, the developing sense of self cannot proceed without the attribute of gender as an integral part of that self. And, even before cognitive capacity has enabled the child to recognize the existence of two sexes, she is necessarily en-meshed in the physical reality of a female body. Primary femininity is made up of the factors of genetics, anatomical-physiological patterning, body-image represen-tation and bodily sensations, emerging ego capacities, primary identification with the mother, and the interactive responsivity between parents and infant. The epi-genetic, psychosexual stages of development intertwine with this closely knit pattern.

PSYCHOSEXUAL STAGES

The psychosexual stages, as described in this chapter, may not look quite familiar. This is because I have allowed myself the liberty of selecting, from a range of revisions and elaborations of Freudian theory, those which seem to me to make the most sense of the observational and clinical material at my disposal. Therefore, after discussing the oral and anal phases, the little girl's pre-Oedipal genital phase will be described. The first part of this phase is the inner genital phase (Kestenberg, 1968, 1975, 1982), in which the small girl's psychosexual focus is on her diffusely perceived "creative inside." The last portion of the pre-Oedipal genital phase is frequently referred to as the "phallic-narcissistic phase" (Edgecumbe & Burgner, 1975). The cumbersome term pre-Oedipal genital was chosen instead (Glover & Mendell, 1982) because the term phallic ignores our present knowledge and reflects the earlier Freudian idea that the little girl has no knowledge of her inner genitals, and views herself as a castrated boy. During the pre-Oedipal genital phase, the little girl is concerned with female anatomical structures, with female fantasies, and with establishing a female identity. Subsequent entry into the Oedipal phase pre-supposes a relatively mature level of relationship to self and object, of drive ac-tivity, and of acceptance of the irreversibility of having a female body. This chapter concludes with a discussion of latency.

Oral phase development involves a receptivity and growing ability to interact with the human and nonhuman environment which the infant is discovering, as well as the physical capacity to derive nourishment and sensual pleasure through the act of sucking and, later, of eating. Spontaneous vaginal lubrication is present during the neonatal period (Kleeman, 1976) and vulvo-vaginal engorgement, prob-ably with genital stimulation, frequently accompanies suckling. Clinical data from adults (Fraiberg, 1972; Greenacre, 1950) illustrate the latent connection between mouth, throat, and vagina. The highly incorporative nature of the act of suckling has a pervasive influence on all later incorporative acts, real and fantasized.

[The] rhythm of introjection and projection becomes a model for similar processes in other parts of the body, for receptivity and release, for the capacity to
retain and expel, to yield, to be filled to capacity and to let go. Later fantasies of
oral intercourse and the equation of food equals baby are based on these primarily oral . . . influences (Kestenberg, 1982, p. 89).

At this early stage of development the little girl begins her first, primitive
internalization of her mother's body image and of her own. The infant's experience
of early mothering is derived both from pleasure in feeding and playing and distress and fury during colic and teething, as well as from her mother's responses to
these events. If the little girl internalizes a mutual feeling of bodily satisfaction
between her mother and herself, the sense of basic self-esteem and well-being in
her body forms the foundation for giving and receiving love in later life.

The mother's handling of her baby girl helps to create beginning mental representations of the infant's earliest, bodily self and also of the mother. She becomes a
lifelong model for her daughter to identify with, to differentiate herself from, and to
bond with. The female infant's earlier maturity from birth, greater empathic capacity (Greenacre, 1948) and heightened awareness of her mother, and her greater need
to "undo" mother's negative moods are major early influences that lead the little
girl to bond even more closely with the mother than does her brother (D. K.
Silverman, 1987a, 1987b). The need to bond with and to "repair" the mother is also
derived from the girl's oral sadism and her primitive, diffuse frustration and envy
of the omnipotent-seeming, bountiful, and depriving mother (Klein, 1932). Thus,
even before the little girl is capable of selectively identifying with her mother as a
genital sexual being, she is laying down the bases for lifelong patterns of dealing
with psychophysical crises in her inner and outer world by means of archaic,
visceral, and sensorimotor identification with her mother.

The second half of the second year of life is particularly fateful for the development of the female child, as it forms a juncture at which a variety of psychosexual,
object-relational, and ego developmental processes interact. This is the confluence
of the anal phase, of the rapproachment subphase of the separation-individuation
phase, of the beginning of relatively free motility and language usage and the
ability to categorize, and of the first awareness of gender differences. As the little
girl's capacity for moving into the world emerges, the earlier mutuality between
mother and child becomes strained. The little girl's urge to control and master her
own moving body, the inside, fecal contents of her body, and the human and
nonhuman objects in her world result both in disharmony with her caretaker who
wants some measure of control over the child, and with the girl's own not yet
always cooperative body. The little girl's greater capacity for and concern with
bonding with her mother, as well as her greater capacity for self-control, results in
her earlier, more consistent, and seemingly easier bowel and urine training, as well
as in her generally greater obedience. However, the very quality of the attachment
to the mother, with its relative emphasis on sameness and diffusivity between
mother and daughter, makes it even more essential for the little girl than for the
little boy to establish separateness and boundary differences, even as it makes it
more difficult. At this time the little girl begins in earnest her "dual, conflicting
tasks of identifying with and separating from her mother's body" (Pines, 1987), a

theme that continues throughout development but is variously elaborated during each psychosexual phase and with each psychophysical crisis.

Hatred of having her movements controlled—her wishes to do what she wants, her large body movements, and her bowel movements—makes the little girl want to lash out at the controlling, depriving mother. Her projection onto the mother of her own hatred, added to the mother's anger and disappointment at her difficult child, result in an exacerbation of fear of loss of the object and of the object's love. Interacting with this, on a bodily level, the child daily sees the reality of the loss of a portion of her own body—her feces. In an attempt to turn passive into active and in identification with the aggressor, the little girl, in order to preserve both her body and her relationship with her mother, turns her anal–sadistic impulses onto her own body. This results in earlier bowel control but also at times in difficulty with constipation or with abrupt expulsive diarrhea. The administration of enemas at this point can both tie the girl to her mother in an eroticized anal-sadomasochistic fashion and severely inhibit her attempt to take control of her body. The precursors of superego begin to form during this phase. They eventuate in a superego both more efficient and more flexible than that of the boy (D. Bernstein, 1983), with a stronger emphasis on the necessity of compromise and sacrifice for the sake of preserving relationships and controlling impulses.

In the climate of upright posture, increasing motility, a beginning cognitive ability to compare and to categorize, yearnings toward both attachment and autonomy, and an increase in genital sensation, awareness, and play (Kleeman, 1975), the little girl discovers the anatomical difference. Fast (1979) conceptualizes this discovery as a gender differentiation process, one of a series of differentiation processes (e.g., differentiation of self and others, of subjective and objective) which necessitate a recategorization of experience and which, once fully understood, can never be consciously rejected.[2] Each differentiation process, including that of gender differentiation, initially results in a sense of limitation and loss. Normally such difficulties are transient, to be replaced by a delimited and more articulated sense of self as female, with a freedom to integrate qualities of femininity within the self and to productively interact with complementary male qualities. However, even in normal development, this resolution does not occur until shortly before the entry into the Oedipal stage.

The female toddler, who generally discovers the penis between the ages of 15 and 24 months, interprets this finding in the light of her current concerns and through the screen of her prelogical cognitive capacities. Understandably, her initial reaction is one of surprise. Mayer (1985) presents the observations and speculations of Emily, a bright and verbal 20-month-old toddler. ''Mummy has a bottom. . . . Daddy has a bottom. . . . Emily has a bottom. . . . Mummy has a vulva. . . .

[2]On an unconscious level, however, severe and irreversible limitations are perhaps never accepted. On this level, the impossibility of possessing the attributes of both sexes, for boys and girls alike, is in the same class as the harsh reality of otherness and of mortality (McDougall, 1985). Kubie (1974) posits a central human drive to become both sexes. Derivatives of this drive are pervasive and particularly difficult to resolve and can manifest themselves in lack of commitment in love and work as well as in hatred and envy toward the opposite sex.

and Emily has a vulva. . . but Mummy, Daddy has something *funny* in his vulva!"
(p. 331). Emily's assumption that "everybody must be just like me" is based on her
experience (everybody has two eyes, one nose, etc.). At 20 months, Emily cannot
conceive of anyone without a genital which opens toward an inner space, and so
assumes that her father must have something in addition to, not instead of, a vulva.
Some months later, she is able to conceptualize differences more clearly and simultaneously declares that she wants a penis for herself and that, "men can't have
surprise drawers, just ladies and girls can" (p. 342).

Too little to understand that differences in genitalia represent belonging to two
different classes of human beings—male and female—the little girl frequently feels
deprived of a concrete something, the penis. The toddler often equates the penis
with a fecal column; the more that issues of possession and control occupy her, the
more she is likely to resent the boy's being allowed to touch, possess, and keep his
fecal product while she is forced to give hers up. Should the possessor of the penis
be a sibling, particularly a new brother, anal phase concerns about loss of the object
and of the object's love are even more likely to condense into the fear of having had
her own fecal penis removed because she was unlovable. Other possible phase-
specific interpretations of a new brother's penis include that of umbilical cord
(Karme, 1981), denoting an attachment to mother that the envious older sister is
denied.

At this stage, anal and genital concerns intertwine with the issues of separation
and individuation, which are played out in bodily context in terms of boundaries
and differentiation. The little girl's genitalia are far less accessible to direct visual
and tactile exploration than are boy's; it is therefore less easy for her to form a
mental representation of them. In addition, the location of sensation is not focused
as it is for the boy; touching the female genital at any point leads to a spread of
sensation to other areas. There is a sensual diffusivity between clitoris, vulva,
urethra, and anus. "The inability to define or locate an experience is in direct
opposition to the child's developmental task of articulating its body and its world"
(D. Bernstein, 1986). This complicates the process of separation-individuation, in
part because it threatens the girl's hard-won mastery over the inside of her body
and in part because it turns her back to her mother to help her master her anxiety
and confusion around her genitals at just the time when she needs to pull away.[3]

Confronted with anxiety over a genital apparatus difficult to define or to lo-
calize sensually, which is too close and too reminiscent of the anal opening and yet
appears to be an opening that cannot be closed, it is understandable that the little
girl may at times wish that she had a penis, which appears to be a concrete,
definable, controllable tool for mastery and independence.

In conjunction with the discovery of the anatomical difference, the little girl has
been noted to increase her fantasy activity and to indulge in quiet, "low-keyed"
play (Galenson & Roiphe, 1976). Her frequent concern with holes, with openings
that don't close, and with phallic-shaped objects reflects her focus on dominant
themes of female sexuality.

[3]Lerner, H. (1976) and M. A. Silverman (1981) speak of the need for parents to assist their
daughters to understand the nature of their genitalia. Lerner presents a particularly concrete
example of a woman incapable of understanding maps and having little sense of direction
based upon her never having acquired a clear "map" of her genitalia.

> Both aspects of female development—the reproductive as well as the sexual function—necessitate the relinquishment of the object and the capacity to possess and to separate, to libidinize both the filling up and the emptying out processes. Female sexuality is indeed a cavity erotism and, therefore, suffers the fate of its forerunner since both involve receptacles . . . through which fullness and loss are repeatedly experienced and tolerated. In this way it resembles much more closely than male sexuality the antecedent anal phase and requires its integration as well as its surpassing (Oliner, 1982, p. 57).

With progressing gender differentiation, the toddler girl becomes increasingly concerned with the inside of her body and with her inner play and thoughts. This development signals the beginning of the inner genital phase in which the little girl, partly through her focus on her inner body and partly out of identification with the admired and envied mother, concentrates on her diffuse, unfocused inner genital sensations and fantasizes a baby inside. An inward focus can be observed in 3-year-old girls, who tend to spend a fair amount of time drawing, painting, and playing with dolls (Frankel & Sherick, 1979). The urgency of the yearning for a doll or a real infant has frequently been noted (Parens et al., 1976). This urge, based on identification with the fertile mother plus the need to externalize diffuse, hard-to-locate genital sensations and perceptions onto a concrete object makes the baby doll an important focus for the little girl. "By assuming the role of a mother to a baby, the little girl recreates not only her own babyhood, but also the mother of her infancy. In this process, she builds an image of her procreative inside, modeled after the shape of a baby" (Kestenberg, 1982, p. 121).

The little girl in the inner genital phase begins to contrast the genital and anal portions of her body and to establish a primacy of the generative feminine inside over the alimentary and excretory organs and functions. In her fantasy, she creates a baby out of food, feces, and urine but always under the sway of the expanding and contracting inner-genital sensate focus and of a continuing (though more refined and always unconscious) awareness of the mother's biological clock and rhythmic cycles. As Blum (1976) states, "The body ego and biological role of the female indicate the metaphorical significance of both inner space and periodic time. . . . Rhythmicity may be a special component of the feminine personality" (p. 18).

The small girl's ability to move out of a pregenital orientation and into the inner genital phase is greatly dependent upon her continuing ability to both identify with and to separate from her mother's body. The quality of the earliest mother–infant interactions and the degree of separation between mother and daughter in large part determine the intensity of desire for and the meaning of pregnancy and of the birth of a child both in the child and in the adult woman (Lester & Notman, 1986). Pines (1982, 1987) points out that there are differences between the desire for pregnancy and the desire for a baby. Frequently, the desire for a child reflects the woman's identification with her mother's maternality and the creation of a positive maternal ego-ideal, while the desire for pregnancy but not for a live child stems from fear of becoming merged with a hostile and yearned for maternal representation. Kestenberg (1976), in a study of pregnant women in analysis, found that during each trimester of pregnancy there was regression to a particular pregenital mode (i.e., oral, anal, or urethral), but that these were all subsumed and integrated under inner-genital development.

The small girl's bodily concerns are organized around making sense of her own genitalia, with their hidden, yet intuited openings and sensations. In taking inventory of her own genital body, the little girl assesses whether there has somehow been damage to her capacity to function, that is, damage to her own female structures or to her fantasized fetus. Concern over the nature of her genitalia, conceptualized in part as a hole with no closure, leads to a central fear that her creative insides can fall out. This anxiety is renewed during psychophysical crises such as menarche and childbirth. Its resolution is a major factor in creating tolerance for physiological changes and for the ebb and flow of the rhythms and cycles of female reproductive life. Still under the cognitive and emotional sway of the preceding, pregenital period of life, the little girl assumes that she is supposed to have male as well as female genitalia. While her concerns about comparing herself to boys are less frequent and intense than her concerns regarding her own inner genitality, she does wonder whether she has somehow lost both penis and testicles.

After an initial assessment of her own female body, the little girl in the next subphase of the pre-Oedipal genital phase is ready to turn her attention to each of her parents as a genital sexual being.

> The differentiation framework suggests that as the girl recategorizes her experience in gender terms changes occur in her relations to each parent. She now learns to relate to each parent in specifically gender terms. She learns to relate to her mother as a same-sex person, to identify with her without losing self–other differentiation. . . . She must learn to relate to the father now as specifically male in relation to her own self as female. These new orientations provide contexts within which she practises and elaborates the differentiated notions of femininity and of masculinity she is developing . . . her relation to the father provides a needed separateness from the mother as she elaborates her identifications with and same-sex relationship to her. The relation to the mother is an independent source of support for her feminity as she develops her cross-sex relation to her father as masculine (Fast, 1979, pp. 451–452).

The little girl has, of course, had a specific relationship with her father since the beginning of life; recent studies demonstrate that infants recognize their fathers almost as soon as they do their mothers. Fathers are frequently looked upon as the more exciting and stimulating parent; Mahler, Pine, and Bergman (1975) write of the father as the "knight in shining armour," who helps the child to separate from the mother. However, as the girl becomes more aware of herself as a genital human being, she turns to her father in the service of "genital self-differentiation" (Abelin, 1971), in order to investigate his sexual aspects in relation to herself.

The little girl's heightened awareness of the male body, particularly of the penis, contributes to her concern about the vulnerability of her own, open genital body. Greenacre (1953) discusses the phenomenon of penis awe, in which admiration, fear, and sexual excitement are mingled. Rees (1986) believes that while representing the father as "phallic aggressor" may in part be a projection of the child's own hostility, it is primarily "an almost inevitable symbolic formation." While the little girl's fantasized anxieties assume a number of forms, the most frequently experienced genital anxiety is penetration anxiety. Barnett (1966) states that, due to the girl's awareness that the vaginal cavity is not protected by voluntary sphincter control, "penetration via that organ remains a constant threat" (p. 131). Greenacre

(1953) describes the girl as terrified by the penis "on account of its size and the fear that to be penetrated by such an organ would be to be split or torn apart by it" (p. 179).

In addition to her fear of penetration, the girl frequently fears becoming overwhelmed by her own sexual response, which may be too strong for her still immature ego structure. "Deep down, she still considers sexual excitement and sexual sensations as dangerous, fragmenting and destructive" (Montgrain, 1983, p. 170). These fears may lead to her defensively, in fantasy, "closing" her creative inside. While some girls turn away from genital stimulation altogether (Barnett, 1966; Fraiberg, 1972; Kramer, 1954), others draw back from vaginal to purely clitoral sensations.

The little girl uses her mother as a background, supportive figure in her task of learning to relate to and deal with the cross-sex attributes of her father. The more comfortable and enjoyable the mother finds the father's phallic qualities, the easier it is for the little girl, in identification with her mother, to overcome her fears. In addition, to the extent that the girl experiences her father as protective of and responsive to her developing femininity, she will actively demand his support for her female qualities and will be able to utilize him to help her separate from her mother sexually when she focuses her attention upon her mother as a genitally sexual person.

Previously, the little girl had been involved in separating from her mother on a pregenital level, as a more independent person. Genital sexual identity is largely dependent on the capacity to identify with the same-sex parent (Edgcumbe & Burgner, 1975). To develop her own sexual identity, the girl needs to selectively identify with certain aspects of her mother's genital sexuality and to discard or modify others. She now carefully studies the mother's behavior as a woman. Consciously and unconsciously, the little girl is interested in and influenced by the mother's feelings about her own sexuality and her female functions and by her feelings about and sexual responses to men. Pregenital identifications with the mother's biological rhythms are continued and elaborated at this point.

In her dual and conflicting need for and fear of separating from her mother, the little girl becomes sharply aware of real or fantasized aspects of the mother that seek to interfere with her development and to keep her dependent on the mother. Both the intensity of the attachment between mother and daughter and the inward-directed nature of female sexuality contribute to the erasing of inner and outer boundaries and result in the girl's fearing she will be destroyed by her mother. This dynamic may be expressed in Kestenberg's finding that the girl is very concerned with issues of death and dying at this time (1975, 1982), and in Frankel and Sherick's (1979) observations of nursery school girls complaining of the mother as rough and mean. Person (1983) finds that fears in the later stages of analyses between female analysts and female patients are often cast in oral terms, with the woman fearing both annihilation and loss of love.

The mother's attitudes around masturbation are particularly significant at this point. In one case, Fraiberg (1972) succeeded in tracing persecutory feelings and accusations toward the mother to the mother's accidentally linking masturbation and danger. According to Torok (1970), masturbation is forbidden by the mother in order to prohibit fantasies of pleasure with the father's penis, thereby blocking the way to genital fulfillment. This is to assure the mother that the daughter, having no penis, will always be loyal to the mother and prevent the mother from lapsing into "bitterness and envy."

The father is used both as a supportive, complementary figure, and as an identificatory figure in aiding the girl to differentiate and separate from the genital mother and to "claim her body as her own." His appreciation of her emerging feminine qualities and his ability to allow her to identify with him (e.g., with the perceived qualities of the phallus as moving through space with force and directed focus) without withdrawing from her, also aid in the integration of qualities perceived as male and as the father's into an overall feminine organization.

The last subphase of the pre-Oedipal genital phase has been labelled "phallic-narcissistic" by Edgcumbe & Burgner (1975). The phallic-narcistic child has not yet entered the Oedipal stage, as the genitals are still used primarily for exhibitionistic, narcissistic and comparative purposes, with sexual wishes and fantasies expressed within an essentially one-to-one relationship.

The girl's fascination with her own and others' bodily appearance and physiological functioning become expressed through both exhibitionism and scopophilia. Unlike the anal-phase child who desires admiration for her body products, the little girl in the narcissistic portion of the pre-Oedipal genital phase demands admiration from others for her bodily prowess, for what she's able to do. In the interest of gaining the admiration necessary for her self-esteem, the little girl uses both the phallic qualities of her father and the inner-genital processes of her mother and herself to bolster her sense of her self and her body-self. She shifts from phallic, thrusting, penetrating, aggressively competitive activity, via the body moving through space, to outwardly placed inner-genital processes, such as displaying active mothering, empathic responsiveness, and artistic endeavors, with one eye always on the response of her objects, whose admiring reactions are her major aim and reward. At this point the girl will compete with anyone for the attention of either father or mother; neither parent is yet given the status of Oedipal conquest or Oedipal rival.

As sexual role definition progresses, establishing a highly individualistic, female identity, the little girl's earlier ability to playfully assume each gender role gradually declines.

> The child has to attempt to come to terms with the differences between the sexes in the physical formation of the genitals, . . . normal development requires a gradual divergence, in boys and girls, of drive derivatives, fantasies, sexual identifications, and modes of relating to the object (Edgcumbe & Burgner, 1975, pp. 162–163).

As she realizes the permanence of genital differences, the little girl compares her body to that of the boy. During the anal phase, the girl envied the boy his large genitals (envy is frequently centered on the large scrotum of the infant boy or the adult male); now the little girl is concerned with performance. The functional superiority of the male genital is particularly apparent when she watches boys direct their urinary stream. Boys delight in displaying this competitive exhibitionistic advantage and girls consider their inability to compete a narcissistic blow.

She envies his possession of a phallic "tool" which can be used either in the service of exhibitionistic or sadistic impulses or for masturbatory pleasure. On the other hand, the girl sees her own body as superior, in identification with her mother's, because it is capable of bearing babies; she experiences her body as safer from harm and therefore better than the body of the boy who risks both physical castration and narcissistic insult due to the placement of his genitalia (Glover & Mendell, 1982, pp. 161–162).

At this moment before the Oedipal phase, the girl's fantasies of pregnancy do not involve bearing her father's child, nor does she yet connect the act of intercourse with pregnancy; rather, it appears to be a self-sufficient, narcissistic fantasy.

Once the little girl has established a relatively differentiated sexual identity out of a melding of inner genital and phallic identifications and on the basis of increasingly articulated object relations and cognitive processes, she has completed the developmental tasks necessary to move into the Oedipal phase of development. Her new ability to imaginatively identify with her cross-sex parent while still defining the boundaries of her female body-self will stand her in good stead when, as an adult, she must empathize with the phallic sexuality of her lover and her male child.

Unlike the girl in the pre-Oedipal genital phase, the Oedipal phase child is capable of maintaining a triangular object relationship, in which she simultaneously is sexually desirous of her father, competes with her mother for the love of her father, and wishes to keep intact the loving, dependent relationship with her mother. Normal nursery school girls consolidate their Oedipal relationships far more quickly and decisively than do neurotic children, whose pre-Oedipal conflicts either delay their move into the Oedipal phase or cause regressive distortions to occur (Edgcumbe & Burgner, 1975).[4]

The little girl's Oedipal attachment to her father is perhaps the most passionate of her life. He is both the heir of her feelings toward the pre-Oedipal mother and the template for her later relationships with men. As she studies ways to intrigue and enchant him, her identification with her mother as a wife and a woman become increasingly differentiated. As her cognitive ability increases she understands for the first time that intercourse leads to impregnation. Her original, pre-Oedipal wish for a baby in identification with the generative mother and as a link between mother, child, and the girl's infant self is supplemented by, and temporarily subordinated to, actively making a baby with her father and thereby having a concrete, permanent link with him.

---

[4]The *reason* for the little girl's entry into the Oedipal phase is frequently raised. At first glance, this may seem like a legitimate question, until one realizes that the little boy's entry into the Oedipal phase is not questioned, nor is the the child's entry into any of the pre-Oedipal phases which follow maturational timetables. The question is a holdover from the earlier Freudian position that the boy's heterosexuality is activated by a psychobiological force, whereas the girl's is activated by a narcissistic injury—the realization of the anatomic difference (Parens, 1976). Frequently, the *timing* of the discovery of the anatomical difference, that is, its advent prior to the Oedipal phase, is presented as though that proved a cause and effect relationship. However, the fact that one event may follow another does not attest to a causal relationship.

At the same time that the little girl continues to love and need her mother, she sees her as a better endowed competitor for the father's favors, and as such hates her and wishes to be rid of her. This conflict generates anxiety over disloyalty and betrayal (frequently projected onto the mother and a major source of the girl's accusations against her) which the girl fears can lead either to the mother's abandonment of her or to the mother's destructive retaliation against her. As the maternal competitor is also the primary source of nurturance, the fantasized destruction takes the form of starvation or annihilation, condensing fears from all preoedipal periods. To appease the mother, the girl may temporarily utilize masculine identifications, thereby attempting to give the mother that which the girl actually wants to take from her—the father and his exciting genitality. Or the girl may retreat temporarily to a pre-Oedipal position where she is again "mommy's baby." Here, so-called negative Oedipal manifestations are used for purposes of conflict resolution, in order to avoid anxieties associated with positive Oedipal wishes. In assuming either of these positions, the little girl may revive anal or urethral penis envy for defensive purposes, as concentration on the lack of a penis or on a fantasized penis protects the girl against punishment for being a female and wanting a man. Thus, penis envy can defensively take the place of desire for the penis. One of the most poignant reasons for difficulty in establishing a positive Oedipal position is the need of both mother and daughter to use each other as their central love object in the absence of the father. Too frequently, this pattern has been interpreted as fixation at a negative Oedipal phase.

> Again we found the constellation of a depressed, neglectful mother, a father absent for long periods, and, when at home, unsupportive of his daughter's positive oedipal moves. The negative oedipal position seemed to be (the) . . . only solution in her struggle to avoid regression from the phallic-drive level and from oedipal relationships in which conflicts about and frustration of positive oedipal strivings were intolerable. It may be seen as part of a more general attempt at adaptation to feared and actual deprivations and losses through an exaggerated and prolonged attachment to the mother (Edgcumbe et al., 1976, p. 57).

In addition, the little girl does have moments of desiring, as well as envying her mother's sexual attributes, moments of erotic desire for her first love object. These homoerotic feelings, along with the little girl's mixture of feelings of sexual competitiveness, power struggle, and narcissistic injury in relation to the mother, result in an intense wish to be envied and admired by the mother. D. Bernstein (1987) notes that a dominant fantasy in women is that of having other women look on at their successes in being beautiful and sexual, thus reversing the actual childhood humiliation. In order for this to happen, the rival must be maintained, rather than destroyed. This represents a condensation of aggression toward and continuing bonding with the maternal rival.

Rejection by the father, however, is the most painful and humiliating narcissistic blow the little girl must face. In her paper, " 'I Can't' versus 'He Won't,' " Barnett (1968) outlines the different positions of the boy and girl during the Oedipal stage. The little boy, intensely aware of the discrepancy in size between his penis and that of his father's, recognizes that he cannot satisfy his mother sexually, much as he wishes to do so. The little girl, on the other hand, although in conflict between her wish to be sexually penetrated by her father and her fear of genital harm, feels that she could be her father's sexual partner, if only he would chose her. No matter how tactful and appreciative of his little girl a father is, it will only ameliorate, not eliminate, her sense of exclusion from the sexual coupling on which she has set her sights, and will confirm her determination to replicate such a desirable relationship when she grows up. According to Bergmann (1982) the little girl abandons her passionate, intense demands on her father for three reasons: first, fear of mother and her punishment; second, because father prefers the mother; and third, because of superego condemnation.

The consolidation of the superego near the end of the Oedipal stage can be viewed as a focal juncture in the process of separating and individuating from parental objects. "The superego, as the culmination of individual psychic structure formation, represents something ultimate in the basic separation-individuation process" (Loewald, 1979, p. 755). By means of internalization of parental attributes, aspects of relationships are transformed into superego qualities and strictures. It is necessary for the little girl to identify with certain of her father's masculine qualities within an overall feminine identity formation in order to assist her in relinquishing him as a libidinal object. Should she not do so sufficiently, she may experience various difficulties, for example, defensive envy of male power and prerogatives in conjunction with an inability to compete with men. Circumscribed identification with the father, at this stage as well as during earlier phases, assists the little girl to individuate. Thus, she is better able to make Oedipal and superego identifications with her mother without fear of becoming overwhelmed by primitive, diffuse identifications.

Due to its pre-Oedipal origins, the girl's superego is marked by the particular qualities of her early identifications with her mother. "The mother is perceived again through infantile eyes; she is diffuse, unstructured, herself. . . . This leads to an internalization of dependence on a superego identification bearing many of the qualities of the resurrected mother . . ." (D. Bernstein, 1983, p. 198). The diffusiveness and internal orientation of the little girl's pre-Oedipal and Oedipal bodily experiences and mental representations are integrated into a specifically female superego structure, marked by flexibility, power, and efficiency of drive control, with emphasis on maintaining relationships as a central content. According to D. Bernstein, the strength of the female superego has its sources in: (a) the resurrected identification with, and fear of, the omnipotent-seeming mother of early infancy; (b) the confusion and diffusion between the genital and anal regions so that the prohibitions of anal impulses are applied to genital sensations and wishes; and (c) anxieties over bodily harm. As described throughout this chapter, fears of bodily harm stem from many sources and assume numerous forms. They include the fear that her creative insides will fall out, penetration anxiety arising from fear of the thrusting phallus, fear of genital mutilation from the jealous mother, and castration anxiety stemming from her infantile conviction that she must originally have been hermaphroditic.

The girl's greater maturity and ego strength, relative to her brother, allow her, in identification with her mother, to form a superego in which there are fewer breakthroughs of drive and less failure to conform to internalized prohibitions or directives.

> At the beginning of latency [there tends to be a picture of female superego functioning] that is different from that observed in boys. The girl's superego operates with less dictatorial harshness and rigidity, less of a tendency to rule by terror and threat of retaliation, and less use of violent punishments to enforce its imperatives than does the boy's. It tends to function more smoothly, quietly, subtly, and effectively in its operation, but there is more of a tendency to masochism, over-control and abnegation . . . too (M.A. Silverman, 1982, pp. 218–219).

Rather than sexuality being dormant during latency, there appears to be progressive consolidation of newly achieved ego and superego modes and capacities, without the continual tensions of new libidinal phase demands. The early latency girl only partly renounces her Oedipal interest in her father. However, her feelings become less sexualized and shift in the direction of warm, affectionate attitudes.In part this grows out of superego prohibitions, in part out of the ego's adaptive and defensive capacities. Neither sexuality nor positive Oedipal feelings are dormant, however. Rejection by the father of her Oedipal longings continues to be a painful narcissistic blow, as evidenced by the core latency fantasy which contains masochistic Oedipal themes, including the wish for and dread of penetration and guilt-induced punishments for wanting to steal father from mother and to kill father for his rejection. Common phobic preoccupations of early latency girls which express these fantasies include the idea of being stabbed or shot by a robber who enters the house to kidnap her. Such masochistic fantasies eroticize suffering and pain (I. Bernstein, 1983).

Masturbation tends to be fought against during latency, in part because of regression to the sadomasochistic anal phase. Although initiated to avoid Oedipal conflict, such regression rarely is effective, and simply adds the girl's shame and disgust at sadomasochistic fantasies to her guilt and fear about the Oedipal fantasies unconsciously attached to masturbation. The girl's hidden genitalia and diffuse excitation make it possible for her to stimulate herself indirectly, while remaining consciously unaware that she is doing so, thus avoiding self-condemnation (Clower, 1976). Rhythmic, total body movement popular among latency age girls both displaces inner genital sensations to the total body and stimulates genital sensations. Her ability to conceal her masturbatory activity from others and even from herself allows her to continue to experience and cultivate sexual sensations without bringing the condemnation of either her superego or authorities upon her. It also presages the adolescent girl's refutation of responsibility for her own sexual experimentation, placing the responsibility on the male.

Latency is a period during which the child consolidates the maternal ego-ideal that she has been developing since the inner genital phase. She attempts to expand her feminine identification by bonding with her girl friends as well as identifying with maternal activity both at home and in the larger world.

> The intense interest which latency age girls have in the mysterious and wondrous forces within them that one day will transform them into sexually mature, menstruating, procreative women with breasts and curves is reflected in their attention to books and stories about remarkable women with fascinating, magical, witchlike powers which they use wisely to help children and people beleaguered by forces of evil. . . . At times the difficulty in waiting for the dormant powers within them to finally emerge from their slumber is too agoniz-

ing, and fantasies are spun out in which limited magical powers express themselves in girls themselves (M. A. Silverman, 1982, p. 214).

In this final moment before puberty with its disruptive libidinal tensions arrives and changes the relatively smooth functioning of latency, the girl has a chance to achieve a relatively mature set of assessments and appraisals about her femininity and to either correct or reinforce distortions from earlier developmental phases.

The physiologically mature female will encounter numerous psychophysical crises, which necessitate specific intrapsychic adaptations and coping skills. They include a tolerance for changes in internal and external body boundaries, as in pregnancy, an acceptance of cyclic rhythms, as in menstruation, and an ability to move flexibly between regressive and mature modes, as is necessary when tending to small children. Freud's view of early female development as secondary to and compensatory for penis envy and castration anxiety is perhaps most inadequate as an attempt to explain the precursors of these extraordinarily subtle and complex mechanisms. This chapter has explored contemporary understandings of the precursors of women's integrative capacities. The dominant themes that have been stressed are identification with, individuation from, and bonding with the mental representation of the mother, contrast and comparison with the complementary male figure, and the increasingly complex and differentiated fantasies and understandings about bodily, particularly genital, boundaries.

REFERENCES

Abelin, E. (1971). The role of the father in the separation-individuation process. In J. B. McDevitt & C. F. Settlage (Eds.), *Separation-Individuation* (pp. 229–252). New York: International Universities Press.

Barnett, M. C. (1966). Vaginal awareness in the infancy and childhood of girls. *Journal of the American Psychoanalytic Association, 14*, 129–141.

Barnett, M. C. (1968). "I can't" versus "He won't." Further considerations of the physical consequences of the anatomic and physiological differences between the sexes. *Journal of the American Psychoanalytic Association, 16*, 588–600.

Bergmann, M. V. (1982). The female Oedipus complex: Its antecedents and evolution. In D. Mendell (Ed.), *Early female development: Current psychoanalytic views* (pp. 175–202). New York: SP Medical and Scientific Books.

Bernstein, D. (1983). The female superego: A different perspective. *International Journal of Psycho-Analysis, 64*, 187–202.

Bernstein, D. (1986). Female genital anxieties: Conflicts and mastery modes. Paper presented at the February meeting of the Division of Psychoanalysis of the American Psychological Association in Xtapa, Mexico.

Bernstein, D. (1987). Female Oedipus complex. In I. Graham (Ed.), *Proceedings of the first Delphi symposium on psychoanalysis and myths* (in press).

Bernstein, I. (1983). Masochistic pathology and feminine development. *Journal of the American Psychoanalytic Association, 31*, 467–486.

Blum, H. (1976). Masochism, the ego ideal, and the psychology of women. *Journal of the American Psychoanalytic Association Supplement—Female Psychology, 24*, 157–191.

Brunswick, R. M. (1940). The preoedipal phase of the libido development. *Psychoanalytic Quarterly, 9*, 293–319.

Chasseguet-Smirgel, J. (1970). *Female sexuality.* Ann Arbor: University of Michigan Press.

Clower, V. (1976). Theoretical implication in current views of masturbation in latency girls. *Journal of the American Psychoanalytic Association Supplement—Female Psychology,* 24,109–125.

Deutsch, H. (1944–1945). *The psychology of women,* Vols. I and II. New York: Grune & Stratton.

Edgcumbe, R., S. Lundberg, R. Markowitz, & F. Salo (1976). Some comments on the concept of the negative Oedipal phase in girls. *The Psychoanalytic Study of the Child, 31,* 35–61.

Edgcumbe, R., & Burgner, M. (1975). The phallic–narcissistic phase. *The psychoanalytic study of the child,* Volume 30 (pp 161–180). New Haven: Yale University Press.

Fast, I. (1979). Developments in gender identity: Gender differentiation in girls. *International Journal of Psycho-Analysis, 60,* 443–453.

Fliegel, Z. O. (1982). Half a century later: Current status of Freud's controversial views on women. *Psychoanalytic Review, 69,* 7–28.

Fliegel, Z. O. (1985). Phallocentricity—How central to psychoanalytic theory? Paper presented at the May 11, 1981 meeting of the Institute for Psychoanalytic Training and Research Panel on Phallocentricity, New York City.

Formanek, R. (1982). On the origins of gender identity. In D. Mendell (Ed.), *Early female development: Current psychoanalytic views* (pp. 1–24). New York: SP Medical and Scientific Books.

Fraiberg, S. (1972). Genital arousal in latency girls. *The Psychoanalytic Study of the Child, 27,* 439–475.

Frankel, S., & Sherick, I. (1979). Observations of the emerging sexual identity of three and four year old children: with emphasis on female sexual identity. *International Review of Psycho-Analysis, 6,* 297–309.

Freud, S. (1925). Some psychological consequences of the anatomical distinction between the sexes. *Standard Edition, 19,* 243–258. London: Hogarth, 1961.

Freud, S. (1931). Female sexuality. *Standard Edition, 21,* 225–243. London: Hogarth, 1961.

Freud, S. (1933). New introductory lectures on psychoanalysis. *Standard Edition, 22,* 112–185. London: Hogarth, 1964.

Galenson, E., & Roiphe, H. (1976). Some suggested revisions concerning early female development. *Journal of the American Psychoanalytic Association Supplement—Female Psychology, 24,* 29–57.

Glover, L., & Mendell, D. (1982). A suggested developmental sequence for a pre-oedipal developmental phase. In D. Mendell (Ed.), *Early female development: Current psychoanalytic views* (pp. 25–60). New York: SP Medical and Scientific Books.

Greenacre, P. (1948). Anatomical structure and superego development. In *Trauma, growth and personality* (pp. 149–164). New York: International Universities Press, 1952.

Greenacre, P. (1950). Special problems of early female sexual development. *The Psychoanalytic Study of the Child, 5,* 122–138.

Greenacre, P. (1953). Penis awe and its relation to penis envy. In R. Lowenstein (Ed.), *Drives, affects and behavior* (pp. 176–190). New York: International Universities Press.

Horney, K. (1933). The denial of the vagina. *International Journal of Psycho-Analysis, 14,* 1–33.

Jones. E. (1933). The phallic phase. *International Journal of Psycho-Analysis, 14,* 1–33.

Karme, L. (1981). A clinical report of penis envy: Its multiple meanings and defensive function. *Journal of the American Psychoanalytic Association, 29,* 427–446.

Kestenberg, J. (1968). Outside and inside, male and female. *Journal of the American Psychoanalytic Association, 16,* 457–520.

Kestenberg, J. (1975). *Children and parents: Psychoanalytic studies in development.* New York: Jason Aronson.

Kestenberg, J. (1976). Regression and reintegration in pregnancy. *Journal of the American Psychoanalytic Association Supplement—Female Psychology, 24,* 213–250.

Kestenberg, J. (1982). The inner-genital phase—prephallic and preoedipal. In D. Mendell

(Ed.), *Early female development: Current psychoanalytic views* (pp. 81–126). New York: SP Medical and Scientific Books.

Kleeman, J. (1975). Genital self-stimulation in infant and toddler girls. In I. Marcus and J. Francis (Eds.), *Masturbation: From infancy to senescence* (pp. 77–106). New York: International Universities Press.

Kleeman, J. (1976). Freud's early views. *Journal of the American Psychoanalytic Association Supplement—Female Psychology, 24*, 3–27.

Klein, M. (1957). Envy and gratitude. In *Envy and gratitude and other works 1946–1961*. New York: Dell, 1975.

Kohlberg, L. (1966). A cognitive-developmental analysis of children's sex role concepts and attitudes. In E. Maccoby (Ed.), *The development of sex differences* (pp. 82–173). Stanford, CA: Stanford University Press.

Kramer, P. (1954). Early capacity for orgastic discharge and character formation. *The Psychoanalytic Study of the Child, 9*, 128–141.

Kubie, L. (1974). The drive to become both sexes. *Psychoanalytic Quarterly, 43*, 349–426.

Lerner, H. (1976). Parental mislabeling of female genitals as a determinant of penis envy and learning inhibitions in women. *Journal of the American Psychoanalytic Association Supplement—Female Psychology, 24*, 269–284.

Lester, E. P., & Notman, M. T. (1986). Pregnancy, developmental crisis and object relations: Psychoanalytic considerations. *International Journal of Psycho-Analysis, 67*, 357–366.

Lewis, M., and Freedle, R. (1973). Mother-infant dyad: The cradle of meaning. In P. Pliner, L. Kramer, & T. Alloway (Eds.), *Communication and affect: Language and thought*. New York: Academic Press.

Loewald, H. (1979). The waning of the Oedipus complex. *Journal of the American Psychoanalytic Association, 27*, 751–775.

Mahler, M., Pine, F., & Bergman, A. (1975). *The psychological birth of the human infant*. New York: Basic Books.

Mayer, E. L. (1985). "Everybody must be just like me": Observations on female castration anxiety. *International Journal of Psycho-Analysis, 66*, 331–348.

McDougall, J. (1985). On the homosexual components of female sexuality. Paper given at the First Carole Dilling Memorial Lecture, Dec. 15, New York City.

Montgrain, N. (1983). On the vicissitudes of female sexuality: The difficult path from "anatomical destiny" to psychic representation. *International Journal of Psycho-Analysis, 64*, 169–186.

Moss, H. A. (1974). Early sex differentiation and mother–infant interaction. In R. C. Friedman, R. M. Richart, & R. L. Vande-Wiele (Eds.). *Sex differences in behavior* (pp. 149–164). New York: John Wiley & Sons.

Oliner, M. (1982). The anal phase. In D. Mendell (Ed.), *Early female development: Current psychoanalytic views* (pp. 25–60). New York: SP Medical and Scientific Books.

Parens, H., Pollock, L., Stern, J., & Kramer, S. (1976). On the girl's entry in to the Oedipus complex. *Journal of the American Psychoanalytic Association Supplement–Female Psychology, 24*, 79–107.

Person, E. S. (1983). Women in therapy: Therapist gender as a variable. *International Review of Psycho-Analysis, 10*, 193–204.

Pines, D. (1982). The relevance of early psychic development to pregnancy and abortion. *International Journal of Psycho-Analysis, 63*, 311–320.

Pines, D. (1987). A woman's unconscious use of her body; a psycho-analytical perspective. Paper given at the Second Carole Dilling Memorial Lecture, Jan. 10, New York City.

Rees, K. (1986). "Perhaps I'll marry mommy!"; another look at masculine identifications in feminine development. Paper presented at the February meeting of the Division of Psycho-analysis of the American Psychological Association in Xtapa, Mexico.

Schafer, R. (1974). Problems in Freud's psychology of women. *Journal of the American Psychoanalytic Association, 22,* 459–485.

Silverman, D. K. (1987a). What are little girls made of? *Psychoanalytic Psychology, 4,* 315–334.

Silverman, D. K. (1987b). Female bonding: Some supportive findings for Melanie Klein's views. *Psychoanalytic Review, 74*(2), 201–215.

Silverman, M. A. (1981). Cognitive development and female psychology. *Journal of the American Psychoanalytic Association, 29,* 581–606.

Silverman, M. A. (1982). The latency period. In D. Mendell (Ed.), *Early female development: Current psychoanalytic views* (pp. 203–226). New York: SP Medical and Scientific Books.

Stoller, R. (1976). Primary femininity. *Journal of the American Psychoanalytic Association Supplement—Female Psychology, 24,* 3–27.

Torok, M. (1970). The significance of penis envy in women. In J. Chassequet-Smirgel (Ed.), *Female sexuality* (pp. 135–176). Ann Arbor: University of Michigan Press.

Chapter 3

Reflections on the Daughter as a Projective Screen
Mother–Daughter Boundaries

JOAN OFFERMAN-ZUCKERBERG

> We knew, of course, that there had been a preliminary stage of attachment to the mother, but we did not know that it could be so rich in content and so long-lasting, and could leave behind so many opportunities for fixations and dispositions. During this time the girl's father is only a troublesome rival; in some cases the attachment to her mother lasts beyond the fourth year of life. Almost everything that we find later in her relation to her father was already present in this earlier attachment and has been transferred subsequently on to her father. In short, we get an impression that we cannot understand women unless we appreciate this phase of their pre-Oedipus attachment to their mother.
>
> —S. Freud, *Female Sexuality* (1931).

The human struggle to separate and individuate from parents begins at birth. With birth comes the loss of psychophysiological symbiosis for both mother and child; with birth comes the beginning of bonding—the foundation of attachment and the beginning of what may be called "relationship."

In pregnancy, through a complicated process of fantasy-wish, revitalization of unconscious memories, and projective identification begin the initial steps toward an aspect of identity for both the mother and child. From the very planning of a child to conception, fantasies related to gender of the child, aspirations attached to gender, and the accompanying ideation and feelings that are part of both parents' collective self-image and unconscious histories have a powerful influence. The

JOAN OFFERMAN-ZUCKERBERG, PH.D. • Founding Board Member and Supervisor-Faculty, Brooklyn Institute for Psychotherapy, Brooklyn, New York; Supervisor, National Institute for the Psychotherapies, Yeshiva University; private practice.

nature of this influence, its chemistry, the role it plays in the general "cybernetics" of mother–child interaction are of interest to me. This chapter focuses on the interaction of female body-gender, mother–daughter relationship, and individuation.

A large piece of our progress as emotionally competent human beings is, in part, measured by the degree to which the self meets successfully the challenges inherent in the phase-appropriate, developmental tasks of individuation. The challenge of individuation for women today is a culturally embedded issue, saturated with a rich historical ancestry and laden with a complexity of feeling. In today's world and in our practices, we are immersed in the struggles women meet in self-definition and development. Very often in this struggle scapegoats or targets of blame are found; rationalizations and displacements arise to help account for feelings of hopelessness, inadequacy, inferiority, or fear. Husbands are often the targets; they may be experienced as the oppressors and may be thought of as manipulative and exploitative. Their ego concerns, demands, and dependency needs are often labeled by women as causative agents as they experience their own frustrations in growth. Children as well, through their myriad demands and needs, their close binding attachment, and growth requirements are experienced, often masochistically by women, as the sadistic forces that prevent self-actualization and change. In the rather obscure and darkened unconscious arena of projection and displacement, much blame and acting out has occurred. Families have been disrupted, children have been abused, parents have run away, evading responsiblities, and family members have been involved in sexual acting out, leading to multiple relationships and to guilt, deception, and despair; these are the realities of today.

It is within this chaotic climate that I feel the need to regain analytic sharpness and clarity with regard to the psychodynamics of individuation, with special regard here to its interrelationship to female body-gender. This focus excludes the rich complexity of male gender psychology and individuation and its interaction with the female. Within this climate of transition, the necessity for psychologists to look deeply and inwardly into the "individual" psychodynamic histories of their patients seems then even more crucial.

The premise of this chapter is simply that mothers experience a relationship between themselves and their daughters that is different from that between themselves and their sons. The experienced differences stem from several important sources. (1) There may be observable differences in the female neonate's constitutional ability to relate, relating used in the generic sense (that is, the early beginnings of what we might call observable differences in eye contact, activity level, and responsiveness to human face and voice). These differences, interacting with other variables, may act as a kind of trigger or stimulus for later projective identifications to occur in the mother. (2) Body-gender "alikeness" may stimulate more "affective resonance," projective identification, self-object merging with corresponding fantasy affect and ideation. (3) This complex of projective identifications can operate as an ongoing obstacle to proper self-object differentiation, thereby slowing down or "complicating" the pace and course of individuation. (4) Finally, this gender-alikeness and tendency to projective identification can make self-body boundaries between mothers and daughters more "permeable" and diffuse, rendering more difficult and complicated the proper development of self-body object "separateness" and the simultaneous network of healthy defensive hierarchies.

I will attempt to substantiate these hypotheses through case illustrations, clinical and empirical data from research, as well as from the ongoing psychodynamics of clinical work. In this way, I hope to clarify and begin to explore the notion of the daughter as a projective screen.

That the birth of a daughter triggers the unconscious in ways different from the birth of a son is intuitively clear enough. How these differences may operate and how in interaction with observable behavioral differences is not as clear. Through what channels are these differences expressed? Shainess (1969) comments on the mother–child relationship by stating that,

> Mothering actions in the human seem to be of a dual nature: one conscious and the second compulsive. The latter erupts from unconscious forces, comparable to imprint-like inclusions which are suddenly triggered by the child's actions, and which are also related to the self-image of the mothering and fathering person (p. 79).

Accordingly, one may ask how the mother's feminine self-image interacts with the already very female child? Menaker (1965) underscores the importance of the mother–child matrix:

> What is of primary importance in this interaction is the mother's mental image of the child—an image that grows with the mother's need to nurture and love her child . . . which forms the background for the quality of character of the ego" (p. 128).

More specifically in terms of the female child, being a grown woman and mother also means having been the daughter of a mother, which affects the nature of her motherliness and quality of her mothering (Chodorow, 1978).

Researchers have observed that, from birth, girls differ from boys in the following ways: they demonstrate less motor activity, are less irritable, and show greater sensitivity to touch, pain, and body contact. By the age of 6 months, girls are more responsive to human faces, showing a longer fixation time to visual stimuli. They are held, cuddled, and talked to more than boys. Infant boys, on the other hand, demonstrate greater visual spatial acuity and motor mindedness than girls, and are encouraged, at least in this culture, to explore the environment. During the 1st year, girls show greater responsiveness to social stimuli and more social orientation, and by approximately 13 months, girls seem to indicate a maximum response to verbal stimulus high in meaning and inflection—implying response to a person. They show earlier language development and greater field dependency, that is, they are less likely to differentiate between figure and ground (Bardwick, 1971).

In a well-designed study (Hittelman & Dickes, 1979), female neonates were found to spend more time than males in eye-to-eye contact, that is, the average length of each eye contact was greater for females than for males. The authors suggest that to the extent that eye-to-eye contact in the newborn is a measure of interaction, to be sure a measure of personal relatedness (however rudimentary), males and females at birth are already relating to the parenting figure in unique ways.

The observation that female neonates spend greater lengths of time in sustained eye contact has implications for bonding, inasmuch as eye contact has been recognized as pleasurable for the mother (Hittelman & Dickes, 1979) and as a "releaser of maternal caretaking." Several studies subsequently have reported that infant girls smile more, earlier, and interact more positively with their mothers (Lichtenberg, 1983).

A report summarizing the proceedings of a panel on the psychology of women at the annual meeting of the American Psychoanalytic Association (Galenson, 1976) claims that "there is increasing evidence of distinction between the mother's basic attitudes and handling of her boy and girl children, starting from the earliest days and continuing thereafter" (p. 159).

Lewis (1976) substantiates the findings of these studies, and concludes that the girl infant may bring to the interaction with the mother more and earlier attachment-seeking behavior. Lichtenberg (1983), in his review of infant research covering the first 2 years of life, makes note of several gender differences: female newborns demonstrate greater responsiveness to taste, greater mouth activity, more tongue involvement during feeding, and a greater overall tactile sensitivity.[1] The empathic, attachment-seeking mother may respond then accordingly to the female neonate's need for oral interaction and comforting. Throughout the 1st year, it is reported, mothers respond to the physical needs of the female child with more contact and more "rescue-like" behavior. For the purposes of this chapter, we may postulate that there may also be as a result of more and prolonged contact, an earlier release of maternal associations, memories, feelings—the stuff of projection, identification, the building material of bonding and attachment.

By early childhood, these constitutional and certainly culturally shaped gender differences find avenues of socialization, and the differences continue: girls are now observed to show less physical activity, less physical aggressiveness, are better able to anticipate parental wishes, are more likely to conform and be rewarded in this culture for goodness. They remain more dependent on others for self-esteem, their self-esteem being based on love and conformity. The boy now is moving more generally in a direction of greater aggressiveness, physical activity, insistent sexual impulses. He is more intent on his own purposes, somewhat unaware of parental demands, and he is being rewarded for achievement, which is his source of self-esteem, independence, achievement, and objectivity (Bardwick, 1971).

From birth, then, the course of individuation for women is different than for men. Mahler, Pine, and Bergman (1975) add that the task of becoming a separate individual seems at 16 to 24 months of age, to be generally more difficult for girls than for boys. Girls are still more engrossed with mother, demand more bodily closeness, and are more enmeshed in ambivalence. Claims to body autonomy are less prominent than in boys. Boys, as described by Mahler, are "more stiffly resistant to hugging and kissing, beyond and even during differentiation" (4 to 7 months) (p. 106).

Mahler et al. attributes the sex differences in the development of a separate sense of self to differential responses of boys and girls to their realization of sex

---

[1]More recently, in a review by Silverman, 1987, studies point to greater alertness, calmness, less irritability, smoother functioning. Also, see Mendell (1988) in this volume, p. 20, for a review of similar findings.

differences, anatomically. "Girls, upon the discovery of the sexual difference, tended to turn back to the mother, to blame her, to demand from her, to be disappointed in her, and still to be ambivalently tied to her" (p. 106). Boys are better able
to turn to the outside world or their own bodies for pleasure and satisfaction and to
fathers as someone with whom to identify.

Kestenberg (1982) has focused on the anatomical differences between boys and
girls and the impact of this difference on the maturation of ego functions and the
subsequent development of sexual identity. Basic to her focus is the anxiety-
provoking nature of inner genital sensations. Inner body integrity and the resultant
maintenance of self–body boundaries seem to be powerful precursors in early
bodily and affective experiences, autoerotically, and in interaction with the mother.
The female sense of inferiority, and all that this denotes, is underscored.

As Erikson (1968) writes, it seems as if females, by virtue of their constitutional,
biological gender, are different in ways that may be conducive to what are considered culturally assigned traditional female roles. This female child seems to show
signs in one culture of greater physiological and psychological emotional "relatedness" (the sine qua non of parenting). Does this given relatedness make more
probable certain projective identification processes in the mother? Erikson's brilliant and now classical observations of children's play constructions seem to substantiate this notion of early difference. The organization of the play space itself
that children construct seems to parallel "the morphology of genital differentiation." The girls' block scenes were typically "interior"; people are within, in static
positions, there are low walls and simple enclosures. Boys' houses had elaborate
walls with cylinder-like protrusions; the scenes were exterior and the people outside, the enclosures were seen in action.

Female somatic design includes the notion of inner space, greater sensitivity to
touch, eye movement, body contact and closeness, sustained eye contact, and
lower activity level. How do these attributes contribute to our understanding of the
female struggle, the female course of individuation and growth, and how do these
observable differences interact with projection, feeling, fantasy, and the mother's
self-system? What does it evoke in the mother?

Winnicott (1971, p. 112) states that, "the mother is looking at the baby and
what she looks like is related to what she sees there." Part of what she sees is a
body like hers. The schema of the body, the core body-sense, develops and is
maintained within the ever-changing alternation and interplay of the body and the
environment by tactile, kinesthetic, and visual stimuli. Eventual self-boundary formation for the infant derives from touch, smell, taste, sight, and the emergence of
motor coordination (Mahler & McDevitt, 1984). Therefore within the early sensori-
perceptive interchange between mother and infant lies the initial groundwork for
subsequent separation–individuation—the physical beginning of the sense of
"being alive." Aiding the developing sense of body-self is activity, beginning with
the sucking reflex and continuing throughout childhood. With an emphasis of
mother–child mutual body sensation as experiences as core phenomena in the
beginning sense of self, it might be useful to draw some possible gender implications. Given the observation that mothers, in our society at least, may from the start
libidinally administer to the female infant differently (for example, more holding,
molding, smiling), would this not alter the rudimentary sense of self in some way
consistent with our other observations, i.e., in the direction of the deeply en-

meshed, prolonged, symbiotic-like relationship characteristic of mother–daughter relationships? Another tentative implication might be that such body-self enmeshment leads to a kind of vulnerability in body-self-boundary, ranging in intensity from developmentally normal to pathological.

What does the mother see and project into this nonverbal being? A mental image? A body-self? What can get distorted? What are the possible pathological repercussions of poor and muddled self–body–object differentiations? Many dynamic configurations come to mind: the daughter may be experienced as a narcissistic mirror and supplier to the mother, the fulfillment of her incomplete individuation and self, the phallic extension, the projected body-self, the Oedipal rival, the masochistic enhancer and symbiotic partner, the ego graft, the therapist, the source of nurturance, the sadistic reminder of her own inadequacy, the feminine limb. Because of the endless projective possibilities (that work in both directions and, hence, may be defined as interactional projection), the daughter may be experienced by the mother as a psychic drain, particularly if the daughter, in her search for a model in the mother, touches off her feelings of inadequacy. The degree to which the mother can provide an effective role model and serve as a competent and rich self-object will determine in large degree mutual feelings of satisfaction, love, and regard.

Often in our practices, the woman who did not have a full, satisfying, "affirming of self" mother may look to the husband for fulfillment, support, and confirmation. This turning to the husband may indeed be therapeutic or can, if conflicted, be a source of further frustration. If the husband is not "enough" and if the woman is psychologically waiting to be rescued or filled, he can be experienced as a target of rage. He may, as well, be ambivalent toward the woman's individuation, her "leaving the home," and be in fact angry and depressed about feeling left behind. This fear and anger may lead to an unconscious or conscious sabotage of growth. Often a woman (in frustration) looks ambivalently to the husband (who may be himself in conflict) for the signal to grow, to make her whole, to connect her to the outside world.

To my mind, as therapists we must underscore in our analytic work the woman's relationship to her history and her own growing self. The first priority is clarity with regard to one's historical relationships. The place to grow can be inside, that is, the home and children, or outside, that is, career or job, or both. The site of growth is somehow less important than the quality of the working through and the clarity of the insight. That is, often women run to the job, "outer space," the man's world, as they define it, believing that that is the only place individuation can occur. Recent work with a professional woman who was always quite active and decided to reduce her workload and focus on her family's growing needs proved dramatically otherwise. For her, slow and continuous growth as a receptive, nurturant, whole, creative woman was felt, enjoyed, and integrated in the home for the first time in her 38 years.

The crippling and damaging effects of excessive and insufficient projective identification and resultant poor empathy are the substance of our clinical work. Numerous case illustrations come to mind and perhaps, to follow the metaphor of this chapter, they may be considered to be images on a screen. The following are a series of brief case images presented to illustrate and underscore female gender individuation dynamics, with an underlying emphasis on body-self phenomena.

The mother who is a perfectionist, conventional, and is overly tuned in to what others think and has rigid expectations and rules of what ought and should be for her daughter's behavior can contribute to the psychology of a daughter who fears getting close to anyone because "they'll want something from me, all of me, and I won't have anything left," and so the daughter spends a good deal of her life in an encapsulated shell, withholding, inhibited, sexually frigid and constrained, fearing that relating brings confinement, criticism, expectation, and possible attack. The patient in this case experienced her mother an an oppressive, critical, and judgmental force. She speaks of her mother as "never knowing me. She does not know who I am." Such a statement is an indicator of the process of projective identification that obscures the emergence of a separately defined identity. The strong parental press in this case also made for damaged self-expression and became an ongoing obstacle to individuation and movement. On the physical plane, this individual suffered from bouts of amenorrhea, in which a core expression of femaleness, i.e., menstruation, was episodically suppressed.

The deeply narcissistic mother, who insists on being the center of attention, may use her daughter as a source of narcissistic supplies rather than relate to her as a whole, separate person. Such a daughter may talk 30 years later of feeling confused about why she's constantly on guard, why she's constantly expecting and feeling that others are exploiting and using her. One such patient compensated for this feeling by insisting on a kind of pseudoindependence. She was, as a result, unable to lean on anyone, particularly men, for fear that she would be "reduced" and used in some way. This patient's first memory of her mother was finding herself on the subway on an errand at a very young age and forgetting why she had been sent. She was to be her mother's messenger, her "extra limb"; she was to serve her will and disregard her own. This woman's life story of early feminist politics, early divorce, harsh physical self-sufficiency and asexuality was in part a pursuance of will and of autonomy. Becoming close meant submission of will and self-annihilation; the course of her individuation was marked by an alternation between masochistic blindness and deep dependency and compulsive, defensive independence.

A pediatrician and mother of an infant illustrates the struggle for individuation, which was colored by a mother's wish for her daughter not to repeat her life consciously but who unconsciously had a sense of pessimism and doom that there could be in fact no choice in life. The mother's family in this case had been wiped out by the holocaust. The patient's mother, a survivor, earned her M.D. but never practiced after having children. The patient experienced her mother as rejecting, depressed, childish, and deeply pessimistic and, at the same time, very ambitious for her to become the working physician she never allowed herself to be. This patient came to me when she was about to drop out of medical school, doubting whether this was her decision. At that time she was compulsively shoplifting and deeply confused and depressed. The powerful and pressing projections had created self-damage in this patient, who felt despair and anxiety regarding who she was. The struggle for this individual to successfully integrate her medical practice and motherhood was admirable but chronically contaminated by an overly intrusive and rejecting mother. What became critical in the treatment was early and ongoing interpretations of the continuous projective process: the patient saw her newborn daughter as a clinging tyrant who would not let her out of the room, a devil who teased at her mother's patience and drained her physically. This patient had to sort out her mother's mixed messages and experience her own fears of abandonment and separation anxiety and ambivalence toward her mother, so as to be able to extricate herself from an ongoing projective displacement onto the new-born child. Interestingly, the second daughter was experienced as cool, distant, and not a cuddler. She gave up nursing early, walked early, and in general became a symbol of independence.

Another patient comes to mind who insists on suffering and victimization. Her mother, a prima donna, had used the patient to enhance her own self-esteem. This patient had masochistically turned against herself in an effort to maintain the bond with her ambivalently loved mother and to avoid the surfacing of her rage. As written in the unconscious script, this patient, now a mother, places in reaction formation her daughters first, only to find herself resenting the deprivation and envy she feels by doing this, and only now feeling the psychic reversal and rage that was an unconscious part of her own childhood. The projective course continued insidiously in this case. The unconscious rage of the mother (i.e., patient) was experienced by her daughter as suffocating, and she found a conversion expression for this in chronic asthma. The other daughter rejected her mother completely as a source of feminine identification, had a series of abortions, and is currently making homosexual object choices.

The mother who claims her daughter as ally, confidante, therapist, friend—who demands of her in obvious and not so obvious ways that she fulfill the traditional female roles in a compliant, compulsive way—"clones" a daughter, and the repercussions may be felt much later. An orthodox Jewish woman, menopausal, whose husband left her, ostensibly for another younger, career woman, mourned her marriage, stating: "I never questioned it. I never expected anything else. I just did for him what he wanted. I loved him and he was my world—there was nobody else. I did what my mother did." Now separated, she experiences herself as a toddler, tasting and touching and exploring the world as an individual. She talks of feeling vital, physically lighter, sexually alive and existentially present in a way she never felt before. Now released from an overtly confined and rather unsatisfying marriage, she says: "Am I crazy?, but I don't care about the future so much. I'm just living now and I never realized how depressed I was." In this case, as in the case to follow, religion and its observance without question became a veil behind which wishes for autonomy and individuation were obscured. Religion acted as a binding force in these cases, a force that safely cemented the ambivalent tie to the mother and made open inquiry into the mother's projective fantasies and wishes hazardous.

Another orthodox Jewish woman had five children. Her mother was a career woman, who subtly neglected her children and both denigrated and idealized the role of mother. This patient remembers spending most of her time in front of a television set with maids tending to her and being served repetitive and boring meals. Her mother's message was that housework and caring for children were unimportant and not worthy of her intellect. What was important was what men have outside—work, self-esteem, money, power—and this can only be had in their world. This woman finds herself 30 years later with five children, married to a devoted orthodox husband who, unlike the mother, makes few demands and is, if anything, too passively dependent on her as an ego support and source of motivation. She came into therapy talking and feeling terribly torn by her wish for a profession and by the realities of her life, that is, her large family. (She had been in a nearly perpetual state of pregnancy, and her children ranged in age from 1 to 7 years.) She resented being a mother because she felt that it was a role that had no self-worth. She was too tired and overwhelmed to have a private practice as a speech therapist (and realistically so). She was paralyzed by conflict, became obese, and had in fact one child that was already showing signs of severe pathology. Her progress in therapy was remarkable, in that she courageously demanded to free herself from her mother's duplicitous messages and influence, and to be herself uniquely. Her relationship to her children is marked by a real effort to understand their individuality and separate talents and strengths. She is demonstrating only now real interest and curiosity in them, a sign of her own individuated self.

Another woman, a child bride, had stepped into her mother's traditional shoes by staying home, cleaning, caring for her children and not asking any questions, ignoring at first any signs of personal discomfort. Eventually the anxiety and ambivalence about this role became so overwhelming that the once successful agoraphobic symptoms did not serve or bind any longer, and crippling arthritic pains took over. They became her constant defense and companion. The self was born in this woman when she began to try to assert herself. Each time she would be beset, though, by overwhelming uncertainty, self-doubt, and massive guilt; everyone became her enemy, including her children and her husband. She claimed no one supported her or gave her respect, and no one could. She held onto her suffering as a powerful defense. This woman's daughter (third generation) gradually managed through therapy to extricate herself from her masochistic, maternal past. However, her presenting symptom of bulimia was clearly in part a symptom of rejection of her feminine body and an affirmation of her mother's perfectionistic standards. In this case, as in so many, mother–daughter merging took expression in body statements and symptomatology in parallel body issues. (The mother was a constant dieter and very self-conscious about weight.) In this case, the mother would actually attribute her own bodily feelings to her daughter, which was a kind of body-dominated neurosis. The daughter, as a consequence, suffered from many body–ego distortions.

Contemporary society is beginning to offer women options for identification. While this is obviously a clear sign of progress, what is simultaneously being made available is means of avoidance of earlier and traditional forms of maternal identifications. Many women today come into our practices not having dealt with their relationships to their mothers because they have simply avoided it, but at a cost.

Regarding this, a patient recently entered therapy with a powerful motivation to understand and cure her sexual frigidity and her anorexia, to uncover and understand the reasons why she experienced intense and ambivalent swings in mood and affect in relationships, and why she had never, at the age of 35, been involved with anyone for any length of time. Her first feeling memory of her mother was of fear and then of a cessation of feelings. "She had come down the stairs and she was standing there, staring at me, ready to punish me, and I knew than that I couldn't feel any more. I would have to become stone." So this patient accommodated herself to her environment through massive affective withdrawal and encapsulation. (Love, attachment, food were considered invaders.) Anyone or anything who would come close enough to elicit feelings was experienced as a threat. Her greatest fear was to become like this cold, unpredictable mother, rigid and controlling. This fear, together with a real structural back disc problem which she had attributed to body contractions experienced from paralyzing fears when abused, prevented her successfully from pursuing marital and motherhood goals. She was starting to think of herself as an invalid on many levels. She focused her energies on a career, and was successful in materialistic ways. She came to me because a kind, decent man loved her and she could not let herself return his love. In this case, one may speculate that the projective identification processes (healthy and unhealthy) were insufficient and excessively asymbiotic. Hence, a more schizoidal picture developed.

Common to all these patients were problems in body-self definition and in body-self separateness and merging. This core conflict was symptomatically expressed in several ways: through overeating and an obsessional relationship to food, through bouts of bulimia and anorexia, through episodes of amenorrhea, through sexual inhibitions alternating periodically with emotionless promiscuity. The need to remain pregnant was in two cases illustrative of a powerful yearning for an early and lost symbiotic attachment to the mother. One patient referred to herself as a hollow, wooden puppet. How could such a creature, all stiff and empty, feel feminine? This sense of emptiness, so often described by female patients, refers back to an early rupture in basic empathy—the self that was never understood, never separated out from the murky, needy, projective unconscious of the mother.

Further clinical illustrations come to mind as indicators of an early and ongoing complexity in mother–daughter relationships, a complexity saturated with ambivalence and projective identification and often specifically expressed in physical terms. S., an obese woman, talks of her mother as a "bear chasing me with the kitchen knife"; the suffocating mother who would "bury me alive." This woman eats to fill the maternal void, but also consciously to violate her mother's critical, perfectionistic standards. S. explained her obesity in part (her eating) as a revenge against the narcissistic wishes of her hated mother, who offered love conditionally based on S.'s fulfilling her requirements to look a certain way. S., in the presence of her mother, often becomes conscious of the wish to enrage her through her appearance; to "never give her the pleasure" of seeing her as she wants. Called a "gutter rat" once in childhood by her mother, S. revengefully reenacts this image.

Another woman, quite obese, often talked of her malevolent mother being inside of her. At 5 years of age, she had been struggling to learn how to swim when her mother said, in exasperation, "Shit floats, why can't you?" Food for her is the warm, full, internal companion. "It takes away the pain, and it's always there." This patient's mother used her simultaneously as the projected "bad self," and as the target for her husband's rage.

Another young woman, a beautiful and intelligent graduate student, speaks with disgust at the thought of pregnancy and birth. It is to her the ultimate invasion, the ultimate degradation signaling distortion, loss of control, a violation of one's very being, and a primitive reminder of her femininity, her dirtiness and impulsivity. This woman's mother was similarly described as base, foul, lacking in controls, primitive, invasive, and controlling. In this family, there was little regard for this patient's body integrity and boundaries. In fact, the father, mother, and daughter would sleep together until this woman was an adolescent.

In like manner, a woman comes to mind who was a law student, and who initially sought treatment because of depression regarding a marriage splintered and diluted by a series of promiscuous love affairs. For this woman, sexual encounters were sought out as a way of affirming, albeit short-lived, self-worth. She shared the parental bedroom for many years and was, hence, an unconscious victim of much overstimulation in the form of physical exposure and parental fantasy. The mother used this daughter "pimp like," set up as a provocateur to stimulate and arouse her husband. Oedipal feelings remained charged and interfered with the proper resolution of the triangular dynamics central to subsequent growth as a mature, heterosexual adult.

On the other end of the continuum is a depressed, menopausal woman whose mother "would not look up at me if she were mopping the floor when I came home from school." Such emotional neglect and absence of projective interaction prompted the wish early in her development to be a mother better than hers, to be there for her children and involved, to create a home. Now experiencing the somewhat emptied nest, she is reexperiencing the deprivation and pain of childhood, the anger and loss, the yearning for a mother to mother her and with whom to identify, a yearning which is putting psychological pressure on the marriage and being symptomatized in a multitude of physical complaints.

How do women participate in their own physical and emotional oppression? The preservation of the mother–daughter bond, however perverse in some cases, seems to be a mandate of nature, and a sensitive respect for this urgent need and traditional attachment is a clinician's responsibility. The safety, security, constancy, and certainty that comes with traditional roles is clear and powerful, as well as the resistance to change and dissolution of familiar object ties, which is involved in moving away from old modes—cultural, intrapsychic, and interpersonal.

From birth throughout the course of a woman's development, her body-gender is assigned. With this assignment come biocultural givens, strong associations in the mother, and a full opportunity to project, identify, and displace. Sometimes these projections are benign and are in fact the very stuff of motherhood; sometimes they are pathological and become the powerful instigating germs of human struggles, as illustrated in the case vignettes.

What seems clear here is that the female sense of self, perhaps from intrauterine life on, is embedded in interaction and interrelationship and parts of that self are projected, introjected, and interwoven in a complicated and highly charged way. From the mother–daughter shared sameness in gender, can come more pathological confusion, fusion, and projection and/or can come exquisite, affectively accurate, and attuned empathic exchange. The female human is powerfully responsive, vis-à-vis a unique relationship to the mother, to a wide array of preverbal, intuitive, and emotional signals that seem lodged in the species itself and are often expressed bodily.

Given this understanding of a female psychology, as therapists, the countertransferential and transferential issues involved in treating women today are even more richly complex. Particularly because of the sociopolitical climate simultaneously denying and affirming male–female differences, the therapist must make a special effort to listen to the individual historical intrapsychic and interpersonal, psychophysiological dynamics. Therapists should not prematurely support or discourage efforts at individuation, identity consolidation, and body-self autonomy.

We must respect the individual pace of individuation and not misinterpret protests arising out of ambivalence toward objects as genuine wishes to dissolve object ties (through acting out, physically and emotionally). We must respect the creative potential of each individual and be open to the notion that emotional growth can occur in the home as well as out. What is important is that there is choice to go in either or both directions. And finally, as therapists of the body-self, we must facilitate the emergence of an identity that can integrate the rich worlds of both motherhood and career—an integration that can more solidly come through clear analytic work, which is simultaneously intrapsychic and interpersonal in nature.

References

Bardwick, J. (1971). *Psychology of women.* New York: Harper & Row.

Chodorow, N. (1978). *The reproduction of mothering: Psychoanalysis and the sociology of gender.* Berkeley: University of California Press.

Erikson, E. (1968a). Womanhood and the inner and outer space. In *Identity, youth and crisis* (pp. 261–294). New York: W. W. Norton.

Freud, S. (1931). Female sexuality. *Standard Edition, 21,* 223–243.

Galenson, E. (1976). Scientific Proceedings—Panel Reports—Panels on the Psychology of Women—Annual Meeting of the American Psychoanalytic Association, 1974. *Journal of the American Psychoanalytic Association, 24* (1), 159.

Hittelman, J., & Dickes, R. (1979). Sex differences in neonatal eye contact time. *Merrill Palmer Quarterly, 25,* 3.

Kestenberg, J. S. (1982). Inner-genital phase—prephallic and pre-Oedipal. In D. Mendell (Ed.), *Early female development: Current psychoanalytic views* (pp. 81–125). New York: S.P. Medical and Scientific Books.

Lewis, H. B. (1976). What are little girls made of? In *Psychic war in men and women* (pp. 61–89). New York: New York University Press.

Lichtenberg, J. (1983). *Psychoanalysis and infant research.* New York: The Analytic Press.

Mahler, M., Pine, F., & Bergman, A. (1975). *The psychological birth of the human infant.* New York: Basic Books.

Mahler, M. S., & McDevitt, J. B. (1984). Thoughts on the emergence of the sense of self, with particular emphasis on the body-self. *Journal of the American Psychoanalytic Association, 30* (4).

Menaker, E. (1979). Masochism and the emergent ego. In Leila Lerner (Ed.), *Selected papers.* New York: Human Sciences Press.

Menaker, E., & Menaker, W. (1965). *Ego in evolution.* New York: Grove Press.

Shainess, N. (1969). Mother-child relationships: An overview. In *Science and psychoanalysis.* New York: Grune & Stratton.

Winnicott, D. W. (1958). *Collected papers: Through pediatrics to psychoanalysis.* London: Tavistock Publications.

Winnicott, D. W. (1971). *Playing and reality.* Middlesex, England: Penguin.

Chapter 4

The Father's Role in the Self-Development of His Daughter

SUSAN ADLER KAVALER

Emily Dickinson's long-simmering hopes for editorial approval were crushed in one blow (Sewall, 1975). She had chosen Thomas Wentworth Higginson, an elder male figure, as her one prime judge. All her hopes for rescue from obscurity were pinned on him. Yet, the imagined ambrosia of praise was dashed with the salt of criticism. Higginson called the poet's poems "spasmodic," a blow from which Emily Dickinson never recovered. Acting like a little girl who can't yet see beyond the sphere of her one and only daddy, Emily Dickinson revered Higginson, her editorial critic, and with his disapproval she sealed herself away for life. She never again attempted publication. Emily's resounding remark of that time haunts us with the formidable subtlety of its stifled inner cry (Ferlazzo, 1976, p. 84)

> A great hope fell
> You heard no noise
> The ruin was within

Outwardly, she became a veiled, and "slightly cracked" (Higginson's words) recluse.

Such devastation of a woman's inner self can only be highlighted by looking at the wounded little girl within the woman. Then we must also go back to the time of the wound.

In that acute moment, when a little girl seeks the warmth of her daddy's smile, if she is met instead with a cold stare or a rigid frown, what happens to her inner self? Does it shatter as it splits off from the now external facade? What parting of self and mask do we cite here?

A daughter cherishes her father, even as he becomes a perverse inversion of

SUSAN ADLER KAVALER, PH.D. • Faculty and Supervisor, National Institute for the Psychotherapies, New York; Psychoanalytic Faculty, Postgraduate Center for Mental Health, Psychoanalytic Institute; Board of Directors and Supervisor, Brooklyn Institute for Psychotherapy; Senior Supervisor and Training Analyst, International School of Mental Health Practitioners.

the longed for adoring dad. He is expected to be adoring, but when his reality doesn't conform to this expectation, the inner image of him can turn sour, turning into judge and critic. By adolescence a father's criticism should be tolerable to his daughter and she should be able to integrate it into a realistic view of him. However, the period of adoration must come first. For some little girls, the adoring father lives only in fantasy, and the reality is continually bleak and disappointing.

Laura is a woman who came for psychotherapeutic treatment with a severe narcissistic disturbance. A memory from the age of 6 years was one of the first communications she extended to me, her therapist. She reported that she was 6 years old when she came home from her first ballet class and paraded herself in her ballet tutu, before her dearest daddy. She twirled herself around the room with glee, anticipating his joy, fluttering with high-rise anticipation. Her father's response was seemingly perfunctory: "Go put on some clothes!" She was cut! Like internal bleeding, the results were subtle, but steadfastly malignant. Some cluster of Laura's blossoming feminity was permanently shaken. So, too, was her potential faith in both her creativity and her love. In Emily Dickinson's words, "The ruin was within."

This kind of female castration is quite incisive, when the adoring mirror in a father's eyes turns to a disapproving glare. It has very little to do with the absence of a penis (although a phallic compensation may be sought). A father's disapproval is viscerally felt. It numbs and chills the upsurge of fluid sensual life in a young girl's body. Like cancer, a girl's inner wound is rarely seen for many years—until, perhaps, her therapist sees it. (A similar example is sighted by Stolorow and Lachman, 1980, case of Jane, "Idealization and Grandiosity.")

THE GOOD-ENOUGH FATHER

Who is the good-enough father? I will attempt to depict him in terms of his early and profound effect on his daughter's growth through various developmental phases. I see him as the man who enters the scene early, for as object relations theory tells us, attachment begins at the beginning of life. A little girl's love for her father blossoms directly out of the pre-Oedipal symbiotic fantasy that she has derived from the loss of the symbiosis with mother.

Susan Spieler (1984) has written an article, "Pre-Oedipal Girls Need Fathers," which states the case quite well. No little girl wants to wait until the Oedipal stage to have a man in her life. Also, if basic gender identity does form from the ages of 18 months (Appleton, 1981) to 3 years (Gilligan, 1982), the interaction with father is an essential part of determining such an identity.

The love affair with father may begin as a father rocks his baby girl infant in his arms. I remember one emphatic description of a mother who was impressed with the tenacious hold that her husband and daughter had on each other, right from the beginning. She said with great authoritative enunciation: "They know the difference! If I held her she would very quickly get restless. If my husband held her, they were both in bliss. They would sit and rock, and rock, and rock for long stretches of time." As she rhythmically simulated the rocking, one had the sense of a long, slow, and undulating caress, with multiple innuendoes, and prolific fantasy formations.

We don't really know how early the fantasies form. Perhaps Melanie Klein is right, and they begin in the first year of life (M. Klein, 1980, 1981). Yet whenever they begin, it is clear that the involvement between father and daughter is initially a tender one, based on potent ties of fantasy-enhanced bonding. This tender connection then gains color from the intensity of sexual and romantic passions.

Pre-Oedipal Years

During the pre-Oedipal years, the good-enough father is actively involved in playing with his daughter, who is at the height of her sensorimotor explorations. A father is much more likely than a mother to toss a baby girl up in the air, catching her unfailingly in his strong protective arms. He may invent games for his daughter, such as one reported by a psychotherapy patient of seating her on one of his legs, and circling her around in the manner of a ferris-wheel. This kind of game can serve as an introduction to later trips to amusement parks, to which a father is more likely than a mother to take his daughter. Why does it happen this way? There is no absolute determinant of this. Yet, "play" is the main activity that distinguishes the father's contribution to child care from that of the mother (Appleton, 1981, p. 8).

During the pre-Oedipal era, the good-enough father not only plays with his daughter and holds her, he also sees her with adoring eyes that mirror and reflect her. Although his wife might provide eyes of empathy and sympathetic understanding, as her baby daughter learns to walk and talk, etc., it is a father who most provides the adoring eyes: eyes that not only watch her but cherish her and imbue her with a feeling of specialness.

A girl's father may be her exclusive audience as she does somersaults across the floor. Also, as her sensorimotor skills take her away from mother, and toward her own individuating activity, it is daddy's eyes that mirror and reflect her path toward increasing autonomy.

Oedipal Era

The good-enough father of the Oedipal era can be seen in terms of a transitional object. He provides a romantic transition from an early symbiotic love with mother to later attachments with other men. It is a little girl's father who reflects and inspires her world of illusion, particularly in terms of romantic fantasies. He sings romantic songs that inspire her, and which convey his own muted eroticism. He may dance with her (like snapshots of Shirley Temple dancing on her cinema daddy's toes), or read her fairy tales. At this stage of development, a father is no longer mirroring his daughter's sensorimotor strivings as much as her psychic and sexual individuation. This is a transition for the Oedipal girl to a later stage of mature dependence, and to mature heterosexual attachments. Later, she will be able to accept a real man, a man who has faults not seen within the romantic ideal. First, however, she must have the romantic ideal of a man through her father's image, and a romantic self view seen through her father's eyes.

It is at this stage that a father may be particularly fond of taking photographs of his daughter, partly because she is so flirtatious and cute as she poses before him at this time. On Valentine's Day, he brings her chocolate hearts. On holidays, he holds her hand, and walks in the parades with her. Maybe she learns to read her first words while sitting in his lap. If her father sees her read and hears her read, she feels recognized. She feels it as "He sees me! He loves me!".

At this stage, a little girl will go beyond somersaults and improvisational gymnastics to dancing and singing. If her father is there to applaud her, she will feel beautiful, that she has a beautiful body and a beautiful voice. If her father turns away from her, she will be hurt. If he shows a smirk of contempt, or verbalizes such mockery or disdain, she will feel awkward and ugly. She may withdraw and seem inhibited, or she may become defiantly flamboyant and exhibitionistic—probably the latter if applause is mixed in with the contempt.

Latency

What is different during the latency period? For one thing, this is the age when a father and daughter can begin to talk together, to have dialogues in which intellectual concepts and moral values develop. It is a time when a young girl can gain recognition and admiration from her father for her intellectual and verbal skills, rather than for being cute and flirtatious. As her intellect is confirmed, she finds new ways of winning approval that can strengthen the sense of her own identity. Later on, this can help free her from too much need for a man's approval. The single most important factor in motivating a woman to intellectually achieve is the degree to which her father recognizes and takes pride in her intelligence. To be truly creative, and to be motivated to create, a woman needs to have a good-enough father who both admires her intelligence and her imagination. This is reinforced along with a sense of femininity derived from the Oedipal period, and becomes the identity of a creative woman.

Beyond mirroring her efforts, and applauding her for her grades in school, the good-enough father must get actively involved with his daughter. Now he can help her with her homework, engage in active dialogues, and express his own opinions so that he enhances his daughter's new capacity for intellectual and moral understanding.

This is also the age of budding creative development. A father needs to encourage the process, not just the product of creation. A father can encourage his daughter to experiment, to take risks, and to sustain the creative effort, even if she flops, and falls on her face occasionally. He can help her sustain the capacity for confusion that is part of the creative process. If he doesn't encourage such experimentation and confusion, the product of creation will become more important than the process, and will abort the creative exploration.

Adolescence

During adolescence, the good-enough father becomes a special "man in the audience" for his daughter's creative pursuits. No longer is his daughter a little girl performing tumblesaults for her father within their private sphere, at home in the living room. Now, she wishes to perform for a wider audience, and her father needs to let go of being her exclusive audience. In the wider audience from whom she now seeks admiration, her father plays a special part. By being in the audience, whether for a dance recital, play, musical recital, or poetry reading, he is showing that he both believes in her and that he is also willing to share her with the world.

In terms of his daughter's intellectual development, the good-enough father needs to be open to entertaining his daughter's polemical disputes at this time. To encourage his daughter's autonomous efforts at forming her ideals and values, a father needs to allow his own ideas to be heard and opposed. He may need to tolerate a good deal of negativism from his daughter, as part of this process. Again, he is a transitional object, but now in terms of allowing himself to be used for his daughter's aggressive opposition. The enabling father allows his daughter to break away from his hold on her as an idealized and eroticized object through her oppositional disputes. This can be a difficult task, because it is so tempting for a parent to peremptorily claim to be right. It can be tempting for a father to claim his age and experience as proof of a lofty superiority. It is much harder to allow his opinions to be open to contradiction, without subtle displays of contempt, or snide warnings, which suggest that his daughter will inevitably come around to his viewpoint once she has grown up or reached his age.

Also, a father is generally expected to assume a role of authority with his daughter. He must be a tender authority, not sacrificing his authority to win his daughter's tenderness and approval. The good-enough father is one who provides firm limits, while simultaneously offering tender regard.

However, tenderness can easily be mixed up with sexual attraction, particularly during this highly charged period of adolescent sexual development. The benign father is able to sense his attraction to his daughter, while able not to be scared into a state of withdrawal, which would be felt as abandonment. Also, he needs not to be overly reactive to the point of seductive acting out. In addition, he must be sensitive enough to the sexual fears aroused in his daughter as she finds his presence stimulating. Although he shouldn't refrain from displays of affection, he needs to restrain such displays if his daughter becomes irritated or uncomfortable. Hopefully, he can empathize with her anxiety, and not interpret her withdrawals as signs of rejection.

PATERNAL FAILURES AND PATERNAL PATHOLOGY

Having viewed the adequate father, let's now take a look at examples that deviate from the model outlined. When does good-enough fathering fail? How does the daughter internalize the failure?

The Inadequate Father

For some women, their fathers are just not there. Yet, unlike death or divorce, where the father is actually absent from the home, in these cases the father is physically present, but emotionally absent, or else is absent and inadequate in highly significant ways.

M. B.'s life lacked any sparkle. Sexual excitement was totally absent from her life. Although she was now in her late thirties, she had rarely dated men. When she did occasionally date, she would try to be nice. Nothing seemed to happen between her and a man. Generally, after one date a man would not call her again. Something seemed to be missing. Actually, her attempt at being nice with a male date was a complete contradiction to her usual high pitched tenor of complaining, bitching, devaluing, and grumpy comments. In a perverse way, this is how she expressed her inner self and her sexuality. As she attempted to be nice with a male date, she negated herself into a placid facade.

M. B. had obviously lacked something fundamental in her relationship with her father, and what was put in its place was not very helpful to her. Somehow she had never gotten that sense of adoration that grows into sexual attraction and flirtatious play between father and daughter. Yet, she did get something in its place. She internalized a combined mother–father personality that constantly devalued, spoiled, criticized, and negated any emotional reality. However, when she really came out in the open with her bitching and moaning, she could be quite funny. Some of her repressed sexuality could even surface when she went full steam ahead with her complaining humor. Unfortunately, she never had a father to enable this sexuality to emerge out in the open.

Just as her sexuality remained repressed, so too did her creative potential. M. B.'s thinking was concrete. Metaphors and images were foreign to her. It seems that the whole right side of her brain was deadened by the lack of stimulation from her father. Constantly, she complained of her limited opportunities in the job market. She was sick of secretarial positions, had a high intellectual potential, and wished she could perform a higher paying job, with more creative possibilities. Yet, her creativity was underdeveloped. She didn't come up with new ideas. She didn't fantasize and imagine things into potential being. The stunting in her character development, thus, affected all areas of her social, work, and creative life. She was chronically depressed.

Another example of an inadequate father can be seen in the case of A. Less extensive than the damage seen in the former case, the effects of A.'s father only affected her sexuality in a limited way, but it was in the area of creative development that the most detrimental effects could be seen.

A.'s father never talked with her. He never took an interest in her activities. She said that the only time when he spoke to her with affection was when she was silent, and helped him with his handiwork, as he puttered around fixing things in their house. Essentially, she had to merge in with him, and be a part of his activities to win any recognition; and the recognition she received was rather muted and patronizing: "You're a good girl!" Any displays of emotion on her part were responded to with the message: "Control yourself. Hold back your passion. Don't allow your lust to show!" So A.'s father was either indifferent to her, exploitative of her as a self-object, or else he was an emotionally constrictive force. As an adult, she felt this in sexual relations with men, where she was inhibited about expressing her sexual desires and needs. Often she ended up frustrated. She was self-conscious, and could become extremely angry at a man if he in any way was frightened by her passion, or expressed a wish to control or suppress her. Sometimes this scared men away or broke off communication. However, A. did have sexual relationships with men, which suggests that there was some covert sexual attraction alive between father and daughter that was not present in the case of M. B.

The area that was most poignantly hit for A. was the creative area. This was seen clearly in a dream. She dreamed that everybody at her job was supposed to write a poem for a competition. While everybody else wrote a beautiful composition, she could only produce a crossword puzzle, a symbol for her stunted creativity. A. related this dream back to her father's message: "Restrain yourself. Don't allow your lust to show!"

In that a father's relationship with his daughter is the most significant factor in whether his daughter becomes a creative woman, it can be seen that the absence of mirroring, stimulation, and sharing of A.'s right-brain creative potential was tied in with her father's lack of interest in any of her activities that were separate from his own. Also, the lack of mirroring and stimulation was related to a lack of her father's involvement with the feminine, imaginative side of her personality.

Both M. B. and A. tended to devalue men more than to idealize them. This pattern may be characteristic of women with inadequate fathers: whereas women with dead or divorced fathers tend to overidealize the image of their fathers. Both patterns cause problems with men, but the latter pattern may enhance creativity.

The Overly Seductive Father

The overly seductive father is often also the abandoning father—the man who tantalizes and then deserts, or the "tantalizing deserter" (Fairbairn, 1952). This was certainly true for C. H., whose father would take her out on "dates," lavish expensive dinners on her, but never see any of her true emotional needs. From the time she was a little girl—certainly during the Oedipal years as well as beyond them— he would have her perform before his friends. He would play the *Blue Danube Waltz*, and have his daughter wiggle her backside to its upturned rhythms, exhibiting hula movements and 5-year-old bumps and grinds. He also erotically stimulated his daughter all through the highly charged Oedipal years by squeezing her genitals, as one would pinch a child on the cheek, uttering comments such as "You're so cute!"

When C. H. was an adolescent, her father left home, divorced her mother, and totally abandoned C. H. along with her mother. This threw her into a massive depression that inhibited her adolescent growth and made competitive issues with her then sexually acting out mother extremely flagrant. As she began to date, she became masochistically addicted to seductive and indifferent men. Her creative development was stunted as well. Although endowed with much potential, her creative capacities were frozen for many years until she was able to experience her rage toward her father in therapy, and to mourn the loss of him. Her overstimulated sensuality was used to cling to men who would tantalize and desert her, as her father had. Her obsession with such men also prevented her from using her expressive abilities in creative pursuits. Instead, she would use her expressive abilities to create hysterical dramas with her abandoning boyfriends.

The famous writer, Anais Nin, was another child of an overly seductive father. Her father would take nude pictures of her when she was in the bathtub (Fields, 1966, p. 99). He aroused her in this erotically stimulating way, and then was possessive of her. Ultimately, he abandoned her. His sexual possessiveness came through in his attitude toward her creativity. He refused to be her "man in the audience" during her developing years. Instead, he accused her of being a whore for dancing in public. He wished to keep her in his own exclusive sphere of seduction. Just as a father can resent his daughter's boyfriends as she moves toward other men in her life, so too can he resent her advances into the wider audience of the world with her creativity. If he acts like a betrayed lover, he is giving her the message that she can't leave him behind, and he is refusing to be a transitional object. Here too, in the life of Anais Nin, seduction and abandonment go together. Though her father wished his daughter to remain exclusively in his narcissistic sphere, and used seduction to hold her, he readily dropped her from his life when he left her mother.

The Narcissistic Character Father

Although all the fathers I mentioned could be seen as narcissistically inclined, I am referring to a specific type of father when I speak of the narcissistic character father. He is someone who lives predominantly through his own reflected image, as it bounces off of his daughter, whom he uses as a self-object for himself. He can use her as an idealized self-object onto whom he projects his image ideal, giving his daughter mirroring only when she becomes what he wants her to be. Also, he can use his daughter as a mirroring self-object from whom he expects adoration and voyeuristic appreciation, which does not allow his daughter very much experience of her own self.

Otto Plath, the father of another famous writer, Sylvia Plath, presents an example of the first type of narcissistic paternal character. When 3 years old, Sylvia was taught to use her precocious intellect in the service of her father's exhibitionism and grandiosity. Similar to the father who had his daughter dance the *Blue Danube Waltz*, Sylvia Plath's father exhibited his daughter before his friends. However, the sexualized aspect was minimized while the intellect became the area of narcissistic pride. Sylvia would recite pollysyllabic Latin terms, winning her father's admiration, as she reflected his golden image before the world.

Sylvia Plath grew up in her "bell jar," as she writes in her autobiographical novel. She was always locked within a role-playing image world. She lived within an intrapsychic hall of mirrors. In her work, she was preoccupied with her stifled and strangled true self, as her infant needy self was blocked off from contact and nurturance, while she adapted to becoming the image of her father's idealized intellectual self. In this way, Sylvia created a false grandiose self that became her overt identity. By being the grandiose "golden girl" for her father's eyes only, she gave up her life and sanity to be a mirroring self-object for her father. Even after his death, she was intrapsychically trapped in this role, this false grandiose self-identity. Perhaps her father's death, when she was only 9 years old, greatly intensified his power as an internal object, an internal object that persistently plagued her with its demands for image reflection.

Although other women have fathers like Otto Plath, they don't all comply so readily with the father's demands. P. was a woman who brought her frustration with such paternal narcissism into a psychotherapeutic situation. There, she told of her protest against her father's efforts to use her as a glamorous portrait to hide behind. She spoke of how her father would exhibit her and her sister before his friends, presenting his daughters as an actress and a dancer. She raved against his lack of concern for what she was really doing in her beginning attempts to act, and against his preoccupation with her as an image. Her protest separated her from him, and kept her authentic self alive.

What are the difficulties of the daughter whose father attempts to use her as a mirroring self-object, as opposed to an idealized self-object? This kind of father is generally preoccupied with the image that he himself is conveying to the world. He may be highly creative himself, often in an exhibitionistic mode of creativity. Basically, he is indifferent to his daughter, except in the part she plays in seeing him, reflecting his idealized self-image, and in adoring him. The absence of her adoration is severely felt. Any creativity on his daughter's part is experienced as competition by the father—competition of a self-annihilating character. It is implicitly disapproved of.

Women with fathers of this nature tend to develop serious creative blocks. Despite innate creative endowment, they will generally remain permanently blocked if they don't seek out psychoanalytic treatment.

Why do they develop such creative blocks? They have unconsciously received the message that to create on their own is equivalent in their father's mind to homicidal murder. To create is to murder their father, because his image of himself as the omnipotent and exclusive grandiose creator is the only self he knows, although it is a false self in being an idealized image that has not incorporated any assimilation of the needy, weak, or uncreative parts of him. His psychic integration has not taken place, and his daughter pays the price as she is called upon to be his grandiose self's sustaining mirror. If she refuses to play out this function, or in any way undermines it with the natural competition of her growth, her father's grandiose self will fragment or deplete, and her father will unconsciously threaten her with his own murderous rage.

The Intrusive Father

Fathers can also be too intrusive for reasons that often relate to narcissistic factors in their character. In an autobiographical novel, titled *The Words to Say It*, Marie Cardinal (1983) describes the analysis of an hallucination within a description of her overall psychoanalysis. Having been terrified to face up to the haunting thing that captivated and imprisoned her, she nevertheless does so, as her analyst sits by waiting. As the hallucination is unmasked, it is discovered that her father photographed his then Oedipal-stage daughter while she was urinating. The developing hallucination is thus found to be related to an acute humiliation, brought on by the sense of pervasive intrusion from her father's telescopic lens. The phallic aspects of this hallucination are not negligible, but the effect on self-impairment is rather total, not confined to sexual development and sexual inhibition. From a self-perspective, the father's voyeurism is felt as perversely demonic. The voyeuristic act installs in the inner world through internalization of introjects a negative view of the child's self. This is a perversion of mirroring, and a very common one with children who grow up with narcissistic defects.

It is particularly significant that the father's intrusion is experienced during the Oedipal period. A little girl is extremely susceptible to overstimulation at this point in time, when her own erotic impulses are intense. Her vulnerability to humiliating feelings of body exposure is also heightened at this time, particularly in relation to a father figure. It may be that Marie Cardinal's father was not a generally intrusive or voyeuristic character, but his act of intrusion came at a time when the tendency to trauma was prevalent. Also, as the subject and author describes her mother, it is clear that she was an excessively intrusive woman, who may have set up the particular vulnerability to this intrusive aspect of the father.

During the Oedipal stage, a girl needs to romanticize her father, not to be actively erotically stimulated by him. His mere presence is erotically stimulating enough.

The Abruptly Withdrawing Father

What effects does it have on a developing woman when her father withdraws from her abruptly? As already mentioned, there are fathers who withdraw altogether, and abandon their daughters. This often happens after divorce, and then there is the even more devastating loss of a father through death.

However, there are also less total withdrawals that affect daughters profoundly. There are emotional withdrawals that can come when the father is reacting to his own idiosyncratic reality. Also, there are emotional withdrawals that come in response to developmental changes in the daughters themselves. Let's look at one example of each.

A. H.'s father was very close to her in those first fundamental years of her life. She knew a tenderness that was particular to her attachment to him, a tenderness that awakened her intensely sensual being during the first 3 years of life. In her analysis, she had vague memories of those early years when her mother would diaper her, and would then bring her over to the bed, where her father was. Her father would pick her up in his arms, and would hug, caress, and cuddle her.

Then a disastrous black wave hit her. This was her perception of the sudden assault of coldness that hit her as there came about a break between her and her father. At 3 years of age—just at the beginning of the Oedipal phase—her father emotionally left her. Later, she was to find out that it was just at this time that her father's father had committed suicide. Yet, of course, at the age of three she had no access to this knowledge, nor could have had any understanding of it; so she had a profoundly injurious experience that wounded her deeply, and from which she drew self-deprecating conclusions. In her subconscious mind, she believed that there must be something wrong with her for this to have occurred. She couldn't possibly know that her father's reaction was not a response to her, but to something outside herself, to something deeply rooted within him. Her Oedipal and latency years were marred by a continual battle with her father, and an intense hatred toward him that she developed as a counter-wall to his wall. Adolescence was even worse. She put on an act of indifference toward any boy whom she was truly attracted to.

During her adult years, her heterosexual life was severely damaged by this time of abrupt paternal withdrawal. For years, she hid behind veils of role-playing facades that she wore as a buffer against potential rejection from a man. Naturally, since she hid her true self, and her true feelings, she set up a self-fulfilling prophesy in which she was always ultimately rejected by a man. Although at first allured by her seductive charms and eloquent dramatizations, a man could quickly tire of her portrayals of the Carmen-like femme fatale, or the sophisticated cynic. Since there was no real contact with a man in light of this incessant role-playing, a man could easily slip away. When this happened, A. H. would feel all the more driven by the compulsion to be continually fascinating. This became a vicious cycle of play-acting and of male rejection.

During analysis, A. H. discovered that her inability to sustain an intimate relationship with a man was very much related to her internal and previously unconscious fantasies that went back to the original trauma with her father. Just at the point when she was truly wanted by a man, a wall of rage would fortify her against him, paralyzing her loving capacities. She would experience this as a thundering "No!" in her brain, and as a sweeping coldness blanketing her body. This was the frozen rage. Behind this wall of rage, however, was the terror. The frozen wall became connected with dream images of a black sea, or a large black wave washing over and annihilating her. Precisely at the moment of potential intimacy with a man—a moment of potential connection—she would draw back abruptly, just as her father had from her, expressing her "No!" by coldness or hostile attack. She was reenacting the trauma with her father, and becoming the active rejector rather than the passive victim. Yet in withdrawing as she did, she inevitably produced the very thing she was defending against, the reexperiencing of male rejection.

Unlike the father who withdraws abruptly due to his own depression (as in this last case), there is the father who abruptly withdraws due to the threat of his daughter's developmental change. The most likely time for the father to withdraw is during his daughter's pubescent years, as she changes in manifest sexual characteristics into a woman.

D. B.'s father withdrew from her just at such a time. However, unlike in the case of A. H., he did not just become cold and distant. When he deliberately attempted to shake off the intense emotional bond that he had with his daughter, he became contemptuously attacking and sarcastically mocking. He maliciously belittled her feminine traits. Up until this time of D. B.'s life, her father could pretend that he had a son. Now, he was unable to deny D. B.'s femininity. So he attacked it! If D. B. tried to hug him, he would garishly cry out, "Get those things off me!," referring to her developing breasts. He would make numerous vulgar comments about her body. She got the message: she was not supposed to have breasts! She tried to hide them. She wore big bulky sweaters, but her breasts never totally disappeared. Also, she felt like a fraud. However, to please her father, she would do anything. He was the love of her life. He was the man whose arms she had always run into—caught up in an ecstatic high—as she saw him all the way down the block. In response to his withdrawal from her, she tried to win him back by developing a masculine image. Not only were her clothes picked to deny the changes in her body, but her manner of walking and moving were also modeled on masculine form. Her sexual identity was affected. It became somewhat ambiguous. She became bisexual, as well, and the diffuseness of her gender identity somewhat reinforced her sex-object choice conflict.

The Incestuous Father

Many women have entered psychotherapeutic treatment with flagrant incest in their backgrounds. Generally, the incest has taken place with either a father, a brother, or a grandfather. S. G. entered psychoanalysis with a history of sado-masochistic relationships with men. During my second meeting with her, she went into a dissociated trance state, and began to reenact an early scene with her father (she was an adopted child). From later reconstructions, it became probable that she was about 3 years old at the time of the original event. There was a little tape in her head of the whole scene. In this scene, her father tells her how much he loves her, and cajoles her with soothing words of approval, as he guides her hands and mouth toward stimulation of his penis. He is kneeling down. "Good girl!," he says, over and over, as she follows his instructions. At the point at which he begins to put his penis inside of her, she shreiks, gets incoherent, and repeats various words over and over again. The shock of this brings her out of her dissociated state, as if coming out of a nightmare due to terror. She promptly forgets and denies the whole thing.

S. G. went through many cycles of erupting with incestuous memories, and of then denying everything. All associations and transferential reactions during her analytic sessions seemed to lead back to her father's incest. Yet, each time she touched it, she pulled away as if she had just been burned. She reenacted the sense of seduction and abuse in the transference by claiming that I was trying to put these horrendous things into her head. What if her father hadn't really done these things? What if her therapist was poisoning her mind? In other words, I became the one who was inwardly contaminating her, sticking the poison penis of analysis inside of her, making her go mad.

Combined with the incestual thoughts and memories was the sense of a special fantasy-enhanced bond with her father. She wished to hold onto her father in an exclusive and idealized way, with repression or denial of the erotic longings and sexual associations. In her inner world she had him all to herself. His actual death only reinforced all this. S. G. could not enjoy sex with a man. Most of the time she was numb and dissociated. She tended to also reenact the abuse with her boy-friends, and would play the masochistic role.

S. G. would seek to hold onto her father by her creative efforts. Her creativity was inspired by the fantasied sense of special communion with her father. She split off the idealized aspect of the relationship she had with her boyfriends after being quickly disillusioned with them, and retained the idealization through her fan-tasied communion with her father, which took place within her creative work, her writing.

Although idealizing the analyst in alternation with projecting the bad object image onto her, the patient felt threatened that analysis would destroy her special bond with her father. In order to hold onto him, and to retain her exclusive bond with him in fantasy, she left analysis. She also simultaneously left her boyfriend and her job. She wanted to devote herself fully to her writing, i.e., to the inner world in which she had her father all to herself—both the ideal father, and the erotically stimulating demon. When she left treatment, she sobbed mournfully, and said that in her heart she knew she'd be back, probably in 2 years. She actually returned in a year. Analysis still represents an intense threat to her incest marriage with her father.

Charlotte Allan (1980) writes about her story of incest with much more bitterness and consciousness than shown by S. G. In her book, *Daddy's Girl*, she tells an autobiographical tale of horrors. Unlike S. G., Charlotte Allan couldn't split off her rage onto random men, or onto a boyfriend. She used writing to face up to her rage, rather than to deny it and idealize her image of her father. In facing up to it, she is strengthened by the hate. Yet, all love seems extinguished. Her father was a brutally possessive man, and there was very little tenderness involved with his sexual demands, although he used seductive foreplay when she was little.

Perhaps because she is less bound by love for her father, Charlotte Allan is more free to write the truth. She writes of how she first submitted sexually for bribes, then later to keep her father's disruptive rage at a minimum, to keep peace in the family. Once she broke away from her father's home as an adult, she received impassioned love letters from her father begging her to return. She was able to ignore these letters. She was not bound, as women often are, to a secret incest bond that gives her a sense of specialness. She seemed to experience her creativity as separate from her father, of her own making. (This is very different from S. G.) Charlotte was able to write of her hatred, and to separate from her father to a degree. Each year she prayed for his death. Eventually, he did die. Yet, at the end of her book, Charlotte is just beginning to really grieve. Hatred alone is never enough. There must be love to mourn, so as to truly separate.

Charlotte Allan's relations with an incestuous father made her relationships with men extremely difficult. She was full of distrust and disgust. Sexual intimacy was always sullied for her. She was convinced that it was her ability to write that kept her from going mad. Through writing she was able to tell her story at last.

P. B. and V. G. are two other women who have graphic incest tales to tell. However, their incestual victimization by their fathers stopped short of sexual intercourse. Their rage saved them. V. G., like Charlotte Allan, reached a point of rage when she was able to draw the line, and keep her father out. She violently bawked, screamed, and wrestled away from her father when he attempted to go beyond foreplay, and to take her into his own bedroom. She sensed what was coming, and she broke away. Her father never actually penetrated her. Ironically, her father's comment at the time when she broke away was "You are unable to deal with growing up!" This was said with a self-righteous air of contempt. To this day, the secret incest remains a secret in V. G.'s family. Fortunately, she is able to tell the story in therapy, and her rage is still available to her.

Other women have repressed incestual scenes, and when they begin to emerge in treatment, they are hysterical and disbelieving—similar to S. G. However, one woman discusses an imagined scene with a grandfather in the basement with awareness that she was highly stimulated, and feels a wish to repeat that which seems perverted to her.

What effect does the incestuous acting out of a father have on the self-image of these women? In each case, there is a sense of being tainted, whether the shame is repressed or not. There is also the grandiose feeling that they had something special that their mothers couldn't give their fathers. There is rage at their mothers for not having protected them, but there can also be a feeling of triumph over them.

As V. G. said, sometimes when her mother was lauding it over her, patronizing her with an air of superiority, she was tempted to retaliate with some caustic comments about her mother's inability to hold on to her man. She never yielded to this temptation. Yet, she was not so scarred that she couldn't think such thoughts. Most women are. Most women repress the grandiosity as well as the shame, and they are then not aware of how the traps they get into are a result of unconscious parts of their sense of self.

One woman, who recently entered treatment with seemingly full awareness of her father's molestations, opened up a session by telling me about a newspaper article she had read. The article reported the story of how an adolescent girl, who had been repeatedly raped by her father, had paid off a friend of hers to have her father killed. With a big smile on her face, the patient said, "That was really creative wasn't it? She actually paid someone to kill him."

The Overly Indulgent Father

The last character type I will discuss is that of the overly indulgent father. He is someone who infantalizes his daughter, and makes it all the more difficult for her to separate from him when the time comes.

There is something uniquely special about the closeness between father and daughter. In his book *Fathers and Daughters*, Appleton speaks of the oasis period that begins in early infancy, and which extends into a woman's adolescence. During those years, a father and daughter can be enormously close. Tenderness, play, and mutual fantasizing enhance their attachment bond. The sense of being special that develops in a daughter, when she feels her father's cherishing adoration in this way, is a very hard thing to give up. It's very hard for the father too, because the tenderness and adoration are mutual.

However, in order for a girl to give up her father as the only man in her life, separation from him is necessary. Social, sexual, and creative development are all inhibited if she can't let go of her father, and move on. Along with giving him up comes the ability to accept realistic criticism of herself, and the giving up of her own grandiose self-image, which is based on her father's idealization.

The father who can't let go of the special idealizing period with his daughter will often use seductive gratification of her wishes and demands as a means of holding on to her. This sets up a situation in which nobody treats her as well as daddy. Other men don't tell her she's wonderful, no matter what she does. She becomes very critical and rejecting of boys her own age, and later of men. All the criticism that a father like this does not encourage toward himself, as he aims to retain his daughter's idealized view of him, will be turned against other men. As his daughter works and socializes with men and attempts to create her own ideals, values, and creative work, she will unconsciously sabotage herself with unrealistic expectations of who she is, and of how she should be treated. She will also convey her contempt to available men who want her, and will convey naive adoration toward unavailable men, who, like her daddy, are out of her range. This creates inevitable conflicts and prevents any realistic relatedness between herself and a man. Along with this, such an overly infantilized and overly idealized daughter will tend to have a distorted view of her own talents and capabilities. She will tend to either greatly overestimate her work (as daddy continues to overestimate her), or she will greatly undervalue it. Large shifts of self-esteem may be evident, with manic highs and depressive lows, as her view of herself, and of her work, shifts from one extreme to another.

Father Loss

The death of a father is too profound an event to go into here. A book devoted to the subject is *Father Loss*, by Elyce Wakerman. One main point stands out. Although a woman may outwardly go through the motions of dating and relating to men, if she has never fully mourned the loss of her father, the idealized image of her father will remain hauntingly with her, and it will prevent her acceptance of other men. Ultimately, she will run from genuine intimacy with a man. She will keep men at a distance. This may be done through criticism and contempt. However, it may also be done through masochistic submission.

There are a few other important points not mentioned by Elyce Wakerman in her book. First of all, for a daughter who is merged in as a self-extension of her father, the loss of her father may be experienced as a loss of her self. The poet Sylvia Plath, who lost her father at the age of eight, writes of how she sealed off her inner self when she lost her father:

> And this is how it stiffens, my vision of that seaside childhood. My father died, we moved inland. Whereon those nine first years of my life sealed themselves off like a ship in a bottle—beautiful, inaccessible, obsolete, a fine, white flying myth (Kavaler, 1984, p. 13).

There was a sharp division at the point of her father's death. It was a division between the sealed-off self and that in contact with the outside world.

Whether a woman has reached a developmental level where it is mainly her relationships with men that will suffer from her father's death, or whether she is at an earlier level in which her entire sense of self will suffer a developmental arrest, the overall dynamics of her internalized relationship with her father will be intensified and magnified by the abrupt and total loss. The compulsion to reenactments will be intensified as well. This is most specificly true when the father is lost during his daughter's childhood years. The earlier the loss, the more serious the consequences can be. Marion Woodman, a Jungian therapist, writes in a book called *Addiction to Perfection* (1982) about the father obsession and complex with a demon lover figure. She states that an obsession with an internalized father object, which prevents a woman from living her life, will be intensified by the father's death. A pathological mourning state is possible when a father lives or dies, but if a father actually dies the resistance to mourning (as mentioned in the description of the overly indulgent father) will be greatly increased. Sylvia Plath is known for her outbursts of narcissistic rage, in which she refuses time and time again to feel the loss of mourning. She holds onto her grandiosity, and in doing so she holds onto her father.

CONCLUSION

When we look at the father's personality, and its effect on the self-development of his daughter, we also have to look at the daughter's capacity to attach herself to her father, to receive the empathic mirroring and contact he provides, and to then move on through a mourning process to separation from him. Father–daughter bonding is fantasy enhanced and is quite tenacious. Consequently, separation may be resisted by both the father and daughter. In moving on to other men, a woman may search continually for the father who never denied her anything, or for the one who never stayed long enough to belong to her. If a father was too frustrating, or too narcissistically damaging, his daughter might search forever for the adoring man whom she never had. Then she will be acutely disappointed when a man's attentions wax or wane, bringing back the experience of earlier injuries. To separate from a genuinely good-enough father is hard enough, and will generally be resisted for some time, but to separate from the adoring father who lives only in fantasy (which is exacerbated when the father is lost prematurely through death or divorce) is still harder. The longed for ideal father lives on, and tantalizingly lingers as an internal fantasy or introject, while ordinary male mortals seem easily tarnished by comparison. Also, fathers who are so narcissistic that they must glow forever in the little girl eyes of adoration never allow their daughters to hate or criticize them; thus, they block their daughter's mourning of the disappointments akin to their own faults. Their daughters, in turn, remain love addicts, who exhibit continual reaction formation reverance in response to their split off, or repressed, rage. They can also rebel, and become single's scene addicts, who continually discard men.

In discussing the father's role in the self-development of women, we have to also take into account the daughter's responsibility to respond and to internalize her father's input into her sexual, intellectual, and creative levels of self-functioning. This involves both the daughter's willingness and her capacity to mourn. She must be able to introject aspects of her father, to use his mirroring and idealizing self-object functions, and to also be able to integrate positive and negative parts of him into her internal male image. This requires a process of assimilation. In order to both differentiate from him, and to integrate his contributing smiles and words into her interior self, she must be able to separate from him through the painful working-through process of the overall mourning process. Although resistance to such mourning may be as much attributable to deficits in mothering as to deficits in fathering, this chapter has focused on the latter.

References

Allen, C. (1980). *Daddy's girl*. New York: Berkley Books.
Appleton, W. S. (1981). *Fathers and daughters*. New York: Doubleday.
Butsher, E. (1976). *Sylvia Plath, method and madness*. New York: Simon & Schuster, Pocket Books.
Cardinal, M. (1983). *The words to say it*. Cambridge, MA: Van Vactor and Goodheart.
Fairbairn, R. (1952). *Psychoanalytic studies of the personality*. Boston: Routledge and Kegan Paul.
Ferlazzo, P. J. (1976). *Emily Dickinson*. Boston: Twayne Publishers.
Fields, S. (1966). *Like father, like daughter*. Boston: Little, Brown .
Gilligan, C. (1982). *In a different voice*. Cambridge, MA: Harvard University Press.
Kavaler, S. (1984). Mirror, mirror on the wall. . . . *Journal of Comprehensive Psychotherapy, 4*, 1–38.

Klein, M. (1981). *Love, guilt, and reparation and other works 1921–1945*. London: Hogarth.

Klein, M. (1980). *Envy and gratitude and other works 1946–1961*. London: Hogarth.

Reich, A. (1973). Extreme submissiveness in women. In *Psychoanalytic contributions*. New York: International Universities Press.

Sewall, R. B. (1974). *The life of Emily Dickinson*. New York: Farrar, Straus and Giroux. Reprinted in 1980.

Spieler, S. (1984). Preoedipal girls need fathers. *Psychoanalytic Review, 71* (1), 63–79.

Stolorow, R., & Lachman, F. (1980). *Psychoanalysis of developmental arrests*. New York: Jason Aronson.

Wakerman, E. (1984). *Father loss*. New York: Doubleday.

Woodman, M. (1982). *Addiction to perfection: The still unravished bride*. Toronto: Inner City Books.

Part II

Female Passages of the Body-Self

Part II of the book deals with female passages of self—a developmental progression of the inner self marked by bodily change and richly saturated in meaning. Sue A. Shapiro posits the idea that the onset and course of menstruation are a challenge to a woman's ego and defenses. The real hormonal changes that occur during the monthly menstrual cycle, together with attending emotional and physical shifts, create an internal state to which the adolescent girl must learn to respond and adapt. Leanne Domash discusses childbearing motivation as a positive force in a woman's psyche, a force that is creative and reparative and is also a powerful blend of the wish to unite, merge, and be separate. In the realm of transitional relatedness are the seeds of both creativity and possible pathology. Both are explicated. Roni O. Cohen reviews comprehensively, from a psychohistorical perspective, psycho-analytic theories of pregnancy, beginning with the early analysts and discussing both the biochemical as well as psychological aspects throughout. Thoughtfully covered as well are the effects of pregnancy on ego functioning as dynamically understood in today's cultural milieu.

Chapter 5

Menarche and Menstruation
Psychoanalytic Implications

SUE A. SHAPIRO

Menarche, as a rite of passage, and menstruation, as an ongoing fact of a woman's life, are central to women's experience. The entry into and exit from reproductive capability seem clearly evident to most women. Until reliable birth control became available in the last century, the menstrual cycle governed women's lives. The phenomenology of the menstrual cycle deserves the attention of psychoanalysts, because of both its presence during 30 to 40 years of women's lives, and the possible clues it offers in understanding the complex interplay of psyche and soma in the generation of psychological experience.

Menstruation is a complex psychosomatic phenomenon and the research concerning it has consequently been subject to the vagaries of politics and fashion. In Freud's time, grounding psychological experience in biology seemed to legitimize the new science of psychoanalysis. However, in today's America, biological arguments are often associated with right-wing efforts to keep certain subgroups, such as women and blacks, in their "proper" place. The current upsurge in research about menstruation is in part a reaction to a number of efforts to deprive women of powerful positions because of their "raging hormones" (Berman, cited in AMA, 1984, p. 65). Not surprisingly then, much current research is decidedly antibiological.

It is my position that each individual stands on her/his own set of coordinates in a field created by physiological (including genetic), sociocultural, and personal–historical factors. To understand any single individual's experience, it is useful to grasp the range of factors that potentially affect that experience. Most individuals are unaware or unconscious of many of the physiological, sociocultural, and per-

The author gratefully acknowledges the help of Claire Basescu and Jackie Weiden in the initial stages of this chapter. She also wishes to thank Susan Blumenthal, Barbara Eisold, and Nora Lapin for their help in reviewing prior drafts of this chapter.

SUE A. SHAPIRO, PH.D. • Clinical Supervisor, New York University, Doctoral Program in Clinical Psychology; Clinical Instructor of Psychiatry, New York University Medical School; Faculty, Manhattan Institute for Psychoanalysis; private practice.

sonal–historical forces that contribute to her/his intrapsychic and interpersonal experience. I am not interested in presenting a unitary explanation of the meaning of menstruation, but rather in elaborating dimensions worth exploring in our patients' experiences. Unfortunately, those who readily accept physiological explanations all too frequently ignore the intrapsychic and cultural factors and vice versa. I am convinced that our task, as psychoanalysts, is best served by remaining open to a holistic understanding of the complexity of forces that may contribute to any particular person's experience.

Women's experience of menarche and menstruation seems to be a complex interweaving of their particular physiology, psychology, and cultural background. We each have our own inherited biochemicial programming which is somewhat altered by our lifestyle (e.g., exercise, diet, frequency of sex, stress). We are each born of specific families which have helped shape our body image, female identity, self-esteem, attitude towards pain, illness, and menstruation. We are also born at a specific historical moment, to a specific constellation of religious, cultural, and social systems of meanings, values, and attitudes regarding female identity, ideal body types, sickness, weakness, menstruation, sex, etc. We each had our own early experiences of our body, discovered our sexuality in our own time, and experienced our own timing in relation to our peers as we approached puberty. These are only some of the factors that contribute to an individual's attitudes toward menstruation.

This chapter explores the nature of menarche and menstruation in an effort to better understand the dimensions of our patients' experiences. First, menstruation will be looked at in a historical/cultural context, next in terms of psychoanalytic theory concerning it, and then information from such fields as endocrinology, social psychology, and developmental psychology that may be blended into a coherent view will be presented. Finally I will present some clinical vignettes to illustrate how these ideas relate to clinical practice.

HISTORY

Menarche has historically been viewed as the start of womanhood. In many cultures, special rites and rituals mark the young woman's passage from childhood. Although our own culture lacks such a rite of passage, parental behavior toward and expectations for the menarcheal girl often change in ways quite similar to those in more ritualized societies. For example, we attempt to confine the social contact of postmenarcheal girls to people of their own social status through fraternities and sororities, debutante and "sweet sixteen" parties to announce social status and availability, and we frequently restrict the movement and activity of adolescent girls (Paige, 1983; Wynne & Frader, 1979).

Until this century, most theorizing about menstruation was done by men who are responsible for many assertions, such as this frequently quoted line from Pliny (79 A.D./1961) on the powers of menstrual blood:

> Contact with it turns new wine sour, crops touched by it become barren, grafts die, seed in gardens are dried up, the fruit of trees falls off, the edge of steel and the gleam of ivory are dulled, hives of bees die, even bronze and iron are at once

seized by rust, and a horrible smell fills the air; to taste it drives dogs mad and infects their bites with an incurable poison (Book 7, p. 549).

Menstruation was viewed with awe in many cultures. Lederer (1968) suggests that a woman's capacity to bleed without dying has been viewed with fear and wonder by men. Some believe that before human beings understood how babies were born, people believed that menstruation produced babies since sex prior to the onset of menses didn't lead to pregnancy. Cultural and religious myths and taboos arose out of this fear and wonder.

Today these myths persist in some religions, including orthodox Judaism and Hinduism in Bali. Although the influence is more subtle among the less religious, demographic variables are still of critical importance in determining menstrual attitudes (Basescu, 1984; Kay, 1981) and in reporting menstrual symptoms (Paige, 1973). Men may have created myths and taboos that reflect their fear or revulsion of menstruating women in response to having been being sexually rejected by them (Lederer, 1968) or fear of women's sexual appetites (Sherfey, 1972). Or human males may be differentially attracted to women during the different phases of their cycle and lack other ways of expressing these unconscious preferences (see McClintock, 1981). Despite the rich anthropological data and the current interest in menstruation, contemporary men's attitudes toward menstruation have received very little attention.

The many pseudo-scientific beliefs concerning menstruation include the suggestions that women should go to bed and not have strenuous exercise or sex during the menses, as well as the contemporary belief that all menstrual-related difficulties are psychogenic and should consequently be ignored. Women have also contributed to misinformation regarding menstruation. Some women, as well as men, have been served by using the excuse "it's just my/your period" to explain away angry outbursts, avoid intimacy, or to be excused from certain activities.

Only recently have women writers openly confronted the menstrual experience. Anne Frank (1955, 1972) innocently describes her experience of menstruation to a friend:

> . . . I think that what is happening to me is so wonderful, and not only what can be seen on my body, but all that is taking place inside. . . .
> . . . Each time I have a period . . . I have the feeling that in spite of all the pain, unpleasantness, and nastiness, I have a sweet secret, and that is why I always long for the time that I shall feel that secret within me again (p. 117).

When Doris Lessing's *The Golden Notebook* appeared in 1962, many women readers felt a shock of recognition when they reached Anna's startlingly frank recounting of her experience during her menstrual period. Lessing's groundbreaking novel ushered in a new directness in the expression of women's experience:

> As I push the stained [from sex] sheet into the linen basket I notice a stain of blood. But surely it's not time yet for my period? I hastily check dates, and realise yes, it's today. Suddenly I feel tired and irritable, because these feelings accompany my periods. (I wondered if it would be better not to choose today to write down everything I felt; then decided to go ahead. It was not planned; I had forgotten about the period. I decided that the instinctive feeling of shame and modesty was dishonest: not an emotion for a writer.) I stuff my vagina with the tampon of cotton wool, and am already on my way downstairs when I re-

member I've forgotten to take a supply of tampons with me. I am late. I roll tampons into my handbag, concealing them under a handkerchief, feeling more and more irritable. At the same time I am telling myself that if I had not noticed my period had started, I would not be feeling nearly so irritable. . . . Now sitting on the bus, I feel the dull drag at my lower belly. Not bad at all. Good, if this first pang is slight then it will be all over in a couple of days. Why am I so ungrateful when I suffer so little compared to other women?—Molly, for instance, groaning and complaining in enjoyable suffering for five or six days. . . . Because, where-as to me, the fact I am having a period is no more than an entrance into an emotional state, recurring regularly, that is of no particular importance; I know that as soon as I write the word 'blood,' it will be giving a wrong emphasis, and even to me when I come to read what I've written. . . . I am thinking, I realise, about a major problem of literary style, of tact. . . . For instance when Molly said to me, with her loud jolly laugh: I've got the curse; I have instantly to suppress distaste, even though we are both women; and I begin to be conscious of the possibility of bad smells. Thinking of my reaction to Molly, I forget about my problems of being truthful in writing . . ., and I begin to worry. Am I smelling? It is the only smell I know of that I dislike. I don't mind my own immediate lavatory smells; I like the smell of sex, of sweat, of skin, or hair. But the faintly dubious, essentially stale smell of menstrual blood I hate. And resent. It is a smell that I feel as strange even to me, an imposition from outside. Not from me. Yet for two days I have to deal with this thing from outside—a bad smell, emanating from me. I realise that all these thoughts would not have been in my head at all had I not set myself to be conscious. A period is something I deal with, without thinking about it particularly. . . . a problem of routine cleanliness (pp. 339–341).

Stopping her thoughts from her mind she makes a mental note that, "As soon as I get to the office I must go to the washroom to make sure there is no smell" (p. 341).

Anne Frank's letter conveys the pride of a young woman in her body that Kestenberg (1975) has emphasized, and we can speculate along with Kestenberg that Anne Frank's menstrual sensations give form and specificity to vaginal sensa-tions and help clarify her body image (see below). Lessing's richly textured account of Anna's experience presents the conflicts and confusion about menstruation that have concerned the last decade of empirical investigators (see below). Lessing openly discusses issues of shame, including concern over smells,[1] the fear that the experience is purely subjective, that it shouldn't be known or discussed in public, and the belief that other women suffer more. Such women are viewed with a strange mixture of compassion, suspicion, and some contempt. In contrast, Lessing reports the moderate physical changes that Anna experiences and the "rational" attitude she adopts toward them.

Contemporary thinking about menstruation is clearly linked with a sense of cyclicity, in a way that would not have been possible until this century. In the last 100 years, the age of menarche has declined dramatically so that while the average age of menarche was 17 in 1850, today it is 12.6 in industrialized countries. In addition, the development of birth control has not only freed women sexually but has also altered their relationship with the menstrual cycle. Thus the average wom-

[1]See, too, advertisements for "feminine hygiene" products to realize that menstruation has become a hygienic crisis in our culture (Toth, Delaney, & Lupton, 1981).

an of 1850 who spent most of her time pregnant or lactating, may have had 30 menstrual cycles during her entire reproductive live. In contrast, the average contemporary woman can expect to have over 300 menstrual cycles. Today's woman is consequently the first in history to have a personal awareness of cyclicity and we are uniquely able to study the impact of cyclical change on woman's behavior. Women are now regularly confronted with periodic changes in behavior, body sensations, and mood which they must assimilate into their ongoing sense of themselves. As Douvan (1970, p. 32) notes, "This regular fluctuation in the body system . . . adds special conflict to the already problem-ridden process of developing a stable self-concept of adolescence . . . It will result in a self-system that is more fluid and vulnerable to environmental influences."

PHYSIOLOGY OF THE MENSTRUAL CYCLE

The physiology of the menstrual cycle is quite complex. The two major hormones (estrogen and progesterone), as well as the minor hormones (androgen, prolactin, prostaglandins, etc.), affect other bodily systems as well as the reproductive system. At the onset of the monthly cycle (traditionally the cycle starts on day 1 of menses), the pituitary gland, in response to a chemical message from the hypothalamus (gonadatropin-releasing hormone), sends follicle-stimulating hormone (FSH) and small quantities of luteinizing hormone (LH) into the bloodstream. When FSH and low levels of LH reach the ovaries, several follicles, or egg capsules, are stimulated, start to grow and to release estradiol. These hormones also cause the lining of the uterus to begin to thicken. As midcycle approaches, estrogen production reaches a high level causing the pituitary to decrease FSH and sharply increase LH. This LH surge, occuring approximately 14 days after the beginning of the cycle, and reliably 14 days before its end, causes the follicle to rupture and release a mature egg into the fallopian tube. This ruptured follicle transforms into a temporary organ, the corpus luteum, which produces progesterone. It is this hormone which is the hallmark of the last half, or luteal phase of the cycle.

Most variation in the length of women's cycles occurs during the follicular phase (first half of the cycle). If fertilization does not occur, the corpus luteum breaks down; the lining of the uterus, lacking sufficient progesterone, stops growing and sheds; and menstruation begins. Figure 1 illustrates the changes in hormone levels during a typical 28-day cycle. Interestingly, androgen levels are at their highest during ovulation. Sexual desire seems to be related to androgen levels, thus this increase in androgen level at midcycle might be nature's way of increasing the likelihood of reproduction. (Leshner, 1978)

It is important to mention some of the systemic effects of these hormones, in addition to their specific roles in the menstrual cycle. Estrogen can increase fluid retention. Progesterone elevates body temperature, and increases tolerance to the presence of a foreign protein such as a fetus or virus. This effect of progesterone might explain the premenstrual decrease in immunity. Abnormal amounts of androgen, caused either by ovarian or adrenal tumors, may cause an increase in facial hair, severe acne, weight gain, and according to some, depression. Prolactin regu-

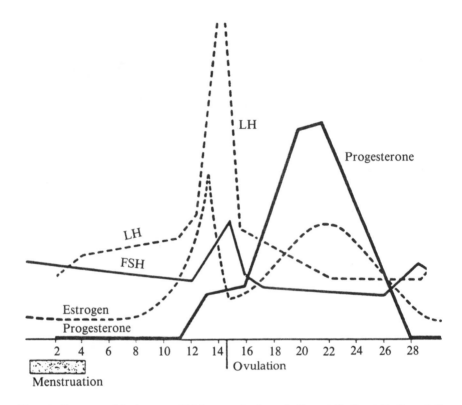

Figure 1. Hormone activity in a normal 28-day reproductive cycle. Stewart, F., Guest, F., Stewart, G., and Hatcher, R., My Body, My Health. New York: Bantam Books, 1981. By permission.

lates breast milk production, but too much estrogen can deregulate prolactin levels. Prolactin has been implicated in some work on psychoses and its level is affected by various mood-altering medications, such as the phenothiazines. And lastly, prostaglandins are a group of hormones whose role in various normal and abnormal processes is under increasing scrutiny. Prostaglandins, which are present in semen, the uterine lining, and many bodily tissues, increase with stress. They can affect many body processes such as blood pressure, body temperature, kidney fluid balance, activity of the gastrointestinal tract, constriction of lung air passageways, arthritis, and uterine contractions. (See AMA, 1984; Lauersen & Stukane, 1983, 1984; Leshner 1978; Stewart, Guest, Stewart, & Hatcher, 1981, for further discussion.)

The menstrual cycle is a delicate balance that is easily affected by both psychological and physiological factors. The effects of psychological stresses may be mediated by the hypothalamus. The interplay between psychology and physiology can be quite complex. For instance, stress is frequently implicated in amenorrhea, or the absence of blood flow, which can however also be caused by central nervous system (CNS) problems, changes in weight, muscle to fat ratio, diet, drugs, and even amount of sunlight. Similarly, excessive bleeding, and breakthrough bleeding can be caused by psychological stress (see Cardinale, 1983) and also by excessive estrogen or estrogen stimulation in a noncyclic pattern.

PSYCHOANALYTIC INVESTIGATIONS OF MENSTRUATION

Scientific interest in the *experience* of menstruation began with Freud. It is important to remember that when Freud first wrote on the subject, women were not yet regularly experiencing a sense of menstrual cyclicity. In some respects his theorizing can be seen as growing out of the tradition begun by Pliny, that of men addressing this topic from the alien vantage point of their own experiences and fantasies.

Horney (1926) has commented that Freud's theory of women resembles the fantasies of the frightened little boy. However, for all the valid criticisms of Freud's views we must acknowledge that the Freudian revolution enabled sexuality to come into the open, and also laid the groundwork for frank discussion of women's experiences. In addition, it should be kept in mind that while Freud worked and wrote, contraception was not readily available, many women still died in childbirth, and thus menarche indeed signaled much of what was painful and dangerous in being a woman. The following brief summaries of psychoanalytic theories focus on those aspects that are relevant to an understanding of menstruation.

Freud proposed that feminine identity developed in response to castration anxiety, penis envy, and a deep sense of inadequacy. Prior to children's observation of the penis (which Freud believed occurred during the early Oedipal period), girls and boys developed in a similarly "masculine" way. He believed that after her observation of sexual difference and subsequent sense of castration, inferiority, and penis envy, the young girl turns away from her mother and toward her father, thus entering the Oedipal complex. In response to this crisis, she also gives up her clitoral (phallic) masturbation, and becomes passive, masochistic, and narcissistic. Her desire for a penis is transformed into a wish for her father's baby. Thus, for Freud, women's maternal strivings were defensive substitutes for her wish for a penis. In this context, menarche was seen as an experience which reawakened castration anxiety, penis envy, and reinforced a woman's masochistic character. This view, which clearly stressed the symbolic significance of menstruation (Freud, 1925, 1931, 1933), was further elaborated with some minor revisions by Bonaparte (1931) and Deutsch (1945).

Freud's theory of women, and by extension the psychoanalytic understanding of menstruation, has been challenged primarily on the developmental–physiological and cultural fronts. The first to question Freud on these issues were Jones (1935) and Horney (1926, 1967) who argued for a primary femininity not derived from penis envy.

While Horney was articulating the idea of a primary feminine identity, she was also developing the cultural line of criticism of Freudian theory (Horney, 1935, 1967). She was joined in this endeavor by Thompson (1942, 1943, 1950) who greatly expanded the scope of this argument. Both women emphasized the impact of cultural prohibitions, expectations, and stereotypes on women's development.

They believed that penis envy arose out of recognition of the real inequities in the lives of the sexes, and that feminine masochism was a response to women's actual social position. Out of their criticisms arose the "cultural" school of psychiatry. (See Miller, 1973, and Strauss, 1985, for their excellent anthologies and discussions of early psychoanalytic theorizing on women.) Their critiques of Freudian meta-psychology and, implicitly, of the patriarchy which gave rise to his theory set the stage for the next wave of feminist psychoanalytic theorists. Chodorow (1978), Dinnerstein (1976), Gilligan (1982), and Miller (1966) emphasize the ways in which women are different but not deficient, and expand our understanding of the effect of culture on women's psychology. They explore the differential impact on boys and girls of women being the primary caretaker during infancy and childhood, and put greater emphasis on pre-Oedipal development and the effect of patriarchal society, and come closest to integrating the cultural school with the new theoretical work coming out of the Freudian tradition. Unfortunately, neither the early cultur-alists nor the new feminist psychoanalytic writings pay much attention to the biological differences between the sexes and the possible physiological substrate to differential experiences. This lack of concern with biology may have been a neces-sary correction to the biological determinism of Freud, and the politically reaction-ary trends fueled by sociobiology, but this extreme distancing from the body weak-ens their theoretical work. So strong has this reaction been that Chodorow, Dinnerstein, Gilligan, and Miller scarcely mention the possible experiential impact of biological differences between the sexes. Although these feminist analysts have not addressed themselves to the psychological effects of menarche and menstrua-tion per se, their insights into women's development and subsequent psychology can inform current thinking on the subject.

In contrast to these theorists, Deutsch (1945) and Kestenberg (1961, 1967a, 1967b, 1968, 1975, 1982) made enormous inroads in attempts at describing the developing sensory experience of the adolescent girl while minimizing cultural effects. Although one may disagree with the theory in which they embed their observations, we are nevertheless richer for their acuity and attention to detail.

Recently, the case for a primary feminine identity (see above discussion of early criticisms of Freud by Jones, 1935, and Horney, 1924, 1926, 1932, 1933) has gained support from the findings of Kleeman (1977), Stoller (1968, 1973a, 1973b, 1977), Galenson and Roiphe (1977), Roiphe and Galenson (1981), Kestenberg (1982), and Money and Ehrhardt (1972). On the basis of infant observation and detailed study of children (Money & Ehrhardt, 1972) and adults (Stoller, 1968, 1973a, 1973b, 1977) with sexual anomalies and gender disorders, we now know that gender identity is established at about 18 months of age. A core sense of femininity is primarily based on parents' ascription of gender and can be established even in the absence of a vagina, or in the presence of a Y chromosome. Thus, a primary feminine identity precedes and is distinct from awareness of the lack of a penis. According to Roiphe and Galenson (1981), the observation of sexual differences occurs between the ages of 16 and 24 months and is not only of critical importance in the ongoing consolidation of self and object representations but also has repercus-sions for cognitive development. (See Person, 1985, and Formanek, 1982, for further discussion.)

Kleeman and Kestenberg note the presence of early vaginal as well as clitoral sensations in young girls. Focused masturbation begins around 14 months (Kleeman, 1977) and continues with various periods of intensification (Kestenberg, 1982) often through latency (Clower 1976, 1977). Masters and Johnson (1966) clearly indicated that "mature" women need not and in fact cannot shift their locus of sexual excitation away from their clitoris to their vagina. Thus, several of the tasks Freud deemed critical in the development of femininity do not in fact occur. There has been, and still is, considerable confusion regarding the development of women's sexuality. Lerner (1977) points out how we perpetuate this confusion through, among other things, parental mislabeling of female genitalia, and to this I would add, therapeutic misrepresentation of "normal" sexual responses.

Especially impressive and extensive is the work by two analytic theorists on menarche and menstruation. Benedek (1952, 1973) and Kestenberg (1961, 1967a, 1967b, 1975, 1982) shifted the focus of psychoanalytic theorizing from the symbolic meaning of menstruation to the impact of the cyclic hormonal changes of the menstrual cycle on women's psychological experience.

Building on the work of Franz Alexander with psychosomatic disorders, Benedek (1952) intensively studied the analytic material of women patients who simultaneously tracked their menstrual cycles. She found that she could accurately predict when these women would ovulate based on the content of their analytic productions. Women in the follicular phase of the cycle tended to be more active, showing increased activity and ambitiousness. During the luteal phase, these women tended to be more receptive. Although her classic study is somewhat flawed by present standards, it testifies to the energetic researching of psychoanalytic hypotheses at that time. Benedeck's efforts to integrate and correlate two different levels of analysis (psychoanalytic and physiological) lay the groundwork for the more sophisticated studies of Kestenberg. Her findings raise the question of whether causality can go in two directions. Thus, for instance, are very ambitious women able unconsciously to increase the amount of time they spend in the follicular part of the cycle? As far as I know, no one has investigated this question.

Kestenberg has made the most elaborate effort to coordinate endocrinological findings with behavioral and psychoanalytic observations. In a series of articles (1967a, 1967b, 1975, 1982), she describes the hormonal and behavioral shifts from infancy through latency, prepuberty, and adolescence. She integrates these data into a comprehensive theory of sexual development. Kestenberg's tendency to minimize or negate the influence of social and cultural factors on psychological development may have limited the integration of her findings into emerging theories of women's development. Her work raises certain questions we have not yet answered. If we ground psychosexual development and simultaneous mood changes in endocrinology, then we should also look for physiological as well as psychoanalytic explanations for various psychopathological outcomes. For example, Kestenberg describes the increased stability that comes to the late adolescent girl when her cycles become ovulatory and a regularity of hormonal fluctuations is established. Given this theory, what are the implications for women who are anovulatory and thus never develop the typical, regular hormonal pattern of mature women? Might this endocrinological abnormality affect their sense of their own femininity and, more importantly, their development of a stable, or mature personality structure? Might some women who are subject to extreme hormonal fluctuations be more likely than other women and men to have the extreme diagnoses of borderline personality disorder?

MENARCHE

Menarche, the beginning of a young woman's menstruating life, and menstruation, as an ongoing fact of her life, have many implications that reverberate through women's psychic lives. Menarche can be viewed as a normal developmental crisis that renews the identification with mother. It is the culmination of a series of pubertal bodily changes which first disrupt and eventually lead to a reintegration of body image. At times it can lead to a sense of pride but at other times to a sense of damage. Unfortunately, girls in our culture don't seem able to rejoice at menarche. Only as women approach menapause do some finally begin to "love" their cycles. Our culture fails to teach girls the miraculous nature of the menstrual cycle perhaps out of fear that they will become pregnant, or simply out of our fear and awe of women's natural powers (Dinnerstein, 1976; Fromm-Reichmann & Gunst, 1973; Sherfey, 1972). In fact the culture puts a premium on denying many signs of adult female sexuality, including body hair, odors, and all signs of menstruation. It is into this apparently hostile, or at least ambivalent environment that a young woman is born.

Menarche marks the initiation of a young girl into woman's time. Just as time is told by birthdays and holidays, for women it can also be measured by menstrual periods. Did I have sex this month? With whom? Am I pregnant? Menopausal? and so on. Thus, menarche gives young women access to organic time, not just on the macro level of aging, or on the subtle micro level of daily biorhythms. Rather, we can say that women live the seasons of the year each month. They may choose to ignore this, and those who are fortunately free of severe menstrual symptomatology may succeed. Or they may choose to tune in and open this window onto their internal state, to fully live this experience. Obviously men also have hormonal fluctuations but they are less able to identify these changes which tend to be less overt. Boys are able to see and touch their external genitals from infancy on, and thus can develop a clearer body representation of their genitals much earlier than girls. After puberty, however, girls may have easier entry into their internal physiological experience.

Women react differently to this organic dimension of time. For some, the changes in vaginal mucus, arousability, water retention, and mood, for example, are clearly within consciousness. Other women are not aware of these changes because they are either less noticeable, or deemed unworthy of attention.

Although the young girl approaching menarche has some notion of her mother's relationship to menstrual cyclicity, much of her experience is intensely private and unarticulated. The pubescent girl knows primarily the public representation of this time/event by her mother and by the culture at large—the specific ideas of her own subculture and the myths and taboos of centuries. To understand her experience, we clinicians need to know something of the time and culture in which she has grown up, as well as the specific nature of her relationship with her mother, and her mother's attitudes toward sexuality and menstruation. In addition to the mother's conscious, stated feelings, the premenarcheal girl has her own, perhaps preconscious awareness of the monthly changes her mother experiences, their subtle meanings to mother and father alike, and the uses and abuses to which her parents have put them.

Most girls get their early information about menstruation from their mothers. This is one reason why parental attitudes toward menstruation and sexuality are critical in the formation of adolescent experience. How do parents feel about their daughter becoming a woman? Are they frightened by her new reproductive capacity? What has been the mother's experience of menstruating? What sort of somatic changes does she have during her cycle and how has she adapted to them?

Interestingly, mothers tend to mislabel their girls' genitalia, referring to it generically as a vagina and neglecting to name the actual external genitalia as vulva, clitoris, etc. (Lerner, 1977). And while mothers usually refer to the internal passage or vagina, they almost universally avoid teaching their daughters to use tampons. Thus, in anticipation of the first period and subsequently at the time of menses, most girls are given sanitary napkins. The use of the napkin, along with admonitions to be especially clean at this time of the month, might increase the likelihood that girls initially regress to an anal experience of menstruation and retain a cloacal idea of their genitals. Thus, menstruation frequently becomes an anal/hygienic crisis. The initial menstrual cycle seems to reintroduce a dependence on the mother and reawakens old conflicts regarding dirtiness and the need to control. The feel of the sanitary napkin may be reminiscent of the feel of the diaper. Shopper (1979) found that most girls begin to use tampons when they are away from home. This act is often a rite of passage which is assisted by a friend and accompanied by fear and excitement. Mothers' reluctance to initially approach their daughter with tampons, despite the fact that they often use tampons themselves, may connote a reluctance to acknowledge that their daughters are sexual beings.

By the time they are preadolescents, both girls and boys have specific, though often erroneous, attitudes and beliefs about menarche and menstruation (Brooks-Gunn & Ruble, 1980, 1982, 1983). During the premenarcheal period, girls may be having subtle precursors of cyclic hormonal changes (Dalton, 1979; Kestenberg, 1961, 1967a). All but the earliest developers hear first about friends' experiences before having their own.

Not until menarche, however, does a girl have her own, personal experience of this central female process. Her future experiences will build on this and change over time as her cycle matures (as we will see, there are physiological changes over time), as she familiarizes herself with it, as her life circumstances and desires change, her culture changes and her biological clock ticks away.

The age and developmental stage at which girls first become aware of menstruation can have a lasting imprint on their experience (Bernstein & Warner, 1984). Age of onset of menarche matters both on the individual level—how prepared a girl is for these changes—and also on an interpersonal, group level—where does she stand in relation to her peers. Researchers have found marked differences in personality development among early and late developers (Berkovitz, 1979; Brooks-Gunn & Ruble, 1980, 1983; Peterson, 1980; Tobin-Richards, Boxer, & Petersen, 1983).

Today there is considerable range in timing of menarche. While early pubertal development enhances boys' self-esteem and standing with peers, both early and late female developers suffer in self-esteem. Early developers tend to become heterosexually involved sooner and, more frequently, have antisocial problems (Miller, 1979). Being "on time," on the same time table as one's peers, is of critical importance for girls, as is appearing "normal." Psychoanalysts have noted that early developers have shortened latencies while late developers have a truncated adolescence. Many researchers have noticed the difficulty with which adolescents talk about and recall early pubertal experiences (Peterson, 1980). Brooks-Gunn and Ruble (1982) note that at the time of menarche, girls are often quite secretive and at first only speak of it with their mothers.

Since there is no sphincter with which to control the menses and the early menstrual cycles tend to be anovulatory and irregular, it takes quite a while before the adolescent can accurately anticipate her menstrual flow. Fears of staining or having accidents are quite common and are increased by the unpredictability of timing and intensity of flow. Adolescents frequently feel as though their bodies don't fit together right (Rosenbaum, 1979). This concern is, of course, a function of the enormous changes in body size and proportions that occur during a relatively short period of time. Psychosomatic preoccupations at this time may also be a function of the strange internal sensations accompanying growth of internal organs and the fluctuating body states reflecting the not yet regulated shifts in endocrine production (Abplanalp, 1980; Daniel, 1983; Dupon & Bingel, 1980; and Warren, 1983).

While Deutsch (1945) felt that menarche per se would have a disruptive effect on the girl's psyche, Kestenberg (1961, 1967a, 1967b) believed that menarche would initially have an organizing effect by strengthening ego structures. Kestenberg asserted that by reducing fantasy and clarifying the girl's sense of her inner space, it would enable her to think more clearly. Weiden's (1984) research tends to support Kestenberg. According to Kestenberg, prepubescent (postmenarcheal but pre-ovulatory) girls show a disorganized emotional lability which is characteristic of a time of gradual adjustment of hormones. For her, puberty is defined by the onset of ovulatory cycles which is a more adjusted and regulated cyclicity of hormonal change. By the time the adolescent girl is 15 or 16 years old, her moods are more predictable and defined than in the previous 3 years. Girls who have had prior difficulties with issues of bodily damage are likely to have serious trouble at menarche.

Clearly, puberty is a time of extreme psychological vulnerability for girls (Barglow & Schaefer, 1979; Giovacchini, 1979; Hill & Lynch, 1983; Rierdan & Koff, 1980; Ritvo, 1977). They must find their way through numerous concerns about body image, sexuality, and autonomy. It is a time of enormous growth but, as mentioned above, it is truly a normal developmental crisis. Thus, many adolescent girls fall into destructive patterns of anorexia nervosa, drug abuse, and promiscuity, while still others suffer more quietly from intense self-consciousness and shyness (Doctors, 1979).

MENSTRUAL DIFFICULTIES

The two major menstrual difficulties are dysmenorrhea (painful periods) and premenstrual syndrome (PMS). Studies note a wide range of prevalence rates for menstrual difficulties, with 25 to 90% percent of all women reporting some degree of premenstrual syndrome and/or dysmenorrhea (this wide range is caused by differences in definition and methodological problems). Dysmenorrhea is the leading cause of missed work and school in the United States, accounting for 140 million hours of missed work each year (Budoff, 1981).

Until recently, most people, including many doctors and therapists, believed that dysmenorrhea (usually involving cramps, backache, and/or nausea) was largely psychosomatic, that is, had an emotional cause. Women's complaints were often seen as signs of weakness, bad posture, physical sluggishness, and neuroses. Even some medical textbooks currently in use state that dysmenorrhea is a symptom of a personality disorder (Budoff, 1981). Increasingly, however, doctors are reversing their position. Dingfelder states that "dysmenorrhea from psychiatric causes is indeed rare in clinical practise. There's no doubt that recurring pain can affect one's attitude towards menstruation. This does not mean that the attitude causes the pain, but quite the contrary" (AMA, 1984, p. 78).

Generally, a normal, ovulatory menstrual cycle is required in order to grow enough endometrial lining to produce painful menses. Thus, most girls will not experience dysmenorrhea during the first year of their cycle but may have extremely painful periods for the next couple of years (Klein & Litt, 1983). Dysmenorrhea often seems to be at its worst during the late teen years, an age when most girls have trouble reporting their difficulties to a doctor and insisting that they be taken seriously. The adolescent may also feel uncomfortable about discussing this topic with parents, and if they do speak of menstrual distress, their parents might respond with misinformation and an attitude that their daughters are being irresponsible.

As psychoanalysts, we need to consider the impact on subsequent ego development of being subjected to either intense debilitating pain or extremely unpredictable shifts in hormone levels during adolescence. (Researchers have found that predictability sharply lessens menstrual distress. See Dan, Graham, & Beecher, 1980, Komnenick, McSweeney, Noack, & Elder, 1981). Until recently, the only "treatments" for dysmenorrhea were birth control pills, which occasionally reduced the problem temporarily, and childbirth, which might alleviate it by enlarging the cervix and thus easing the flow of blood. Many women were not helped by either of these methods.

Dysmenorrhea is now treatable. An increasing amount of evidence suggests that prostaglandins play a major role in primary dysmenorrhea. Levels of prostaglandins are affected in many ways, one of which is stress. When prostaglandins are administered to normal women, they cause uterine cramping. However, menstruating women who are given antiprostaglandin medication report that their menstrual cramps subside and, contrary to prior psychoanalytic expectations, they have no symptom substitution. The severity of this problem should not be underestimated by those of us fortunate enough not to suffer severe cramps. Some women have such severe cramps that they do not recognize the onset of heavy labor, which they have been told will be like a very severe period.

It takes several years for full hormonal regulation to take place, and the relative amounts of hormones apparently continue to change throughout a woman's life, perahps accounting for the delay in reported onset of PMS until a woman is in her late 20s or 30s. We do not yet have a clear picture of the prevalence, causes, and treatment of PMS. There is as yet no agreement on a physiological cause for PMS, nor even a clear definition of it.

Methodological problems abound in studies of PMS, whether they have been undertaken by endocrinologists or by social psychologists who tend to have more sophisticated research strategies. As yet there is no agreed upon set of clinical features that clearly delineate PMS from dysmenorrhea or disorders of the paramenstruum. As Table 1 indicates, many symptoms occur in both phases of the cycle. There is reason to suspect that PMS is not a unitary phenomenon. Some women describe an enormous sense of relief when their menses begin, while others suffer from PMS symptoms for the first 2 days of their periods. Although there is enormous variation in the physical and emotional symptomatology associated with the menstrual cycle, many physiological and psychological studies have treated women as though they were all alike. As a result, potentially significant findings are often annulled by extreme variation and bimodal distribution of responses.

The menstrual cycle is indeed a psychosomatic and somatopsychic event. It is psychosomatic because the events and timing of the menstrual cycle are governed by the physiological changes of the endocrine system, which is mediated by the CNS through the hypothalamic–pituitary axis. Thus, stress can and does interfere with the secretion of hormones. However, these hormones are intimately associated with moods and with other physiological processes which also affect mood. For instance, the bloating, weight gain, and constipation associated with the premenstrual period can affect mood. Some of these symptoms seem to be inherited

Table 1. *Commonly reported symptomatology during premenstrual and menstrual phases of the menstrual cycle in nonpatient populations*

Pain	Physical symptoms	Mood	Behavior
Headache	Breast swelling	Depression*	Performance deficits
Backpains	Abdominal bloating	Irritability*	Impaired concentration
Stomach aches†	Edema of extremities	Anxiety	Sleeping difficulties
	Weight gain	Restlessness	Absence from work
	Exacerbation of acne	Tension	Confinement to bed
	Increased thirst	Lethargy	Medical consultation
	Increased appetite	Emotional lability	Analgesic use†
	Food cravings		
	Constipation		
	Diarrhea		
	Dizziness		

Source: Fielding, D. and Bosanko, C., Psychological aspects of the menstruum and premenstruum. In A. Broone and L. Wallace (Eds.), *Psychology and Gynaecological Problems*, London: Tavistock, 1984. By permission.

Studies reviewed: Coppen and Kessel (1963); Sutherland and Stewart (1965); Moos (1968); Widholm and Kantero (1971); Timonen and Procope (1971); Schucket, Daly, Herrman and Hinerman (1975); Bergjø, Jenson and Vellar (1975); Sheldrake and Cormack (1976); Rouse (1978); Taylor (1979).

*Associated with premenstrual phase reported as occurring in more than 30 per cent of subjects in mor than two studies.

†Associated with menstrual phase reported as occurring in more than 30 per cent of subjects in more tha two studies.

[e.g., identical twins reared apart have the same amount of blood flow and report similar symptoms (Chern, Gatewood, & Anderson, 1980)].

From social psychology, we know that reports of presence or absence of symptoms may not reflect actual existence of underlying physiological changes (Basescu, 1984). Thus, there are cultural, psychological, and environmental factors that influence readiness to report PMS sympoms; these factors make it all the more difficult to establish the true presence of the disorder. In other words, a large percentage of women may experience premenstrual changes that are not severe enough to override some predilection for denying them. Other women may be prone to label even mild discomfort as PMS if they think they are in the appropriate part of their cycle.

Some women in analysis, who were previously unaware of any rhythmic changes in moods, have begun to notice a periodicity to their depressions, elations, or times of irritability. Many women must have well over a decade of experience with menstruation before they fully recognize their cycle. This delay is multidetermined. Menstrual cycles change over time, and are usually not regular for the first 2 years. Even after some stability has been achieved, cycles remain vulnerable to changes in life-style, diet, stress, etc. (Smolensky, 1980). Many adolescents are too anxious to keep track of their cycles and a month seems like a very long time to them. Most women stay fully involved in their daily activities, regardless of severity of menstrual symptomatology. The types of coping strategy used by these women may be related to amount of actual menstrual symptomatology and to their attitudes toward menstrual-related difficulties. Attitudes of denial or focusing on menstrual difficulties often seem to be learned from one's mother (Basescu, 1984). Currently, professional women fear that their hard-earned and tenous position in the business world will be jeopardized if they show signs of discomfort during the paramenstruum. Frequently, the woman of today will say, when asked about menstruation, that it is not a problem and that she has no thoughts about it. Responses to this question are linked to cultural differences.

In fact a study of menstrual cycles and weekly cycles found that men had as many "off" days as women but their cycles were more variable and they usually were not aware of them as such (Rossi, 1980). An extreme example of this is the man reported on by Stone (1980) who was treated with lithium for a 28-day cycle for depression. His cycle followed the moon.

There is no widespread support for the view that affective changes in the cycles are accompanied by cognitive or performance decrements (Golub, 1981; Graham, 1980; Peterson, 1979). However, many women feel that they do not concentrate as well and have other cognitive and/or performance changes during the paramenstruum. Perhaps this is simply a function of mood changes (Parlee, 1980). There is evidence that some tasks are performed best in the luteal phase, others in the follicular phase. Testing performance changes is difficult, in part because there is some diurnal as well as monthly variation in task performance. Speed, concentration, memory, and fine motor tasks are all affected differently in different individuals. Opera singers try not to perform during the paramenstruum because their voices drop. Musicians often experience depersonalization or changes in their sense of rhythm; athletes may find their timing is off; and other such effects have been noted.

Various neuroendocrinological hypotheses have been suggested to explain

PMS. Halbraeich, Ben-David, Assael, and Bornstein (1976) suggest that PMS arises from an excess of the pituitary hormone, prolactin. Janowsky, Bereis, and Davis (1973) believe PMS arises from the activation of the renin-angiotensin aldosterone system. Others, including Reid and Yen (1981), have implicated endorphin and melanocyte-stimulating hormone in its etiology. Others suspect that it is the relative proportion of estrogen and progesterone that is causal. Still other researchers, building on the work of Schacter, suggest that the best approach to the paramenstruum is to consider it as creating a general change in stimulus responsiveness, or arousability, which will intensify both good and bad affects depending on circumstances (Brooks-Gunn & Ruble, 1980; Parlee, 1980). In my own practice, I find that patients' affects are frequently intensified during the paramenstruum. This intensification is useful with patients with blunted or stilted affect because it magnifies their generally muted emotional state. With borderline patients, it is often helpful for both patient and analyst to realize the likely hormonal cause of the intensification of already intense, labile affects.

As psychoanalysts, we should take considerable care not to further the oppression of women to which the medical profession has sometimes contributed. When contemporary medicine doesn't know the answers, doctors are often all too willing to lay the blame on the patient's psychological difficulties. Too often psychoanalysts have been eager to accept the power for once granted them by medicine, and consequently will speak of the character pathology or poor female identity of women who suffer menstrually or premenstrually. This is especially easy at a time when no definitive understanding of premenstrual experience exists. We must be alert to this temptation and avoid the all-too-frequent occurrence of either overmedication or overdiagnoses of women, freely admitting instead our continuing ignorance in the face of real symptoms and real complaints, both physical and interpersonal. We can say with a fair degree of certainty that there is enormous individual variation in menstrual symptomatology, hormonal cyclicity, and consciousness of that cyclicity. Individual differences in the menstrual experience of researchers and psychoanalysts, as well as their theoretical biases, may account for differences in the slant of their research and theorizing. We know that menstrual attitudes and experiences are complex, multidetermined, quite variable, and strongly shaped by women's initial experiences around menarche. In our clinical work with individual patients, we can further explore this complex phenomenon.

CLINICAL ILLUSTRATIONS

The following examples illustrate the complex interaction between physical and psychological factors. Elaine is an example of a woman whose gynecological difficulties—severe pain during intercourse and severe menstrual discomfort—had been treated prior to psychotherapy as purely physical problems which could only be ameliorated by childbirth. After 1½ years of therapy we discovered that she had been raped by her father at age 10. Once this traumatic memory was recovered she lost her symptoms, which had been labeled endometriosis.

I recently began work with another incest victim who recalls that when her period first arrived, she thought "If I have to bleed like this always, I want to die."

She had no menstrual discomfort per se and never understood the intensity of her reaction until recently, in therapy, she again had the thought that she wanted to die. This thought occurred shortly before recalling some new details of her sexual abuse. She then realized that the menstrual bleeding had threatened to trigger her memories of prior vaginal bleeding secondary to penetration as a young girl. She reports that many incest survivors found menarche traumatic. Not only did they not want to become more sexual but also they, like my patient, became threatened by the blood itself and the memories it triggered. Adolescents who were physically traumatized, by either genetic or subsequent damage, are frequently intensely distressed by the onset of menses. They have such a damaged sense of their physical self that menses can only be seen in this negative light.

While the woman Elaine, described above, had intense psychological reactions that at times masqueraded as physical problems (see, too, Cardinale, 1983), Jane is an example of a patient who indeed had an undiagnosed physical problem that was masquerading as severe psychopathology. Jane is a woman with a long history of hospitalization as an adolescent. Diagnosed borderline, she had had nine therapists by the time I saw her at the age of 18. She was a poly-drug abuser, often exceedingly depressed, with a terrible family background, very self-destructive, and with terrible self-esteem. Among other concerns were her weight, her skin, and that she never felt like a woman. She always dressed like a younger adolescent in baggy clothing to hide herself. At times she complained about the hair on her face. At first I thought this complaint simply demonstrated her general overconcern with her body and her use of bodily dissatisfaction to assert her negative self-esteem. However, when Jane's dermatologist suggested that she do something about the hair on her face I began to wonder more seriously about what actually was causing it. She also had painful periods and severe depression premenstrually. I suggested we try to determine the cause rather than treat the hair problem cosmetically. I sent her to a gynecologist and specifically requested an endocrine workup to rule out Stein-Leventhal syndrome.

The gynecologist discovered that she did have this syndrome and had been producing too much testosterone. Jane has now been on birth control pills for the last year. Perhaps Jane's physiological imbalance was responsible for some of her feeling that she wasn't a normal girl. It is conceivable, but I think less likely, that the imbalance developed secondary to her psychological concerns. Jane's weight is now stable, her skin is remarkably improved, as is her overall psychological and behavioral functioning. She has been able to keep a job for more than a year and no longer has extreme mood swings. In addition, for the first time in her life, she has been able to have sex more than once with the same man and without being drunk. Many factors have contributed to Jane's problems in living and her partial improvement, but the hormonal imbalance and its subsequent correction seem to be among them and warranted our attention.

Another type of patient with severe menstrual problems poses a more complex picture. One woman asked, during an initial consultation, what I knew about PMS since she had been on progesterone for more than a year. Her symptoms were so severe that she found it necessary to keep a list of all the people she offended 2 weeks of each month so that she could call them and apologize after her period came. She, like other patients, described the onset of menses in the same poetic way people describe the relief of the monsoon. Suddenly her mood would change, things wouldn't seem so bleak, she wasn't in a rage, and she could relax. Gradually, the picture became more complex as her periods themselves became more painful and menses no longer offered any relief. Ibuprofen (Motrin), an anti-prostaglandin, no longer helped. A visit to another gynecologist provided the answer this time. She had stenosis of the cervix possibly secondary to DES or to her treatments for venereal wart. A brief surgical procedure provided relief.

This woman puzzled and frustrated me. She was very masochistic and described her physical pain so vividly and in such gory detail that I felt assaulted and became quite unsympathetic over time. A formerly strict Catholic, she was laden with conflicts about her sexuality and body sensations. However, most of her gynecological difficulties began in earnest when in the course of trying to become pregnant she discovered that she was a DES baby and would therefore not only have fertility problems but would also need to be on the alert for cancer. Her paramenstrual problems and discomfort, which had previously been bearable, now became the center of her painful existence. Similarly, a woman who had been medically abused during labor and whose baby had been permanently damaged by malpractice, now finds her premenstrual period much more intense than before.

It is difficult with these women to tease apart the psychological and changing physical causes (which after all do vary over time) for their distress. Despite the obviously complex psychological component in the last two cases, both women were helped considerably by dietary changes and supplemental doses of vitamin B_6. Regardless of the cause of the distress, some form of physical (dietary, vitamin) treatment may prove to be effective. However, it is also quite possible that my active concern and offering of a specific form of help, rather than the specific nature of the treatment, was the ameliorative factor. Frequently, this interest and concern has been contrasted by patients with their parents' or spouses' disinterest.

Several other clinical findings or avenues for further study deserve mention. The considerably higher rate of diagnosed borderline disorders in women raises the question of misdiagnosed PMS or some other hormonal imbalance (see the example of Jane, above). In fact many of the "bad" borderline behaviors appear most often during the paramenstruum. Stone (1980) describes several women whose diagnosis seemed to change during their cycle, and who lost their borderline features when treated for PMS. He suggests the need for more research in the area of faulty regulation of diurnal, monthly, and seasonal cycles in some people prone to depression and notes that this dimension seems to interact at times with the continuum of MAO (monoamine oxidase) production to lead to some serious depressions.

A neglected area of study is the impact of the therapist's cycle on her work and on her patients' cycles. I find that often the women patients with whom I am most intensely involved begin to have their periods in synchrony with me or I with them. Then when negative transferential material comes up or they become more separate, we go our separate monthly ways. This might be a repetition of some adolescent synchrony experienced with their mother. This fascinating feature of menstrual cycles has been extensively studied by McClintock (1971, 1978, 1981). Briefly, research has found that women who are in close proximity, for example mothers and daughters, often have their periods at the same time. This synchronization is apparently governed by phermones.

In general, menstruation often becomes the avenue for opening up in the transference, in therapy, a previously unexplored dimension of the mother–daughter relationship. The therapist's expressed or inferred reactions to the patients' menstrual complaints often trigger memories of earlier conflicts with her mother. Concerns over staining, unpreparedness for menses, and ignorance about cyclicity all may emerge in the consulting room and become opportunities for exploring failed assimilation of bodily changes and failed parental empathy. Thus, some of my patients seem to establish their sense of monthly timing in the course of their analysis. They will enter a session fearful of pregnancy, scared of sudden staining, or suddenly caught without a tampon, and spontaneously begin to review, in my presence, the previous menstrual month. In the course of this narration it often emerges that even those women who are quite responsible about birth control are quite disconnected from any sense of monthly time. Their concerns over pregnancy seem not only reflections of their ambivalence about childbearing but also a way of indicating their lack of ownership and confusion over their bodies. As therapy progresses, these women become more tuned in and responsive to the needs of their bodies and their changing states.

In summary, I have explored major findings from various disciplines concerning menarche and menstruation in an effort to better understand my patients' experiences. I believe that more work is needed on the interface of the physical and psychological self lest we further frustrate and mystify our patients' efforts to understand and own their experiences.

REFERENCES

American Medical Association (1984). *Womancare*. New York: Random House.

Abplanalp, J. M. (1980). The psychoendocrinology of the menstrual cycle. In A. J. Dan, E. A. Graham, & C. P. Beecher (Eds.), *The menstrual cycle*, Vol. 1 (pp. 209–222). New York: Springer.

Barglow, P., & Schaefer, M. (1979). The fate of the feminine self in normative adolescent regression. In M. Sugar (Ed.), *Female adolescent development* (pp. 201–213). New York: Brunner/Mazel.

Basescu, C. (1984). *Attitude about menstruation in mothers–adolescent daughter pairs*. Doctoral dissertation, Yeshiva University, New York.

Benedek, T. (1952). *Studies in psychosomatic medicine*. New York: Ronald Press.

Benedek, T. (1973). *Psychoanalytic investigations*. New York: Quadrangle Press.

Berkovitz, I. H. (1979). Effects of secondary school experience on adolescent female development. In M. Sugar (Ed.), *Female adolescent development* (pp. 173–198). New York: Brunner/Mazel.

Bernstein, A. E., & Warner, G. M. (1984). *Women treating women*. New York: International Universities Press.

Bonaparte, M. (1931). Passivity, masochism, and femininity. *International Journal of Psychoanalysis, 16*, 325–333.

Brooks-Gunn, J., & Ruble, D. (1980). Menarche: The interaction of physiological, cultural and social factors. In A. J. Dan, E. A. Graham, & C. P. Beecher (Eds.), *The menstrual cycle*, Vol. 1 (pp. 141–159). New York: Springer.

Brooks-Gunn, J., & Ruble, D. (1982). The development of menstrual-related beliefs and behaviors during early adolescence. *Child Development, 53*, 1567–1577.

Brooks-Gunn, J., & Ruble, D. (1983). The experience of menarche from a development perspective. In J. Brooks-Gunn & A. Peterson (Eds.), *Girls at puberty* (pp. 155–178). New York: Plenum.

Brooks-Gunn, J., & Peterson, A. C. (Eds.) (1983). *Girls at puberty*. New York: Plenum.

Budoff, P. W. (1981). *No more menstrual cramps and other good news*. New York: Penguin.

Campbell, E. R. (1984). In favor of menstruation. *Mothering*, 27–29, Summer.

Cardinal, M. (1983). *The words to say it*. Cambridge, Mass.: Vanvactor and Goodheart.

Chern, M. M., Gatewood, L. C., & Anderson, V. E. (1980). The inheritance of menstrual traits. In A. J. Dan, E. A. Graham, & C. P. Beecher (Eds.), *The menstrual cycle*, Vol. 1 (pp. 123–130). New York: Springer.

Chodorow, N. (1978). *The reproduction of mothering: Psychoanalysis and the sociology of gender*. Berkeley: University of California Press.

Clower, U. L. (1977). Theoretical implications in current views of masturbation in latency girls. In H. Blum (Ed.), *Female psychology* (pp. 109–126). New York: International Universitites Press.

Dalton, K. (1979). *Once a month*. Claremont, CA: Hunter House.

Dan, A. J., Graham, E. A., & Beecher, C. P. (1980). *The menstrual cycle*, Vol. 1 New York: Springer.

Daniel, W. A. (1983). Pubertal changes in adolescence. In J. Brooks-Gunn & A. Peterson (Eds.), *Girls at puberty* (pp. 51–72). New York: Plenum.

Deutsch, H. (1945). *The psychology of women*. New York: Grune & Stratton.

Dinnerstein, D. (1976). *The mermaid and the minotaur: Sexual arrangements and the human malaise*. New York: Harper & Row.

Doctors, S. (1979). *The symptom of delicate self-cutting in adolescent females: A developmental view*. Doctoral dissertation, Yeshiva University, New York.

Douvan, E. (1970). New sources of conflict in females at adolescence and early adulthood. In E. Walker (Ed.), *Feminine personality and conflict* (pp. 32–44). Belmont, CA: Brooks/Cole.

Dupon, C., & Bingel, A. S. (1980). Endocrinologic change associated with puberty in girls. In A. J. Dan, E. A. Graham, & C. P. Beecher (Eds.), *The menstrual cycle*, Vol. 1 (pp. 131–140). New York: Springer.

Fielding, D., & Bosankio, C. (1984). Psychological aspects of the menstruum and premenstruum. In A. Broome & L. Wallace (Eds.), *Psychology and gynaecological problems*. London: Tavistock.

Formanek, R. (1982). On the origins of gender identity. In D. Mendell (Ed.), *Early female development* (pp. 1–24). New York: Spectrum.

Frank, A. (1972). *The mind of a young girl*. New York: Pocket Books.

Freud, S. (1925). Some psychic consequences of the anatomical distinction between the sexes. In J. Strachey (Ed. & Trans.), *The standard edition of the complete psychological works of Sigmund Freud*, Vol. 19 (pp. 243–258). London: Hogarth.

Freud, S. (1931). Female sexuality. In J. Strachey (Ed. & Trans.), The *standard edition of the complete psychological works of Sigmund Freud*, Vol. 21 (pp. 223–243). London: Hogarth.

Freud, S. (1933). Femininity. In J. Strachey (Ed. & Trans.), *The standard edition of the complete psychological works of Sigmund Freud*, Vol. 22 (pp. 112–135). London: Hogarth.

Fromm-Reichmann, F., & Gunst, V. (1973). On the denial of women's sexual pleasure: Discussion of Dr. Thompson's paper. In J. B. Miller (Ed.), *Psychoanalysis and women* (pp. 86–94). New York: Penguin.

Galenson, E., & Roiphe, H. (1977). Some suggested revisions concerning early female development. In H. Blum (Ed.), *Female psychology* (pp. 29–58). New York: International Universities Press.

Gilligan, C. (1982). *In a different voice*. Cambridge, MA: Harvard University Press.

Giovacchini, P. L. (1979). The dilemma of becoming a woman. In M. Sugar (Ed.), *Female adolescent development* (pp. 253–272). New York: Brunner/Mazel.

Golub, S. (1981). Sex differences in attitudes and beliefs regarding menstruation. In P. Komnenich, M. McSweeney, J. A. Noack, & N. Elder (Eds.), *The menstrual cycle*, Vol. 2 (pp. 129–134). New York: Springer.

Graham, E. A. (1980). Cognition as related to menstrual cycle phase and estrogen level. In A. J. Dan, E. A. Graham, & C. P. Beecher (Ed.), *The menstrual cycle*, Vol. 1 (pp. 190–208). New York: Springer.

Halbreich, U., Ben-David, M., Assael, M., & Bornstein, R. (1976). Serum-prolactin in women with premenstrual syndrome. *Lancet, 2*, 654.

Hill, J. P., & Lynch, M. E. (1983). The intensification of gender-related role expectations during early adolescence. In J. Brooks-Gunn & A. C. Peterson (Eds.), *Girls at puberty* (pp. 201–228). New York: Plenum.

Horney, K. (1924). On the genesis of the castration complex in women. *International Journal of Psycho-analysis, 5*, 50–65.

Horney, K. (1926). The flight from womanhood. *International Journal of Psycho-analysis, 7*, 324–339.

Horney, K. (1932). The dread of women. *International Journal of Psycho-analysis, 13*, 348–360.

Horney, K. (1933). The denial of the vagina. *International Journal of Psycho-analysis, 14*, 55–70.

Horney, K. (1935). The problem of feminine masochism. *Psychoanalytic Review, 12*, 241–257.

Horney, K. (1967). *Feminine psychology.* New York: W. W. Norton.

Janowsky, D. S., Berens, S. C., & Davis, J. M. (1973). Correlations between mood, weight, and electrolytes during the menstrual cycle: A reninangiotensin-aldosterone hypothesis of premenstrual tension. *Psychosomatic Medicine, 35*, 143–154.

Jones, E. (1935). Early female sexuality. *International Journal of Psycho-analysis, 16*, 263–273.

Kay, M. A. (1981). Meaning of menstruation to Mexican-American women. In P. Komnenich, M. McSweeney, J. A. Noack, & N. Elder (Eds.), *The menstrual cycle*, Vol. 2 (pp. 114–123). New York: Springer.

Kestenberg, J. (1961). Menarche. In S. Lorand & H. Schneer (Eds.), *Adolescents.* New York: Hoeber Press.

Kestenberg, J. (1967a). Phases of adolescence. Part 1. *Journal of American Academy of Child Psychiatry, 6*, 426–463.

Kestenberg, J. (1967b). Phases of adolescence. Part II. *Journal of American Academy of Child Psychiatry, 6*, 577–611.

Kestenberg, J. (1975). *Children and parents.* New York: Jason Aronson.

Kestenberg, J. (1982). The inner-genital phase—Prephallic and pre-oedipal. In D. Mendell (Ed.), *Early female development* (pp. 181–226). New York: Spectrum.

Kleeman, J. (1977). Freud's views on early female sexuality in the light of direct child observation. In H. Blum (Ed.), *Female psychology* (pp. 3–28). New York: International Universities Press.

Klein, J. R., & Litt, I. F. (1983). Menarche and dysmenorrhea. In J. Brooks-Gunn & A. Peterson (Eds.), *Girls at puberty* (pp. 73–88). New York: Plenum.

Komnenich, P., McSweeney, M., Noack, J. A., & Elder, N. (1981). *The menstrual cycle*, Vol. 2. New York: Springer.

Lauersen, N. H., & Stukane, E. (1983). *Listen to your body.* New York: Bernel Books.

Lauerson, N. H., & Stukane, E. (1984). *PMS: Premenstrual syndrome and you.* New York: Pinnacle.

Lederer, W. (1968). *The fear of women.* New York: Grune & Stratton.

Lerner, H. F. (1977). Parental mislabeling of female genitals as a determiniant of penis envy and learning inhibitions in women. In H. Blum (Ed.), *Female psychology* (pp. 269–284). New York: International Universities Press.

Leshner, A. L. (1978). *An introduction to behavioral endocrinology.* New York: Oxford University Press.

Lessing, D. (1962). *The golden notebook.* New York: Bantam, 1981.

McClintock, M. K. (1971). Menstrual synchrony and suppression. *Nature, 229*, 225–244.
McClintock, M. K. (1978). Estrous synchrony and its mediation by airborne chemical communication. *Rattus norvegicus. Hormones and behavior, 10*, 264–276.
McClintock, M. K. (1981). Major gaps in menstrual cycle research: behavioral and physiological controls in a biological context. In P. Komnenich, M. McSweeney, J. A. Noack, & N. Elder (Eds.), *The menstrual cycle*, Vol. 2 (pp. 7–23). New York: Springer.
Masters, W. A., & Johnson, V. (1966). *Human sexual response*. Boston: Little, Brown.
Miller, J. B. (Ed.) (1973). *Psychoanalysis and women*. New York: Penguin.
Miller, J. B. (1976). *Towards a new psychology of women*. Boston: Beacon Press.
Miller, P. Y. (1979). Female delinquency: Fact and fiction. In M. Sugar (Ed.), *Female adolescent development* (pp. 115–140). New York: Brunner/Mazel.
Money, J., & Ehrhardt, A. (1972). *Man and woman, boy and girl*. Baltimore: Johns Hopkins University Press.
Paige, K. (1973). Women learn to sing the menstrual blues. *Psychology Today*, pp. 41–46, Sept.
Paige, K. E. (1983). A bargaining theory of menarcheal response. In J. Brooks-Gunn & A. Peterson (Eds.), *Girls at puberty* (pp. 301–322). New York: Plenum.
Parlee, M. B. (1980). Changes in moods and menstrual levels during the menstrual cycle in special naive subjects. In A. J. Dan, E. A. Graham, & C. P. Beecher (Eds.), *The menstrual cycle*, Vol. 1 (pp. 247–263). New York: Springer.
Person, E. (1985). Some new observations on the origin of femininity. In J. Strauss (Ed.), *Women and analysis* (pp. 250–264). Boston: G. K. Hall.
Peterson, A. (1979). Female pubertal development. In M. Sugar (Ed.), *Female adolescent development* (pp. 23–46). New York: Brunner/Mazel.
Peterson, A. (1980). Puberty and its psychosocial significance in girls. In A. J. Dan, E. A. Graham, & C. P. Beecher (Eds.), *The menstrual cycle*, Vol. 1 (pp. 45–55). New York: Springer.
Peterson, A. (1983). Pubertal change and cognition. In J. Brooks-Gunn & A. Peterson (Eds.), *Girls at puberty*. New York: Plenum.
Peterson, A., & Wittig, M. A. (1979). Differential cognitive development in adolescent girls. In M. Sugar (Ed.), *Female adolescent development* (pp. 47–59). New York: Brunner/Mazel.
Pliny (1961). *Natural history* (H. Rackham, Trans.). Cambridge, MA: Harvard University Press.
Reid, R. L., & Yen, S. S. (1981). Premenstrual syndrome. *American Journal of Obstetrics, 139*, 84.
Rierdan, J., & Koff, E. (1980). The psychological impact of menarche: integrative versus disruptive changes. *Journal of Youth and Adolescence, 9*, 49–58.
Ritvo, S. (1977). Adolescent to woman. In H. Blum (Ed.), *Female psychology* (pp. 127–138). New York: International Universities Press.
Roiphe, H., & Galenson, E. (1981). *Infantile origins of sexual identity*. New York: International Universities Press.
Rosenbaum, M. B. (1979). The changing body of the adolescent girl. In M. Sugar (Ed.), *Female adolescent development* (pp. 234–252). New York: Brunner/Mazel.
Rossi, A. S. (1980). Mood cycles by menstrual month and social week. In A. J. Dan, E. A. Graham, & C. P. Beecher (Eds.), *The menstrual cycle*, Vol. 1 (pp. 56–71). New York: Springer.
Sherfey, M. J. (1972). *The nature and evolution of female sexuality*. New York: Random House.
Shopper, M. (1979). The (Re) Discovery of the vagina and the importance of the menstrual tampon. In M. Sugar (Ed.), *Female adolescent development* (pp. 214–232). New York: Brunner/Mazel.
Smolensky, M. H. (1980). Chronobiologic consideration in the investigation and interpretation of circamenstrual rhythms in women. In A. J. Dan, E. A. Graham, & C. P. Beecher (Eds.), *The menstrual cycle*, Vol. 1. New York: Springer.

Stewart, F. Guest, F. Stewart, G., & Hatcher, R. (1981). *My body, my health*. New York: Bantam.

Stoller, R. J. (1973a). The sense of femaleness. In J. B. Miller (Ed.), *Psychoanalysis and women* (pp. 260–272). New York: Penguin.

Stoller, R. J. (1973b). The 'bedrock' of masculinity and femininity: Bisexuality. In J. B. Miller (Ed.), *Psychoanalysis and women* (pp. 273–284). New York: Penguin.

Stoller, R. J. (1977). Primary femininity. In H. Blum (Ed.), *Female psychology* (pp. 59–78). New York: International Universities Press.

Stone, M. (1980). *The borderline syndrome*. New York: McGraw-Hill.

Strauss, J. (Ed.) (1985). *Women and analysis*. Boston: G. K. Hall.

Sugar, M. (Ed.). (1979). *Female adolescent development*. New York: Brunner/Mazel.

Thompson, C. (1941). The role of women in this culture. *Psychiatry, 4*, 1–8.

Thompson, C. (1942). Cultural pressures in the psychology of women. *Psychiatry, 5*, 331–339.

Thompson, C. (1943). Penis envy in women. *Psychiatry, 6*, 123–125.

Thompson, C. (1950). Some effects of the derogatory attitude towards female sexuality. *Psychiatry, 13*, 349–354.

Tobin-Richards, M. H., Boxer, A. M., & Peterson, A. C. (1983). The psychological significance of pubertal change: sex differences in perception of self during early adolescence. In J. Brooks-Gunn & A. Peterson (Eds.), *Girls at puberty* (pp. 127–154). New York: Plenum.

Toth, E., Delaney, J., & Lupton, M. J. (1981). The menstruating woman in the popular imagination. In P. Komnenich, M. McSweeney, J. A. Noack, N. Elder (Eds.), *The menstrual cycle*, Vol. 2 (pp. 104–113). New York: Springer.

Warren, M. P. (1983). Physical and biological aspects of puberty. In J. Brooks-Gunn & A. Peterson (Eds.), *Girls at puberty* (pp. 3–28). New York: Plenum.

Weiden, J. (1984). *Menstrual attitudes, self and body image, and overall psychological adjustment in pre and post menarcheal girls*. Doctoral dissertation, Adelphi University.

Wynne, L. C., & Frader, L. (1979). Female adolescence and the family: a historical view. In M. Sugar (Ed.), *Female adolescent development* (pp. 63–82). New York: Brunner/Mazel.

Chapter 6

Motivations for Motherhood and the Nature of the Self–Object Tie

LEANNE DOMASH

The tension between the wish to merge and the wish for separateness exists throughout life with a rhythm that, at certain points, accentuates one, then the other. Mothering embodies this duality: the wish to unite and the wish to be distinct and autonomous.

The essence of good-enough mothering is the establishment of a nonpathological (flexible) self–object tie: a bond that is close but that has perspective, that blurs boundaries when necessary, yet rapidly reconstructs them if need be. This is similar to Winnicott's discussion of the mother's "active adaptation" to her child's needs (Winnicott, 1953, 1955). Loewald (1960), too, speaks of the need for the parent to stay in tune with the child and even one step ahead to foster growth and development. While there has been discussion by the above authors and others (Benedek, 1959, 1970; Blum, 1977), there is still insufficient emphasis on articulating the underlying motivations for motherhood, particularly in the positive sense. Female psychology continues to struggle to divest itself in a definitive manner from the phallocentric picture painted by Freud. His view stressed femininity as a defense, a reaction to the disappointment of not being male, and not as a primary, legitimate expression of self.

This chapter explores the motivations for the mother–child tie, discussing the creative, adaptive factors involved and also instances at which it has become pathological and rigid. In part, this depends on how much the act of mothering is for the woman a new act, that is, an opportunity for growth, and therefore a potential rebirth. This, in turn, permits the psychological birth of a unique child with an individualized self. In contrast is the mother for whom parenting falls more under the realm of the repetition compulsion, causing her to relate in rigid, stereotyped ways, not allowing for the spontaneous in herself or the child. Most mothers

---

LEANNE DOMASH, PH.D. • Consulting Psychologist, Beth Israel Medical Center, New York City; Adjunct Assistant Professor of Psychiatry, Mount Sinai School of Medicine; private practice.

consciously hope for the former and it is the clash between the two, present to some extent in all mothers, that causes greater or lesser conflict.[1]

In a practical sense, this discussion of motivation may be useful as an analytic framework for therapists who work with women who are either contemplating motherhood or who are already mothers. It may help them explore feelings so as to enhance the healthier end of the continuum and reduce the grip of the repetition compulsion.

What complexity of factors contributes to the formation of the mother–child tie and what happens to this tie in normal parenting versus pathological parenting? What motivates the mother to undertake the enormous demand and range of response required of her? The contrasting images of the fetus inside the mother versus the dramatic expulsion at birth sets the scene for what is to come. A mother is expected to nourish and be very close to the child yet separate at the right moments to facilitate normal growth.

It is interesting to speculate how much the strong urge to have a child—this sense of primary creativity—is based on biological factors, hormonal or otherwise. At the very least, one could suppose that when the strong wish for a child is present, it may be transmitted into chemical messages in the brain, which are then felt as a bodily need for a child. Many women have described this to me. These feelings contribute, for example, to the frustration and sadness of infertility. Many of these women describe a bodily hunger for a child. Entertaining the opposite possibility, that there is a basic biological urge for children, makes evolutionary sense, but remains in the realm of interesting speculation.

What factors might be involved when a woman has a marked fear of having a child? Numerous issues may be important, of course, but several possibilities include fear of bodily changes, insufficient identification or denial of identification with the mother, and denial of the aging process. Motherhood is a psychophysiological passage: the body image is vastly altered in pregnancy and in many cases, in the postpregnancy period also. These processes intensify the woman's identification with her own mother. Her mother is no longer the woman with the aging body while she has the younger, more perfect one. Pregnancy and motherhood is a passage into the world of mothers as well as an acceptance of the aging process as reflected in women's bodies.

Can there also be a straightforward decision in a woman not to have children with no particular conflict regarding feminine identification? This would be an important group of women to study to see if the fulfillment that childbearing and raising provide is simply satisfied in other ways, such as in a love relationship or in creative work; or if these women carry with them multiple conflicts that interfere with the wish to have children. Another possibility is that these women may be low on the need to express some of the aspects of fulfillment that mothering provides, and high on other needs.

---

[1]Conflicts regarding the mothering role were studied empirically by Zuckerberg (1972, 1980). Using the Pregnancy Thematic Apperception Test, she demonstrated that, in pregnant women, when there was a discrepancy between conscious and unconscious attitudes, somatic symptoms occurred most frequently and level of excessive worry was high.

EXPRESSION OF PRIMARY CREATIVITY

A very healthy motivation for wanting a child is the wish to use one's creative energies, the urge to create, which can be expressed as the mother helps shape the personality of her child. This includes in Rank's (1932) terms the acceptance of the child's individual will as the expression of his or her unique personality. The creativity of the mother is to sense the child's proclivities, help enhance them, while leaving them the exclusive property of the child.

The expression of creativity is at its height in the transitional area of experiencing between mother and child. Motherhood is rich in its constant shifts between merger and separateness in this realm of transitional relatedness. It is this need in the woman to find expression for these dual urges that is a primary motivator for motherhood. The area of transitional relatedness, so well described by Winnicott (1953), is the area of illusion, the potential space of creativity which has the "suspense of the absolute" (Muensterberger, 1978). This is an intermediate area of the real and the imagined, called by some "the location of magic." It has moments when inside and outside are one, when our focus is broad and encompassing. At other times, we focus in a narrow and distinct sense and we see the child as very separate. It is frequently this kind of experiencing that gives life its deeper meaning whether in parenting, in loving a partner, in enjoying cultural experiences, or in fact, in the act of creativity.

Chodorow (1983) in a sense is saying something similar, that women become mothers to reestablish the symbiotic bond with their own mother, a wish that is not allowed legitimate expression in current society outside the mother–child bond. However, I am emphasizing the rich potential in transitional relatedness, which I would not call symbiotic, because it contains both the idea of merger *and* the idea of separateness. It contains the potential for creativity and growth, while "symbiotic" implies stasis.

Transitional relatedness includes the ability on the part of the mother to just "be" with the child (in whatever way this is phrased), and to understand, to empathize, to nurture; in common language, it means to "hang out" and see what develops. I remember a film prepared by Stern (1984) on mother–child interaction. It was a series of encounters between normal mothers and their children in a play situation. There was one dyad that particularly expressed this ability. The mother was relaxed and calm, yet playful. She was not particularly concerned with the camera, as some of the other mothers had been, nor with the achievements of her child. In fact, in the beginning sequence, the child was about 6 months old and fussing. The mother expressed herself nicely when she said lovingly yet almost casually, matter of factly, "we'll just do whatever we have to do," meaning in terms of adaptation and comfort. Later in the sequence, when the child was about 12 months and making conversational sounds but not yet talking (in fact sounding more like a chicken than a person), the mother very naturally mimicked her tone and sounds. It was in tune and effortless. She seemed to be able to truly "hang out" with the child. This is a somewhat "silent" quality; the ability to "be" and be background to another, to be a quiet support without the need for personal comfirmation.

This ability to "be" with the child helps mother and child traverse the important path, described so poetically by Winnicott (1969), from transitional experiencing to object usage. In the former, the child feels the mother to be part of his or her own body. Mother and child participate in an illusion or realm of transitional experiencing that is prior to the clear realization of self and other differences and is the forerunner of later ego strength and creativeness. In the latter, object usage, the child finally experiences the mother as separate. The child destroys the object as a subjective object and the object now becomes real. The child's sense of positive existence now takes this difference between mother and child into account and is, in some sense, based on it.

In the transitional area, creative experiencing is open and fluid and profoundly heightened. As the infant moves toward object usage there is a simultaneity of destruction, love, and survival with a core affect of joy. This is a nondefensive appreciation of otherness which may grow into concern.

This urge to create—this willingness to "be"—is related to a possibly universal wish to surrender or an act of faith. Faith is a way of experiencing with one's whole being, a core sense of creativeness. It is a giving of body and soul to an act, a kind of blanking out of ordinary consciousness where the sense of self is submerged in an oceanic feeling. It is an act of transcendence. The act of faith is described by Winnicott (1953), Eigen (1981), and Ghent (1983), and others. This leap of faith, this immersion, fosters the breakdown of inner rigidities of organization and, therefore, facilitates growth. There can be a surrender of the false self and a longing for and perhaps even a rebirth of the true self. It is a self-healing process that can occur in this sometimes overwhelming act of being a mother.

As the mother helps the infant traverse this rich course from transitional experiencing to object usage, she too will have complementary experiences of bathing in the creativity of transitional experiencing and later feeling the joy of knowing her child, with all his/her complexities, as an increasingly separate other, whom she can deeply appreciate. The mother goes through a parallel experience of faith. This experience can be so rich as to feel this is the "stuff" that gives life its meaning.

Put less poetically, Benedek (1959) speaks of the actual structural changes that occur in the mother as a result of her interaction with her child. In each critical period, the child revives in the mother her related developmental conflicts. She now has the opportunity for achieving new levels of integration as these conflicts are worked through and new internalizations are developed. Thus, parenthood is a continuation of the developmental process.

ACCEPTANCE OF THE LIFE CYCLE

Good mothering, of course, draws also on the past. A very healthy aspect is the remembrance of happy, even idyllic, moments in one's own childhood and the wish to recreate these and enjoy them vicariously. It is a recreativity of childhood innocence, an innocence that is treasured and yet must be left behind. Blos (1984), for example, speaks of the need for the son to mourn the pre-Oedipal father with whom he had many periods of happiness, in order to continue to grow and work through Oedipal conflicts.

Yet, in parenting, one can at times have this period back again. It is, at least for moments, a return to this preconflictual time. An example is a patient who commented when she was pregnant that she remembered with great nostalgia long bicycle rides she would take through shady tree-lined streets when she was about 11 years old. She remembers this as one of the most peaceful times of her life. It was a time of beginning feelings of mobility, enjoyment of nature yet before the anxieties of adolescence. She hoped for just such moments for her child. Freud (1914) spoke of a similar process, but in less positive terms, when he stated, "That which the fond parent projects ahead of him as his ideal in the child is merely a substitute for the lost narcissism of childhood."

As parenthood helps us mourn our childhood (yet paradoxically recapture it), it also helps us accept our own mortality. This fulfills our need for continuity and acceptance of our place in the life cycle. It helps us meet with courage the existential fact that we all will die. Rather than a denial, this is an acceptance of the seasons of our lives.

Developmental Roots

What are the early developmental roots of the girl's wish for a child? Kestenberg (1977), Stoller (1977), and Blum (1977) raise the issue of primary femininity: that the wish for a child grows out of the girl's early identification with the mother. Kestenberg speaks of the pre-Oedipal maternal phase named inner genital which is the cradle of maternality in both sexes. Stoller describes a primary femininity in two phases, the first contributes an early and nonconflictual sense of femaleness and the second a more richly textured sense arising out of the conflicts of the Oedipal period. Blum speaks of motherhood as an important aspect of fulfillment of the ego ideal in women and therefore felt to be a vital expression of feminine nature.

This is in contrast to the famous issue raised by Freud (1925) that woman's wish for a child is the result of penis envy. Freud (1931, 1933) then himself appeared to modify his views stating how little he understood women and also began to emphasize the major influence of the girl's pre-Oedipal attachment to her mother. But then later (1937, 1940) he returned to approximately the same paternalistic viewpoint as in 1925. Of course, the concept of penis envy has undergone significant change from the "bedrock" concept of Freud's to now an expression of many possible meanings, itself frequently a deriviative of earlier, pervasive narcissistic injuries (Grossman and Stewart, 1977; Satow, 1985).

Kestenberg, Stoller, and Blum have added a necessary new view of motherhood, one that correctly legitimizes femininity as primary and significant in itself and not as a defense against the disappointment of not being male. However, the fact that envy of the male exists in some women is undeniable, as does of course the reverse (Jaffe, 1968). Usually experienced as envy of the male's power, penis envy is considered in an object relational format by Horner (1985). Horner discusses how the woman may want to live vicariously through the male, not herself wanting to do the "work" that the power requires. Then she may marry or have a boy child with this as the underlying motive. Rather than the primary motive for motherhood as described by Freud, I view this as a pathological motive which needs careful consideration and hopefully can receive enough resolution so that a sufficiently positive environment can be provided for the male child.

Need for Reparation

Next on the continuum of health is the need to make reparation, that is, the need to heal the wounds of a less than desirable relationship with one's parents. This includes the capacity for concern (Winnicott, 1963) mingled with a background of guilt. In attempting to heal the relationship with the parent, one is also repairing that aspect of the self.

This is related to the frequently strong wish in people for two children, this unconsciously being the wish to repair the missing aspects with each of the two parents. Particularly poignant examples are when a woman has had a problematic relationship, for example, with her mother, and then longs for a female child with the hope of making reparation. But then when confronted with the child, the new mother becomes intensely conflicted, leading to a postpartum depression of serious magnitude. I have described a similar case elsewhere (Domash, 1985).

Interferences with Mothering

Another disorder in parenting is when specific conflicts from the past interfere with current parenting, a kind of transference to the child. The motivation here may be viewed as a need to repeat the past. However, the conflict is frequently circumscribed and, therefore, relatively easy to work through. For example, a patient in consultation described her persistently mildly anxious, overprotective attitude toward her son. When asked about her background, she revealed that when she was 2 years old, her brother was killed by falling into an unrepaired area on her family's property that her mother had been remonstrating her father to repair. Her brother was walking behind his father when this happened. His father had continued walking and suddenly realized the boy was not behind him, only to find that his son had fallen into a ditch in the unrepaired area and died. It was relatively easy to work with this mother because she was quite intact, and once this connection was verbalized she was able to quickly move toward giving the child genuine independence. Her child flourished.

Another example is a woman who had been in analysis for 4 years when she gave birth to her son. She had had long-standing conflicts of penis envy and penis awe, admiring, overvaluing, and envying the male and his phallus while concomitantly devaluing herself. She felt ecstatic after her son was born and temporarily freed of these past feelings of self-contempt. Her overvaluation of the male now centered on her own son whom she felt as an extension of herself. In her unconscious, she now had what she had longed for her whole life. She was in danger of overvaluing her son's abilities and not permitting sufficient separation to develop, as then she would lose the treasured maleness. Although a profound conflict, this was still a relatively specific or circumscribed one, so that it could be discussed and gradually sufficiently resolved that her son was free to develop.

Another example is a young mother of three children. She was a very good, in fact devoted, mother in most respects, but woven in with her motherliness was an angry statement to her own mother: that she could outdo her, that she could succeed where her own mother had failed and, further, that proving this would be her revenge. She felt a lack of acceptance and acknowledgment from her own mother although there had been many positive identifications as well, some of which were repressed, which allowed her to be as good a mother as she was. This extra edge of anger caused complications in her mothering. She tended to take on more burdens than necessary to prove her superiority and to anguish more than necessary when her children failed to accomplish a developmental task "on schedule" as this proved her inferiority. When the competition with her mother was analyzed in detail, she was able to gradually relinquish the use of her motherliness as a weapon against her own mother (and at times herself) which in turn helped lift some of the repression of the positive identifications with her own mother.

More severe disorders are found in mothers who have, rather than specific conflicts, pervasive character disorders. This is frequently seen in the woman with strong masochistic traits. She may wish to be punished by the child for what she feels guilty about in her relationship with her own parents. The mother will assume a persistently masochistic position, now perhaps even for having had a child herself. In her relationship to her child she condenses the impulse to have a child and perhaps exceed or displace her mother with her defense of masochistic suffering. The defense provides both a punishment for the impulse and a disguise for the fact that, to some extent, she has successfully expressed the impulse. The motivation for motherhood in these women is, at least in some part, self-punishment.

Ghent (1983) holds the view that when the act of faith (described previously), that is, the passionate longing to surrender, becomes perverted, this becomes masochism. Surrender then becomes submission. The person longs for contact in a deep way, but by an impinging other. In Ghent's view, the masochism is an attempt at self-cure. When, however, this dynamic develops between mother and child, the relationship becomes very disturbed.

Blum (1977) in speaking of motherhood makes the distinction between self-sacrifice and masochism. He writes that there is no masochism in good mothering; this would only encourage children to be sadists. Rather, the sacrifices the mother makes are in terms of a guiding ideal: the ego ideal. We know what we want to be and what is good for our child and we try to live up to it. To whatever extent this can be achieved, assuming the goal is not too idealized, self-esteem flourishes. To live up to this goal is to achieve one's ideal way of being.

Another very difficult, at times seemingly intractable problem is the narcissistic parent who has a very rigid way of relating to the child. The essence of good parenting is a flexible self-object tie. The tie with the narcissistic parent is very rigid and tends to remain the same rather than shift as the years go on. Maternal motivation here includes the inappropriate use of the child as a self-object to express, bolster, or even deny aspects of the self.

One frequent manifestation is a wish to continually and inappropriately indulge the child as an aspect of the self. One woman patient spoke about her younger son who was now 35 as if he were still a precious child to be coddled, who could not be expected to persevere at a job and who needed continual pampering from her. She too was pampered by her husband, for whom she had contempt, and had been unable to pursue a work situation despite having wanted to. She extended to her son the same indulgences (and handicaps) she grants that special part of herself. This can be so gratifying for the mother who has the need for this indulgence that it is hard to alter.

A related and even more destructive disorder is the narcissistic and/or borderline parent who dissociates the negative aspects of the self onto the child, so well described by Slipp (1973). In punishing the child, she can ignore this in the self.

A final and extreme category would be a mother who wants a fantasy realization of what never was, a mother who wants her child to be an omnipotent parent who is going to take perfect care of her. A further extension of this example are mothers who commit child abuse, as this unconscious fantasy of perfect parenting from the child meets with inevitable disillusionment.

In summary, motherhood has multiple motivations which can encompass a range from the sublimely creative, the creation of a unique and free individual, to the saddeningly pathological, as in child abuse. The good-enough mother has an opportunity to satisfy her need for primary creative expression, for union and individuality, for the recreation of childhood innocence, and for her need for reparation. She, at times, may also act out specific repetition compulsions with her child which yield fairly easily to either self-reflection or analysis. The more disturbed woman may have pathological needs for self-punishment and for bolstering of self-esteem, including a need to project negative aspects of the self onto the child. In the extreme, the mother needs to reverse the mother/child role with the mother assuming the role of the child. While all motivations are present in varying degrees in all mothers, it is the preponderance of those drives on the healthier end of the continuum that allows us to raise good-enough children.

REFERENCES

Benedek, T. (1959). Parenthood as a developmental phase. *Journal of the American Psychoanalytic Association, 7*, 389–417.

Benedek, T. (1970). Parenthood during the life cycle. In E. J. Anthony and T. Benedek (Eds.), *Parenthood: Its psychology and psychopathology* (pp. 185–208). Boston: Little, Brown.

Blos, P. (1984). Son and father. *Journal of the American Psychoanalytic Association, 32*, 301–324.

Blum, H. (1977). Masochism, the ego ideal and the psychology of women. In H. Blum (Ed.), *Female sexuality* (pp. 157–192). New York: International Universities Press.

Domash, L. (1985). Tragedy, masochism and the heroic confrontation. Unpublished paper.

Eigen, M. (1981). The area of faith in Winnicott, Lacan and Bion. *International Journal of Psychoanalysis, 62*, 413–433.

Chodorow, N. (1983). *The Reproduction of mothering: Psycho-analysis and the sociology of gender.* Berkeley: University of California Press.

Freud, S. (1914). On narcissism: an introduction. *Standard Edition, 14*, 91. London: Hogarth, 1957.

Freud, S. (1925). Some psychical consequences of the anatomical distinction between the sexes. *Standard Edition, 19*, 243–258. London: Hogarth, 1961.

Freud, S. (1931). Female sexuality. *Standard Edition, 21*, 223–243. London: Hogarth, 1961.

Freud, S. (1933). New introductory lectures on psycho-analysis. *Standard Edition, 22*, 3–182. London: Hogarth, 1964.

Freud, S. (1937). Analysis terminable and interminable. *Standard Edition, 23*, 211–253. London: Hogarth, 1964.

Freud, S. (1940). An outline of psychoanalysis. *Standard Edition, 23*, 141–207. London: Hogarth, 1964.

Ghent, E. (1983). Masochism, Submission and Surrender. Colloquium, New York University Postdoctoral Program in Psychoanalysis, December 2, 1983.

Grossman, W. I. & Stewart, W. A. (1977). Penis envy: From childhood wish to developmental metaphor. In H. Blum (Ed.), *Female sexuality* (pp. 193–212). New York: International Universities Press.

Horner, A. (1985). Falling in love and the idealization and sexualization of the power attributed to men. Annual Meeting of the American Psychological Association, Los Angeles, Calif.

Jaffe, D. S. (1968). The masculine envy of women's procreative function. In H. Blum (Ed.), *Female psychology* (pp. 361–392). New York: International Universities Press.

Kestenberg, J. (1977). Regression and reintegration in pregnancy. In H. Blum (Ed.), *Female sexuality*, (pp. 213–250). New York: International Universities Press.

Loewald, H. (1960). On the therapeutic action of psycho-analysis. *International Journal of Psycho-analysis, 41,* 1–18.

Muensterberger, W. (1978). Between reality and fantasy. In S. Grolnick (Ed.), *Between reality and fantasy: Transitional objects and phenomena* (p. 10). New York: Jason Aronson.

Rank, O. (1932). *Art and the artist.* New York: Knopf, 1958.

Satow, R. (1985). A question of bedrock: is penis envy the bottom line? *Psychoanalytic Review, 72,* 265–275.

Slipp, S. (1973). The symbiotic survival pattern: A relational theory of schizophrenia. *Family Process, 12,* 377–398.

Stern, D. (1984). Film shown in course The Interpersonal World of the Infant, New York University Postdoctoral Program, Spring.

Stoller, R. (1977). Primary femininity. In H. Blum (Ed.), *Female psychology* (pp. 59–78). New York: International Universities Press.

Winnicott, D. W. (1953). Transitional objects and transitional phenomena. In *Playing and reality* (pp. 1–30). New York: Penguin, 1980.

Winnicott, D. W. (1955). Clinical varieties of transference. In *Through pediatrics to psychoanalysis* (pp. 295–299). New York: Basic Books, 1958.

Winnicott, D. W. (1963). The development of the capacity for concern. In *The maturational process and the facilitating environment* (pp. 73–82). New York: International Universities Press, 1965.

Winnicott, D. W. (1969). The use of an object and relating through identifications. In *Playing and reality* (pp. 101–111). New York, Penguin, 1980.

Zuckerberg, J. (1972). An exploration into feminine role conflict and body symptomatology in pregnancy. Unpublished doctoral dissertation. New York: Long Island University.

Zuckerberg, J. (1980). Psychological and physical warning signals regarding pregnancy. In R. L. Blum (Ed.), *Psychological aspects of pregnancy, birthing and bonding* (pp. 151–205). New York: Human Sciences Press.

Chapter 7

Psychoanalytic Aspects of Pregnancy

RONI O. COHEN

Among the psychophysiological crises in a women's life, pregnancy holds a unique position. Like menarche and menopause, it is a crisis because it revives unsettled psychological conflicts from previous stages and requires psychological adaptations to achieve a new integration. Like menarche and menopause, it represents a developmental step in relationship to the self (as well as here in relationship to the mate and child). And like menarche and menopause, pregnancy sets off an acute disequilibrium endocrinologically, somatically, and psychologically (Bibring, 1959).

On the other hand, pregnancy alone of the major female developmental milestones is not a physiologically inevitable part of the maturational process. It is often actively sought and self-induced, finite, raising questions about the propelling and compelling forces behind the drive, as well as the psychological consequences of successful conception. Freud (1931) wrote of pregnancy as a gratification of a women's basic wish, and, as such, saw no evidence of its creating conflicts. In fact, he described maternity as a period of calm, reflecting an inner peace emanating from the sense of fulfillment. Others have cited devotion to perpetuation of the species (Deutsch, 1930), biological imperatives (Benedek, 1970; Erickson, 1968), and psychophysiological determinants of identification (Greenacre, 1953; Kestenberg, 1956) to account for the urge for motherhood.

This chapter is divided into two major parts. The first part, "Femininity and the Wish To Have a baby," covers the biological, psychological, and psychosocial determinants of femininity, feminine identification, and the wish to have a baby from the viewpoint of Freud and other early psychoanalysts, and the more current theorists. The second part, "The Pregnancy," covers the biological and psychological impact of pregnancy, the cognitive and emotional state induced, the conflicts aroused, and the distinctions between a normal and a pathological pregnancy state.

RONI O. COHEN, PH.D. • Clinical Instructor of Psychology, Department of Psychiatry, Cornell Medical Center; Supervisor, Payne Whitney Clinic; Seminar Faculty, The Psychoanalytic Society of the Postdoctoral Program; private practice.

Femininity and the Wish To Have a Baby

Early Analysts

Freud (1925, 1933) was the first to construct a theory of female psychosexual development. He drew his conclusions retrospectively from the memories, fantasies, and dreams of hysterical adult women, not having had the benefit of direct observation of very young children nor the systematic observational studies of others. He knew the value of observational research, and encouraged his followers, particularly his female followers, to study children directly. Allowing for the incompleteness of his knowledge about females, Freud (1933) speculated that they matured in the following way: girls have a masculine development through the third year of life; they, like boys, scale the oral, anal, and phallic phases of development with their organizing drives and unique means of conflict resolution. It is only when the girl becomes aware of the anatomical difference between herself and boys (at about 3 years of age) that the developmental routes of the two sexes diverge. At that point, girls experience what he called castration shock; that is, they feel envious of the highly valued penis, defective and deprived by virtue of its absence, and enraged at their mother for depriving them of this prize. As a result, they turn from their mother as their love object to the father who has the penis they want. Realizing they cannot have a penis, girls accept a child as a substitute for it. This engenders an identification with the mother to whom the father gives babies.

To Freud, femininity is a consequence of disappointment, deprivation, and defeat. It comes as a result of girls accepting their inferior status vis-à-vis men and resigning themselves to their defectiveness. Femininity, as such, is a defense against castration, and is defined by masochism, passivity, penis envy, and a weak superego. Penis envy is a basic truth, and, therefore, is not susceptible to further anaylsis. The wish for a child is a compensation for anatomical inferiority.

There was little opposition to Freud's formulation among the psychoanalytic ranks. However, from the beginning, there have been differences of opinion as to where lies the emphasis. Ruth Mack Brunswick (1940), for example, reiterated Freud's statement that early on both boys and girls want to be able to have babies like the omnipotent mother. Although neither Freud nor Mack Brunswick goes into detail about the effect of that wish on future behavior, Mack Brunswick does make the point that the wish for a baby precedes the wish for a penis, and that that wish plays a prominant role in the unconscious life of a child.

Deutsch (1944) also traces the wish for a baby through psychosexual stages, and she concurs with the idea of the idealized penis being the stimulus for maternal yearning. In fact, she says that the investment in the vagina is based solely on that organ's function in relation to the penis. What she adds to Freudian thought on maternity is the existence of an instinct derived from a devotion to the continuance of the species which accounts, in part, for wishes to be a mother (Deutsch, 1930).

The most significant shift in emphasis came in 1933 when Jones suggested the likelihood of there being a primary wish for a child, a wish inclusive of the fantasy of making a child from the incorporated penis, but not the fantasy of the child as a substitute for it. Jones went on to question the intensity of the female's preoccupation with the penis, attributing its idealization to frustration with the mother and breast, and suggested instead that, in fact, girls were more involved with their own internal organs than the external one of the male. Idealization of the penis, he said, is a defense against anal–sadistic impulses toward the father which threaten her only remaining love object. Jones was not alone in his divergence from Freud. Horney and Thompson also disagreed with the primacy of penis envy, and Horney (1933) made the point that if Freud were right, women would resent pregnancy as an artificial substitute instead of relishing it as an instinctual achievement.

Current Theories

Out of these beginnings, the idea of a unique and basic feminine nature and line of development grew. Although not using his observations of girl's early nature to postulate basic femininity, Freud (1933) did write that girls are different from boys from the start. He described the differences as those of "genital structure and other bodily differences" (on which he did not elaborate) and differences in their nature, as well. Girls are "less aggressive, defiant, and self-sufficient; greater in need of affection . . . more dependent and pliant . . . more intelligent and livelier than boys" (p. 117).

More than 40 years later, Stoller (1976) offered a theory of a basic and immutable sense of femaleness, a "core gender identity" which he called "primary femininity," defined by him as conflict-free and egosyntonic. Contributing to its development, are biological, psychological, and environmental factors. Biological forces include the neurophysiological organization of the fetal brain as well as the sex assigned at birth. Other factors include the parents' attitude about the infant's sex, biopsychic phenomena created by handling and postnatal conditioning, and sensations from the genitals. The particular resolution of castration shock and Oedipal conflict also contribute to the sense of femininity.

Evidence for the existence of primary femininity comes from a number of sources. Authors have pointed to the distinctive way little girls as young as 2 years of age move, hold themselves, daydream, play games, relate to clothes (Erickson, 1968; Stoller, 1976), and play with dolls—the last of which is evidence of a pre-Oedipal identification with mother (Galenson & Roiphe, 1976). Further conclusive evidence is the way they react to learning of the existence of the penis; that is, that it is exactly because of her irrevocable sense of herself as female that she is disappointed and envious of what she knows she can never have (Stoller, 1976). Current thinking is that, in any case, it isn't that the girl wants a penis instead of a vagina, but that she wants both (Chehrazi, 1986).

Erickson (1968) also advocates an instinctual basis for maternal feelings. He attributes instinctual maternal feelings to females' having a sense of their "inner space." He observes that very young girls are aware of this and of their potential for reproducing, and that from an adaptive viewpoint, it stands to reason that this would be the primary reality rather than would a missing external organ. In contrast to Freud, Erickson sees femininity as a positive life force enriching the lives of women, and essential to survival of the species. In other words, he speaks of the female's "inner potential . . . competent pursuit of activities consonant with possession of uterus, ovaries, and vagina," and her "ability to stand and understand pain as a meaningful aspect of human experience in general rather than masochistic pleasure in pain" (p. 275).

Although Freud (1933) dated the female's awareness of her anatomical difference from boys to age 3, he believed these differences were not fully known, particularly the existance of the vagina and reproductive organs, until puberty. He thought that memories of adult women of early vaginal sensations were, in fact, displacements from other libidinal zones, and that femininity emerged from pregenital or phallic wishes until puberty when the reproductive organs reached maturity (Freud, 1924).

Much information to the contrary has been collected since. Horney's (1933) clinical experience led her to conclude that an unrecognized vagina was a "vagina denied." Greenacre (1950), Galenson and Roiphe (1974), and Kestenberg (1956, 1976) attest to clinical and research data revealing early awareness of the vagina and internal organs in girls. Greenacre describes increasing genital sensations between the 2nd half of the 2nd year and during the 3rd year. Galenson and Roiphe place genital awareness even earlier. Confirming Roiphe's (1968) thesis of an early genital phase between 16 and 24 months, they found, in a study of 70 children, heightened and qualitatively distinctive genital awareness between 15 and 19 months. In addition, vaginal awareness in girls of this age has been reported by mothers who observed their infants putting a finger into the vagina.

Today, there is little question that the vagina and masturbation play an important part in developing the body image of little girls (Clower, 1976; Williams, 1977), and that the visual body image contributes to the development of a female identification. It is a given also that females have, as Notman (1981) says, "an individual and distinct genetic composition and anatomical structure with the potential for further development in a recognized feminine direction under the influence of specific hormones which are present prenatally and postnatally" (p. 192).

The acceptance of the girl's having a primary sense of femaleness has not, however, discredited the concept of penis envy, but has indeed dramatically altered its significance in the female's development, i.e., its place in triggering the Oedipal conflict, as a stimulus for having a baby, and as a motive for turning to the father. While the early analysts saw the narcissistic injury suffered by virtue of recognizing their "genital inferiority" as underlying subsequent female development (Freud, 1925), the current view is that penis envy is a phase-specific developmental phenomenon, reemerging and worked through again at each developmental stage. The working-through is facilitated by having a good-enough mother, a growing level of cognitive capacities and awareness of the genitals, and by resolving the Oedipal conflict and identifying with the mother (Chehrazi, 1986). The idealization of the penis facilitates the wish to be penetrated and impregnated, and pregnancy presents an additional opportunity for focusing on what the female has rather than on what she does not have.

Kestenberg (1956) integrates her ideas of early vaginal and inner organ tension into a theory of development that includes a pre-Oedipal, inner genital phase that begins to prepare the female biologically and psychologically for motherhood in the early years. She believes the reproductive organs play a major role in the development of mature femininity. In opposition to Freud, Kestenberg believes vaginal sensations are felt alongside those of other zones from the beginning. She says the female discovers her vagina for herself manually during the first year, after already having experienced the pleasure of genital manipulation through bathing and cleansing by her mother. From the beginning, there are vague kinesthetic cues from the internal organs which send out waves of excitation during breast feeding; the process of incorporation and ejection of mother's milk interacts in a rhythmic way with the mother's lactation, and promotes an association between the oral and genital zone when in synchrony; when they are not, the discrepancy promotes differentiation. During the next phase, a connection is made between the anal and genital zones. The tendency to contract vaginal muscles when anal sphincters are contracted tends to fuse the two muscle systems kinesthetically. In fact, early vaginal sensations are often confused with anal and urethral tensions (Greenacre, 1958). Play and fantasy in the anal phase is highly significant in the development of maternal feelings, i.e., there is a fantasy which joins the body's process and productivity and the creation of feces. The concept of the fecal product can easily be understood as the anal baby.

During this phase, the girl feels that everything is hers: father's and brother's penis, and if mother is pregnant, the mother's baby, and she struggles to learn to differentiate between what is hers and what is not. Girls, more than boys, tend to play with holding back urine and feces which, among other things, leads to a sense of fullness—perhaps an early sensation which is later sought in filling up the vagina.

At about 2 years of age, the female enters what Kestenberg calls the urethral phase. In this phase, the girl's interest shifts from the product to the process; that is, from wanting to retain for the sake of keeping her possession, to wanting to practice retaining and letting go for the sake of the achievement of control over her body. The penis is idealized at this stage because of its superior ability to control the flow of urine. The little girl is becoming more focused on babies and maternal feelings, playing dolls and turning passive to active by feeding, bathing, and dressing them, as well as herself, at her own convenience and, thereby, gaining a sense of mastery at a time when she senses only vague and confusing sensations from the inner genitals.

Following the urethral phase, vaginal excitations become important in and of themselves. In retrospective analyses, Kestenberg (1956) found that at about 3 years of age, the child enters the inner genital phase, and the incorporative and excretory functions of the body become subordinated to the still vague, inner genital sensations. At this time, the female is struggling with her conflicting wishes to grow up and have babies and to remain a baby herself. It is during this phase, comparable to the phallic phase in boys, that she solidifies her identity with her mother and consolidates herself as female. Identification with the maternal figure is an important determinant of feminine identification and the wish for a child (Galenson & Roiphe, 1976; Mahler, Pine & Bergman, 1975). In order to be, as well as to conceive of herself as a good-enough mother, she must have a positive maternal ego ideal (Blum, 1976). That ideal is promoted both through having been well mothered, and through the father's confirming her feminine identity and supporting the formation of a maternal ego ideal (Jones, 1935). Fantasizing having a baby is a joyful part of this growing identification. At sometime in her 4th year, however, she suddenly has the sense that she's lost it, a precursor to the fears of women in pregnancy of losing their baby. She becomes enraged at her mother for hoarding babies and, perhaps defending against that, wishes to give mother a real baby.

At 4 years, the child enters into an active negative-Oedipal phallic phase, denying her vaginal orifice, her reproductive capacity, and her wishes for a baby, and experiences intense feelings of penis envy and identification with the father.

She is highly aware of her clitoris now and fantasizes its growing into a penis. En route from the negative to positive Oedipal, the child practices identification with both mother and father. The pre-Oedipal mother fostered maternal behavior; the positive Oedipal promotes heterosexuality in an identification with the mother as rival for the father. The highly valued penis is the means to impregnation which is wished for in order to recreate the mother and father (Jacobson, 1968) and as evidence of father's love. Incidentally, some analysts (Parens, Pollock, Stern, & Kramer, 1976) have suggested substituting the term "genital phase" for the "phallic phase" in girls, as the latter name suggests the girl's lack of awareness of her own genitals, which has been convincingly disproved, and her feeling that she has nothing subsequent to renouncing her clitoris. In fact, at this stage, girls seem to fantasize having both a vagina and a penis (Greenacre, 1950; Kestenberg, 1956). Even more accurate might be "early genital phase" (Chehrazi, 1986) or "pre-Oedipal genital phase" (Glover & Mendell, 1982).

Kestenberg's theory of psychosexual development includes a description of latency and adolescence, and gives new meaning to the developmental significance of pregnancy. In latency, there is a repression of hormones and inner genital drives, which creates the opportunity for integration of the ideals of motherhood and heterosexuality. Adolescence brings with it a new version of the inner genital phase and development of adult female genitality. At this time, there is a preoccupation with the development of breasts and with menstruation, and renewed rage at the mother for the loss of the negative-Oedipal baby.

In addition, she is experiencing dramatic biochemical changes. Her body is producing two groups of gonadal hormones: estrogen which, as the follicle-ripening hormone, stimulates the development of ova, and lutein, also called progesterone, which prepares the uterus for implantation. Research has shown that these biochemical phenomena have psychodynamic correlates which are new for the adolescent, and require adaptation and adjustment (Benedek, 1970). The new rhythms of her body foster new psychic rhythms, which may take a while to become established and create havoc with her sense of self-confidence until they do. More specifically, during estrogen secretion, emotions seem to be object seeking, promoting mating and procreation. Ovulation reverses the process, tending the woman toward introversion, passivity, and a sense of relaxation and well-being. The receptive and retentive tendencies seem to be the emotional manifestations of a biological need for motherhood, and, as such, seem to represent further evidence to contradict the early analyst's theory of a baby as substitute for the missing penis.

Furthermore, each phase-specific task prepares the female psychologically for motherhood. She matures through the regulation of her biochemistry and related sensations, and begins to integrate menstruation with inner genital tension. This results in the critical association of menstruation with pregnancy rather than with castration. Menstrual cramping prepares her for the pain of childbirth, increasing her tolerance for pain, self-sacrifice, and endurance. And finally, she transforms her wish for her father and his baby into the wish for a heterosexual attachment to an appropriate man. A reignition of Oedipal conflagration gives the adolescent the opportunity to sublimate her wishes to be impregnated by her father, and to turn sensuous yearnings for him into affection. The third opportunity to work through the inner genital phase occurs during pregnancy, and is discussed in the following section.

What I have attempted to do in this section is describe a number of theories of femininity and motivations for motherhood. They include those that ascribe influences from the biological, psychological, and environmental realms. More specifically, the theories covered include the early analysts' idea of baby as substitute for the missing penis, the biological imperative, pregnancy as the realization of one's biological potential, and the evolutionary imperative. These motivations have been observed in pregnant women by myself and others (Zuckerberg, 1980). In many women, pregnancy seems to be an attempt to solve both pre-Oedipal and Oedipal conflicts through the reworking of the mother–daughter relationship. For example, for some women, having a baby is a new edition of early doll play, in that it is used as an opportunity to master a passive position by taking charge of their own baby. Through activity, the mother redoes her relationship with her own mother by identifying with the baby, and heals some of the open wounds of her childhood. For others, having a baby is an attempt to provide themselves with unconditional love, and assurance of their lovability. In a new version of the wish to give mother a baby in defense against rage toward her for hoarding babies (see page 107), some women want a baby as a gift for an errant husband with hopes of putting the marriage back on course. Other motivations include a replacement for a lost or deceased love object; solidifying the sense of herself as a female by proving her femininity and sexuality; a wish to recreate mother and father and, in the process, provide immortality to her parents and herself; to further work through the inner genital task of growing into an adult woman; an attempt to extricate herself from her parents; and the competitive wish to outdo her mother by being a better mother to her own child than her mother was to her. As Kestenberg (1977) says, as pregnancy becomes possible, various childhood wishes which heretofore fluctuated in intensity come to the fore and press for fulfillment. In addition, it is clear that more than one psychological force may be in operation at any one time. Here, I am referring to Waelder's (1936) concept of multiple function, in which he said that a behavior may serve a number of psychic functions or may be a solution to a number of problems. Pregnancy, in other words, may be motivated by, and a gratification of, a number of psychic pressures.

The Pregnancy

In discussing the changes set in motion by pregnancy, I will return to the concept of pregnancy as a crisis and explain what it is that makes it so.

Biochemical Aspects

The word crisis means, in general, a decisive time, a turning point in the course of something. Here it is used in the sense of a critical biological and psychological event in the development of a woman, which involves dramatic and profound physiological and psychological changes requiring adjustment and adaptation in order to reach a higher level of integration and maturation.

Benedek (1970) describes pregnancy as an extension and exacerbation of the leutin phase of the reproductive cycle (previously discussed) with particular biophysical and characteristic psychological repercussions. Biochemically, conception alters metabolism by increasing production of the gonadal hormones estrogen and progesterone which, as previously pointed out, play a large role in the turmoil of adolescence. The hormonal changes affect central monoamine metabolism, alter catecholamine excretion and plasma tryptophan, deplete reserves of vitamin B_6 and serum folate, and increase serum prolactin and platelet monoamine oxidase activity.

Research studies have demonstrated a relationship between some of these phenomena and mood fluctuations, although findings are preliminary (Gise, 1967). Naturally, the woman is not aware of these biochemical changes, nor of some of their more subtle effects, such as an increase in the REM cycle of sleep and changes in electroencephalograph (EEG) and hypothalamic activity. The behavioral manifestations of these internal changes are the characteristic complaints of early pregnancy: changes in temperature regulation (some women complain of always being cold; one woman said she felt there was a short in her thermostat because of the delay in her body's adjusting to temperature changes), fatigue, and, in about 50% of women, morning sickness.

Psychologically, the lutein-phase effects are also exacerbated; that is, there is an increase in primary narcissism which manifests itself in a greater sense of well being, an increase in receptive-retentive tendencies and maternal feelings, and a greater integrative capacity of the ego in healthy women, as well as a decrease of anxiety in anxious women (Benedek, 1970). These characteristics are no doubt what impressed Freud when he observed that pregnant women exude a sense of calm and well being.

In addition to these biological and biologically induced forces, which promote continuation of the species, pregnancy stimulates psychological reactions which, if confronted and resolved, will promote maturation of the individual, as well as a potentially healthier pregnancy, delivery, postpartum reaction, and mother–infant relationship (Heinstein, 1967). If not successfully dealt with, they create a variety of problems for the woman, the infant, and the marital couple.

Psychological Aspects

The pregnant state exerts a regressive pull, reawakening repressed wishes and fears, which demand readjustment of psychic priorities and the working through of unresolved infantile conflicts. Fortunately, the state creates not only the germs of the disease, but also the environment for the cure. While the regression induces symptoms that even in relatively healthy women look like a borderline psychosis, the regression also produces a receptive and introspective state highly responsive to therapeutic efforts (Bibring, 1959). More specifically, on interview, pregnant women give evidence of magical thinking, premonitions, depressive reactions, primitive anxieties, introjective and paranoid mechanisms, and incomplete repression. They report feeling more sensitive to and fearful of confrontation, overreacting to emotionally charged issues such as child abuse, abortion, and missing children, and appear to be more superstitious and phobic than they were prior to the pregnancy (Coleman, 1969). Some complain of difficulty concentrating, and find themselves preoccupied with daydreams and behaving autistically (Coleman, 1969; Jarrahi-Zedeh, Kane, Van de Castle, Lachenbruch, & Ewing, 1969).

Researchers have also reported increased depression (Kumar & Robson, 1968), and increased dependency needs (Pines, 1972). Their responses on the Rorschach inkblot test give evidence of emotional lability, psychic upheaval, and reactive worries and concerns (Zuckerberg, 1980). And while it is difficult to imagine the adaptive value of some of these symptoms, it is clear that self-absorption may very well be a critical state for the narcissistic refueling vital for adaptation (Zuckerberg, 1980), and that the incomplete repression and highly introspective state contribute to a speedy and successful resolution of psychic conflict.

Adjustive Tasks

Many authors have organized their thinking about the psychological aspects of pregnancy around the three trimesters. This is a natural division, as each has somewhat characteristic physiological dynamics and, as a whole, represent a sequence of events that stimulate universal conflicts and issues. Each trimester has particular themes that can be seen as recapitulating the psychosexual stages of development, while issues from the stage before or the stage to come are also present, though not dominant. In addition, the pregnancy can be viewed as another opportunity, though certainly not the last, for the woman to reexperience and work through the early steps of development, i.e., autism, symbiosis, separation/individuation, and rapproachment. I discuss this further a little later.

First Trimester. Following the first spontaneous reaction to the discovery of a wanted pregnancy, whether it be joy, anxiety, or amazement, the women's thoughts, fantasies, and feelings often focus on the foreign object that has settled into her body. The biological symbiosis of conception demands the psychological integration of the self with another, and as such, is a repetition of the mother's first relationship with her own mother. This time it is she who must accept a foreign object, representing both the fetus and the sexual partner, as part of the self. The adjustive task of the trimester is to accept the intrusion and incorporate it into the image of oneself (Bibring, 1959).

The major theme of the first trimester is an oral one (Benedek, 1970; Deutsch, 1944; Jessner, Weigert, & Foy, 1970; Kestenberg, 1976). In the first month there are the dramatic anatomical changes spoken of earlier, which no doubt interact with psychological conflicts to produce the somatic symptoms often, but not always, observed. Many women have nausea to one degree or another with or without vomiting. Deutsch (1924) and others have spoken of vomiting as representing the wish to expel the fetus and a rejection of the mothering role. The ambivalently felt fetus is primarily an extension of the ambivalently felt self, and as such may represent either the loving or loved self or else the aggressive, devouring self (Benedek, 1970). Indeed, many women have anxious fantasies of being devoured by the fetus (Jessner et al., 1970). The oral theme is also represented by the tenderness and engorgement of the breasts and food cravings which can be symbolic of wishes for reincorporation and affirmation of fecundity (Deutsch, 1924). The woman at this stage is also described as somewhat autistic in the sense of inwardly directed and preoccupied with herself, and as previously mentioned, this state is likely facilitative of integration and maturation.

While these oral themes seem to predominate, the complexity of human behavior demands a more complex theory. Kestenberg conceptualized pregnancy as a time of reemergence of the inner genital stage with the intertwining of oral-genital, anal-genital, and urethral-genital as predominant modes during the first, second, and third trimesters, respectively. At bottom, she says, is acceptance and rejection of the inner genital. This means that the conflict is between the regressive wish to be the baby and to enjoy the luxury of passively receiving external supplies while renouncing the genital because of guilt over sexuality and pregnancy, and being an adult woman responsible for her sexuality and capable of nurturing another. Many women experience a revival of old yearnings for supplies from a mother who has proved incapable of giving them. Past lessons are relearned promoting resolution and development. A woman in a pregnancy group which I lead laughed over her renewal of futile efforts which she'd thought she had long abandoned. Laughing represented an achievement, as it meant she had worked through and relinquished some of her enormous rage.

For most women, feelings of successfully surpassing their mothers bring shame and guilt as well as pleasure, and to the extent this is true they experience anxiety about announcing the event to their mothers. Working through of these conflicts leads to comfort with and integration of her new identity, as well as a rapproachment and less ambivalent relationship with her mother. Through this she achieves comfort in her new sense of being part of a mother–child duo. In addition, resolution can lead to greater acceptance of her own dependency needs and acceptance of and pleasure in her husband's support and protection.

Second Trimester.   In the second trimester, one sees a combination of oral, anal, and genital themes. Some believe the dominant theme is anal-sadistic, with issues of control and dominance primary (Kestenberg, 1976; Jessner *et al.*, 1970); others contend that orality continues to be primary (Chertock, Bonnaud, Borelli, Donnet & Revault d'Allonnes, 1969). Oral themes do continue. Nutrition is a primary concern, with mother focusing on her diet and what she should and should not ingest. She has fantasies of the baby's character, as well as his or her health being affected by what she eats. She continues working through dependency issues, anticipating and fearing the loss of her dependency supplies from her husband and parents.

Her body is growing and changing, and how she feels about that is affected by a number of factors; intrapsychic, interpersonal, and cultural. A major factor is how she felt about her body as she was growing up, and particularly as she developed into a woman. Another issue is her investment in her figure, and how she imagines the pregnancy will affect that for all time. Interpersonally, her husband's continuing interest in and sexual attraction to her or not has a significant effect on her feelings about her body, as does the attitude of her sociocultural group. The latter may consider pregnant women better unseen or, conversely, as radiantly beautiful.

Although it seems to be changing, the attitude in Western society has been that pregnancy is a social stigma—probably because of the embarrassment over its sexual implications—and at best should be underplayed and desexualized. In fact, maternity clothes, until very recently, have been largely derivative of toddler styles, with smocking at the chest and little bows at the peter pan collar, rather than modified versions of sophisticated and sexy women's fashions. Acceptance of her body is one step among others in the transition of her identity; it leads to an integration of herself as a sexual female and nurturant mother.

It is during the second trimester that the fetus moves, kicking and changing position in the womb and, by so doing, disrupts the symbiotic union just enough to stimulate the fantasy of the fetus as a real organism separate from the self. This begins the slow process of acceptance of anatomical separation at delivery. Knowing from her own bodily experience that the baby is alive, the woman experiences relief from earlier anxieties related to her wish/fear of expulsion. She may also feel that rather than being in possession and control of her body, she is victim of this other being which has taken possession of her.

Kestenberg (1977) found second-trimester women's dreams and fantasies revealing anal-sadistic regressive trends that are characteristic of the inner genital stage of childhood and adolescence. Superstitions abound and she feels her diet, her behavior, and her emotions exert a powerful influence over the fetus. Some women experience the fetus as an internal penis compensating them for the pain of the earlier castration. They feel strong and god-like in their possession of masculine powers (Chasseguet-Smirgel, 1976). Others feel at times disturbed over the fetus' influence over them and their body.

Genital themes are stimulated by the mother's growing body, which exposes her sexuality to the world. Exhibitionistic conflicts come to the fore, with some women delaying wearing maternity clothes and others becoming reclusive. One patient in my practice rationalized having put herself on a high protein, low fat, and low carbohydrate diet in order, we eventually discovered, to avoid growing out of her regular clothes.

These middle months appear to be a time of maintainence and relative stability. The early months of dramatic hormonal changes with accompanying physiological disturbances have passed; and delivery is still relatively remote. The psychological task of the trimester is maintainence of stable maternal attitudes through retention (Kestenberg, 1977).

Third Trimester.   Preparation for relinquishing the baby is the primary work of the third trimester. Separation-individuation and abandonment are major conflicts. The body contributes to the readiness by increasing production of estrogen and progesterone, which leads to an increase in physical discomfort. The fetus' weight triples, changing the maternal center of gravity and causing backaches and feelings of clumsiness. The diaphragm is pushed up by as much as an inch, causing breathing difficulties; the stomach is displaced, resulting in indigestion; and pressure on the bladder causes frequent urination. Pressure on her other organs can cause hemorrhoids and varicose veins. Braxton Hicks contractions become increasingly persistent as the trimester progresses; at best, they are distracting and at worst, painful. The baby's movements, as well as pressure to urinate, disturb sleep.

These are compelling reasons to welcome delivery, and they facilitate the resolution of the separation, and assuage guilt over wanting it over with. Psychologically, the body's preparation for delivery disturbs the sense of mother–fetus unity.

The oral theme continues through the third trimester. Over the months of the pregnancy, the successful mother has become more and more identified with the fetus, and fears its being forced from the safety of the womb. Abandonment anxiety is displaced onto the sexual partner; fear of rejection by one's parents for the triumph increases worries about one's ability to take care of both baby and the self.

The birth of the child was described by Hegel as the death of the parents (deBeauvoir, 1953). Psychologically, many women experience their pregnancy as a death knoll to their own sense of childhood. Some feel the birth foreshadows their own death, as they are being replaced as a child by their own child. One patient graphically illustrated this by describing her life as symbolized by an oval running track complete with the quarter-mile sprint extension. She felt the oval represented her life from birth to marriage, the extension represented the marriage, and the end of the extension childbirth, which would be the end of her life.

Anal issues continue as well with the retention–expulsion theme. The task is to separate psychologically from the fetus without expelling it prematurely. Being able to anticipate relinquishing the biological symbiosis, resolving the guilt over wanting to sever it, and recognizing the infant as a separate person while maintaining the psychological symbiosis are crucial for good mothering. Kestenberg reformulates some of these themes as urethral issues. She says they are stimulated by the anticipation of breaking water and fears of delivering the baby prematurely while urinating. Many women feel helpless about not having control over where and when water breaks and labor begins, and they fear losing other body parts and fluids along with the baby, as well as losing their minds.

As labor and delivery approaches, conflicts of genital-Oedipal origin become dominant. Sexual intercourse is often avoided during the last trimester, in some cases because of guilt for enjoying sex and fearing damage to the fetus as punishment, and in others because of the fantasy that the fetus, representing the envious parent, is watching. In fact, recent studies have shown the fears of coitus in the last weeks are unwarranted in that women continuing intercourse with orgasm do not have increased incidence of fetal complications (Walbracht, 1984).

Fears of childbirth are almost universal (Weiss & English, 1957) and begin in childhood with ideas of being cut open, torn, split apart, bloody, and messy and of dying. Many women fear the episiotomy with its genetic origins in castration anxiety (Raphael-Leff, 1981). Labor and delivery also stimulate fears of being damaged, as well as exhilaration, relief, denial, regression, depression, all of which are considered normal (Turrini, 1980). While many of these fears appear to be Oedipal in origin, Kestenberg (1976) feels that they are under domination of the inner genital, and, in fact, are often disguising pre-Oedipal wishes for mother and baby.

Marital Adjustment

Implicit in the foregoing is the idea that the months of incubation provide the time for the new mother to prepare herself for new identifications and new roles. She has pre-Oedipal conflicts around dependency, separation, and castration anxiety in relation to feared body damage, and Oedipal concerns and anxieties about maternal adequacy, growing up, and assuming new roles. She has also had to cope with revived feelings about past abortions, stillbirths, and previous pregnancies which, even if normal, are somewhat traumatic in that the memory traces of anxiety and pain remain in the preconscious or unconscious (Turrini, 1980).

To the degree that this process causes upheaval distinguishes the normal from the troubled pregnancy. And to the degree this causes upheaval is the degree to which stress is put on the marriage and other important relationships. The father-to-be is naturally having to make adjustments of his own, and the incubation period provides him, as well, with the time to work out his new identity and new roles. The adjustments he makes will, in turn, have an important effect on his wife. He is part of, but also separate from, the intimate relationship between his wife and the fetus. He stands by while his wife is fussed over and often feels "Hey, how about me?" Some men make unconscious efforts to be a more integral part of the pregnancy process and to defend against feelings of alienation. In one Lamaze class, a father was found among the women on the floor doing the preparatory exercises rather than standing by with the other men. And many men are known to put on weight and even to have morning sickness during their wives' pregnancies.

Another experience that is difficult for many men is finding themselves in the new position of being married to a mother. Her changing body often stimulates anxiety over incestuous wishes, and sexual relations are consequently strained, or in some cases, avoided. Her husband's negative reaction to her growing and evolving body obviously has serious repercussions for how the woman feels about her own body, herself, and how she feels about her husband. Both partners in the marriage are undergoing redefinition of themselves as individuals and in relation to each other. The pregnancy gives each the opportunity to work out the new roles they will play in relation to the baby and to each other.

Couples have characteristic ways of relating to one another based, among other things, on the projection of introjected objects. Impending parenthood often disrupts the homeostasis, calling for readjustment and accommodation. Early sibling issues, as well as later Oedipal issues, are raised within the marriage. The father's feeling of being excluded from the fetus–mother dyad creates jealousy and resentment which, in turn, can exacerbate latent or explicit fears in the wife of being punished for her sexuality and fecundity. The new pregnant woman, on the other hand, may experience her husband as an intruder in the biological and psychological symbiosis she is enjoying with her fetus, and react in a way which exacerbates his feelings of exclusion and stimulates sibling-like rivalry between the father and the fetus. The mother's sibling rivalry can also be stimulated by the father's excitement and interest in the new baby.

Conflicts in the marriage grow when both partners are in need of support at the same time and, for that reason, neither is capable of giving to the other. Fortunately, however, these regressions and reintegrations seem to be highly flexible and fluid rather than fixed, making it likely that at least some of the time one or the other will be capable of providing the understanding and support needed by the other. This is fortunate for the fetus, as well as for the couple, for the fetus' very survival depends on these healthy trends. The diminution of the woman's natural ambivalence toward the pregnancy and toward the fetus' survival depends on her husband's support and his wishes for the infant's survival. The husband's understanding and attention has a significant ameliorative effect on his wife's anxiety and conflicts. Facilitating their successfully providing mutual support is the bond formed by the couple's having together created a new life and their working together to create a receptive environment for their new child and a place for each other as a mother and a father.

The Difficult Pregnancy

While there is no question that the biological and psychological aspects of pregnancy constitute a crisis, most women traverse the territory with relative ease. Some have more difficulty. Physically, they have trouble maintaining the pregnancy. They may suffer excessive nausea and vomiting (hypermesis gravidarum) which is likely to represent a wish to expel the child. They may have breakthrough bleeding, leaking of amniotic fluid, spontaneous abortion, hypertension, inappropriate weight gain, gastrointestinal complaints, and general aches and pain. Psychologically, any of these normal concerns and worries in an exaggerated form suggests a troubled pregnancy: excessive worries about bodily damage or damage to the baby; compulsive rituals or obsessive ruminations, agoraphobia, acute anxiety, anhedonia, emotional lability, or an indifference to the pregnancy and a neglect of the normal preparatory activities (Zuckerberg, 1980).

What often seems to be the basis of a psychopathological response to the pregnancy is a disturbed identification with the mother-to-be's own mother. A woman in my practice developed hypochondriasis during her pregnancy, focusing on every beat of her heart and twitch in her chest, and becoming convinced she was going to have a heart attack. She was the fifth of five children born 2 years after the only other girl, to a masochistic, self-sacrificing woman who doted on her three sons and trivialized the girls. The patient had idealized her mother during her childhood to defend against her extensive aggressive feelings toward her, but was aware that she didn't want to be like her. She became an architect, married in her mid-thirties, and became pregnant without ever having felt a particular yearning for child. In discussing the hypochondriasis in relation to her feelings about her mother, she realized that in fact she was doing what her mother had done, playing the victim and threatening to die. She realized that her symptom was an identification with her mother in defense against her wishes to separate from her and deny their similarity, and an expression of her aggression in that her death would deprive her mother of a daughter and a granddaughter. The fears of a heart attack were also in fact a displacement of her fear of childbirth, which she felt would kill her as the phallic woman she fantasized herself to be. Working through her resistance to a maternal identification helped eliminate the hypochondriasis and pave the way for a relatively smooth pregnancy and birth.

Other women direct their aggression toward the fetus, experiencing it as a monster or cancerous growth, or toward the impregnating male. The husband's reaction to his wife can have a distinctly ameliorative effect or not, depending on his ability to cope with her aggression.

The potential for this degree of regression, in general, would suggest a poor prognosis. But in fact, treatment with pregnant women has been shown to be quite successful (Bibring, 1959). Pregnant women are unusually receptive to therapeutic intervention, and symptoms seems to easily disappear with minimal supportive treatment. This seems to be because of their accessibility to their own fantasies and inner life (Coleman, 1971; Zuckerberg, 1980) and their powers of insight and understanding of their own symbolism (Raphael-Leff, 1981). In addition, their motivation is high as they are often anxious to resolve their conflicts before the baby is born. The rewards are also quite gratifying. Successful delivery of a healthy baby has been shown to raise self-esteem and make women feel a great sense of accomplishment. They feel more feminine and grown up, and have a new sense of independence in relation to their own mothers. The bond to their husbands and new families is strengthened with the loosening of old ties to their families of origin, and they often feel capable of relating to their parents in a new, more mature and healthier way. They also feel excited about the opportunity to raise their children as they wish they had been raised, thereby healing the old wounds and decreasing the old pain. It is clear, from the foregoing, that successful resolution of the many conflicts revived by pregnancy promotes a new maturity which increases the woman's sense of herself as an adult, as well as her capacity to be a good mother.

REFERENCES

Barnett, M. (1968). "I can't" versus "he won't." Further considerations of the psychical consequences of the anatomical and physiological differences between the sexes. *Journal of the American Psychoanalytic Association, 16*, 588–600.

Benedek, T. (1952). *Psychosexual tendencies in women.* New York: Ronald Press.

Benedek, T. (1970). The psychobiology of pregnancy. In E. Anthony & T. Benedek (Eds.), *Parenthood: Its psychology and psychopathy* (pp. 137–151). Boston: Little, Brown.

Benedek, T., & Rubenstein, B. B. (1942). *The sexual cycle in women.* Washington, D.C.: National Research Council.

Bibring, G. (1959). Some considerations of the psychological processes in pregnancy. *Psychoanalytic Study of the Child, 14*, 113–119.

Bibring, G., Dwyer, T. F., & Huntington, D. S. (1961). A study of psychological processes in pregnancy and of the earliest mother child relationship. *Psychoanalytic Study of the Child, 16*, 9–24.

Blum, H. (1967). Masochism, the ego ideal and the psychology of women. *Journal of the American Psychoanalytic Association, 24 (Suppl.)*, 157–191.

Brazelton, T. (1969). *Infants and mothers.* New York: Delacorte Press.

Chasseguet-Smirgel, J. (1970). Feminine guilt and the Oedipus complex. In *Female Sexuality.* Ann Arbor: University of Michigan Press.

Chasseguet-Smirgel, J. (1976). Freud and female sexuality: The consideration of some blind spots in the exploration of the "dark continent." *International Journal of Psycho-analysis, 57*, 275–286.

Chehrazi, S. (1986). Female psychology: A review. *Journal of the American Psychoanalytic Association, 34*, 141–162.

Chertok, L., Bonnaud, M., Borelli, M., Donnet, J. L., & Revault d'Allonnes, C. (1969). *Motherhood and personality.* Philadelphia: Lippincott.

Chodorow, N. (1978). *The reproduction of mothering: Psychoanalysis and the sociology of gender.* Berkeley: University of California Press.

Clower, V. (1976). Theoretical implications of current views on masturbation in latency girls. *Journal of the American Psychoanalytic Association, 24 (Suppl.)*, 109–126.

Coleman (1969). Psychological state during first pregnancy. *American Journal of Orthopsychiatry, 39*, 788–797.

Coleman, A. (1971). First baby group. *International Journal of Group Psychotherapy, 21*, 74–83.

Deutsch, H. (1924). The psychology of women in relation to the function of reproduction. In R. Fliess (Ed.), *The psychoanalytic Reader, 1948* (pp. 192–206). New York: International Universities Press.

Deutsch, H. (1930). Significance of masochism in mental life of women. *International Journal of Psycho-analysis, 11,* 48–60.

Deutsch, H. (1944). *The psychology of women,* Vol. I. New York: Grune & Stratton.

Deutsch, H. (1945). *The psychology of women,* Vol. II. New York: Grune & Stratton.

Erickson, E. (1968). Womanhood and the innerspace. In *Identity, youth and crisis* (pp. 261–294). New York: W. W. Norton.

Freud, S. (1917). On the transformation of instincts as exemplified in anal erotism. *Standard Edition, 17,* 125–133.

Freud, S. (1924). The dissolution of the Oedipus complex. *Standard Edition, 19,* 173–182.

Freud, S. (1925). Some psychical consequences of the anatomical distinction between the sexes. *Standard Edition, 19,* 243–258.

Freud, S. (1928). Fetichism. *International Journal of Psycho-analysis, 9,* 161–166.

Freud, S. (1931). Female sexuality. *Standard Edition, 21,* 221–243.

Freud, S. (1933). Femininity. *Standard Edition, 22,* 112–135.

Freud, S. (1940). An outline of psycho-analysis, *Standard Edition, 23,* 141–207.

Galenson, E. (1976). Report of panel on early infancy and childhood. *Journal of the American Psychoanalytic Association, 24,* 141–160.

Galenson, E., & Roiphe, H. (1974). The emergence of genital awareness during the second year of life. In R. C. Friedman, R. M. Richart, & R. L. Van de Wiele (Eds.), *Sex differences in behavior* (pp. 223–231). New York: John Wiley & Sons.

Galenson, E., & Roiphe, H. (1976). Some suggested revisions concerning early female development. *Journal of Psychoanalytic Pregnancy, 24* (Suppl.), 29–59.

Gise, L. H. (1967). Psychiatric implications of pregnancy. In S. A. Richardson & A. F. Guttmacher (Eds.), *Childbearing: Its social and psychological perspectives* (pp. 229–233). Baltimore: Williams & Wilkins.

Glover, L., & Mendell, D. (1982). A suggested developmental sequence for a preoedipal genital phase. In D. Mendell (Ed.), *Early female development—current psychoanalytic views* (pp. 127–174). New York: Spectrum.

Greenacre, P. (1950). Special problems of early female sexual development. In *Trauma, growth, and personality* (pp. 237–257). New York: International Universities Press.

Greenacre, P. (1953). Penis awe and its relation to penis envy. In R. M. Lowenstein (Ed.), *Drives, affects, behavior* (pp. 176–190). New York: International Universities Press.

Greenacre, P. (1958). Early physical determinants in the development of the sense of identity. In *Emotional growth* (1971) (pp. 113–127). New York: International Universities Press.

Heinstein, M. (1967). Expressed attitudes and feeling in pregnant women. *Merrill-Palmer Quarterly, 13,* 217–236.

Horgan, D. (1983). The pregnant woman's place and where to find it. *Sex Roles, 9,* 333–339.

Horney, K. (1933). The denial of the vagina. *International Journal of Psycho-analysis, 14,* 57–70.

Jacobson, E. (1950). Development of the wish for a child in boys. *Psychoanalytic Study of the Child, 5,* 139–152.

Jacobson, E. (1975). On the development of the girl's wish for a child. *Psychoanalytic Quarterly, 37, 4,* 532–538.

Jarrahi-Zadeh, A., Kane, F. J., Jr., Van de Castle, R. L., Lachenbruch, P. A., & Ewing, J. A. (1969). Emotional and cognitive changes in pregnancy and early puerperium. *British Journal of Psychiatry, 115,* 797–806.

Jessner, L., Weigert, E., & Foy, J. (1970). The development of parental attitudes during pregnancy. In E. Anthony & T. Benedek (Eds.), *Parenthood: Its psychology and psychopathy* (pp. 209–244). Boston: Little, Brown.

Jones, E. (1933). The phallic phase. *International Journal of Psycho-analysis, 14*, 1–33.

Jones, E. (1935). Early female sexuality. *International Journal of Psycho-analysis, 16*, 263–273.

Kestenberg, J. (1956). On the development of maternal feelings in early childhood. *The Psychoanalytic Study of the Child, 11*, 257–291.

Kestenberg, J. (1976). Regression and reintegration in pregnancy. *Journal of the American Psychoanalytic Association, 24 (Suppl.)*, 213–250.

Klein, H. R., Potter, H. W., & Dyk, R. B. (1950). *Anxiety in pregnancy and childbirth.* New York: Hoeber.

Kumar, R., & Robson, K. (1978). Preliminary communication: Previous induced abortion and ante-natal depression in primaparae. *Psychology and Medicine, 8*, 711–715.

Lampl-de Groot, J. (1927). The evolution of the Oedipus complex in women. *International Journal of Psycho-analysis, 9*, 332–345.

Mack, Brunswick, R. (1940). The pre-Oedipal phase of the libido development. *Psychoanalytic Quarterly, 9*, 293–319.

Mahler, M., Pine, F., & Bergman, A. (1975). *The psychological birth of the infant.* New York: Basic Books.

Miller, T. (1976). *Toward a new psychology of women.* Boston: Beacon Press.

Money, J., & Erhardt, A. (1972). *Man and woman, boy and girl.* Baltimore: Johns Hopkins University Press.

Notman, M. (1981). Changing views of femininity and childbearing. *Hillside Journal of Clinical Psychiatry, 3*, 187–202.

Notman, M., & Nadelson, C. (1978). New views of femininity and reproduction. Paper delivered at the American Psychiatric Association, Chicago, May 1978.

Parens, H., Pollock, L., Stern, J., & Kramer, S. (1976). On the girl's entry into the Oedipus complex. *Journal of the American Psychoanalytic Association, 24 (Suppl.)*, 79–108.

Pines, D. (1972). Pregnancy and motherhood: Interaction between fantasy and reality. *British Journal for Medical Psychology, 45*, 333–342.

Raphael-Leff, J. (1981). Psychotherapy with pregnant women. In B. Blum (Ed.), *Psychological aspects of pregnancy, birthing and bonding* (pp. 174–205). New York: Human Sciences Press.

Rapoport, R. (1963). Normal crisis: Family structure and mental health. *Family Practice, 2*, 68–80.

Rheingold, J. C. (1964). *The fear of being a woman.* New York: Grune & Stratton.

Roiphe, H. (1968). On an early genital phase with an addendum on genesis. *The Psychoanalytic Study of the Child, 3*, 348–365.

Stoller, R. (1937). Overview, the impact of new advances in sex research on psychoanalytic theory. *American Journal of Psychiatry, 32*, 241–251.

Stoller, R. (1976). Primary femininity. *Journal of the American Psychoanalytic Association, 24, (Suppl.)*, 59–78.

Turrini, P. (1980). Psychological crisis in normal pregnancy. In B. Blum (Ed.), *Psychological aspects of pregnancy, birthing and bonding* (pp. 135–150). New York: Human Sciences Press.

Waelder, R. (1936). The principle of multiple function. *Psychoanalytic Quarterly, 5*, 45–62.

Walbracht, G. S. (1984). Sexuality during pregnancy. *American Family Physician, 5*, 273–275.

Weiss, E., & English, O. S. (1957). *Psychosomatic medicine*, 3rd ed. Philadelphia: W. B. Saunders.

Wenner, N. K., Cohen, M. B., Weingart, E. W., Kvarnes, R. G., Dhaneson, E. M., & Fearing, J. M. (1969). Emotional problems in pregnancy. *Psychiatry, 32*, 389–410.

Williams, J. (1977). The emergence of sex differences. In J. Williams (Ed.), *Psychology of women* (pp. 121–157). New York: W. W. Norton.

Winnicott, D. W. (1965). Providing for the child in health and crisis. In *The maturational process and the facilitating environment* (pp. 64–72). New York: International Universities Press.

Winnicott, D. W. (1970). The mother-infant experience in mutuality. In J. Anthony & T. Benedek (Eds.), *Parenthood; Its psychology and psychopathy* (pp. 246–255). Boston: Little, Brown.

Zuckerberg, J. O. (1980). Psychological and physical warning signals regarding pregnancy. In B. Blum (Ed.), *Psychological aspects of pregnancy, birthing and bonding* (pp. 151–173). New York: Human Sciences Press.

Part III

From Body-Self to Other

From passages clearly intrapsychic of self-body, we travel to passages more clearly interpersonal. Naomi Berne focuses on birth and delivery as clear markers of the transition to parenthood. She notes the fascinating way in which the pregnant woman's psychology parallels the physiological changes in her body: from fetal symbiotic merging to quickening, the beginning of a separate object within the self; to delivery, physiological separation, and the rupture of symbiosis. Nature's wisdom is such that nursing reinstates the lost symbiosis through active nurturance.

Leanne Domash explores the cataclysmic effects on the personality of the mother during the postpartum period. She discusses shifts in ego functioning that lead to instances of both heightened creativity and, at the other extreme, to a resurgence of intense psychopathology. Mary Beth Cresci writes about the nursing experience, a dramatic event, which profoundly affects the evaluation of a woman's identity. In the nursing experience, the mothering identity begins and becomes an important part of subsequent self-consolidation. David Kliot provides the physician's perspective. He reviews the emotional components of labor and delivery and enriches our understanding through his sociohistorical review of childbirth approaches since the turn of the century.

Chapter 8

Psychology of Childbirth

Naomi Berne

The onset of labor and its culmination in delivery clearly mark the moment of transition to parenthood. The birth of a child transforms the internal and external realities of the mother as well as relationships within and between families and generations. Labor and delivery, because they constitute the moment of the transformation, are imbued with undeniable drama and importance. However, childbirth can also be viewed as a point along a continuum which begins before conception and moves through pregnancy, labor, delivery, the confinement period immediately following the birth, and the beginnings of the developing relationship with the child. As the pregnant woman advances through these phases, we see a continually changing pattern of relationships with the fetus growing inside her, with her mate, with her own parents, and with the environment.

The complexity of the childbirth experience, in its mechanistic as well as transcendent aspects, eludes easy analysis. The mother's experience remains rooted in her underlying psychodynamics, but her experience of the events requires an examination of the interaction between psychodynamics and the unique aspects of the childbirth experience itself.

The extraordinary way in which the pregnant woman's psychology parallels the physiological changes in her body is one of the most fascinating aspects of a study of the entire process. In the earliest months of pregnancy, the fetus, unfelt and unseen, remains psychologically merged with the mother, an integral part of herself. Quickening disrupts this unity and transforms the fetus into a separate object within the self. From this point to delivery, the part of the woman which is the baby begins to be perceived as a separate object and thus begins the psychological preparation for the physiological separation—the birth. The mother's perception of the pull on her body and her increasing physiological discomfort continue to aid in the transformation of the fetus into a separate being whose real existence as a person is approaching. The ultimate termination of this internal unity and the final separation from the "so long familiar and cherished content of the body" (Haas,

---

NAOMI BERNE, PH.D. • Consulting Psychologist, Alcott Montessori School, Scarsdale, New York; Psychologist, Pleasantville Cottage School, Pleasantville, New York; private practice.

1952) gives the childbirth experience its unique quality. The core problem specific to this final phase is that of attachment–loss–reintegration or more specifically, separation from the contents of the body, the dissolution of the symbiotic union, and finally, reintegration in the postpartum period. The examination of this aspect of the entire childbirth experience before all others reflects the primacy of these issues in the unfolding of the actual birth experience.

Childbirth is often described simply as a significant maturational step in the adult life of a woman. In its most elemental form, it can be experienced as the ultimate physical challenge and struggle, second only to death in the anxieties and fears it evokes. The juxtaposition of life affirmation and death finds its roots in the experience of separation from the significant other which brings with it, in its extreme form, the threat of dissolution and nonexistence. Delivery is associated with pain and bleeding which generally characterize dangerous and/or life-threatening situations involving bodily injury and damage. The awareness of one's solitary participation in an event that is frightening yet inevitable is likely to evoke fears of fatality. At the root of these most primitive fears lies the pregnant woman's own body, in its past strengths and weaknesses, and in its as yet untested ability to undergo and withstand extreme physical pressures. The dreams of pregnant women, particularly during the last trimester, reflect these bodily uncertainties on unconscious, symbolic levels. Jones (1978) noted a large number of references to architectural structures in the dreams of pregnant women and suggested that these reflected the dreamer's "inner representations of the uterine environment." In addition, many images of damaged architectural structures were noted, perhaps representing the fear of body damage caused by the fetus. Many researchers (Deutsch, 1973; Gillman, 1968) report dreams of labor and delivery being totally bypassed. The baby is dreamed to simply emerge magically from the mother's body or another person is dreamed as giving birth to the baby. Dreams of fully developed children represent a wish that the child is already beyond the dangers of early infancy but also that he/she arrives in the world by magic and is not delivered in the usual, perhaps threatening, way.

Experience of Labor and Delivery

Realistic appraisal of the processes of labor and delivery indicates that it is not without risk. Although now rare, childbirth can result in death for the mother and/or child, and actual bodily changes are not limited to the stretching of organs and muscles with an eventual return to the prepregnant state. Bleeding is inevitable and tissues can be torn. Increasing incidence of caesarean birth clearly heightens fears related to body damage. However, beyond all realistic appraisals, emerge fears and anxieties rooted either in the phases of the pregnant woman's early development reawakened by the birth process or in the physical sensations unique to the process. The labor and delivery experience is a supreme test of the woman's basic trust and confidence in her own body in its most natural and elemental form. This sense of trust emerges at least partially from the woman's experience of being handled and nurtured in her own infancy so that the woman's approach to her own childbirth experiences recapitulate those of her own mother. The pregnant woman's experience of her own body not being good enough to satisfy her own mother may well be related to a fear that her body simply cannot produce a baby.

Primitive response patterns of receiving, retaining, and releasing rooted in oral, anal, and genital stages are revived in the birth process. The increasing discomfort of the mother during the last stages of pregnancy, as well as the woman's heightening awareness of the separate human being within, reinforces an expulsive trend (Deutsch, 1973). However, separation fears and the mother's reluctance to part with the loved contents of her body set up a dynamic reminiscent of the child's struggle for sphincter control. The woman's anxiety about "making a mess," both physically and experientially, can be traced to anal conflicts. The fate of the retentive–expulsive tendencies remains partially determined by the symbolic meaning of the lost fetus, i.e., the valued lost self or the bad, devouring self. In the psychoanalytic view, the soon-to-be-lost fetus becomes the penis soon to be lost through castration and the prospect of an episiotomy reinforces these castration fears. Analogies to the experience of sexual intercourse can be found in the intense activity–climax–rest rhythms, as well as the total dominance of physical sensations in both experiences.

The pregnant woman, as labor progresses, becomes increasingly dominated by the physical process itself. The normal progession of labor generally involves decreasing intervals between contractions and intensification of the pain of each contraction until the point of crowning (appearance of the crown of the baby's head at the cervix). At this point of peak stretching of the cervix, the woman may feel most "opened up" and vulnerable, but the anxiety tends to be eclipsed by the total dominance of physical sensations to which the woman must be able to surrender. The loss of genital sensation can awaken primitive images (Raphael-Leff, 1980) of a single internal cavity which will give up its total contents, including the female genital, at the moment of birth. The felt need of the woman to push the baby out, intertwined with the involuntary expulsive pressure as the baby moves through the birth canal, combine to reinforce this image. This fantasy carries the threat of castration and loss of femininity awakened by the episiotomy.

The domination by physical sensation is reinforced by the physical situation and surroundings. These simulate a sensory deprivation experience with its usual immobility, physical confinement, and isolation from others. This in turn gives rise to a sense of disorientation and loss of the sense of time and the normal sequence of activities in the external world. More recent use of birthing rooms and the presence of the family members at the birth clearly can counteract some of these complex influences. However, the dread of breaking down, of being physiologically and emotionally exposed by a series of phenomena over which one has little control, is most acute during this period.

Attachment and Differentiation

The physical and symbolic union with the fetus and its subsequent dissolution is the core dynamic of the childbirth experience. Even before the moment of conception, the fetus (and fantasied baby) becomes the repository of the dreams and wishes of the parents which encompass the strengths and talents of the child, as well as those of the parents themselves who are responsible for the very conception of this special child. The fetus most frequently represents part of the loved self and indeed, dreams are reported in which the child is the mother herself (Stukane, 1985). The loss of this unique union brings with it the potential loss of this part of the loved self and the death of the fantasy baby. However, the intense need to maintain the symbiotic union is threatened by the increasing physical burden of the maturing fetus and its "meta-individuation" through the establishment of patterns of movement, positions, etc., which soon become familiar to the mother. Deutsch (1973) described the development of hostile, expulsive impulses toward the baby within conflicting with the powerful need to maintain the union. Kestenberg (1977) suggests that the underlying aggression of the last trimester is transformed into the strength and activity required of the woman in labor. Fear of death and/or deformity of the fetus may represent the projection of this hostility onto the fetus with the ultimate punishment to the mother for her rejecting and negative thoughts about the child.

Attachment–differentiation issues are central to the mother's ability to master the increasing anxieties and fears surrounding the impending birth. Intrapsychic reorganization involves shifts between self- and object-cathexes with the ultimate healthy resolution residing in the acceptance of the child as a separate object along with a deep identification with the new child as well as with the woman's own mother. Disturbances in the cycle of attachment–differentiation experienced by the pregnant woman in relation to her own mother may reappear in the form of increased anxiety about the impending birth. The dissolution of the symbiotic union may reawaken fears of vulnerability, damage, and abandonment. Women who have previously chosen to terminate a pregnancy may experience a re-emergence of feelings of guilt with retaliation taking the form of increased fears for the baby's or their own health. Family mythology surrounding childbirth, particularly the birth experiences of the pregnant woman's own mother, can color her experiences because of the pregnant woman's increasing identification with her own mother as the pregnancy proceeds. After the birth, the mother's own attachment and differentiation experiences will again be reworked as her own infant develops and proceeds through the very same stages.

Issues of Individual Personality Organization

Intrapsychic issues discussed thus far form the unconscious psychological substrate upon which are superimposed the conscious anxieties and fears specific to the labor and delivery processes. These latter are shaped both by the core problems intrinsic to the process as well as by the individual woman's personality attributes and organization as they are called up to handle what is perceived as an extraordinary challenge to the woman's sense of competence, autonomy, and strength. Childbirth as an inevitable psychophysical event takes complete control of the senses and as such, awakens conflicts around control over one's own body as well as over the environment. The woman's characterological tendencies toward activity and passivity, dependence and independence, are elicited by the simultaneous experience of power and submission inherent in the event (Deutsch, 1973).

The birth process is one involving powerful physical sensations which change over time but continue to dominate the experience because of their unchangingly high intensity. The ability to cope with the experience without undue anxiety and fear requires a fluidity of psychological organization that allows for an alternation between regression and more defensive control as the stage of labor requires it. Thus, just as a weak defensive structure with poor ego boundaries and poor self- and object-representations place women at risk for traumatic birth and postpartum experiences, characterological defensive rigidity can place undue stress on the woman in labor.

The intensity and nature of the woman's need for control over her own body and/or her environment are critical to the childbirth experience. The woman is forced into a helpless, immobile position, so that for some, maintaining control constitutes an enormous challenge. The woman may question whether she is strong enough to master this challenge, and the birth experience becomes a test of competence carrying with it the potential for narcissistic injury. The woman may experience deep feelings of inferiority if she cannot perform in a way she feels she should. For some, prepared childbirth methods offer a means of asserting control over the unknowable experience ahead. For others, the inability to tolerate the anxiety drives them to insist on decision-making power on every detail. Clearly, the woman who is able to tolerate a loosening of her need for control without totally losing control is most likely to complete the process with a sense of mastery, or perhaps even triumph.

The alternation of active effort and passive endurance is intrinsic both to preg-nancy and to the labor and delivery process. The high levels of energy and activity observed in many pregnant woman, particularly toward the end of the third tri-mester, may represent a reaction against the passive endurance of the long waiting period and a means of warding off the increasing fears of the labor and delivery. Zuckerberg (1984, personal communication) has suggested that this overactivity serves the magical function of filling time so completely that the delivery simply cannot take place. During the delivery itself, the first stage of contraction and increasing dilation requires primarily passive endurance and surrender to the phys-ical sensations. In the second or expulsive phase, intense physical and psychologi-cal activity is demanded. Indeed, the degree to which the birth experience itself is construed as an active accomplishment and how this realization is related to uncon-scious conflicts around activity–passivity is likely to color the woman's behavior and her choices concerning prepared childbirth, anesthesia, etc. Deutsch (1973) speculates that the pursual and mastery of the feared experience despite the intense suffering has cathartic effects which contribute to the sense of joyful accomplish-ment as a woman. On the other hand, Kitzinger (1978) suggests that a psychologi-cal retreat from the experience and an inability to respond to its complex and changing demands can play a role in the actual elongation of labor.

Childbirth is a solitary experience in the deepest, most fearsome sense, but the pregnant woman must be able to trust those around her and allow herself to depend on and/or accede to their judgment if appropriate. Intensification of fears and anxieties during labor and the increasing focus on internal physical sensations to the exclusion of most environmental stimuli require that the woman be able to approach the experience with the belief and knowledge that others are available to support and help her if necessary. The extremely passive, infantile woman may find apparent comfort in others around her but may ultimately revert to ragefully demanding help and freedom from her pain. However, even the most psychologically healthy woman may react with anger and irritation during the second or transition state of labor. At this point, the physical sensations are so powerful and seemingly unceasing that there is a tendency for the woman to project the feelings evoked by the overwhelming inner sensations onto those around her and she may become angry and demanding. Clearly, at any point in the process where the fears and sensations threaten to overwhelm, a woman may demand anesthetic, thereby avoiding further intensification of the anxiety and the physical discomfort.

In years past, the power of the family mythology surrounding childbirth experiences could not be overemphasized. The routine use of total anesthesia resulted in a kind of alienation from the entire childbirth experience for whole generations of women. This has become anathema to modern women whose goal is often total aware participation in the event. The radical changes in roles and expectations for woman accompanied by increasing use of prepared childbirth techniques have loosened the powerful connection between a particular woman's experience and that of her own mother. However, it is likely that the mother's thoughts and transmitted feelings, particularly if extreme, remain important in the formation of the pregnant woman's approach to the birth of her child. Blum (1978) describes a maternal ego-ideal, a substructure of the ego-ideal, which is composed of the "woman's internalizations of how she would like to be as a mother." This concept can easily encompass the pregnant woman's notions of how she should be performing during the birth of her child, particuarly in comparison to her own mother. The rigidity of this maternal ego-ideal clearly will affect the woman's feelings of mastery of the experience.

ROLE TRANSFORMATIONS

The childbirth experience marks the transformation from girl to woman or from woman to woman/mother. For some, it is seen as the ultimate test of femininity, while for others it involves a transformation from woman in the erotic sense, to mother, in its maternal rather than erotic aspect. Modern conceptions of womanhood which put a premium on assertiveness, control, and independence and deemphasize the roles of childbearing and child rearing clearly exacerbate conflicts around these transformations. Discussion of these self-image changes are beyond the scope of this chapter. However, the way in which these transformations are effected is dependent in large degree on the woman's identification with her own mother which is considerably strengthened by the childbirth experience. Indeed, the woman has now become a mother herself and in a crucial sense, has become her own mother's equal. The position of nurtured and protected child is no longer hers as it once was and the new equality and identification can be both comforting and frightening. Hopefully, the intense identification can inspire feelings of strength and competence as a woman and, during the delivery itself, can counteract fears of vulnerability and death. If the woman's own mother can be accepted as a prototype of the maternal figure, childbearing and child rearing will be less conflicted and problematic. However, the new equality can stimulate competitive strivings, particularly in relation to the birth process, with a desire to outperform mother and/or a real fear of usurping her position. Guilt feelings aroused by these strivings may intensify fears of death in childbirth as retaliation for these impulses. Zuckerberg (1980) has discussed the woman's fear of abandonment resulting from this competitive struggle, and indeed, the woman's need for a mother substitute following childbirth may emerge partially to assuage these fears. It is interesting to note that the mother who now becomes a grandmother and provides the traditional unconditional acceptance of her grandchild can actually provide nurturance for the new mother because the child has become an extension of her.

The Male Partner

The male partner's role in the childbirth process is both a concrete and a symbolic one in contrast to that of the pregnant woman's mother whose actual participation in the process is usually minimal. In recent years, the role of the male partner has expanded considerably with increasing numbers of couples choosing to have male partners present during the birth. Tanzer (1976) reported that women who chose natural childbirth where husbands were present during the birth reported having "peak experiences" more often than women whose husbands were not with them. Freud theorized that carrying a child represents the gratification of the woman's basic Oedipal wish, i.e., the incorporation of the penis of the father, and as such, is responsible for the reported state of bliss of the pregnant woman. Kestenberg (1977) speaks of a pre-Oedipal maternal urge to create and nurture a child in a dyadic relationship. Indeed, Stukane (1985) reports that some pregnant women dream of being in a shared pregnancy with their husbands. Thus, it is possible that in the delivery, the ultimate gratification of the Oedipal wish, or the wish to bear and care for a child within the dyadic relationship, comes to fruition and is even further intensified by the husband's presence, contributing to the peak experience. In terms of the actual realities of the experience, the support and sharing clearly attenuate many of the fears discussed previously and thus allow the woman increased opportunity to use her strength for positive mastery of the experience.

The sharing role, if adopted by the male partner, allows him to begin the reestablishment of a unity that has been inevitably transformed by the woman's unique relationship to the human being growing inside her and her own self-image transformations from girl to woman and woman to woman/mother. Indeed, genuine jealousy of the developing fetus may contribute to the father's desire and/or need to remain with the mother during the labor and delivery. The evolving relationship between the new mother and her male partner is beyond the scope of this chapter. However, it is clear that the participation in the experiences allows the father to establish himself as a partner in one of the crucial life experiences of the woman, and the establishment of this bond may overshadow any of the more fleeting impressions of the experience itself relating to the woman's behavior during the labor and delivery. Possible pride in the woman's "performance" during the birth may well be expressed in the shared pride in the newborn and may only later be incorporated into his evolving appraisal of the woman in both her erotic and maternal roles.

The role of the male partner in both its symbolic and practical aspects is often shared with the woman's obstetrician. His role in the birth process can evoke fantasies of the all-powerful father who is capable of quieting the woman's fears and alleviating her pain. He may become the fantasied giver of the child and during the labor and delivery is generally looked to as the person who can and is willing to alleviate the woman's suffering. The male partner, on the other hand, may well become the target of anger and irritation at certain points during the labor. Kitzinger (1978) suggests that the obstetrician or midwife may become parent surrogates who reawaken the ambivalent feelings toward the woman's own parents. Their presence can also assuage the woman's anxieties about her impending separation from the fetus/baby.Residual anger and guilt feelings toward the woman's own mother can be assuaged by the pain of birth and resolved by the doctor who will, through his actions, put an end to the situation creating them. However, the extreme dependence on the doctor may trigger ambivalent feelings which are expressed in hostility and anger, particularly in women who experience childbirth as a test of strength and individual competence.

The birth experience, although cataclysmic, is not remembered in detail. The fears, anxieties, and pain tend to be subjected to a kind of amnesia which allows the memory of only concrete and/or peripheral aspects of the event. It is almost impossible to conjure up either the physical sensations or emotional state. Clearly, the pain remembered may bear little resemblance to the actual pain, if they could be measured. A great deal more may be forgotten than remembered. In this sense, the experience is not dissimilar from other experiences of intense physical pain. However, the aftermath of most other pain experiences involves at its best the cessation of pain and repair of the body. After childbirth, not only is pain halted and the body repaired, but the woman has brought forth a new life, surely one of the most extraordinary and rewarding life experiences, one that often pales beside the experienced pain, even that of a natural vaginal birth. Deutsch (1973) emphasizes the intrinsic role of pain in the childbirth experience, stating that the ultimate "transfer of emotions from the woman's ego to the child as object is prepared partly during the act of birth" and that this is weakened in totally painless deliveries. She speculates on the increasing alienation of women from the birth process and from their newborn if they have been anesthetized so that delivery was experienced as painless. Leifer's (1980) study of first pregnancies provides some support for these speculations, although much research needs to be completed before definitive statements can be made on this issue. Women who choose to give birth without anesthesia and are trained in Lamaze or other prepared childbirth techniques are clearly subjected to intense physical pain. However, they most often report extremely rewarding birth experiences and tend not to dwell on the pain (Tanzer, 1976). This phenomenon points up the complexities of the pain experience, which remain beyond the scope of this chapter.

Summary

The experience of childbirth transforms the pregnant woman in countless complex ways. As she moves through labor toward the delivery, physical and emotional energies must be mobilized to cope with both the physical challenges as well as the inevitable anxieties about the event itself and the new role and relationships which result. Others must and can support her but the experience is ultimately a solitary one, overwhelmingly dominated by unfamiliar sensations and fearsome in its inevitability. Overlapping identifications between woman, child, and mother require reworking of earlier intrapsychic conflicts, particularly those involving separation and loss, individuation, dependence–independence, and passivity–activity. The unique intensity of the experience results in significant shifts in self-image, personal roles, and relationships for the new mother and those around her. Current conceptions of female identity have added another dimension to the exploration of the entire process. Clearly, the childbirth experience, both elemental and extremely complex, shapes and reshapes lives in the most intricate and immutable ways.

REFERENCES

Blum, H. (1978). The maternal ego ideal (unpublished paper, New York).
Deutsch, H. (1973). *The psychology of women*, Vol. II. New York: Bantam Books.
Gillman, R. D. (1968). The dreams of pregnant women and maternal adaptation. *American Journal of Orthopsychiatry, 38*, 688–699.
Haas, S. (1952). Psychiatric implications in gynecology and obstetrics. In L. Bellak (Ed.), *Psychology of physical illness* (pp. 90–118). New York: Grune & Stratton.
Jones, C. (1978). Unpublished Ph.D. dissertation. In E. Stukane (Ed.), *The dream worlds of pregnancy*. New York: Quill Press, 1985.
Kestenberg, J. (1977). Regression and reintegration in pregnancy. In H. Blum (Ed.), *Female psychology* (pp. 213–251). New York: International Universities Press.
Kitzinger, S. (1978). *The experience of childbirth*. New York: Penguin.
Leifer, M. (1980). *Psychological effects of motherhood: A study of a first pregnancy*. New York: Praeger.
Raphael-Leff, J. (1980). Psychotherapy with pregnant women. In B. Blum (Ed.), *Psychological aspects of pregnancy, birthing and bonding* (pp. 174–205). New York: Human Sciences Press.
Stukane, E. (1985). *The dream worlds of pregnancy*. New York: Quill Press.
Tanzer, D. (1976). *Why natural childbirth?* New York: Schocken Books.
Zuckerberg, J. (1980). Psychological and physiological warning signals in pregnancy. In B. Blum (Ed.), *Psychological aspects of pregnancy, birthing and bonding* (pp. 151–174). New York: Human Sciences Press.

Chapter 9

The Postpartum Period
Analytic Reflections on the Potential for Agony and Ecstasy

Leanne Domash

There is frequently a cataclysmic effect on the personality of the mother during the postpartum period as she adjusts to her infant and the now enlarged family unit. The new mother is experiencing significant hormonal shifts and physiological changes, including some subtle rebound effects (that is, certain mechanisms were turned off during pregnancy and afterward get turned on again and overshoot the mark). The mother is in the midst of forming a very close bond with her baby, referred to as "primary maternal preoccupation" (Winnicott, 1956). If she is nursing, another complex set of hormones is being released.

Yet she has just lost the most profound symbiosis possible: life growing inside her body. This is a time when buried conflicts regarding her own mother can surge forward. Similarly, because of her heightened state, other conflicts can become very sharpened and demand resolutions. There are also, of course, the issues of readjustment with her husband, the formation of larger family unit, and if applicable, the weaving together of career and family.

Heightened Sensitivity and Increased Creativity

This shared phenomenon, affecting all woman postpartum in varying degrees, results in a state of heightened sensitivity, including a loosening of defenses. One can think of it as a temporary shift to increased right-brain functioning which allows the woman richer access to her feelings and intuition. There is an availability

Leanne Domash, Ph.D. • Consulting Psychologist, Beth Israel Medical Center, New York City; Adjunct Assistant Professor of Psychiatry, Mount Sinai School of Medicine; private practice.

of primary process material as the new mother becomes less structured, partially as a necessity of being close with her baby.

This state of heightened sensitivity has great potential—from increased creative functioning at the one end of the continuum to heightened psychopathology at the other end. This continuum is similar to the creativity—madness relationships that have frequently been suggested (Karlsson, 1968), i.e., that there is a heightened or unusual sensitivity in some people that, depending on the degree of ego strength and extent of environmental support, can lead to unique, creative self-expression or to personality deterioration. In some women, we may see each aspect expressed at different times. (An intriguing example is Virginia Woolf; see Bond, 1984). She alternated between periods of intense creativity and periods of severe depression. Here I am saying that women, after giving birth, have an echo of this unusual sensitivity and potential.

Tanzer (1976) spoke of childbirth in a similar fashion. She described two extremes: women who experience childbirth as a peak experience and those who focus mainly on the pain, pointing to natural childbirth and Lamaze as helping to facilitate the former. In a recent critique of Lamaze technique, Wideman and Singer (1984) address the complexity of factors that may facilitate this, including the social support in the Lamaze groups and the possible stimulation of endorphins through the use of relaxation and breathing techniques. There may be a number of specific factors that foster a positive birthing experience, many of which are not yet understood.

Similarly, there may be many factors that facilitate a positive or creative experience in the postpartum period. These include (1) the extent of the new mother's positive identification with her own mother, (2) the mother's capacity to regress in the service of the ego or to enter what is called transitional space, (3) the mother's capacity to be a mother of symbiosis (id mother) versus the later mother of individuation (ego mother), (4) the effects of certain unconscious fantasies surrounding the child, that is, whom the child unconsciously represents, (5) the amount of emotional support the mother receives, and (6) the possibility that nursing may stimulate the production of endorphins (the small peptides with opiate-like receptor activity localized in various areas of the brain), a hypothesis that requires further exploration. Similarly, women who are under stress, whether from a very difficult child, marital problems, or intrapsychic conflicts, are prone to depression and may also possibly inhibit endorphin production.

While acknowledging that some of each aspect, that is, the increased creativity on the one hand and the increased tendency toward depression on the other, is present in most mothers, for the purposes of discussion, this paper explores both extremes. In the following paragraphs, I give examples of facilitation of creative functioning from my own experience of working with patients after I gave birth. I experienced doing analytic work in a more loosely organized state of consciousness, with a heightened sensitivity to nonverbal cues and an increased ability to utilize visual imagery regarding patients. Although I discuss how an analyst might use the greater availability of primary process material, there are a myriad of possible avenues women postpartum could explore. Obvious areas are writing, acting, visual arts, music, and business ventures, including taking a new direction in an already established profession, as more of our inner selves are available to contribute to such explorations. Similarly, although I experienced an increase of visual images regarding patients, another person might experience this in relation to musical tunes, poetry, or any number of other means of personal expression.

The example of increased creative functioning will be contrasted with a case example of a patient who, after giving birth to her daughter, entered an intense, malignant regression. Included is a discussion of her underlying vulnerability and how the alterations in ego functioning interacted with this to allow the full rage at her mother to erupt. The tumultuous working through of a spiteful, negative transference was necessary before any resolution of feelings toward the mother could be achieved. Lastly, there is a discussion of the physiological changes following giving birth and how these may interact with the psychology.

ADAPTIVE REGRESSION

Ego functions are altered as the mother cares for her infant (Domash, 1981). There is the adaptive regression to meet the infant's needs. Early memories are evoked. Many forgotten perceptions and sensations rush in from the past, as the past inevitably floods into the present. These fragments of thoughts and images contribute to an opening up, a loosening of rigid boundaries, and a lowering of the stimulus barrier. There is also the heightened kinesthetic sense from holding the child. This all allows, if the process is going well, new aspects of the mother to become assimilated and integrated.

The ability to regress in an adaptive manner includes the ability to merge momentarily, not only without fear of loss of boundaries, but as an actual sustenance to one's identity. This I see as a creative act, one that is especially required of the mother in the postpartum period but that continues throughout the mother–child relationship as part of the empathic process. This includes the complementary task of then changing focus and seeing child as unique and separate in his or her own right. It is this ability to shift in focus, the balance of which changes with each developmental stage, that is difficult but crucial in mothering. It may be a kind of ability to shift in focus that is required in many creative acts. One momentarily merges with one's subject matter in the act of creating, then steps back to objectively revise, reshape, and polish the product.

In another context, Rockwell (1985) describes this ability or type of experiencing in terms of moving from one city to another. She described an almost constant, subliminal process of scanning the environment for familiar shapes and impressions. This is the pleasure in finding the familiar in the unfamiliar. (This might be akin to the new mother seeing her own mother or father in the child and being able to take pleasure in this.) This kind of experiencing takes place in the transitional area described by Winnicott (1953) where inside and oustide are one. In this process there is both the merging with old primary identifications and separation and formation of new objects.

In the immediate postpartum period, the mother's ability to tolerate the inevitable and necessary regression will help determine how creatively or pathologically she will experience this period. She must be able to tolerate her greater awareness of primary process and embrace it. This will enhance her ability to be a good mother of symbiosis who is essentially an id mother (Kaplan, 1978). She must allow her boundaries to blur as she merges with the infant and tends to and cares for his or her body. Ease with the body and bodily sensations is crucial as is joy in physical contact. Greater access to the unconscious fosters these abilities. It also mirrors the inevitable feeling of chaos in the home environment immediately after giving birth and helps the mother tolerate it. That is, the primary process material of the mind mirrors the temporary disruption in the family environment with its strange sleeping patterns, unpredictability, need to go on hunches, conflicting messages, and demands.

I remember years ago, when I was a consultant to a neonatal intensive care unit, I was struck by what I felt was the dreamy, and at times chaotic, primary-process-like atmosphere there. I did not then appreciate that these nurses had to be in a continuous postpartum state to meet the needs of the infants, many of whom had exceptional problems. To reach the nurses in any meaningful way as a consultant, I had to try to enter this emotional atmosphere which seemed like a Fellini film and very contrary to any organized and logical approach to problems. What puzzled me then is now so clear. These women were perpetually adapting to newborn infants who were even more needing of mothering than normal, healthy babies.

IDENTIFICATION WITH ONE'S OWN MOTHER

Another important postpartum factor is the degree of positive identification with one's own mother. The extent of this resolution will crucially relate to how easily and readily the new mother accepts her role. The little girl at the end of the separation–individuation phase completes the first phase of identification with her mother where the functions of the mother are internalized, including her soothing function. This permits the firm establishment of object constancy. The second phase is at the conclusion of the Oedipus when there is an even richer identification with her sexual and relational aspects (Stoller, 1977). These developmental, as contrasted with defensive identifications, are crucial for positive female development.

The identificatory process, when moving along well, also develops a deeper appreciation of what one's own mother went through, an increased sense of forgiveness, and a wish to make reparation not only in our care of the baby but also, for the mother-therapist, in a deeper sense of dedication to our patients. There grows in the mother, as she sees how impossible it is to be a perfect mother, a greater tolerance of paradox and ambiguity which, since the unconscious consists of paradoxes, aids unconscious perception.

Problems can arise, however, at various stages of the identification process that interfere with this optimal development. Horner (1984) describes a significant impasse in feminine development called "refusal to identify," indicating those women who cannot identify with their mothers. This interferes with both the resolution of the separation–individuation process and the Oedipus complex. Its function is to protect gender identification and the ego ideal. This insufficiency is the basis for an ongoing dependency on the object and generates fears of abandonment, separation anxiety, and depression. I would add it also makes the assumption of the maternal role conflicted in the extreme. When a woman with this problem becomes a mother, her strong need *not* to identify with her own mother is immediately challenged. When the need is intense, the woman can be thrown into a state of agitation and panic. In addition, beneath her conscious refusal to identify with her mother are frequently more primitive, global identifications (incorporations or introjections) which she has repressed. These may surge forward as the personality in the postpartum period is less well defended. These may threaten to overwhelm her and she then feels even less adequate to care for her child. This situation is likely to produce a postpartum depression.

In contrast, the woman who has adequate identifications with her mother can weather the flux of this period with the solid sense of positive identification. The sex of the child may also influence the degree of pathology experienced. For example, a woman who refuses to identify with her mother may fare better with a male child than a female as she may feel less *like* her mother with a son and therefore her defense can remain partly intact.

EXAMPLE OF INCREASED PSYCHOPATHOLOGY

The case of Carol is an example of a failure in the identificatory process leading to an inability to mother and a significant depression. The patient, Carol, after the birth of her first child, a daughter, entered a protracted, malignant regression involving what I viewed as spectacular, spiteful suffering as well as an attempt to render the analyst impotent. Carol was 35 years old and had been in analysis 6 years at the time of the crisis. She had been married for 2 years when her daughter was born. Until this point, she had made steady gains both in her professional life as a writer and financial analyst and personally in her marriage. Her transference had been positive and idealized, which on the one hand sustained and strengthened her, but on the other did not allow for sufficient expression of her rage at and longing for her mother, about whom she was profoundly conflicted.

Carol began to take a tragic downslide after the birth of her daughter. A negative transference developed in which Carol attempted to "hurt" the analyst by the intensity of her suffering and refusing to "eat" or digest any of the analyst's interpretations. What emerged was a complex dynamic: intense rage at her depressed mother for not adequately caring for her as well as a subsequent inability to now be different from her depressed mother and thus risk separation from her. She felt paralyzed in this suffering state both because of an inability to separate as well as an intense guilt about any possible attempt. She had managed to suppress these conflicts in an enforced pseudo-maturity originally fostered by her mother and which had held together rather well until now.

At this point, Carol's life outside the analytic sessions was characterized by intermittent panic states during which she experienced terror, hysteria, and desperation. She was functioning only marginally in her career and had increasingly significant difficulties caring for her daughter. Suicidal thoughts were recurrent.

How did the alterations in ego functioning following childbirth affect Carol? Rather than adaptive, her regression became malignant. She could not relate empathically to her child's needs because of her own agitated depression. The sight of the infant invoked her own neediness which had gone unfulfilled. The more loosely organized state of consciousness following childbirth had then permitted the rage which had previously been well controlled to surface. She finally had her encounter with her mother, vis-à-vis the analyst. The regression became malignant in that she felt so spiteful that she attempted to cling to me in a state of intense suffering, never to improve and never to leave. She hoped to reverse the early pseudomaturity fostered by her own mother and *never* have to leave me. No forgiveness of her own mother was possible until this rage could be worked through which was the subject of many subsequent months of analysis.

In terms of an analysis of Carol's object relations, she had not successfully negotiated the separation-individuation phase and had refused to identify with her mother. As discussed by Horner (1984), it is crucial to distinguish the primary identifications of early object relations from later identifications. The former is a gross identification that serves as an ego defense against object loss. The latter refers to identification as a process leading to a change in structure of the ego. Carol had the former type of identification. She clung in a primitive way to an early identification with her suffering, depressed mother as a defense against loss. This was one aspect of her masochism, as a defense of the ego against separation (Menaker, 1953). Carol was able to eventually move from the gross early identification with her mother to the selective later identification, allowing her to adequately mother her child and successfully compete as an adult female.

Postpartum depression is a complex syndrome with some writers stressing psychological factors almost exclusively (Bental, 1965; Blum, 1978) while others investigate biological factors and the role of hormone levels (Adler & Cox, 1983; Dalton, 1971; Gelder, 1978). Many cases likely combine aspects of the psychological and the hormonal. Incidence is very hard to determine as many cases are not reported. Statistics on postpartum psychotic depression (comprising a small group of the broader category of postpartum depression) indicate only 1% based on hospital inpatient records, while in fact incidence including nonhospitalized patients is closer to 12% (Braverman & Roux, 1978).

EXAMPLE OF FACILITATION OF CREATIVITY

The following is an attempt to use the greater availability of primary process thinking in the postpartum period in my work as an analyst. To use the heightened sensitivity after childbirth, as early as the first contact with a patient, I would try (and still try) to listen in as playful a way as possible, as a child would. I take special notice of the voice, including the rapidity of speech, the rhythm, the pitch, the intonation. I try to articulate my first impression. I observe what the person wears, how he or she moves, his or her posture and facial expression, and lastly, how he or she makes me feel.

For example, shortly after I returned to work after giving birth, a woman came to see me for a consultation regarding marital problems. My initial impression was how small she was, a little like a scarecrow; but she also had an all-American, wholesome aspect with her blond-streaked hair and white-toothed smile. She sat in a prim manner, crisp and self-contained. As she discussed her marital problems, she was mocking of her husband and apparently was prone to gossip and laugh about him with her friends and was doing this now with me. Her understanding of her situation appeared startlingly superficial. Her husband has good days and bad days. Their marriage was good for a while, then bad. They were no longer communicating, but she had decided she could not raise her children alone. How could I help her "use" her husband better? Her peculiar detachment and flippant, matter-of-fact efficiency were chilling.

She induced in me an initially cynical attitude. Formerly, I might have stopped there and perhaps begun to wonder about the etiology of this. Instead, I relaxed, and let my thoughts go. Some troubling images came to me. "You don't need me, I don't need you." "Fill me up with money, I'll fill you up with answers." I felt I was being viewed as a coin-operated, psychological answering machine. Then I thought I knew how she felt with her husband. He'll fill her up with material things. She'll do mechanical things for him. Several additional sessions confirmed a lack of closeness and a superficiality (her word) in the depth of relationships in her original family, which had been replicated in her marriage.

Interestingly, this patient had other, somewhat contradictory aspects about her. She had an underlying sense of strength. She appeared organized, capable, cheerful, and fairly undefensive. She had a long marriage of 13 years, and three children. She did want to "save" the marriage. I modified my initial impression to include her strengths and lived with these different aspects of her as they became clarified in subsequent sessions. My ability to accept paradox and let the material unfold had increased.

My use of visual images regarding the patient was greatly increased in the postpartum period. That is, I relaxed, assumed a receptive attitude, and let an image of the patient come to me, as described by Hammer (1968, 1972). In the example of the patient just discussed, my image of her during the first interview was of a crumpled, slightly soiled, tan and white striped, thin dishtowel. In verbal terms this suggested to me banality, mediocrity, self-absorption, or colloquially speaking, dirty dishes and soap operas. However, I had another view of her as a piece of brilliantly colored, strong, yellow and white striped cloth, with the white stripe thickly woven and raised from the material. Is this not her efficiency at its best, its definiteness and clarity, especially when mixed with warmth and vibrancy? Here is strength and vitality under her resigned, cynical depression.

How generalizable is this tendency toward facilitation of creativity? It is logical that this period has potential for enhanced creative functioning. As mentioned, the postpartum period is a time that requires the mother to attend to nonverbal cues, including tactile and kinesthetic sensations and sensitivity to moods and feelings. Arieti (1976) described this type of communication as "endoceptual," which refers to the amorphous, private quality of it, sensed but hard to put into words. The endocept may be defined as a primitive organization of past experiences, memory traces, images of things, and of movements. These previous experiences are repressed, but continue to have an indirect influence.

The endoceptual thinking required of the mother is specifically linked to the inspirational stage of the creative process. At that time there is an openness to receiving unconscious impulses and their derivatives (Kris, 1952). There is a transient dissolving of ego boundaries; one gives oneself up to sensory perceptions.

The kind of "thinking" required may include feelings, words in primary process form, fantasies, form, shapes, textures, and colors. Spitz (1965) has stated that, for the most part, adults, with the exception of the artistically gifted, have lost the ability to use this type of perception. It would seem that this is a latent capacity which, given sufficient conditions, will be re-aroused when the new mother relates to her infant. If the mother chooses to, she can probably extend this to another activity and consciously attempt to use this state for inspiration. It is a time of increased access to unconscious processes and heightened empathy, so that certainly psychotherapeutic work (as well as many other areas) can benefit. It may be of special help to the woman who has attained a high level of proficiency in a field and can use this period to sufficiently break rigid or conventional structures to allow greater access to spontaneous or original thinking.

Related to this, the postpartum period can be a time for development of divergent thinking, in the nature of searching and readiness to pursue different directions. It is the ability to retain many hypotheses and ideas in the mind before prematurely coming to conclusions. Divergent thinking is required for creativity (Guilford, 1957; Horner, 1968). Convergent thinking, which is directed toward one right answer, is probably more typical of greater states of equilibrium than is found in the postpartum period. Therefore, even a woman who tended to be a convergent thinker might shift postpartum and begin to be able to entertain hypotheses formerly not possible. For a woman who chooses to use this capacity in her work or creative life, it can be a time of generation of ideas and ways to problem solve, applicable to many types of artistic, business, or scientific situations.

PHYSIOLOGY OF THE POSTPARTUM PERIOD

What are the physiological events that occur postpartum and how are they related to the psychological events? Whereas the physiology can be stated and some interesting correlations can be demonstrated, very little conclusive information is actually available about the relationship between the physiology and the psychology of the postpartum period.

1. How is the biology affected by the psychology and vice-versa? As an example of the former, workers in the field of behavioral endocrinology are investigating the following possibility. Paired rats are being studied as the female gives birth and the male watches. There is the suggestion that there is some sympathetic alteration in the neuroendocrine system of the male rodent, that the male's level of prolactin (the hormone which in the female assures the continuous secretion of milk) rises as he watches the female give birth. That is, his witnessing or being aware of her giving birth evokes a hormonal change. This may have implications for Lamaze training and co-parenting concepts.

2. Is there a continuum of experience possible in the postpartum period ranging from the euphoric to the painful, as researchers have demonstrated for childbirth itself (Tanzer, 1976)? Wideman and Singer (1984) in a critical review of research done on the Lamaze method suggest that the secretion of endorphins and enkephalins may be affected by the manipulation of physiological processes such as

respiration and neuromuscular responding that occur in Lamaze technique. This perhaps, in part, accounts for the more positive, at times euphoric, view Lamaze takers have toward the whole birth experience, themselves, their mates, etc.

3. That nursing provides the emotional pleasure that enhances the mother/child bond is well accepted. Does nursing also provide a physical experience of pleasure that fosters the intensely close relatedness required in this early period? In pregnancy, the placenta secretes hormones which allow the ligaments to accommodate the growing fetus. Are there biological factors in the postpartum period also that make the mind more capable of symbiotic relatedness in this early period when boundaries need to be blurred? Put simply, are there bodily correlates to the mother's psychological experience of "emotional symbiosis"?

What is the role of endorphins, the small peptides with opiate-like receptor activity localized in various areas of the brain, in the nursing experience? Is the body more sensitive or more able to produce endorphins in the postpartum period? Does the release of oxytocin stimulate endorphin production? It is known that endorphins stimulate the production of prolactin necessary for the initiation of lactation (Grandison & Guidotti, 1977). This is evidence for a link between endorphin production and lactation. Is it possible that the converse is the case also, that lactation stimulates endorphin production?

4. As a related and/or separate variable, what is the possible role of fantasy, conscious or unconscious, in the stimulation of endorphin production? Perhaps the very nature of the fantasy may have differential impact on behavior based on alteration of endorphin production. The host of conscious and unconscious fantasies in the mind of the new mother suggests this is an important variable to explore. I was not able to find any research on this point. However, work on imagery and its positive effect on healing, as reported by Simonton & Matthews-Simonton (1975), for example, suggests that guided imaging has physiological consequences.

The nursing experience will be considered in detail because, in this author's opinion, the pleasure experienced from it, on both the emotional and physiological level, likely contributes to the mother's ability to enter a "blissful" experience with her child and is therefore more likely to provide the good symbiosis necessary in the first months of life. It is interesting that the rule of thumb is a 6-month period of nursing to get maximal nutritional benefit. There may be great bodily wisdom in that this corresponds to the time when mother and child should be in a state of close union, a metaphorical and physical symbiosis. The role of endorphin stimulation in nursing needs further investigation. Is the body more sensitive to endorphin production in this period to help the mother enter the necessary ego state? As mentioned, it is known that endorphins stimulate the production of prolactin necessary for the initiation of lactation.

What happens physiologically during the nursing experience? Both oxytocin and prolactin are important in lactation, prolactin probably more for the initiation of lactation and oxytocin for its maintenance. The milk ejection reflex is a neurohormonal mechanism regulated in part by CNS factors. Suckling triggers the discharge of oxytocin from the posterior pituitary gland that is carried to the breast in the blood. Oxytocin acts on the myoepithelial cells around the alveoli, causing them to contract, and thus pushing out the milk into larger ducts where it is more easily available to the baby. When nursing is initiated, a prompt and short-lasting release of prolactin occurs. Prolactin is a protein hormone secreted in the anterior pituitary gland. Numerous hormonal and neuropharmacologic factors influence the secretion of prolactin, including endorphins.

The physical responses of the mother to this, unless there is a serious interference, is pleasurable. As pointed out by Newton and Newton (1950), the survival of the human race, long before the concept of duty evolved, depended on satisfactions gained from two voluntary acts of reproduction, coitus and breast feeding. These had to be sufficiently pleasurable to ensure their frequent occurrence. In fact, the physiological responses during coitus and lactation are allied. Uterine contractions occur during nursing (Moir, 1934) and sexual excitement (Kinsey and others, 1953). Nipple erection occurs in both (Newton, 1958; Masters, 1960). Milk ejection has been observed to occur in some women during sexual excitement and the degree of excitement is related to the degree of ejection (Campbell and Peterson, 1953). Extensive breast stimulation is involved in breast feeding and breast stimulation alone can induce orgasm in some women (Kinsey et al., 1953). Emotions aroused by both sexual excitement and breast feeding involve skin changes. Sexual excitement causes marked vascular changes in the skin (Masters, 1960). Nursing raises body temperature in mammary and submammary skin areas (Abolins, 1954). The baby, too, appears aroused. The reactions are more clearly observable in older babies whose total body shows signs of eagerness (Newton and Newton, 1967). There are rhythmic motions of the hands, feet, fingers, and toes. Erection of the penis is common in male babies. After feeding, there is a relaxation that is characteristic of the conclusion of satisfactory sexual activity. This sensuous enjoyment is likely to increase the baby's desire to suckle his mother frequently and thus stimulate the secretion of milk. It would seem that this physiologic experience of pleasure would help the mother enter the necessary calm, blissful state required to provide optimal physical and emotional symbiosis.

Aside from the nursing experience, what are the major hormonal and physiological adjustments postpartum? During pregnancy the levels of estrogen, progesterone, and prolactin all rise to many times higher than prepregnancy levels. In addition, human placental lactogen is being produced. Immediately after birth, the levels of estrogen, progesterone, and human placental lactogen fall. The secretion of prolactin continues (with a short, brief drop immediately after birth) which is important in the stimulation of milk production.

There are numerous additional anatomic and physiologic readjustments (Monheit, Cousins, & Resnik, 1980). There are major changes in the cardiovascular system, including an enormous loss of fluid affecting all the hormones which regulate salt and water balance. This includes a decrease in blood volume and in cardiac output. Heart rate, blood pressures, and oxygen consumption are also affected. These parameters return to prepregnancy levels 6 weeks postpartum. Similarly the marked changes that occurred in the urinary tract, adrenal gland, liver, and reproductive tract also return to basal pregnancy levels.

There is the resumption of cyclicity, menstruation, and the secretion of the neurohypophyseal hormones which regulate sex hormone production and ovulation. If the mother is nursing, this is usually delayed. Nursing itself involves the secretion of two additional hormones, oxytocin and prolactin.

In some of these instances there may be a rebound effect, that is, a mechanism was turned "off" during pregnancy, and then when turned "on", overshoots the mark. For one, the placenta may produce steroids which suppress certain adrenal cortical steroids. The removal of the suppressive effect could also cause a rebound in excessive production of potentially psychosis-inducing steroids, producing a kind of hypomania and excitement. Another rebound effect occurs because during pregnancy there is greater carbohydrate absorption because of the utilization of fuels by the placenta. Afterwards carbohydrates are harder to absorb, possibly producing greater states of awareness. Possibly either of these two rebound effects, in small degrees, might lead to states of heightened awareness or a feeling of being "high"which was a component of what I was describing in my postpartum experience working with patients.

The emotional effects of many of these changes are not yet known and/or perhaps can occur in so many permutations that it is hard to generalize. A related finding is that excessive prolactin is associated with depression in the postpartum period (Jones and Jones, 1981). Prolactin is secreted in large amounts during periods of stress and non-Rem sleep, possibly the type of sleep a mother might experience from waking up many times a night with a difficult infant. However, although the correlation has been found between excessive prolactin and postpartum depression, it is hard to know if it is merely a correlation or a causative factor.

This shared phenomena of loosening defensive structures and increased availability of primary process thinking gives us an important potential both for sensitive caretaking of our children and of extending this to other areas as well. Previously the link had not been made from creative parenting to creative endeavors elsewhere. For example, Winnicott (1956) in discussing primary maternal preoccupation makes it seem like a "psychosis" of limited duration (several weeks) suggesting initial and complete absorption with the child, probably a merger phenomenon, which then abruptly ends. He clearly states how rich and creative this experience is for the child, without which he is irreversibly damaged. Yet this rich resource that the mother has available to her, this ability to create emotional life, is portrayed as if it is a time-limited and possibly psychotic-like experience. Rather, I would emphasize that it is a capacity that the new mother has, that she continues to have it at least for the first year, although in gradually attenuated form. From this, she can deepen her creative capacities in general, both in regard to her child and also in regard to other activities.

How can a woman protect herself from being flooded by this primary process material? In addition to her knowledge that the regression is a universal phenomenon, it is crucial for the new mother to structure time for herself apart from the baby so as to allow "space for the ego". This will strengthen her ability to flexibly enter and leave transitional space. However, the traversing of the postpartum period ultimately depends on how accepting we are of our mother in ourselves, awareness of which will naturally intensify after giving birth. The degree to which we can selectively and creatively choose identifications, rather than globally incorporate all aspects, including those we do not want, will decide how comfortable we are with this greater sensitivity postpartum. It is those women who have been fleeing from identification with their mother and denying their attachment most of their lives who comprise one of the groups most vulnerable to postpartum depression.

References

Abolins, J. A. (1954). Das stillen und die temperatur der brust. *Acta Obstetricia et Gynecologica Scandinavica, 33,* 60–68.

Adler, E. M. & Cox, J. L. (1983). Breast feeding and post-natal depression. *Journal of Psychosomatic Research, 27,* 139–144.

Arieti, S. (1976). *Creativity: The magic synthesis,* New York: Basic Books.

Bental, V. (1965). Psychic mechanisms of the adoptive mother in connection with adoption. *Israel Annals of Psychiatry, 3,* 24–34.

Blum, H. (1978). Reconstruction in a case of postpartum depression. *Psychoanalytic Study of the Child, 33,* 335–362.

Bond, A. H. (1984). Virginia Woolf: Manic-depressive psychosis and genius. An illustration of separation–individuation theory. *Journal of the American Academy of Psychoanalysis, 13,* 191–210.

Braverman, J., & Roux, J. F. (1978). Screening for the patient at risk for postpartum depression. *Obstetrics and Gynecology, 56,* 731.

Campbell, B., & Petersen, W. E. (1953). Milk let-down and orgasm in the human female. *Human Biology, 25,* 165–168.

Dalton, K. (1971). Prospective study into puerperal depression. *British Journal of Psychiatry, 118,* 689–692.

Domash, L. (1981). Facilitating the creativity of the psychotherapist. *The Arts in Psychotherapy, 8,* 157–163.

Gelder, M. (1978). Hormones and postpartum depression. In M. J. Sandler (Ed.), *Mental illness in pregnancy and puerperium.* London: Oxford University Press.

Guilford, J. P. (1957). Creative abilities in the arts. *Psychology Review, 64,* 110–118.

Grandison, L., & Guidotti, A. (1977). Regulation of prolactin release by endogenous opiates. *Nature, 270,* 357–359.

Hammer, E. F. (1968). *Use of interpretation in treatment technique and art.* New York: Grune & Stratton.

Hammer, E. F. (1972). The creative process in treatment. *Journal of Contemporary Psychotherapy, 4:*81–86.

Horner, A. (1968). Genetic aspects of creativity. In C. Buhler and J. Massarik (Eds.), *The course of human life* (pp. 123–139). New York, Springer.

Horner, A. (1984). *Object relations and the developing ego in therapy,* 2nd ed. New York: Jason Aronson.

Jones, H. W., & Jones, G. S. (1981). *Novak's textbook of gynecology,* 10th ed. (p. 52). Baltimore: Williams & Wilkins.

Kaplan, L. (1978). *Oneness and separateness: From infant to individual.* New York: Simon & Schuster.

Karlsson, J. L. (1968). Geneologic studies of schizophrenia. In D. Rosenthal and S. Kely (Eds.), *The Transmission of Schizophrenia.* Oxford, England: Pergamon Press.

Kinsey, A. B., Pomeroy, W. B., Martin, C. E. & Gebhard, P. H. (1953). Sex behavior in the human female. By staff of Institute for Sex Research, Indiana University. Philadelphia: W. B. Saunders.

Kris, E. (1952). On preconscious mental processes. In *Psychoanalytic explorations in art.* New York: International Universities Press.

Masters, W. H. (1960). Sexual response cycle of human female. *Western Journal Surgery, 68,* 57–75.

Menaker, E. (1953). Masochism: a defense reaction of the ego. *Psychoanalytic Quarterly, 22,* 205–220.

Moir, C. (1934). Recording the contractions of human pregnant and non-pregnant uterus. *Transactions of the Edinburgh Obstetrical Society, 54,* 93–120.

Monheit, A. G., Cousins, L., & Resnik, R. (1980). The puerperium: anatomic and physiologic readjustments. *Clinical Obstetrics and Gynecology, 23,* 973–984.

Newton, N. (1958). Influence of let-down reflex in breast feeding on mother/child relationship. *Marriage and Family Living, 20,* 18–20.

Newton, N. & Newton, M. (1950). Relationship of ability to breast feed and maternal attitudes towards breast feeding. *Pediatrics, 5,* 869–875.

Newton, N., & Newton, M. (1967). Psychologic aspects of lactation. *New England Journal of Medicine, 277,* 1179–1187.

Rockwell, S. (1985). Illusion and identity: The Wordsworthian experience of merging as sustenance for identity. Meetings of the Division of Psychoanalysis of the American Psychological Association, New York, April.

Spitz, R. (1965). *The first year of life.* New York: International Universities Press.

Stoller, R. (1977). Primary femininity. In H. Blum (Ed.), *Female psychology* (pp. 59–78). New York: International Universities Press.

Tanzer, D. (1976). *Why natural childbirth?* New York: Schocken Books.

Wideman, M. V., & Singer, J. E. (1984). The role of psychological mechanisms in preparation for childbirth. *American Psychologist, 39,* 1357–1371.

Winnicott, D. W. (1953). Transitional objects and transitional phenomena. In *Playing and reality* (pp. 1–30). New York: Penguin, 1980.

Winnicott, D. W. (1956). Primary maternal preoccupation. In *Through paediatrics to psychoanalysis* (pp. 300–305). New York: Basic Books, 1958.

Chapter 10

The Nursing Experience
A Clinical Study

MARY BETH M. CRESCI

The woman's experience of breast-feeding her infant is a natural extension of two other profound female experiences: pregnancy and childbirth. These three interrelated functions, the capacities to bear children, to bring them into the world, and to provide the newborn with life-sustaining nutriment, are reproductive capacities limited to the female sex. They are all creative processes in the original meaning of that term, since without them the basic genetic unit formed by a man and woman at the moment of conception would be unable to develop into a growing fetus, a newborn infant, and a healthy child. Thus, these capacities are essential to the creation and maintenance of new life and the preservation of our species.

To some extent, all of these processes have been altered, and in some cases significantly distorted, by social pressures and advances in medical technology. While we are far from the society pictured in *Brave New World* in which mothers have become obsolete and the test-tube baby has no bond with a loving, caring parent, we have seen significant changes in all three of these reproductive capacities in earlier societies and most particularly in the last 50 years as social and medical advances have occurred so rapidly in our own society. It is now technically possible for another woman to bear the potential mother's embryo, in instances in which the mother herself cannot physically withstand the stress of pregnancy. In spite of a recent emphasis on natural childbirth, the use of various analgesics and anesthesias and the dramatic increase in the use of caesarian section have altered the experience of childbirth for many women, making it no longer a consciously experienced, cooperative effort between the mother, the child, and the medical professional.

Probably the reproductive aspect most affected by social change and medical advances has been the mother's decision to breast-feed or bottle-feed her baby. In earlier times, mothers had few alternatives to nursing their child. Wet nurses were

MARY BETH M. CRESCI, PH.D. • Faculty, Senior Supervisor, and Assistant Director of Training, The Psychoanalytic Institute, Postgraduate Center for Mental Health, New York City; Supervisor, National Institute for the Psychotherapies; Board member, Faculty, Supervisor, Brooklyn Institute for Psychotherapy; private practice.

available to the wealthy, but generally a child whose mother could not nurse was much less likely to survive. However, during the past 50 years, factors have combined to discourage women from nursing their babies. Several social trends have minimized the woman's role as a nursing mother, whether it be the emphasis on the woman's breast as a sexual allurement combined with the belief that breast-feeding ruins the shape of the breast or the new acceptance of women working outside the home in settings where access to the baby throughout the day for the purposes of breast-feeding is not facilitated. The technological advance that made these social changes possible was the development of prepared baby formulas which closely approximate the known components of breast milk. These trends were sufficiently successful in encouraging women to forego breast-feeding that, in 1955, a national survey showed that only 29.9% of mothers breast-fed their 1 week-old infants, while in 1970, the figure was an even lower 24.9% (Ross National Mothers Survey MR 77-48, 1981). When it is further realized that there is a dramatic decline from the number of babies breast-fed at 1 week to the number breast-fed at 1 to 6 months of age, it is evident that these already low figures for 1-week-old babies are indicative of a much lower rate for older infants. For instance, a 1975 study reported by Foman (Lawrence, 1985) showed that 20% of the babies were breast-fed at the 2 to 3-month interval while only 5% were breast-fed at the 5 to 6-month interval. Clearly, in the middle years of this century, the great majority of babies were either not breast-fed at all or not breast-fed for any significant period of time.

The last 10 years have seen a significant shift away from bottle-feeding and back toward nursing (Bentovin, 1976; Brown et al., 1960; Buxbaum, 1979; Committee on Nutrition, 1976; Entwisle et al., 1982; Gunther, 1976; Hatcher, 1982). Again, social and medical trends have combined to make this new direction popular. The medical issue has been the finding that breast milk has immunological and other properties that are not available from formula (Lawrence, 1985). There has also been an emphasis on the importance of early bonding of mother and child (Kennell & Klaus, 1979), and nursing has been seen as a means of encouraging physical closeness which strengthens the emotional bond between mother and child. The demographic data thus show a rise from the low of 24.9% in 1970 of 1-week-old babies who were breast-fed to 49.7% in 1979 and 56.4% in 1981. The data further indicate that this change to breast-feeding is most evident among educated and middle-class mothers, although the duration of breast-feeding is contracted by the mother's return to work.

I do not intend to suggest that breast-feeding is essential for the healthy growth of a child or for the development of a close attachment between mother and child. Breast-feeding is certainly only one among many factors in determining the health of the child and the quality of maternal care. Rather, I consider the issue of the nursing experience among women who do choose it, thus making it an important developmental task in their adult life.

Becoming a mother and nursing are profound experiences that dramatically affect the life of the woman. The woman's ability to tolerate the many new demands and to enjoy and benefit from the many new experiences of this role are of great importance in her own psychological and emotional development. The experiences of childbearing and nursing can be seen both as a developmental crisis whose outcome reflects capacities and difficulties that are already present in the mother-to-be and as a new opportunity to reassess and redefine old patterns of behavior and understanding. In so doing, the new mother, sometimes consciously but frequently unconsciously, inevitably reexamines her own experience as a child, particularly her experience of being mothered. She then chooses for herself, often unconsciously, a role that incorporates much of that experience but that may also attempt to be different in some respects. Thus, for most women the successes they believe they have achieved and do achieve in creating a healthy, happy baby throughout the mothering process are vital to their identity as women and as complete human beings. The nursing experience for many women is an integral part of the process of consolidating the woman's self-identity as a successful mother.

THE WOMAN'S EXPERIENCE: THEORETICAL

What are the developmental issues that the nursing mother is reassessing and redefining from her own personal history? The psychoanalytic literature is not as helpful in this area as one might hope. Freud (1925) did not see the little girl's development as being profoundly influenced by her awareness that she would one day be able to be pregnant, have children, and nurse them from her own breasts. He did not view these capacities as being significant in their own right but only as substitute gratifications that could in some way compensate the little girl for not having a penis. Thus, her awareness of the lack of a penis and her envy of the father's penis were the primary experiences, while the capacity to have a child was seen as the best means at the little girl's disposal to capture a penis in the form of a baby, particularly a boy child. The mothering capacity had little value of its own.

Freud (1905) focused on nursing as a primary experience mostly in terms of the infant's early experience of orality. He suggested that the child's need for food was a self-preservative drive which compelled the child to move from an initial state of primary narcissism and autoerotism (i.e., nondifferentiation of self and others and gratification through hallucination and self-stimulation) to a relationship with the first part-object, the breast. This oral-dependent relationship was called anaclitic because the child's hunger drive, which was a basic need, provided the occasion for the first object-related component of the sexual drive, namely, oral pleasure through sucking and biting, to develop. This aspect of Freud's theory assumes that a nursing relationship exists between mother and infant. However, it does not focus on the quality of the actual relationship between the mother and child from the child's perspective, nor does it consider the meaning of this experience for the mother herself.

Some later psychoanalytic theories placed greater emphasis on the child's experience of the mother during early development. Melanie Klein (1957) saw the child's oral hunger as the basis of the envy and greed that the child develops for the many products the mother's body contains, including babies and penises in her womb and milk in her breasts. Other object-relation theorists saw the child as being object-seeking by nature. They focused on satisfactions in the early feeding situation as a prototype for experiencing self and other. Reference is made to the "good breast" or "bad breast" depending on whether or not the infant feels sated and content.

Winnicott (1975) refers to the mother–infant dyad as a "nursing couple," pointing out that there is no such thing as an infant apart from its relationship with its mother. He assumes that the mother will nurse and suggests that the infant's experience will be qualitatively different in unknown ways if the baby is bottle-fed. Winnicott includes the suggestion that the mother requires considerable support from her husband and others in her environment if she is to maintain this "primary maternal preoccupation," which is so necessary for the child's healthy development.

Interestingly, in spite of the significance given to the mother–infant relationship and the nursing experience in particular, little emphasis is given even in these theories to the mother's experience during the mothering and nursing process. This lack of emphasis on the mother herself reflects a general bias away from considering issues of development beyond the stages of early childhood.

More recently, there has been an increasing interest in the literature in understanding female development on its own merits rather than as a variant of male development. Stoller (1976), for instance, suggests that the development of femininity in young girls be divided into two phases. He sees the first phase as one of "primary femininity" which is not conflictual in nature and focuses on self-identification as a female and a desire to look like a female. The second phase, the result of Oedipal conflict, "produces a richer femininity, not merely one of appearances, but one enriched by desires to perform with the substance, rather than just the facade, of femininity" (p. 77). This substantive femininity would include the desire and capacity to be a mother and to have and to rear children. In this theory, then, the female reproductive capacities become significant goals in their own right, rather than as a substitute for the penis. The theory does not, however, explain how or why the later, conflictual Oedipal stage fosters the trend toward a "substantive" femininity.

There have also been a few psychoanalytic studies of pregnancy and the early mother–child relationship from the point of view of the adult woman. Bibring, Dwyer, Huntington, & Valenstein (1961) studied the personality changes undergone during pregnancy. They concluded that pregnancy is both a developmental crisis and an essential part of growth which must "precede and prepare maturational integration." They describe "the core of the adjustive task" of pregnancy as the resolution of the pregnant woman's relationship to her own mother. They say that,

> Pregnancy seems to affect this relationship in a characteristic way. . . . It's as if the attitudes in this relationship established as solutions of childhood experiences are abandoned and replaced by various new forms of identification with their mother. . . . In the case of successful maturation they develop into a conflict-free, useful identification with the mother as the prototype of a parental figure (p. 18).

Another aspect of development that Bibring et al. identify during pregnancy is the movement from a phase of "enhanced narcissism" early in pregnancy in which the baby is seen primaryily as a narcissistic part of the self to the moment of quickening when the baby begins to be seen as a "new object within the self." They describe a healthy resolution of this aspect of pregnancy as having

> the distinctive characteristics of a freely changeable fusion—varying in degree and intensity—of narcissistic and object-libidinal strivings, so that the child will always remain part of herself, and at the same time will always have to remain an object that is part of the outside world and part of her sexual mate (p. 22).

Bibring et al. also conclude that these developmental tasks are not completed when the mother gives birth but rather get resolved slowly as the child itself develops within the family unit.

There are, in addition, a few studies that consider the psychological effect of nursing itself on the mother (Kauffman, 1979; Newton, 1955; Watson, 1949). While rejecting the bonding-attachment theory of Kennell and Klaus, Brody (1981) does suggest that the early nursing experience has a considerable value for the new mother. She suggests that it helps to maintain the mother's relatedness to the newborn, thereby augmenting the mother's body pleasure and self-esteem.

Several authors have also considered some of the reason for women's failures and difficulties with breast-feeding. Lerner (1974, 1979) found that many of her female patients who began nursing their babies received unsupportive, ambivalent messages from their husbands and mothers. Lerner suggested that the woman's success at nursing emphasized the accomplishments of the woman and inadvertently tipped the balance in the marital relationship from one in which the woman was the dependent partner to one in which the husband felt threatened by her mothering capacities (see also Waletsky, 1979). There were also subtle messages from the new mother's own mother that suggested the mother was jealous of her daughter's accomplishments. In response, the new mother began to have difficulties with nursing and considered giving it up.

Lerner's data suggest that both men and women hold an image of their own mother as an extremely powerful mother on whom their survival depended in childhood. Thus, the nursing mother is challenging her own mother's omnipotent position and possibly incurring her wrath and destructiveness. In addition, the husband whose wife is nursing may fear and envy his wife for her creative capacities, thus renewing childhood conflicts in his case as well. To avoid being overwhelmed with envy and fear of his wife's resemblance to his own powerful mother, the husband may unconsciously attempt to undermine his wife's success in nursing. These data suggest that both the genetic factor of early childhood experience and the mediating factor of the present-day husband–wife relationship are important in enabling the new mother to have a pleasurable, successful nursing experience.

In conclusion, we are now moving away from the original psychoanalytic hypothesis which subsumed a little girl's interest in becoming a mother under the primary importance of penis envy. We instead postulate the desire to become a mother as having a primary importance of its own and as having nonconflictual origins, based on identifications with the mother and experiences of being mothered, as well as conflictual origins, such as Oedipal competition with the mother. In addition, pregnancy, childbirth, and nursing are important aspects of adult femininity which provide developmental opportunities of their own. They give the adult woman the opportunity to feel competent as a woman with a well-functioning body and the capacity to care for another. To successfully complete these new tasks, the woman will most likely have to rework and integrate issues from previous developmental stages. Success in nursing, for instance, may arouse the new mother's fear of challenging her own mother's omnipotent imago and of provoking a retaliatory destructiveness from her mother. The woman's nursing capacity may also arouse the husband's fear of her mothering capacities and thus cause him to be unsupportive of her. These problems interfere with successful resolution of the woman's mothering experience.

CASE STUDY

The developmental tasks and opportunities related to childbearing and the nursing experience were dramatically illustrated to me by an analytic patient who became a mother and nursed her child within the same time period that I also had a child and nursed him. The intricacy of experiences which the conjunction of these events produced allowed us to work in the analysis on a number of themes in an intense manner, themes that are often represented in analysis in a more symbolic or derivative form. In the process, the meaning and importance of the nursing experience was underscored, both as experienced by the infant and by the mother.

Ms. R., a married, overweight school teacher in her mid-thirties, had been referred to me for analysis at a time when she was experiencing considerable difficulties in her marriage and her professional development. She had seen a male analyst for several years in her early twenties, but this time she had specifically requested a female analyst, something she had feared in the past. She seemed to think that working with a woman would be more difficult but possibly also more helpful than working with a man because she expected it to arouse more directly the mixture of love–hate feelings she experienced toward her mother. An initial defensive view of women as weaker, more emotional, and less analytic than men was soon superseded by an intense focus on me as a woman who could choose to be supportive and loving or rejecting and cruel.

Ms. R. was an only child born of working-class parents. She described her father as a withdrawn, noncommunicative man who remained uninvolved with her care and upbringing. While she admired her father's ability to distance himself from his domineering wife, she resented the fact that he withdrew and left her feeling defenseless against her mother's attacks.

In contrast, Ms. R. described her mother as extremely intrusive and volatile, capable of physical violence and verbal abuse. Ms. R. considered her connection to her mother to be so fragile and yet so important for her survival that any sign of independence would sever this connection and would most assuredly kill one or both of them. Though she suffered from abuses in the relationship, Ms. R. feared even more the moments when her mother seemed to withdraw from her altogether.

Ms. R.'s present-day obesity suggested a history of conflicts regarding feeding. This proved to be the case. Ms. R. was nursed by her mother for only a few days after birth because the hospital staff told her mother that she was not gaining weight properly. Ms. R. remembered first being offered food and then being criticized for overeating. A good example was her memory from the age of 8 years of being given some money to buy a snack while in a cafeteria with her mother. She chose apple pie and a soft drink. When she returned to the table, she was severely criticized by her mother for choosing fattening foods. Her mother asserted that a normal child would have bought healthy snacks, such as an apple and milk. Ms. R. felt, indeed, that her greediness made her abnormal and unlovable and thus explained why her mother so frequently criticized and rejected her.

A particularly significant pattern in the relationship between Ms. R. and her mother, one which is somewhat evident in the above-mentioned example, was the mother's tendency to encourage Ms. R. in pursuing ambitious, even unrealistic, goals or desires, only to dash her hopes completely in a cruel, sadistic fashion. One poignant example was Ms. R.'s great desire at about age 12 to have a pony as a birthday gift. On her birthday she was first given as a gift an accessory which Ms. R. believed to be saddle bags for a pony, but she was presented with a bicycle instead.

An even more long-term and sustaining ambition was Ms. R.'s desire from an early age to become a doctor. Her mother had agreed that she could become a doctor and assisted her in collecting a large stack of medical school catalogues which Ms. R. browsed through regularly. Ms. R. was a good student in high school. However, when she approached her mother in her senior year about applying to college, she was told that the family had no money to send her to college and that she would have to go to work when she graduated. This disappointment was very disorienting for Ms. R. who had organized herself so completely around the goal of becoming a doctor. She went into a severe depression shortly after leaving high school and was hospitalized briefly. Eventually, she entered analysis, worked and attended school at night, and obtained a teaching credential.

At the time Ms. R. began her analysis with me, she had been married for several years to a man who was a successful professional. While the relationship was basically stable, Ms. R. tended to experience her husband as withdrawn and unavailable, and she often saw this withdrawal as sadistically motivated. She assumed that he found her unlovable and purposely shunned her. She tried at times to break through his withdrawn state by being warm and maternal, but these efforts made her feel as though she was doing all the giving and getting little in return.

As this time Ms. R. was also trying to recover from a devastating career setback in which she had not received tenure in her teaching position. She felt her work had not been properly appreciated by her superiors because of personality conflicts in which she had unwittingly become embroiled. She was struggling to find a more satisfactory position.

Treatment

During her first year of analysis, Ms. R. made positive strides in finding a job and in resolving her marital difficulties. Our primary focus in the treatment was on her transferential wishes to be completely supported, appreciated, and understood by me, wishes that she felt were being frequently undermined by behaviors on my part that she interpreted as showing a lack of interest and commitment toward her. As we explored her swings in mood, she became increasingly aware that she had a fantasy of being merged with me as the "good mommy," which was interfered with whenever I acted in ways that she considered antithetical to her needs or wishes. With this patient, "empathic failures" were common, and the self-object transference which often operates as a silent aspect of the treatment (Stolorow & Lachmann, 1986) was for her a prominent feature. Any disruption resulted in substantial fragmentation of her fragile sense of self.

Early in the treatment, Ms. R. had expressed a strong wish to have a child. She had as yet not gotten pregnant, and she imagined that this was related to the emotional conflicts in her marital relationship. She reasoned that in such an unpromising emotional climate it would be very difficult for herself or her husband to be fertile. She took it as a sign that their relationship was improving when she did get pregnant about a year after she began analysis.

Ms. R. greatly enjoyed her pregnancy. She felt she now had an excuse for being overweight and actually gained hardly any additional weight during the pregnancy. She felt fulfilled as a woman and also quite literally "filled up" with something good, namely, the baby. She saw herself in many ways as a bountiful earth-mother full of good things to nurture the ultimate goodness, the baby. She also felt a sense of unity and merger with this new life-force within her. She made plans to go on maternity leave from her job during the last few months of the pregnancy and found a part-time teaching position at a local college which she would assume a few months after the baby's birth.

During the last few months of the pregnancy, a number of problems arose. Ms. R. had some symptoms related to toxemia, which did not ultimately prove dangerous but shook her view of herself as a perfect childbearing mother. Then, shortly before the delivery date, her husband was in a car accident and suffered a severe whiplash which incapacitated him for several weeks. The delivery itself was more stressful than Ms. R. had imagined. After a long period of labor that was not progressing, she agreed to a Caesarian section. She was unconscious during the delivery. When she awoke she learned that the baby was a healthy girl. Ms. R. was extremely disappointed that the child was not a boy. Given the nature of the delivery procedure, she felt cheated of experiencing the birth. She fantasized that the baby she was given was not actually hers but a substitute for a boy baby she had really delivered.

Most importantly, Ms. R. experienced the delivery as a forcible taking from her of the wonderful baby she had possessed within her body. The delivery had interrupted the sense of perfect merger she was experiencing and produced a separate child instead. Thus, in many senses she experienced the delivery and birth of her baby as a separation and loss rather than an accomplishment and an addition to her life.

The nursing experience was a substantial compensation to Ms. R. for the loss of the internal baby. She again felt closely connected to her child and extremely pleased that she could provide her daughter with food and love. The baby thrived, and Ms. R.'s confidence in her capacities as a woman and mother were restored. The rupture in the unity between mother and child, which the process of birth had produced, seemed to have been repaired. A disquieting factor was that Ms. R. found nursing painful on one breast because of an inverted nipple, but this fact was minimized in the light of the pleasure at having so much to give her baby.

About 2 months after the baby was born, Ms. R. began her new part-time teaching job. The job proved to be much more demanding than she had anticipated, badly shaking her fragile sense of professional competence. In addition, the experience of being separated from her baby was quite traumatic. Ms. R. felt as though a part of her was missing when she was separated from her daughter. Additionally, she now had to deal with her mother's criticism of her mothering skills when the mother came to care for the baby in her absence. On the one hand, Ms. R. worried that her mother would neglect the child and, on the other, she was quite sensitive to criticisms her mother made about the baby and herself. The presence of the mother made Ms. R. feel that she was losing her importance as the primary mother figure and that the strong connection between her and the baby was again in danger of rupture.

The combined stresses of job and motherhood, often unacknowledged in the attempt to feel supremely capable in both areas, eventually resulted in a delusional state in which Ms. R. feared that her baby was dead. In compensation she imagined that she was herself a baby and I was her new perfect mother. A brief period of hospitalization resulted during which Ms. R. became stabilized with medication and supportive therapy.

Following her discharge, Ms. R. was able to make a slow but steady recovery. However, one of the damaging results of the hospitalization was that the nursing was interrupted and was not able to be resumed despite Ms. R.'s best efforts to do so. Although she was still producing milk, the baby had become used to a bottle and was no longer interested in nursing. It was quite a narcissistic injury to Ms. R. to feel that her maternal gifts were being rejected by her baby. In her eyes, another serious blot had been placed on her capacities as a woman.

The months following the hospitalization were very crucial for the analysis as well as for Ms. R.'s recovery of her self-esteem as a mother and worker. She had been able to experience my concern and support during the period of the hospitalization, but she felt a loss of trust in my ability to take care of her because I had not prevented the breakdown itself. I had, in fact, not recognized how disoriented she was becoming in such a short period of time. I was subsequently much more aware of early signs that she was feeling overwhelmed by a sense of inadequacy and lack of support. By arranging for medication and a temporary leave of absence from her part-time work at a critical time, Ms. R. was able to avoid further hospitalization in the next several years. Ms. R. continued to be anxious about her mothering capacities toward her daughter, specifically with regard to the fact that her daughter preferred the bottle to solid food. However, Ms. R. was increasingly able to enjoy her daughter and to receive pleasure from her daughter's growth and development.

Many issues regarding her own self-regard as a mother and underlying feelings of unsatisfied needs as a child came to a head when Ms. R. discovered that I was pregnant about 6 months after the birth of her child. It is not uncommon for a therapist's pregnancy to call up feelings that the patient experienced both as a child and as a new parent herself, and such was certainly the case with Ms. R. A brief period of pleasure in our "sisterhood" in sharing the mothering experience was followed quite rapidly by a variety of angry, hostile feelings. One source of these feelings was a sense of sibling rivalry that Ms. R. felt with my baby. She felt that she had lost a fantasized unique position as my only child and that I would inevitably take time and attention away from her to devote to the new baby. The fact that I was planning to take a 6-week maternity leave after the baby was born served to corroborate her feelings of abandonment. These feelings of anxiety that I would abandon her were indicative of the concerns we had been discussing already regarding any interruption that Ms. R. experienced in the treatment. Now these feelings became quite focused on the pregnancy and my nursing capacities of which she was deprived since she was not actually my child.

Another disturbing aspect was that Ms. R. fantasized that my capacities as a mother were greater than hers. She imagined that I would have a better experience of childbirth than she had had and that my child would be a boy. Thus, in addition to feeling envious of the baby in regard to the amount of nurturance and attention it would receive from me, she also felt directly competitive with me in my role as a woman and mother.

All of these themes were very dramatically played out in regard to my nursing experience. Ms. R. was anxious to learn if I was indeed nursing my baby. On the one hand, my ability to nurse signified to Ms. R. that I was a good mother and would, therefore, have nurturing supplies to offer her, as well. On the other hand, this meant that my baby was receiving better mothering than she had received as a child. Additionally, she was concerned that my ability to nurse signified that I was being a better mother than she was being and that I was enjoying the experience much more than she had.

Ms. R.'s ability to consciously experience these feelings and work them through with me in her analysis proved to be very growth producing. Some time after she had stopped nursing her own baby and while I was still pregnant, she began to fantasize that she was a baby nursing from me. She would imagine that she could have warm, loving, pleasurable sessions in which everything was peaceful and no adult cares or past conflicts would interfere. She resented any interpretations from me almost regardless of their content because they interfered with her imagined state of oneness with me. She considered my silence to be a reflection of the fact that we were in harmony with one another and understood each other intuitively. She would comment on the quiet and tranquility in my office and be reluctant to discuss problems that might be bothering her because they would ruin the perfect mood that had been created. Both during the sessions and between sessions she would imagine that she was a little baby, nursing at my breast and "slurping milk" from me.

These moments of perfect bliss and unity were cruelly interrupted, in Ms. R.'s eyes, by the fact that the session had an end. Ms. R. focused her anger and frustration particularly on the breaks in treatment, both for summer vacation and for maternity leave. However, even though her anger was focused on these extended moments of abandonment, Ms. R. actually went through a similar crisis each week as we approached the last session of the week and were to have a 3-day break in the treatment. These weekly cycles produced considerable feelings of loss and abandonment which were displayed in terms of panicky feelings between sessions. Ms. R. would then call me full of anxiety and wanting the reassurance of hearing my voice. Although I kept the conversation brief, she felt pleased that I had been available to her and felt that I did care about her.

Interpreting the issues related to Ms. R.'s panicky feelings did not at first seem to help. We did take some additional steps, such as arranging for a psychiatric consultation for backup medication, and Ms. R. did recognize that she was attempting to hold onto me as a "good mother" throughout the week, including between sessions. Her anger, as well as her fear, was very high around the aforementioned vacation periods. There was an effort to arrange coverage for her, but her feelings of being abandoned and of being unimportant to me were such that she could not accept help very easily from others. These were substantial narcissistic blows which could only be partially alleviated by my understanding and interpretations and limited availability by phone.

When we resumed analysis after the birth of my child, the nursing fantasies were pervasive. The need to feel at one with me was quite strong. Yet, there were soon some gradual shifts in the transference and the content of the material. At this time, Ms. R. was involved in a difficult job situation in which she was being evaluated to move from a temporary to a permanent teaching position. In addition, her husband's company was merging and his position was threatened. In spite of these reality problems, however, the calls from Ms. R. abated. She began to show greater ease in discussing material from all levels of experience, from the seemingly superficial to more deep and intrapsychic. Her awareness of me as someone other than a "good mommy" also increased, as reflected by her intense curiosity about details of my life and her desire to find flaws in my capacities as a wife and mother. She seemed much more observant of me as a person, commenting on my appearance and conjecturing about my life outside the office. In addition to the critical aspect of the comments, there was a certain freedom in her style and a sense of daring about them that she greatly enjoyed.

These shifts became very evident to both of us when I was away for a brief vacation. Ms. R. did not feel her usual need to call me while I was away. When I returned she commented that she liked being on her own and had felt some reluctance to come to the first session after the break. I mentioned that this reaction was very different from previous breaks. She then talked about imagining nursing from me and having so much milk that she could "slurp" from my breasts. She said she felt I might be embarrassed to have her talk like this because she was being so personal. The actual comment she made about nursing was not at all different from other comments she had made, but her concern that it was personal and might embarrass me was new. I told her this and said that I felt the comment sounded less natural than it had in the past. She acknowledged this and began to discuss her feeling of being more sure of herself and less needy of me. Possibly the fact that both of us had indeed survived the separation of my maternity leave and had been reunited without incident had allowed Ms. R. to loosen her strong insistence that I be the constantly available "good mommy" with breasts full of nurturing milk. She now seemed able to tolerate some differentiation between us, a fact that would have been too threatening earlier. She seemed to have less need for the "nursing," yet she did not want to give it up entirely or feel it was completely unavailable to her. A symbolic weaning had begun, but naturally Ms. R. wanted it to be gradual rather than abrupt.

The movement toward feeling better about herself has continued, while the need to have my role greatly circumscribed to that of a perfect, nurturing mother has abated. I pointed out to Ms. R. the more free, open-ended way in which she was bringing material to the session. She saw this as a different perception of me in that she no longer assumed I would know or understand things without verbal communication. She experienced this as a separateness, something that might have frightened her in the past but that now seemed fairly comfortable and even exciting. These changes were reflected in a dream that Ms. R. had at this time:

> My mother and I were cleaning something together, perhaps in a plane. We were mopping white stuff up off the floor, something like Crisco. I felt pleased there was so much of it and that I could get it all cleaned up.

The dream indicated that Ms. R. was seeing herself as an equal of her mother, thereby signaling her greater positive feeling about herself as a woman and mother. The white stuff might represent breast milk, and certainly its abundance was quite evident in the dream, probably an indication that Ms. R. saw herself as having more goodness inside her. The emphasis on cleaning might be an attempt to gain control of her own body products and of the mother's nurturing products as well. The sense of accomplishment that Ms. R. felt was very strong and suggested greater capacities to resolve issues of envy and greed in a less cruel and sadistic fashion. In a sense, if there was so much nurturance to go around, Ms. R. would not have to be so greedy in order to get satisfaction. She could easily "get it all." The mother in the dream may also represent the analyst, with whom Ms. R. is now feeling more connected as an adult woman and more cooperative in performing a task together.

Discussion

Ms. R.'s experiences in becoming a nursing mother, as troubled as they were in many respects, serve to highlight the inner meaning and developmental significance that the nursing experience has in a woman's life. For one thing, her experience tends to corroborate the concept that pregnancy and motherhood are not simply compensatory experiences for the lack of a penis. The sense of being filled up by the pregnancy and by the production of milk seems very fulfilling as marks of womanhood and the possession of a well-functioning woman's body without reference to male experience.

We might also ask to what extent Ms. R.'s experience bore out Stoller's contention that primary femininity is nonconflictual, based mostly on identification with the mother, but that substantive aspects of femininity such as childbearing are based on Oedipal competition with the mother. In many ways, Ms. R.'s wish to have a child and to be a mother were based on positive identifications with her mother. However, conflictual feelings about competing with her mother in these capacities created substantial anxiety for Ms. R. The fact that her nursing experience was initially a much more positive one than her mother's had been created substantial anxiety for Ms. R. in challenging what Lerner referred to as fantasies of the omnipotent maternal imago and in creating fears of retaliation from the mother. Certainly, Ms. R.'s sensitivity to her mother's criticism and her own heightened awareness of her mother's failings were indicative of competition with her mother.

I would not, however, limit these conflictual aspects to the level of Oedipal development. Rather, the conflicts around pre-Oedipal issues were very evident with Ms. R. and may well be so with many women as they experience motherhood and nursing. In particular, Ms. R.'s difficulty with pre-Oedipal issues of merger and separation related to her baby and her narcissistic investment in motherhood and nursing are common issues for most new mothers. The studies of Bibring *et al.* (1961) of pregnant women showed an unusual incidence of disturbance on personality tests administered in the first trimester of pregnancy. The test results showed substantially less pathology after the fourth month when quickening had occurred. Bibring postulated that prior to quickening, the growing fetus is experienced as a merged part of the self, whereas afterward it is seen as a more separate entity. Her study suggests that total lack of differentiation is more threatening to the self than a sense of two being in close, intimate connection. Similarly, Brody (1981) postulated that the nursing experience enables the mother to feel a continuation of the connectedness with the infant after delivery.

For Ms. R., this sense of merger or connectedness was particularly conflictual. Based on her own childhood experiences, her desire for merger was so great and her fear of loss and abandonment was so strong that Ms. R. found any disruption in connectedness to be traumatic. Her tendency during the pregnancy to ignore questions about her state of health and her emotional unpreparedness for the caesarian delivery suggest a reluctance to relinquish the internal baby. Her general lack of foresight about plans for child care and return to work are consonant with an unconscious fantasy that she and the baby would remain physically merged indefinitely. The nursing became an important perpetuation of the wish for merger with the baby. The interruptions of returning to work and of having her mother provide childcare intensified the feeling of of having been abandoned by her newborn child. As a result, Ms. R. experienced in a more intense manner the sense of loss when separating from one's baby that most mothers feel.

Thus, it appears that some of the conflicts at least were pre-Oedipal in nature. The wish for merger and the fear of loss were pre-Oedipal conflicts that Ms. R. had not resolved. These conflicts suggest that it may not be possible to classify the pre-Oedipal experience as nonconflictual and the Oedipal experience as conflictual.

Another question to consider is the extent to which the mothering and nursing experiences are a recapitulation of childhood issues and to what extent they are new developmental tasks that provide the opportunity to redefine oneself. Certainly both aspects are important. Ms. R.'s approach to her pregnancy and nursing was similar in many ways to her efforts to become a doctor or get a pony. In these cases, she set goals and aimed for them in an ambitious manner, only to have her hopes severely dashed. In the case of becoming a mother, the state of motherhood and nursing was seen as a blissful realization of many fantasies. The reality, however, was quite different and unexpectedly stressful. In Ms. R.'s case, the discrepancy was so great that a delusional state resulted. While the impact may not be as great, the sense that motherhood and nursing are not so idyllic once the baby is born is a very common reaction.

Given her experience in analysis, Ms. R. had an opportunity to experience symbolically the act of nursing from both the role of provider and that of recipient. In the analysis, as the nursing baby she was able to experience the fear of abandonment by her mother, the concern that her greediness would be destructive, the strong intensity of her desires to be merged and provided for, and the concern that she was unlovable and would never be able to achieve her goals. While these issues were specific to Ms. R. and are not necessarily common to all women, the fact that they did occur in relation to her pregnancy and nursing and were themes in the transference does suggest that the new mother in many respects must rework her own experience of being mothered and her own patterns of dealing with an anxiety-producing situation.

In considering the degree to which nursing is a new developmental task, the importance of the sense of self-esteem that a woman derives from nursing can be emphasized. While the production of the new baby itself is most often experienced as a great accomplishment, the ability to nurse is a considerable enhancement of one's mothering capacities. This was certainly the case with Ms. R. Heretofore, she had had little sense that she could have so many good, valuable things inside her. Up until then her excess pounds indicated that she had a lot of substance, but not a substance of real value. Now she was not fat, she was pregnant, and eating food was now appropriate because it produced not fat but a baby and the breast milk on which the baby nursed.

The fact that Ms. R. was unable to resume nursing after her hospitalization was certainly a blow to the positive sense of self which Ms. R. had developed in seeing herself as a bountiful, nurturant mother. While she still was producing milk and thus did not need to see herself as deficient in this respect, she did have to deal with the distressing fact that her baby did not want what she had to offer. She feared that she must be producing bad milk if the baby preferred the bottle to the breast. This may be an extreme example of a syndrome that frequently occurs when mothers realize they have milk and yet their let-down reflex or the baby's lack of vigorous sucking creates an unsuccessful nursing situation. In many of these cases, the baby is ultimately weaned to a bottle, and the mother feels she has been rejected and found wanting by her baby. Certainly it is important that these mothers have the opportunity and necessary support to reassess their capacity as mothers on criteria other than those of providing the baby's nutrition directly from their own bodies.

In the context of a new experience, nursing allows the mother to be the active agent in providing nurturance to someone else. As such the woman sees herself as having new capacities which will satisfy her wish to be a capable adult woman. The realization that she has something good to offer her baby enables her to be tolerant of the constant demands of the baby. In spite of no longer being able to nurse, Ms. R. did become invested in her daughter and did see her role as a mother to be very significant. She recognized that she could care for her daughter whether or not she nursed. This—more than a blind reliance on the nursing capacity alone—gave her a sense that she had many good, valuable products within her. Her capacity to love her child was less tangible but certainly more significant than any other gift she might have offered her child.

REFERENCES

Bentovin, A. (1976). Shame and other anxieties associated with breast-feeding: A system theory and psychodynamic approach. In *Breast feeding and the mother*, Ciba Foundation Symposium 45 (pp. 159–178). North Holland, Amsterdam: Elsevier, Excerpta Medica.

Bibring, G. L., Dwyer, T. F., Huntington, D. S., & Valenstein, A. F. (1961). A study of the psychological procession in pregnancy and the earliest mother-child relationship: 1. Some propositions and comments. *The Psychoanalytic Study of the Child, 16*, 9–24.

Brody, S. (1981). The concepts of attachment and bonding. *Journal of the American Psychoanalytic Association 29*(4), 815–829.

Brown, F., Lieberman, J., Winston, J., & Pleshette, N. (1960). Studies in choices of infant feeding in primiparas. *Psychosomatic Medicine, 22*(6), 421–429.

Buxbaum, E. (1979). Modern woman and motherhood. In T. Karasu & C. Socarides (Eds.), *On sexuality: Psychoanalytic observations* (pp. 61–72). New York: International Universities Press.

Committee on Nutrition. (1976). Commentary on breast-feeding and infant formulas, including proposed standards for formulas. *Journal of Pediatrics, 57*, 278–285.

Entwisle, D., Doering, S., & Reilly, T. (1982). Sociopsychological determinants of women's breast-feeding behavior: A replication and extension. *American Journal of Orthopsychiatry, 52*(2), 240–260.

Foman, S. J. (1975). What are infants fed in the United States? *Pediatrics, 56*:350.

Freud, S. (1905). Three essays on the theory of sexuality. *Standard Edition, 7*, 125–245. London: Hogarth.

Freud, S. (1925). Some psychical consequences of the anatomical distinction between the sexes. *Standard Edition, 19*, 243–258. London: Hogarth.

Gunther, M. (1976). The new mother's view of herself. In *Breast-feeding and the mother*, Ciba Foundation Symposium 45 (pp. 145–158). North Holland, Amsterdam: Elsevier, Excerpta Medica.

Hatcher, S. L. (1982). The psychological experience of nursing mothers upon learning of a toxic substance in their breast milk. *Psychiatry, 45*, 172–181.

Kauffman, I. (1970). Biological considerations of parenthood. In E. J. Anthony & T. Benedek (Eds.), *Parenthood* (pp. 3–55). Boston: Little, Brown.

Kennell, J. H., & Klaus, M. H. (1979). Early mother-infant contact. *Bulletin of the Menninger Clinic, 43*(1), 69–78.

Klein, M. (1957). Envy and gratitude. In *Envy and gratitude and other works, 1946–1963* (pp. 176–235). London: Hogarth.

Lawrence, R. (1985). *Breastfeeding: A guide for the medical profession*, 2nd Ed. St. Louis: C. V. Mosby.

Lerner, H. E. (1974). Early origins of envy and devaluation of women: Implications for sex role stereotypes. *Bulletin of the Menninger Clinic, 38*(6), 538–553.

Lerner, H. E. (1979). Effects of the nursing mother-infant dyad on the family. *American Journal of Orthopsychiatry, 49*(2), 339–348.

Newton, N. (1955). *Maternal emotions*. New York: Paul B. Hoeber.

Ross National Mothers Survey MR77-48 (1981). Columbus, OH: Ross Laboratories.

Stoller, R. J. (1976). Primary femininity. *Journal of the American Psychoanalytic Association, 24*(5), 59–78.

Stolorow, R., & Lachmann, F. (1986). Transference: The future of an illusion. *The Annual of Psychoanalysis, 7/8*, 19–37.

Waletsky, L. R. (1979). Husband's problems with breast-feeding. *American Journal of Orthopsychiatry, 49*(2), 349–352.

Watson, N. D. (1949). Why can't I nurse my baby? *Psychiatric Quarterly Supplement, 23*(2), 353–359.

Winnicott, D. U. (1975). *Through paediatrics to psycho-analysis*. New York: Basic Books.

Chapter 11

Emotional Aspects of Pregnancy and Childbirth

DAVID KLIOT

CULTURAL ATTITUDES: PATHOLOGY VS. PHYSIOLOGY

In all known human societies, there are recognizable patterns of behavior specifically related to the birth of a child. Cultural beliefs and traditions create and shape these patterns of behavior, and although the importance of childbirth is evident in all cultures, there is wide variation in approach to childbirth. Some cultures regard childbirth as a normal, natural, physiological process and a joyful part of ordinary everyday life. For example, DuBois (1944), observing the women of Alor, comments: "One gathers the impression that birth is considered an easy and casual procedure. This does not mean that difficulties never occur, but it does indicate that this society has not emphasized such difficulties." Likewise, the Jarava women of South America give birth in a passageway or shelter in full view of everyone, even small children. Among the Navajo Indians (Southwest United States), birth was seen as a social event and moral support from anyone was welcomed.

The frank approach of some cultures to childbirth has been reflected in the games the children play. Pukapuka preadolescents of the Pacific Islands used coconuts to represent babies. "After a pretend cohabitation, the girl-mother stuffed the coconut inside her dress and realistically gave birth to her child, imitating labor pains and letting the nut fall at the proper moment" (Beaglehole & Beaglehole, 1939).

In contrast to such open, happy attitudes, some cultures feel the need for extreme privacy and even secrecy about birth. Childbearing may be regarded as an illness, with anxiety and fear the pervading emotions to accompany the anticipation of difficulty and disaster. The Cuna Indians of Panama, for example, expect a pregnant woman to visit a medicine man daily and to receive medication throughout pregnancy and labor. Cuna children are kept in ignorance as long as possible;

DAVID KLIOT, M.D. • Clinical Associate Professor of Obstetrics and Gynecology at the State University of New York Health Science Center at Brooklyn; Attending at Obstetrics, Methodist Hospital; private practice.

'ven forbidden to watch births of domestic animals (dogs, cats, and pigs) & Newton, 1972). Ideally, they are not informed about sexual intercourse or childbirth until the last stage of the marriage ceremony. To maintain secrecy, many cultures have led children to believe that some animal, such as a stork or a dolphin, will bring the mother her baby.

Many different peoples see childbirth as a time of particular vulnerability when supernatural and malevolent spirits are at work. Thinking of birth as dirty or defiling has been reported from widely scattered regions all over the world, and was especially strong in parts of Asia. Special places or "birthing huts" at some distance from the village are not uncommon. In parts of India, not only is the woman considered impure, but anyone touching her during labor is considered contaminated and is isolated as well. Vietnamese mothers reportedly avoid going out for months after delivery so they will not bring bad luck to others.

Our own Hebrew and Christian traditions share the belief that birth is unclean. In the Torah of the ancient Hebrews, the portion of Leviticus 12 is devoted to the ritual purification of women after childbirth (Levin, 1960). The Catholic Church also has a special ritual for new mothers, although this observance is falling into disuse.

Our own contemporary American culture has also been accused of having the attitude that childbirth is an illness. In 1963, Atlee described the attitudes of his colleagues as follows:

> We obstetricians seem to think and act as if pregnancy and labor constitute a pathologic rather than a physiologic process. Our entire basic medical education is so obsessed with pathology that it is practically impossible for us to think of any woman who comes to us as other than sick (p. 514).

In 1981, U.S. Public Health Advisor Paul Ahmed went even further to say, "Professional literature in the field of health care has tended to view pregnancy as a sickness—biologically, psychologically and sociologically" (Ahmed & Kolker, 1981).

Howard Brody and James Thompson (1981), in an article in the *Journal of Family Practice*, compare what they call "maximum strategy of modern obstetrics" to military maneuvers, in which one approached a problem as if the worst possible outcome is to be expected. This approach, applied to routine obstetrical care, has not been documented with superior clinical results. Maximum strategy in medicine in general is "promulgated partly by an intraprofessional reward system that gives very little credit for a large number of normal patients handled with appropriate care . . . but imposes heavy opprobrium upon the failure to treat adequately one patient with a rare or unexpected complication."

The view of pregnancy and childbirth as a state of illness or of health has been periodically revised, depending less on the state of medical knowledge than the cultural views of childbirth, medicine, and woman's role in society.

FEMALE MIDWIVES

Looking back to colonial times, one finds that English practices and customs were followed, which made childbirth the exclusive province of women. Female friends, relatives, and perhaps a midwife were gathered (often by the husband) to give the event a social aspect. During colonial times, midwives were not considered a part of the medical establishment; they performed a special social and somewhat religious function. There was no formal training; instead, the fund of knowledge was shared and passed among the midwives themselves or to those who were interested (Wertz & Wertz, 1977).

The importance that the midwife (meaning "with women") held is attested to by the fact that several colonial towns provided housing for her with salaries or special privileges to guarantee her presence and her services. Maternal mortality rates for colonial New England were better than Great Britain's for the same period. It has been postulated that healthier conditions prevailed in the colonies. Americans enjoyed a better, more dependable supply of food and were spared the unsanitary effects of urban congestion.

THE MALE PHYSICIAN

A "new midwifery" was introduced to the colonies in the middle of the 18th century when American men returned with a medical education from abroad. The 19th century saw the gradual replacement of the female midwife in the United States by the male physician. Although traditional midwifery continued in France, England, and the Netherlands, American childbirth developed differently due to the dynamics of the expanding American society. The medical profession grew quickly. American mobility left fewer stable communities to provide the networks of support that existed in communities where midwives flourished. Also contributing to this change were shifts in cultural attitudes about the proper place and activities for women in society and the changing taste of middle and upper class women who looked to the male physician for greater safety and more respectability. Wertz and Wertz (1977) state,

> "Expecting and laboring women lost a great deal from the exclusion of educated female birth attendants . . . although no doubt doctors were often sympathetic, they could never have the same point of view as a woman who had herself born a child and might be more patient and discerning about birth processes . . . and would not, of course, lay on the male prerogative of physical and moral control of birth" (p. 73).

The respectable place to give birth, however, was still at home. Nineteenth century maternity hospitals were for the poor or lower classes, and carried the danger of puerperal fever and the stigma of being an unconfined, homeless woman.

VICTORIAN FEMININITY

In Victorian America there was enhanced concern over pain in childbirth, which probably had its origin in a combination of physical, psychological, and social conditions. The culture expected women to be frail, delicate, and vulnerable, and to openly express their aches and illnesses. Health and physical capability were equated with vulgarity and coarseness and even considered uncivilized. Fashions dictated corsets to constrict the waist to an ideal 15 to 18 inches. A practice of binding the waists of preadolescent girls resulted in permanently deformed rib cages. Lack of exercise, improper diet, and stuffy rooms also contributed to physical disability.

The introduction of anesthesia to relieve the pain of childbirth met opposition on several fronts. A religious argument was that no one had the right to remove Eve's punishment. It was also suggested that suffering during childbirth was useful as a means to limit future conceptions. Another theory was that suffering was essential for the development of motherly love. Such opposition held less credibility after Queen Victoria elected to use chloroform for the birth of Prince Leopold in 1853 (Chabon, 1966).

Finally, Niles Newton (1965) observes, 100 years later, that "cultural femininity" as measured by conventional psychological masculinity–femininity tests correlates negatively with biological femininity, i.e., interest in and success at the tasks of mothering, confident delivery, successful breast feeding, and related attitudes and behaviors. She has noted that in the female reproductive triad of coitus, birth, and lactation, there is a tendency in our society to place special emphasis on the first, presumably because of its special pertinence to the adult heterosexual relationship and to ignore the sexual aspects of the latter two.

Birth in the Hospital

As the 20th century progressed, puerperal fever was under control, use of anesthesia was sanctioned, and there was general agreement among informed women and physicians that hospital birth was preferred. It appeared to offer the best of the old methods such as the practical services (nursing, housekeeping) associated with social childbirth in addition to new skills that were less easily obtained, promising greater safety and more comfort (Wertz & Wertz, 1977).

Ironically, despite these promises, the change of scene forced a change in attitude. Whereas birth at home was usually attended by friends and relatives and considered a normal, healthy process (despite its dangers), childbirth in the hospital was now associated with doctors, nurses, and illness. Gradually, after 1930, problems in the new trend began to surface; doctors were concerned because hospital births had not produced notably better results (New York Academy of Medicine Committee on Public Health Relations, 1933; White House Conference on Child Health and Protection, 1933), and some women began to declare that medical treatment and institutional care had deprived them of important birth experiences by treating every birth as a potential problem.

Prepared "Natural" Childbirth

Grantly Dick-Read (1954) provided support for the concept of prepared, natural childbirth with his view of normal childbirth as a natural, joyous process that need not be painful if a woman was emotionally prepared. To this day, evidence is still collecting to support his fear–tension–pain theory.

Preparation for childbirth is of increasing popularity in our culture because so many childbearing women and couples have had little or no exposure to the birth experience. Perhaps it was our regard for privacy that kept it out of the school curriculum for so long. Certainly the media (movies and television) capitalized on the difficult, dramatic, and anxiety-producing aspects of childbirth. In rural societies, there was something to be learned in the breeding, birthing, and raising of farm animals. As our society became more industrialized, family size decreased and childbirth moved away from the experience of the family. Word of mouth carried superstition and tales of frightening experiences.

A woman's experience is very personal and is subjected to many influences (particularly by her relationship with her own mother). Pregnancy is a developmental period in which a woman must resolve old conflicts such as dependency, autonomy, and Oedipal issues. Bibring notes that confusion may exist in differentiating oneself from one's mother as well as one's fetus.

There is, during the course of a healthy pregnancy, a pattern of reconciliation with one's mother. This relationship continually improves and by the third trimester most women look back upon a happy childhood and see their own mother as someone who is good and giving. If there are difficulties in resolving maternal conflicts, a woman's relationship with her husband may compensate. The resolution of maternal ambivalence is crucial for the woman's sense of self and child (Ballou, 1978).

Studies show a relationship between anxiety during pregnancy, difficult labor, and delivery, and neonatal problems (Clark & Affonso, 1976; Notman & Nadeslson, 1978).

Anticipatory Guidance

Anticipatory guidance is the cornerstone of comprehensive and preventive psychological care and probably has a critical relationship to labor, delivery, and postpartum care. Areas of psychosocial functioning to be explored early in pregnancy are (1) the woman's concerns and expectations about pregnancy, childbirth, and motherhood; (2) her capacity for adapting to strain and stress; and (3) the nature of her social support system. In gathering information, it is best to avoid questions that could be answered by yes or no such as, "Was everything all right in your last pregnancy?" A better question would be, "Could you tell me what your last pregnancy was like for you?" After the woman's expectations and concerns have been explored, there is a basis for taking steps toward education, guidance, support, and reassurance (Brown, 1979).

Education for Childbirth

Preparation for childbirth in the United States is principally based on Grantley Dick-Read's natural childbirth and the psychoprophylactic or Lamaze approach. Many programs are eclectic and draw from different sources. Individual instructors may introduce modifications they have found personally effective.

Generally, the goal is to enable the mother to control or at least cope with an unmedicated labor, to teach her how to use her body to ease and shorten delivery. Since fear is related to tension and pain, the attempt is to reduce fear as much as possible by a thorough education. Each stage of labor and delivery (effacement, dilation, transition, expulsion) is discussed with respect to both physical and emotional changes that can be expected. For each stage, specific breathing techniques are suggested to help the woman work with her body. The couple is taught how to help the woman relax her muscles, both to conserve energy and prevent tension buildup. During the early stages of labor, she is encouraged to relax her body and concentrate on coordinating breathing technique with contractions. By taking each contraction individually, she develops confidence in her ability to maintain control and distract herself from the full impact of the pain.

The couple is forewarned about transition (cervical dilation of 7 to 10 cm) and possible reactions to it (shivering, irritability, nausea). It is the stage at which she is most likely to want to give up maintaining control. Understanding that having reached this stage is an accomplishment, that it is of relatively short duration, and the emotional support and encouragement from staff and husband at this time can enable her to continue to cooperate in expediting the expulsion of the baby.

In an effort toward greater realism, childbirth films are usually shown and the couple is taken on a tour of the labor and delivery rooms. A couple recently delivered is invited to speak of their experiences (Macfarlane, 1977). Expecting couples attending classes often find comfort in their common interests, appearance and concerns, and even express that they "feel more normal."

Husbands educated to assume their time-honored role as birth assistants may come to the delivery prepared with techniques to handle such discomforts as backaches, cramps, and thirst. They coach, encourage, and support their wives. Many couples find this a moving experience which brings them closer together as parents, enriching their love for each other and the newborn (Simons & Pardes, 1977).

Studies have shown that women who are educated for childbirth and are accompanied by a support person during labor and delivery fare better statistically in terms of shorter labor, fewer complications, less anesthesia, better neonatal outcomes, greater pleasure, and more positive initial response to their babies (Charles, Norr, Block, et al., 1978; Flowers, 1978; Haire, 1981; Henneborn & Cogan, 1975; Howells, 1972; Hughey, McElin & Young, 1978; Kennell & Klaus, 1976; Morris, 1972; Scott & Rose, 1976; Sosa, Kennell, & Klaus et al., 1980).

The success of prepared childbirth, however, depends on the couple's choosing this approach and being adequately prepared and synchronized. Difficulties arise when there is disharmony between the couple's wishes and hospital rules or between the respective needs of the husband and wife. The husband barred from attending his wife may feel frustrated and impotent, while the wife may be angry, anxious, and resentful toward a husband who she feels abandoned her to suffer in a strange hospital environment. On the other hand, the husband coerced through direct or subtle pressure into attending his wife may be unduly stressed, and the effect may be quite detrimental to the family (Ballou, 1978).

THE FATHER EXPERIENCE

The couple's personal needs and attitudes are paramount. Historically, the custom of expecting the husband to assist in childbirth and the custom of excluding the husband completely may be marked by the "couvade ritual" (from the Frenc. word *couvage*, meaning to hatch) (Chabon, 1966). This centuries old ritual is a magical practice in which the husband pretends to experience labor and childbirth at the time his wife is due. A significant number of expectant fathers in our culture actually experience symptoms resembling those that their wives experience during pregnancy and labor. Unlike the ritual couvade, the couvade syndrome is not a pretense. The symptoms experienced by the husband may occur without any awareness on his part of their association with his wife's condition. Trethowan's study (1972), comparing expectant fathers with a group of similar men whose wives had not been pregnant during that previous year, showed that the expectant fathers were more likely to be affected by symptoms and also suffered from a significantly greater number of symptoms. The number of expectant fathers experiencing loss of appetite, nausea, toothaches, indigestion, and abdominal pain reached statistical significance. Also significant was the relationship between physical and psychiatric symptoms and between physical symptoms and the degree of anxiety felt over the wife's pregnancy (which was often unperceived by the father). The couvade syndrome, which may, on rare occasion, even include abdominal swelling and, more commonly, sympathy labor pains, characteristically will disappear after the birth of the child.

Estimates of the incidence of the couvade syndrome range from 9% to more than 33% of expectant fathers (Blum, 1980).

Ritual couvade has been explained as sympathetic magic to protect the mother and child and simultaneously to establish the child's paternity. Explanations for couvade syndrome include: (1) identification and empathy with the wife; (2) parturition envy or jealousy of her ability to bear a child; and (3) reaction against his own ambivalence and hostility (whereby the symptoms serve to protect her from his aggression).

Anticipatory guidance should be provided for the expectant father or the main support person as well as for the expectant mother. Interviews with the father should be held early and in the presence of the expectant mother. It is important to clarify issues, especially if the pregnant woman is uncertain about events or her response to them. The father's attitudes, expectations, and concerns should be evaluated. His importance in the childbirth process should be stressed. Opportunity to ask questions should be available and the caregiver should present as a supportive resource person (Brown, 1979).

MATERNAL STRESS AND ANXIETY

Although maternal anxiety and stress are inevitable, providers of maternity care should have heightened awareness of their possible consequences and attempt to minimize the effects through psychological management. Most stress is psychologically based and mediated by personal interpretation. What is moderately stressful for one individual may have little effect on another because of varying perceptions of stressful situations. People differ markedly in the quality and extent of their personal, financial, professional, spiritual, and interpersonal resources, which all contribute to one's response to stress.

Animal studies have demonstrated the deleterious effect of environmental disturbances on labor and perinatal mortality (Adamson, Mueller-Heubach, & Meyers, 1971; Morishima, Pedersen, & Finster, 1978; Newton, Peeler & Newton, 1978; Shnider et al., 1979). Animals also have mechanisms for adapting to environmental stress. For example, a deer at term would select a secluded area to give birth where she would not be vulnerable to predators while she was relatively defenseless during labor and delivery. However, if while she was in labor a pack of dogs caught her scent and began chase, her fear would cause her to secrete epinephrine, which in turn would act to diminish uterine contractions and aid her flight. When danger passed, she would be able to proceed with parturition (Flowers, 1978).

Fears and anxieties of a woman at term may initiate the secretion of epinephrines (catecholamines) inappropriately. The study by Lederman, Lederman, Work et al. (1978) correlates self-reported anxiety to dysfunctional labor in the absence of other complications. Results of the study indicated that anxiety at the onset of the second stage of labor was significantly correlated with high plasma epinephrine levels and longer labors. Higher norepinephrine levels, however, were significantly correlated with shorter labors. The placental vascular bed is extremely sensitive to the constrictive effects of epinephrine, which can lead to a decrease in uterine contractility and decreased utero placental circulation, presenting potential fetal hazard.

Newton et al. (1979) in a study of psychosocial stress and its relation to premature labor, conclude that pregnancies resulting in premature labor are far more likely to have been stressful than pregnancies which are full-term.

Crandon (1979) associates high maternal anxiety with the following obstetrical complications: preeclampsia, forceps deliveries, prolonged labor, precipitate labors, postpartum hemorrhage, retained placenta requiring manual removal, and fetal distress in the forms of fetal tachycardia, bradycardia, and meconium staining. Although stress and anxiety are increasingly recognized as powerful factors in labor and childbirth, much has yet to be known.

MINIMIZING STRESS AND ANXIETY

There is evidence that women who express their anxieties do better than those who deny or repress their conflicts (Uddenberg. et al., 1976). Disturbing dreams are a common symptom of the last trimester (Flowers, 1972). A 1972 study showed that women who reported dreams with themes of anxiety had shorter labors than women reporting dreams without anxiety. Ventilation or discussing fears and concerns can provide considerable relief from tension and distress. Brown (1979) throws light upon how this operates. Putting troublesome feelings or thoughts into words is accompanied by a change in perspective. One can view the concerns with more distance than when they remain highly personal, subjective, unshared preoccupations. Part of this shift in perspective comes from giving the concern a concrete form through verbalization. Once a difference in perspective is achieved, a number of coping mechanisms can be utilized; some may be initiated by the patient, others by the listener.

The therapeutic value of ventilation depends on the listener's response. The attitude of the listener is critically important, for much of the value derives from acceptance and support. Interest, concern, and seriousness should always be apparent.

Reduction in intensity of feelings is an important component of ventilation. Putting emotions into words, whether the feelings are distressing (anxiety) or pleasurable (sexual pleasure), reduces their intensity.

Patient concerns must be treated with respect regardless of how absurd or unrealistic they may seem. For the woman with morbid or irrational fears, related factual information should be provided in detail. Information can give one a sense of mastery over unfamiliar, uncomfortable, and potentially dangerous situations. For some people, information gathering and focusing on details is a successful way of relieving anxiety and may serve to refocus attention from morbid thoughts of death and deformity onto the details of the physiology of labor and delivery.

In working out a particular anxiety, clarifying the source can be particularly beneficial; it serves to demystify the anxiety and to give one a sense that it can be mastered. Often expectant women whose friends or family have had a bad experience or problem baby have heightened anxiety.

Although pregnancy generally does not produce emotional problems, it can heighten existing ones. If anxiety symptoms interfere with the patient's normal functioning, psychiatric referral is in order and, with the patient's permission, collaborative comprehensive care should commence.

Maternal satisfaction with the labor and delivery is an important goal in itself and seems to be a function not so much of the obstetrical setting as of the match between the setting and the mother's personal needs and attitudes (Brody and Thompson, 1981). Maternal dissatisfaction plays a major role in the current public criticism of obstetrical practices.

NEW APPROACH TO U.S. BIRTH PRACTICES

Beginning about 1940, the medical dominance of birth began to be challenged. Advocates of "natural childbirth" wished to rely more on nature and less on the arts of medicine. Once medicine had tamed birth's dangers and the birth control movement allowed for voluntary motherhood, women questioned the safety of drugs during delivery. They questioned whether obliviousness, which for their mothers signified liberation, was best for their child and for their own birth experience.

In the 1950s, Dr. Lamaze adapted and introduced the psychoprophylactic method of childbirth to Western culture. In 1959, Marjorie Karmel, an American woman delivered by this technique in Paris, sparked American interest with her book, *Thank You, Dr. Lamaze,* and the natural childbirth movement took wings in the United States.

In 1956, La Leche League was formed, the first formally structured organization directed at helping women with birth-related problems. These women reacted against the lack of professional assistance available for women who wanted to nurse their babies. Many of the original members attribute part of their success in nursing their later children to returning to the home to give birth. This challenging approach to obstetrics as commonly practiced in the United States accompanied by a new and joyful attitude towards birth and biological feminine functions seems to have come from a revised view of womanhood after World War II, which Betty Freidan (1963) has called "the feminine mystique."

Women's magazines of the 1940s and 1950s extolled home and maternity; the birth rate soared. The women's health movement gained momentum in the 1960s, and the 1970s saw a proliferation of explicit criticism launched against U.S. childbirth practices by articulate and creative feminist leaders such as Doris Haire (1973), Suzanne Arms (1975), Gena Corea (1977), and Ehrenrich and English (1973).

The issues concerned both attitudes and procedures. That the obstetrician delivers the child and is thanked was not quite right. The corrected attitude is that the obstetrician attends the mother who delivers the child with a tremendous sense of her own accomplishment (Tompson, 1976). Questions were raised concerning the efficacy of the lithotomy position, the use of drugs, shaving of pubic hair, fetal monitoring, induction of labor, episiotomy, increasing number of Caesarean sections, breast-feeding, and options in birth opportunities (Youngs & Ehrhardt, 1980).

There was an outcry against the routine use of many procedures intended to be employed only when medically justified. The "dehumanizing" experience of the institutional setting was accused of inhibiting the birthing process, thereby leading to the justification of medical interference.

Childbirth is an emotional and physical crisis of unparalleled intensity. For many women it is a turning point in their lives. It is the moment the expecting couple has been anticipating for 9 months. They have been coping with a changing physical and psychological reality. The extent to which they were able to support each other's confidence and emotional growth during pregnancy will be a factor in the way they respond to childbirth. Their own inner security, their image of themselves and their sexuality, and their acceptance of the unborn baby are also significant. Another important factor in the experience of childbirth is the degree to which the expectant mother can surrender herself to her basic bodily urges during labor and delivery. Any factors that may inhibit the woman can complicate labor; if she is embarrassed or humiliated by an unfriendly or critical attitude or if she feels as though she is on display as unfamiliar faces come and go and examine her private parts she may react with tension. On the other hand, the intimacy of a familiar setting with trusted birth attendants and especially one close support person (often the husband) can provide the sanction that will allow her to let go of her inhibitions and actively expedite the birth process.

There seems to be general agreement that the best outcomes are obtained by following women's preferences (Notman & Nadeslson, 1978) and that each birth should be tailored to the personal, familial, and cultural as well as the medical needs of the participants.

Strangely enough, the 1930–1932 maternal mortality report for New York City partially fixed responsibility for an outrageously high proportion of avoidable deaths on the expectant mother.

> Responsibility lies with: 1) the medical profession as a whole; 2) the individual
> members of that profession; 3) society—as represented in organizations formed
> for the improvement of the health conditions of those dependent upon public
> health; and 4) finally with the woman herself—to demand what she is trained

and educated to recognize as proper and quality care" (New York Academy of Medicine Committee on Public Health Relations, 1933).

ALTERNATIVE BIRTH STYLES

Delivery styles in which the woman has a great deal of control and participation are associated with reduced anxiety and pain during labor, enhanced satisfaction with the childbirth experience, and increased attachment to the infant (Brown, 1979).

The alternative birth movement began as part of a more generalized movement by women to regain control over their own bodies, to make childbirth more of a family affair, and as a reaction to "excess of technological management." Women began to search both for obstetricians who were willing to support their attempts to birth with a minimum of medical interferences and for the proper environment, which could offer nonstressful surroundings, emotional support, and the backup of technical care, if required.

Stimulated by clinical studies (Banta & Thacker, 1978; Brackbill & Broman, 1979; Brown et al., 1972; Caldeyro, 1978; Caldeyro et al., 1975; Haverkamp et al., 1976; Mehl, 1978) and consumer demands, hospital innovations now may include fathers or another support person in the labor and delivery room, unrestricted attendance of the father during and after labor and delivery, combined labor–delivery–recovery home-like "birthing" rooms, rooming in with newborn sibling visitation, inhospital childbirth education classes, and special staff training to encourage psychological and practical staff support for current childbirth techniques, family-centered childbirth, breast-feeding, and also family-centered procedures for Caesarean birth.

Strong feelings that physician-attended births may lead to excessive interference with natural processes plus the added incentive of reduced cost have contributed to the growing popularity of out of hospital births. Programs such as New York's Maternity Center Association rely on nurse-midwives to provide low risk patients with prenatal care and to attend their deliveries. They have obstetricians and hospital backup services.

The number of home births has doubled in less than a decade. David Stewart, Director of the National Association of Parents and Professionals for Safe Alternatives in Childbirth (NAPSAC), estimates that between 1 and 2% of all births nationwide are home births. Home-birth proponents stress family bonding as an important reason for their preferences. A pilot study has shown that the presence of siblings promoted a positive attitude toward birth and warm family feelings. The baby is more easily accepted and there is less jealousy and sibling rivalry (Maynard, 1981; Tompson, 1977). Researchers at the Mount Zion Alternative Birth Center in San Francisco, however, are finding no evidence of reduced sibling rivalry in studies conducted over the past 5 years. Emphasis is placed on the fact that children's experiences depend on the quality of their family lives with many complex factors contributing ("Children Witnessing," 1981). The popular and widely circulated *Woman's Day* magazine, in an article that focused on home births, cautions that "family birth" is not for everyone—or indeed for most people. It is not for families who are uncomfortable with nudity or are formal and reserved in their relationships. It is not for all children and certainly should never be urged upon those reluctant to participate (Maynard, 1981).

Choice, together with risk screening, is an important consideration for the management of labor and delivery. High risk technology applied to low risk women has detrimental effects (Ahmed & Kolker, 1981).

In a study of the Leboyer method of delivery (Figure 1), the one significant difference noted was that women expecting a Leboyer delivery had a significantly shorter first stage of labor (Nelson, Enkin, et al., 1980). In an editorial, Duff (1980) pointed out that family preferences were important aspects of childbirth and need consideration. It is likely that a Leboyer approach or other attitudes and behaviors may influence feelings and shorten labor.

Position for Childbirth

At present, there is an increased interest in alternatives to the lithotomy position for delivery. In most preindustrialized societies, delivery takes place in the squatting, kneeling, or sitting positions, taking full advantage of the forces of gravity during contractions. The lithotomy position has been criticized for neglecting this advantage and for the compression of the uterus against the inferior vena cava aorta, iliac arteries, and ureters which interfere with circulation and urinary output. A study by Newton and Newton (1960) disclosed that women who deliv-

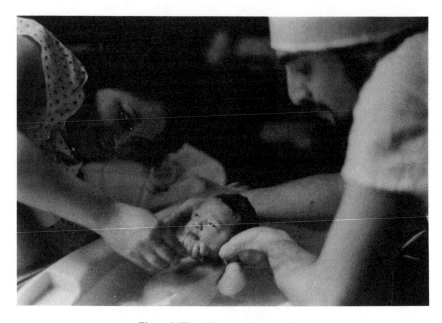

Figure 1. The Leboyer method of delivery.

ered in a propped up position (30° to 45° from horizontal) tended to take a more active part in labor and delivery, pushed more actively in the second stage of labor, required less anesthesia and analgesia, and showed more pleasure at the first sight of their babies. The lateral recumbent, or Sims' position, while not currently popular in the United States, was recommended in early obstetric texts and is still commonly utilized in Great Britain, Ireland, and Scotland (Figure 2) (Edgar, 1912). Modern variations of the delivery chair have been designed in the United States (century chair) and Sweden to avail laboring women of a choice in sitting position for delivery (Haukeland, 1981).

A Latin American collaborative study found that 95% of their mothers chose to labor in a vertical position and reported greater comfort in a lateral, sitting, or standing position to supine. Women laboring in a vertical position had a median duration of the first stage that was shorter by 45 minutes (25%). Primigravida labor was shortened still more by 78 minutes or 36%. Although early amniotomy shortened labor by 28%, it is associated with fetal heart rate deceleration, caput succedaneum, and increased molding of the fetal head.

Maternal bearing down during the second stage may lead to fetal hypoxia and acidosis if prolonged. Women who bear down as they feel the need usually do so within the physiological limits of 5 to 6 seconds. The second stage proceeds more slowly, but there is no compromise to the fetus and there is more time for the perineum to stretch to reduce the need for episiotomy (Caldeyro, 1978; Caldeyro et al., 1975).

Ambulation during the first stage of labor has been shown to improve uterine action, encourage more rapid engagement of the fetal head, enhance maternal satisfaction (as assessed by a "mood or emotion thermometer") and enhance breast-feeding and lactation (Pitkin and Zlatnik, 1980).

ATTACHMENT

It is now recognized that events surrounding childbirth can have significant effects on bonding or the attachment of both parents and infant. The newborn can smell, see, and follow, shows visual preferences, and responds preferentially to the mother's voice. The period immediately after delivery is seen as an optimal time for parent–infant interaction. Both are in an increased state of alertness and have an increased potential for stimulating each other reciprocally (DeChateau & Wiberg, 1977; Flowers, 1978; Macfarlane, 1977; Salk, 1970). In a conference on maternal attachment, Dr. Ross Parke referred to Margaret Mead's observation that fathers are a biological necessity but a social accident, and called for "bringing the father back into the family from the start and demonstrating that he is a social as well as a biological necessity (Klaus, Leger, & Trause, 1975; Parke, Power, Tinsley et al., 1979).

THE HIGH-RISK PREGNANCY

Events surrounding a high-risk, premature, or Caesarean section delivery preclude the active participation of the mother. Such deliveries require extra effort to

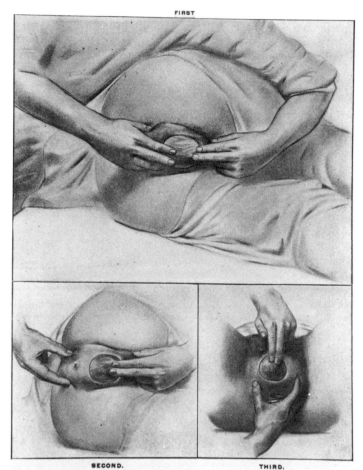

FIRST

SECOND.   THIRD.

FIG. 635.—PERINEAL PROTECTION, SHOWING THREE METHODS.

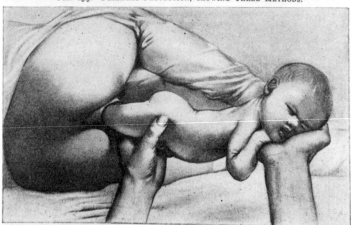

FIG. 641.—SUPPORTING THE CHILD DURING THE EXPULSION OF THE TRUNK AND LEGS.
Note that the trunk is grasped at the pelvis, leaving the chest and abdomen free
from pressure.

Figure 2. Sim's position.

help the parents understand what is happening in order for them to get back some feeling of control. When there is a problem after delivery, the parents need to know immediately. The truth at that time is usually less stressful than the mother's fantasy and, if shared immediately, conveys the impression that the physician is aware and under control. A brief explanation at first is best, for example, "Your child has difficulty breathing; he is being taken care of." Not sharing the information is more likely to be due to the physician's feelings of stress.

In the high-risk pregnancy, morbid fears and negative feelings, often transient in a normal pregnancy, predominate. If all goes well, most families reorient and attach to the neonate. Occasionally a family does not readjust their thinking and will perceive the child as sick and vulnerable, which may predispose the child to that role in life (Green & Solvit, 1964).

If the newborn is ill or stillborn, families need time to grieve. A normal child born before the parents have had a chance to resolve their grief is more likely to be overprotected. Six months is rarely long enough. The time required is usually 12 to 24 months (Sosa & Cupoli, 1981).

POSTPARTUM DISORDERS

Postpartum blues are so common (50 to 80% prevalence) that they can be considered among the normative postpartum experiences. Postpartum psychosis is rare and will appear within the first 2 to 4 weeks postpartum. Factors contributing to postpartum emotional problems may be genetic, organic, psychological, social, or iatrogenic. Men usually do not relate their emotional disorders to the childbirth, but may exhibit problem behavior, such as lack of cooperation and/or support, or negativism. The subtle interplay of postpartum disorders can tend to make the perinatal period "a breeding ground of marital and parental maladjustment (Ahmed & Kolker, 1981).

An important facet of postpartum adjustment is the mother's need to remember the details of her child's birth. Some women feel the need to go over the details of their experience repeatedly, often to the boredom of their listeners. Grandmothers may recount details of their childbirth experiences with amazing accuracy, yet be forgetful of more recent events. One interpretation centers about the need for acceptance and achievement. A woman with a sense of failure may be hampered at her next childbirth experience. The sense of achievement from a good birth experience is a very strong stimulus for greater self-esteem and later effective functioning.

CONCLUSION

Emotional components of labor and birth receive the greatest emphasis from nonobstetrical organizations and publications. Accumulating evidence of the significance of psychological factors has begun to take added importance in the practice of obstetrics. Much remains unknown. In 1946, Heyns reported that the Bantu women of South Africa deliver their babies spontaneously through pelves so small that Western women would need to be sectioned. Were the Bantus so socially conditioned to be able to accomplish uterine contractions extraordinary enough to force the molding of the baby's head to allow vaginal birth? Heyns believes that "simple dystocia, due to contracted bony passages, can almost be eliminated by fostering the will in the parturient to deliver herself" (p. 405).

Birth attitudes and birth behavior are curiously intertwined in what today is popularly called a "catch-22" arrangement. Newton and Newton (1972) observe "the availability of forceps and Caesarian sections depends on cultural attitudes which accept the idea of a nonspontaneous birth. In turn, the widespread use of operative procedures may decrease the desire to push the baby out spontaneously."

No one would agree to forego any of the advances of modern obstetrics, yet there is the criticism that technologizing birth is dehumanizing. On the other hand, ignoring medical risks may result in unnecessary pain and loss. There is a real challenge to effectively integrating both the viewpoints of nature and technology to the best advantage.

References

Adamson, K., Mueller-Heubach, E., & Meyers, R. E. (1971). Production of fetal asphyxia in the rhesus monkey by administration of catecholamines to the mothers. *American Journal of Obstetrics and Gynecology, 109*, 248.
Ahmed, P., & Kolker, A. (1981). Coping with medical issues. In P. Ahmed (Ed.), *Pregnancy, childbirth and parenthood*. New York: Elsevier.
Arms, S. (1975). *Immaculate deception*. Boston: Houghton-Mifflin.
Atlee, H. B. (1963). Fall of the queen of heaven. *Obstetrics and Gynecology, 21*, 514.
Ballou, J. W. (1978). *The psychology of pregnancy*. Lexington: D. C. Heath & Co.
Banta, H. D., & Thacker, S. (1978). *The premature delivery of medical technology: A case report*. Hyattsville: National Center for Health Services Research.
Beaglehole, E., & Beaglehole, P. (1938). *Ethnology of Pukapuka*. Bernice P. Bishop Museum Bulletin, *150*, Honolulu.
Blum, B. (1980). *Psychological aspects of pregnancy, birthing and bonding*. New York: Human Sciences Press.
Brackbill, Y., & Broman, S. (1979). *Obstetrical medication and development in the first year of life*. Bethesda: National Institutes of Health.
Brody, H., & Thompson, J. R. (1981). The maximum strategy in modern obstetrics. *Journal of Family Practice, 12*, 6, 966.
Brown, et al. (1972). Relationship of antenatal and perinatal psychologic variables to the use of drugs during labor. *Psychosomatic Medicine, 34*, 119.
Brown, W. A. (1979). *Psychological care during pregnancy and the postpartum period*. New York: Raven Press.
Caldeyro, B. R. (1978). The influence of maternal position during the second stage of labor. In P. Simkin & C. Reinke (Eds.), *Kaleidoscope of childbearing*. Seattle: Pennypress.
Caldeyro, B. R., et al. (1975). Adverse perinatal effects of early amniotomy during labor. In L. Gluck (Ed.), *Modern perinatal medicine*. Chicago: Yearbook Medical Publishers.
Chabon, I. (1966). *Awake and aware*. New York: Dell.
Charles, A. G., Norr, K. L., Block, C. R., et al. (1978). Obstetric and psychologic effects of phychoprophylactic preparation for childbirth. *American Journal of Obstetrics and Gynecology, 131*, 44.
"Children witnessing childbirth." *New York Times*, 21 Sept., 1981.
Clark, A. L., & Affonso, D. D. (1976). *Childbearing: A nursing perspective*. Philadelphia: F. A. Davis.
Corea, G. (1977). *The hidden malpractice*. New York: Morrow.

Crandon, A. J. (1979). Maternal anxiety and obstetric complications. *Journal of Psychosomatic Research, 23,* 109.

DeBois, C. (1944). *The people of Alor,* Minneapolis: University of Minnesota Press.

DeChateau, P., & Wiberg, B. (1977). Long term effect on mother–infant behavior of extra contact during the first hour of postpartum: II. A followup at three months. *Acta Paediatrica Scandinavica, 66,* 145.

Dick-Read, G. (1954). *Childbirth without fear.* New York: Harper Bros.

Duff, R. (1980). Care in childbirth and beyond. *New England Journal of Medicine, 302,* 685.

Edgar, J. C. (1912). *The practice of obstetrics.* Philadelphia: P. Blakiston's Sons.

Ehrenreich, B., & English, D. (1973). *Witches, midwives and nurses.* Old Westbury: Feminist Press.

Flowers, C. (1978). Psychological preparation for childbirth. *The Female Patient 3* (2), 49–52.

Flowers, C. E. (1972). Hormones and the emotions during and after pregnancy. Presented at a Symposium on Physiologic Bases for Emotional Disorders in Women at the New York Academy of Medicine, New York, October 1972.

Friedan, B. (1963). *The feminine mystique.* New York: W. W. Norton.

Green, M., & Solvit, A. (1964). Reactions to the threatened loss of a child: A vulnerable child syndrome. *Pediatrics, 34,* 58.

Haire, D. (1973). The cultural warping of childbirth. *Environment and Child Health, 19,* 171.

Haire, D. (1981). Improving the outcome of pregnancy through increased utilization of midwives. *Journal of Nursing and Midwifery, 26*(1), 5.

Haukeland, I. (1981). An alternative delivery position: New delivery chair developed and tested at Kongsberg Hospital. *American Journal of Obstetrics and Gynecology, 141,* 115.

Haverkamp, A., Thompson, H. E., & McFee, J. G. (1976). The evaluation of continuous fetal heart rate monitoring in high risk pregnancy. *American Journal of Obstetrics and Gynecology, 125,* 310.

Henneborn, W. J., & Cogan, R. (1975). The effect of husband participation on reported pain and probability of medication during labor and birth. *Journal of Psychosomatic Research, 19,* 215.

Heyns, O. S. (1946). The superiority of the South African Negro or Bantu as a parturient. *Journal of Obstetrics and Gynecology of the British Commonwealth, 53,* 405.

Howells, J. G. (1972). *Modern perspectives in psychological obstetrics: Modern perspectives in psychiatry, 5,* New York: Brunner & Mazel.

Hughey, M. J., McElin, T. W., & Young, T. (1978). Maternal and fetal outcomes of Lamaze and prepared patients. *Obstetrics and Gynecology, 51,* 643.

Karmel, M. (1959). *Thank you, Dr. Lamaze.* Philadelphia: Lippincott.

Kennell, J., & Klaus, M. (1976). *Maternal-infant bonding.* St. Louis: C. V. Mosby.

Klaus, M., Leger, T., & Trause, M. (1975). *Maternal attachment and mothering disorders: A round table.* Sausalito: Johnson and Johnson Baby Products Co.

Lederman, R. P., Lederman, E., Work, B. S., et al. (1978). The relationship of maternal anxiety, plasma catecholamines and plasma cortisol to progress in labor. *American Journal of Obstetrics and Gynecology, 132,* 495.

Levin, S. (1960). Obstetrics in the Bible. *Journal of Obstetrics and Gynecology of the British Commonwealth, 67,* 490.

Macfarlane, A. (1977). *The psychology of childbirth.* Cambridge, MA: Harvard University Press.

Maynard, F. (1981). Childbirth as a family affair. *Woman's Day* (January 13).

Mead, M., & Newton, N. (1967). Cultural patterning of perinatal behavior. In S. A. Richardson & A. Guttmacher (Eds.), *Childbearing: Its social-psychological aspects.* Baltimore: Williams & Wilkins.

Mehl, L. (1978). Research on alternatives in childbirth. What can it tell us about hospital practice? In L. Stewart & D. Stewart (Eds.), *21st century obstetrics now!,* Vol. 1. Marble Hill, MO: NAPSAC.

Morishima, H., Pedersen, H., & Finster, M. (1978). The influences of maternal psychological stress on the fetus. *American Journal of Obstetrics and Gynecology, 131,* 286.

Morris, N. (1972). Psychosomatic medicine in obstetrics and gynecology. Third International Congress, London.

Nelson, N. M., Enkin, M., et al. (1980). A randomized clinical trial of the Leboyer approach to childbirth. New England Journal of Medicine, 302, 655–660, 685.

New York Academy of Medicine Committee on Public Health Relations (1933). Maternal mortality in New York City: A study of all puerperal deaths, 1930–1932. New York: Oxford University Press.

Newton, N. (1965). Maternal emotions: A study of women's feelings toward menstruation, pregnancy, childbirth, breastfeeding, infant care and other aspects of their femininity. New York: Hoeber.

Newton, N., & Newton, M. (1960). The propped position for the second stage of labor. Obstetrics and Gynecology, 15, 28.

Newton, N., & Newton, M. (1972). Childbirth in cross-cultural perspective. In J. Howells (Ed.), Modern perspectives in psycho-obstetrics. New York: Brunner & Mazel.

Newton, N., Peeler, D., & Newton, M. (1978). Effects of disturbances on labor. American Journal of Obstetrics and Gynecology, 8, 1096.

Newton, R. W., et al. (1979). Psychosocial stress in pregnancy and its relation to the onset of premature labor. British Medical Journal 2(6187), 411–413..

Notman, M. T., & Nadelson, C. C. (1978). The woman patient: Medical and psychological interfaces, Vol. 1, Sexual and reproductive aspects of women's health care. New York: Plenum.

Parke, R. D., Power, T. B., Tinsley, B. R., et al. (1979). The father's role in the family system. Seminars Perinatology, 3(1), 25.

Pitkin, R., & Zlatnik, F. (1980). The yearbook of obstetrics and gynecology 1980. London: Yearbook Medical Publishers.

Salk, L. (1970). The critical nature of the postpartum period in the human for the establishment of the mother-infant bond: A controlled study. Diseases of the Nervous System, 31, 110.

Scott, J. R., & Rose, N. B. (1976). Effect of psychoprophylaxis: (Lamaze preparation) on labor and delivery in primaparas. New England Journal of Medicine, 294, 1205.

Shnider, S. M., et al. (1979). Uterine blood flow and plasma norepinephrine changes during maternal stress in the pregnant ewe. Anesthesiology, 50, 524.

Simons, R. C., & Pardes, H. (1977). Understanding human behavior in health and illness. Baltimore: Williams & Wilkins.

Sosa, R., & Cupoli, M. (1981). The birthing process: The effects on the parents. Clinical Perinatology, 8(1), 206.

Sosa, R., Kennell, J., Klaus, M., et al. (1980). The effect of a supportive companion on perinatal problems, length of labor, and mother-infant interaction. New England Journal of Medicine, 303, 597.

Tompson, M. (1976). Why do responsible, informed parents choose home births? In D. Stewart & L. Stewart (Eds.), Safe alternatives in childbirth. Chapel Hill: NAPSAC.

Tompson, M. (1977). Family bonding: Why families should be together at birth and why we chose birth at home. In L. Stewart & D. Stewart (Eds.), 21st century obstetrics now! Marble Hill, MO: NAPSAC Publication.

Trethowan, W. H. (1972). The couvade syndrome. In J. Howells (Ed.), Modern perspectives in psycho-obstetrics. New York: Brunner & Mazel.

Uddenberg, N., et al. (1976). Reproductive conflicts, mental symptoms during pregnancy and time in labor. Journal of Psychosomatic Research, 20, 575.

Wertz, R. W., & Wertz, D. C. (1977). Lying in. New York: Collier-Macmillan.

White House Conference on Child Health and Protection (1933). Fetal newborn and maternal mortality and morbidity. New York: Appleton-Century.

Youngs, D. D., & Ehrhardt, A. A. (1980). Psychosomatic obstetrics and gynecology. New York: Appleton-Century-Crofts.

Part IV

Later Developmental Themes

It is not until menopause and the possible onset of grandmothering occur that the body clearly sets off a new set of triggers to the unconscious and a new set of challenges to the self in transition. Dale Mendell looks at menopause through the analyst's eyes by interviewing a number of psychoanalysts about their menopausal patients. Using dreams and fantasies as vehicles of understanding, Mendell outlines thematically menopause as a marker for aging, as a period of constructive reevaluation, and a mourning for lost opportunities and lost fecundity, which in turn can bring about a reaffirmation of present and future. Ruth Formanek stresses as well the "good news" about menopause, reviewing older conceptualizations based on the "libido dethroned" theory and increased susceptibility to insanity. Menopause can bring with it welcome relief from premenstrual syndrome, cramps, and the possibility of unwanted pregnancy.

Chapter 12

A Study of Menopausal Women in Analytic Treatment

DALE MENDELL

There has been a considerable dearth of psychoanalytic literature on menopause. At first glance this is surprising, since menopause is an inescapable fact in the life history of women, a psychophysical passage replete with layers of multiple meanings. As such, it would appear to be a treasure trove for psychoanalytic investigation of the vicissitudes of development and of the interaction between a biological event and its numerous diverse psychic manifestations.

HISTORICAL OVERVIEW

There are, however, reasons why the topic of menopause has been neglected in the analytic literature. For one thing, until quite recently, only Erikson (1959) recognized developmental stages in the adult. For other theorists, adulthood was seen as a developmental end station. Rather than being viewed as a series of milestones and transformations, the normal adult changes were seen as steps toward loss of psychic function and the inevitability of death. In this climate, it was not surprising that analytic treatment of people in the second half of their lives was not encouraged. Analysts shared Freud's (1905) pessimism about the "elasticity of their mental processes" and about their capacity to utilize the transferential potentialities of the analytic situation except for regressive repetition of dependent patterns.

This deprivational bias in regard to adulthood and aging, in which even positive midlife changes are considered to be stimulated by the fear of loss of

I would like to express my appreciation to Laurice Glover, M.S.S., for her most valuable assistance.

DALE MENDELL, PH.D. • Faculty and Supervisor, The Psychoanalytic Institute, Postgraduate Center for Mental Health, New York City; Senior Supervisor, Training Analyst and Faculty, Training Institute for Mental Health; Senior Supervisor, National Institute for the Psychotherapies; private practice.

physical and psychic functioning, was applied doubly to the menopausal woman. Seen from a classical Freudian perspective, female development is secondary to and compensatory for male development; as she was considered to be a "little man" from birth, the girl was viewed as being forced into femininity by a series of shocks, from the discovery of the penis through menarche, defloration, and childbirth. Seen from this theoretical vantage point, it was logical to view women as losing their femininity with their reproductive ability rather than progressing to a normal, later life stage of female development. Indeed, menopausal women were viewed by early theorists as clinically depressed, abandoned by external and internal objects, and in both a psychic and hormonal state of delibidinization.

This pessimistic and cavalier view of the menopausal woman was in complete accord with that of the larger medical, academic, and social culture. With very little in the way of research to support such conclusions, until relatively recently the menopausal woman was considered to suffer from a host of diverse symptoms, both psychic and physiological, which rendered her a burden to herself and to her family. It is only within the last two decades that the subject of menopause has been studied in a sophisticated and extensive fashion from physiological, psychosocial, and cross-cultural perspectives. The new findings contradict many long-standing assumptions, some of which had been repeated in analytic literature. For example, only two physical symptoms—vascular changes, such as "hot flashes," and a thinning and loss of elasticity of the vaginal wall and surrounding mucosa— are attributable to the hormonal changes of menopause. The degree of *physical* distress is independent of psychological adjustment; clinical depression is rarely seen at menopause and is likely to occur only in those women who had experienced previous depressive episodes. (See Greene, 1984, for a comprehensive review and Chapter 13, this volume, for a summary of these findings.) It has also been pointed out that earlier, less sophisticated research has confounded the effects of aging and of menopause per se, thereby distorting conclusions about menopause (Notman, 1979).

Within psychoanalysis itself, there have been extensive changes in formulations both about developmental stages in adulthood and about normal female development. (See, e.g., Greenspan & Pollack, 1980, on aging, and Blum, 1976, and Mendell, 1982, on female development.) The emphasis on normal midlife developmental changes and transformations and on the primary, rather than compensatory, nature of femininity have engendered a current climate in which analytic investigation of menopause is particularly feasible.

The stimulating, pace-setting work from the social and biological sciences forms a frame and a complement to analytic investigation of menopause, but can never substitute for clinical material. Information obtained from the subjective reports and behavioral data of large numbers of women has the advantage of statistical reliability, but neither aims for nor is able to examine latent meanings or interrelations among aspects of psychic functioning. To date, however, reports in the analytic literature on menopausal women, in addition to being sparse, have been confined to the generalizations of a single clinician, on the basis of a limited number of cases. The present study is intended to add to the scant literature on menopause by using a somewhat broader data base and a slightly different perspective.

Menopausal Women in Psychoanalysis

For this study, a number of psychoanalysts were interviewed about their menopausal patients. This design was utilized in an attempt to expand beyond the boundaries of a single clinician's personal and theoretical biases and countertransference distortions, while retaining the desired aim of garnering menopausal themes from many levels of awareness as expressed in patient's dreams, fantasies, and transference material.

Review of Pertinent Literature

Before proceeding to a report of the study, I will briefly review selected pertinent literature from the writings of Deutsch, Benedek, Bibring, and Lax. Deutsch (1945) viewed the climacterium as "one of the most difficult tasks of woman's life" (p. 456). Narcissistic disappointment and mortification in the face of vanishing beauty and sexual life can engender "intensified libidinal needs" and "narcissistic self-delusions of youthful looks." Women also develop an urge for a baby before "the gates close"; this activity may represent a compensation for "partial death—as servant of the species" (p. 459). These and other "active" manifestations of the denial of the deterioration of sexual and reproductive life in some women are responded to by depression in others. Some degree of depression is seen as normative during climacterium. These depressed moods, connected to feelings of inferiority, are reminiscent of pubescence, so much so that Deutsch's prognosis for climacterium is based on the course of puberty. Envy and competition with son's wives, frequently of pathological proportions, is awakened with regression to Oedipal issues. "Narcissistically beautiful" women supposedly fare better than others due to their continued self-love. Successful treatment is difficult, as the patient can be offered little in the way of substitute gratification. Deutsch's idea that "the flow of feminine emotional life vanishes" (p. 461) is clearly based on the early analytic assumption that femininity is secondary and compensatory and that with the loss of reproductive capacity a woman losses her femininity.

Like Deutsch, Benedek (1950) views the normal climacterium as analagous to puberty in that internal physiological changes cause considerable stress. Benedek sees even more evidence of emotional disturbance and strain in the climacterium than at menarche. For Benedek, there is a regression of the ego's integrative capacity and a reduction of its capacity to love, due to declining hormonal production. Disappointment in the changing and declining self engenders feelings of inferiority and self-accusation which may lead to severe depression. As hormonal supports decline, there is a frequent narcissitic preoccupation and a desexualization of emotional needs. Unlike Deutsch, Benedek emphasizes the progressive adaptations which are made during climacterium. Even desexualization is seen as providing new aims for psychic energy; "emancipation from sexual competition and fear of sexual rejection" is viewed as "releasing talents" (pp. 26–28). Benedek states that any symptoms are determined by the individual's method of mastering psychic tension; she particularly considers pre-Oedipal and Oedipal identification with the mother to be of note. Benedek overemphasizes the role of hormonal depletion on the psyche of the menopausal woman; currently such a view is regarded as over-simplifying complicated interactions among a number of biological and psychological processes.

Bibring, Dwyer, Huntington, and Valenstein (1961) regard menopause, like puberty or pregnancy, as a period of crisis, representing important biological developmental steps and having in common characteristic psychological phenomenon. All three normative developmental crises revive psychological conflicts of earlier developmental periods and all require new and different solutions. These principal steps in human growth, as biologically determined maturational crises, are inevitable. For example, once a woman reaches menopause, childbearing is ended. Bibring criticizes Deutsch and Benedek's emphasis on pathogenesis, and sees the crisis of menopause as a normal and essential part of growth, which precedes and prepares for further maturational integration. The revival of repressed fixations makes them available for new solutions.

Lax's (1982) thesis is that during the crisis of climacterium there are average expectable stresses resulting in an expectable depressive reaction which manifests itself in sadness, a sense of loss, and mourning for one's vanished youthful self. This depressive reaction varies in nature and intensity with a number of factors, among them the severity of physiological symptoms, past experiences, and psychic structure, ego strengths and the current life situation. Depression is viewed as normative in response to loss, rather than pathological, and, as a prerequisite for maturation, climacteric is seen as a narcissistic assault, due both to an inability to bear children and to feelings of reduced well being due to physiological changes. Lax warns against denial as preventing the working through of a mourning process which normatively contributes to a move toward adaptation and greater psychic maturity. Lampl-de Groot (1980), on the other hand, believes that depressive reactions during menopause are neurotic, and that "coping well" is the normative mode.)

While there is an emphasis on depression, narcissitic depletion, and loss in the conceptualizations of most of the theorists cited, there is also a noticeable shift between early and later writers in the direction of viewing menopause as a normative developmental crisis that holds the possibility for mature resolutions and transformations rather than as a deprivational state with little room for further growth. This change in thinking parallels the recent interest in the field in adult developmental stages and their adaptational modes.

Description of the Study

For the present study, psychoanalysts who were treating menopausal patients by means of psychoanalysis or psychoanalytic psychotherapy were asked to talk about their patients.[1] There were 13 patients in the study. The criterion for acceptance in the study was that of having been perimenopausal (having zero to one menstrual periods during a given year) at some point during treatment. At the time

---

[1] In the interest of preserving patient confidentiality, I am unable to thank by name the colleagues who graciously donated their time to assist me with this project.

of the interview all 13 women were either perimenopausal or postmenopausal by definition. None had had a surgical menopause and only two had received short courses of estrogen replacement therapy. All patients were white and middle-class. Demographically, three patients were divorced or single and childless, four were divorced or single and had children, one was married and childless, and five were married with children. Using broad diagnostic categories, seven can be described as neurotic and six as having borderline or character disorders.

As the sample size was small, it was thought best to control the parameter of analyst gender; therefore, all analysts were female. I conducted each of the open-ended interviews. The procedure consisted of asking each analyst to discuss the selected patient. The only other initial request was that the analyst report the first patient dream that occurred to her, on the assumption that the analyst's free associations when asked to discuss a menopausal patient would lead her to a dream in which menopausal issues were significant; this assumption appears to have been justified. Interviews lasted from 1 to 2 hours. In general, analysts spontaneously touched upon many of the issues noted in the literature. Toward the end of the interview, I asked specific questions about issues that had not been discussed or that I felt had not been discussed sufficiently. (A checklist of issues to be covered is included in the appendix of this chapter.)

Because of the relative smallness of the sample, the fact that I was the only interviewer and investigator, the subjective and selective picture that analysts form of their patients, and the very fact that all subjects were analytic patients, these findings about menopausal themes must be regarded as tentative. To partly correct for my status as sole investigator and interpreter of the material, I submitted all patient dreams to Laurice Glover, M.S.S., who is especially knowledgeable in the area of women's dreams; her interpretations have been integrated into the body of this report.

Findings and Discussion

Dominant themes that emerged from this study include:

1. Menopause is viewed as a "marker" of aging, and is a compelling catalyst toward evaluating the past and anticipating and attempting to shape the future.
2. There is regret at lost capacities and opportunities, particularly in the areas of sexual fulfillment, sexual competition, and the ability to have children.
3. There is a heightened sense of awareness of the body, with reactivation of feelings and memories of earlier developmental phases; concurrently, identifications with the mother's reproductive and sexual states and attitudes are heightened and renewed.
4. There are specific, unique meanings of menopause for each individual woman, based on her particular adaptive and defensive intrapsychic structure as well as on her past and current life circumstances. Thus, for example, fluctuations in self-esteem did not follow any general pattern, but rather reflected each woman's particular dynamics.

Additional findings include the following: clinical depression occurred only in those women who had had prior depressive episodes; lack of interest in or capacity for sexual pleasure was not evidenced; energy levels in postmenopausal women were perceived as tending to remain the same or to increase; and the least mentally healthy patients tended toward the extremes either of exaggerating or denying the fact and meanings of menopause.

Menopause as "Marker" for Aging

All patients in this study view menopause as a "marker" for aging. Whether clearly articulated or strongly denied, each woman demonstrates through latent communication that the menopausal experience is connected with ideation related to aging. There is a sense of time passing more swiftly, of the future appearing more finite than it had previously, and of the necessity for reevaluating one's past life. There is a marked tendency toward expressing regret at missed opportunities and a fear that there may never be a chance to make up for them. At the same time, there is a definite trend toward attempting to overcome past limitations and to live as fully as possible in the future.[2] These concerns are manifested in a wide variety of ways, depending on the patient's psychic structure, her ego capacity, her life history, and her current internal and external reality.

Regret at Lost Capacities

The most common cause for regret is the loss of the capacity to become pregnant and to have babies. Eleven of the thirteen subjects expressed marked preoccupation with babies. Some of the time this was experienced consciously, either in heightened interest in infants or in expressions of grief at the end of the capacity to bear children. Much of the time, however, it emerged mainly or wholly in dreams, in which themes of pregnancy and possessing babies were prominent, both on a manifest and latent level. For example, a married, childless woman dreams:

> Shall I make that quiche? I have all the ingredients needed. I notice a funny shaped ingredient, sort of like a tree with branches like peapods. This is just the right thing to put in to make the quiche myself. What I was doing was not so hard.

This dream appears to be a reparative fantasy for the lost ovarian function.

Dreams and fantasies of being pregnant or of having babies occur throughout life and express a variety of concerns that reflect both individual and developmental stage considerations. Jackel (1981) views pregnancy fantasies as a means of undoing loss, either the loss of an object or a physical loss. It is understandable that reparative fantasies should figure prominently in the dreams of menopausal women as the loss is both a physical one (the ability to bear children) and the loss of an object (the fantasied new life). In this small sample, dreams concerning pregnancy and babies are distinctly more frequent than they are during other phases of life

---

[2]A heightened focus and sense of urgency is also reported by the therapists of older patients (Greenspan & Pollock, 1980). This is but one respect in which it may be difficult to differentiate the effects of the menopausal experience from the general effects of aging.

and appear to symbolically express yearning and regret far more often than they express other possible meanings, e.g., rebirth.

While there is an assumption in the literature that childless women are far more distressed by the ending of childbearing capacity than are women who have borne children, in this sample the intensity and frequency of the unconscious wish for a baby was independent of whether or not a woman had children. In addition, it was independent of whether or not a woman would have welcomed actually becoming pregnant. Indeed, some patients assumed they were pregnant when they skipped a menstrual cycle, and were disheartened when forced to recognize that the skipped cycle was due to menopause rather than to pregnancy. One patient fantasized that she was pregnant even though she had been having hot flashes for some time and welcomed the idea of being pregnant even though she was in no position to raise another child. In spite of conscious goals, the sense of loss of a historically prized function resonates intrapsychically.

The theme of a new inability to compete for a man with younger, more sexually attractive women was almost as frequent as the theme of mourning for lost fecundity. While these are separate and distinct themes, they are frequently confounded. For many women in the study, the ability to bear children represents feminine desirability. The pain of feeling that she can no longer compete with younger, fertile women for a man is a major cause for some women to regret their inability to procreate. One patient said, "I am a barren woman; men will no longer be interested in me." A confounding of the theme of competition with younger women and the urge for a pregnancy was found in a patient with three grandchildren who became envious of the pregnancy of a relative of her husband's. She dreamed that her husband was bringing a young girl into the house, where the patient was cleaning; he ordered the patient to leave the house. Another patient became envious of her daughter-in-law's pregnancy, which revived her feelings of loss of the Oedipal competition to the mother who has both father and baby. The new Oedipal configuration of the patient, her son and her daughter-in-law was recreated at a point when her own inability to have babies revived an old sense of losing out competitively.

Unlike much of the analytic literature, where delibidinization has been seen as accompanying menopause, lowered sexual desire was seen infrequently in the women in this sample. Far more frequent were feelings of regret at missed opportunities in their past sexual lives and fear that they will not have a chance to make up for them. A few women appeared to have become less fearful of male sexuality with the arrival of menopause; this may have something to do with their new freedom from worry about pregnancy, but seemed to have more to do with feeling less helpless and vulnerable in relation to men sexually. Women who feel at a particular disadvantage in terms of competing for a man express bitterness at the uselessness of their own sexual desire. While some women feared an end to their sexual lives due to negative feelings about their attractiveness and power to compete, only one patient, who had a particularly ungratifying sexual relationship with a psychotic husband, felt relieved at the possibility of stopping sexual relations.

Menopausal Woman's Identity with Her Mother

Starting with early childhood, women identify with their perception of their mother's inner bodies. During each developmental stage, on both conscious and unconscious levels, they revive memories, impressions, and emotional resonances with their mother's reproductive states and their attitudes about those states. The patients in this study tended to be strongly influenced by their impressions of their own mother's menopause. As the mother's menopause frequently coincided with the patient's early adolescence, it left a strong impression on her perception of femininity. One woman, for example, realized only when she became menopausal that her mother had been menopausal at the time the patient began menarche. The mother had become withdrawn, depressed, and inaccessible to the patient at the very moment that the patient needed understanding, support, and reassurance for her budding sexuality. In spite of having been unaware at the time that the mother was going through menopause, with the advent of her own menopause the patient felt filled with loss. She complained that menopause was "this sick trick that life has played upon me when I was about to bloom." She felt that her body was failing her, that it was the end of being feminine and creative, and that men would be less interested in her. Above all she feared losing all the important people in her life, including her analyst. It became clear that the intensity of her sense of loss was in large part a revival of her sense of losing her mother during the mother's own menopause.

Intrapsychic Experience

The menopausal experience, as a normal psychophysical crisis, tends to turn a woman's focus inward upon her inner body and backward to conscious or unconscious comparisons with earlier physical developmental moments. Dream symbols express bodily representations and an awareness of bodily functions to a greater extent than is seen in younger adult women except at heightened times of body awareness, such as pregnancy. Many women indicate that they experience the unpredictibility of menstrual flow, both in timing and intensity, which normally accompanies perimenopause, as a loss of urinary or anal control. The physiological, intermittent, light bleeding (staining) revives feeling memories of childhood developmental stages.

Specific intrapsychic concerns were the determining factor in deciding which psychosexual phase was most salient. Some patients recreated in fantasy the latency period, as though the closest experience to being postmenopausal occurred prior to menarche. Some dealt with their anxiety about male genital sexuality, as though the cessation of menses gave them an opportunity to rework early genital anxieties. Other patients sought to cope with menopausal stresses by reviving memories and coping strategies from the anal period, when they learned to control both hostile competitors and the insides of their own bodies. Phallic resolutions were attempted, but quickly rejected in this small sample of women. For one patient, on a latent level, the awareness of the changes in her body was reminiscent of the anxiety she'd felt at the beginning of menses when she had felt angry and helpless at the loss of control of her body and its beloved familiarity and the symbolic and actual loss of her childhood.

Case Study

I am presenting a verbatim portion of an interview with an analyst both to provide an example of the raw data from which the themes in the paper are drawn and to illustrate a number of these themes. The patient had been a nun from 18 years of age. She had a distant but affectionate relationship with her father and a cold, strained, and difficult one with her mother; her ultimate decision to leave the Church was partly motivated by her feeling of being held prisoner from being the woman she could be.

When she noticed symptoms that her period was decreasing and it was happening once in 3 months, there came the first dream that there were spots—she would not tell me what kind of spots—on her dress and that these spots had to be removed—they were ugly spots. So that alerted me to ask about her period and then I learned that her period was very spotty. Soon there came a dream of a baby. There was a baby; there were two blankets and both blankets were not enough to cover the baby. She related that to herself, as the baby who was not adequately covered by father and mother in terms of the kind of care that she wanted, not the kind of care that they gave her, and that led to her regret that because she had led so many years as a religious sister and, now that she was menopausal, that *she* would not be able to care for a baby. Soon there were other dreams: that she was with her mother in a small room and that she was taking down curtains that had to be taken down and that she knew that she had to replace them with new curtains, which was a change of life. Menopause is a change of life; she knew her mother went through this. Her mother had to take down curtains and get new curtains for herself, and here is she also having to do this for herself. And it's also curtains for one form of life, and another life beginning.

This was followed by a dream of going in a car with two babies; she did not know who was driving the car. Again there was deep yearning and regret for the babies she never had and now would never have.

Then there came several dreams of rooms which were being enlarged and redecorated, which was the valuation of herself as compared to the feeling of being devalued. Also, she was going to enter a room, but the doorknob was a beautiful golden colored ball which was a symbol of my earrings. She said that the analytic process had helped her enter a new sense of being female—she was entering a new threshold. This is when she decided to leave the convent—the process is called exclaustration—and yet continue her religious work. I asked her what was she going to do and she arrived at the idea that she would like to have a profession and that would give her the best sense of fulfillment.

After this, she had a dream of two babies—that theme is repeated—underlining the fact that she now knows she would like to have two children but she would never be able to have them—a deep sense of regret and mourning. Then, several other dreams of rooms and journeys. But, the healing aspect: when she terminated treatment, she was in her third year of graduate school. The dream then of accepting the fact that she was menopausal and was no longer a devalued woman but that she was a free woman and sexual was a beautiful dream where she had a jewel case in her hand. It was red and many of the jewels were the jewels that I had worn which she had liked and would have liked to have, and these jewels were in that red velvet jewel case. And she was able to hold it on a bicycle; she was riding a bicycle, but the jewel case was in front of her on the handlebars, securely fixed to the handlebars, and she was riding along quite happy. And it meant to her that she was a really wonderful, valuable woman, that there her inner genital was a jewel case. And the bicycle between her legs meant that now she was ready to have a relationship with a man. Thinking about the jewel case, the jewels are the male genitals, the jewel case is the female genitals, and she is able to accept not just her sexuality but a conjunction between hers and male sexuality, and there is a conjunction between that and her mother's and father's sexuality, because her identification with her analyst has super-seded her identification with her antisexual mother.

In this excerpt, a number of the themes previously discussed are easily discern-ible. For this patient, as for all the patients in this study, menopause is a watershed experience, emphasizing the approach of age. She feels an increased sense of urgency in regard to making positive changes in her life. Patients like her, who do not use denial as a major defense and who have sufficient ego resources, are able to reorder and reorganize functions on a higher level of adaptation after a period of regret and sense of loss.

The theme of mourning for lost fecundity is seen clearly in this patient. Both waking and dreaming, she regrets her lost opportunities doubly, in the form of two babies. Her wishes to be a mother and have babies, and to redo her own deprived childhood by identifying with the babies she would like to raise better than her parents had raised her, have to be relinquished.

The theme of identification with the mother's genital sexuality is particularly clear in this patient. She is able to identify with her own mother in accepting and moving on from the psychophysical event of menopause. But she is also able to reject the perceived antisexual aspects of her mother and instead internalize her view of her analyst as a woman comfortable both with her sexuality and with her menopausal status. This identification with her analyst may contribute to the clear distinction this patient, unlike many others, makes between losing the capacity for motherhood and losing the ability to be sexually desirable. The patient's dream of "ugly spots" on her dress appears to symbolize earlier episodes of spotting, but it is difficult to know precisely which bodily products are primarily involved.

INDIVIDUAL REACTIONS—VARIATIONS ON A THEME

A portion of the feelings of loss and grief seen in the patients in this study appears to stem from the fear of change and sense of loss of one's former self that is seen at all points of transition between developmental stages. As menopause is also seen as a marker for aging, the anxiety over bodily changes associated with the cessation of menses frequently becomes translated into concerns over minor medi-cal problems. In contrast to Lax's findings, most women in this sample focused less on a sense of reduced physical well being or on feelings of physiological assault on the body and far more on the fear that even minor physical symptoms were signs of impending age-related physical changes. In general, they felt well, did not complain about or dwell on symptoms, and were not hypochondriacal. However, they were uneasy about their ability to maintain their present and past sense of their physical selves.

Only the most disturbed women in this study reacted to menopause with hypochondriacal preoccupation or with extreme denial. This finding does not refer to the severity of actual menopausal vascular symptoms, e.g., hot flashes, which are physiologically determined and vary in severity from individual to individual. It refers, rather, to the adaptation made to the perception of menopause. Indeed, actual menopausal vascular symptoms were rarely the subject matter of hypochondriacal preoccupation. Denial was utilized in an attempt to maintain rigid narcissistic defenses or to defend against the threat of separateness which accompanied an abrupt awareness of growing older, as though these women were growing old before they had grown up. The separation concerns in these women were intense enough to differ in both quality and quantity from the reworking of early issues found in all subjects. For example, the only lesbian in the sample stated that menopause meant that her life was over, as she could no longer be anybody's little girl. Two women with severe borderline pathology became extremely hypochondriacal and had morbid obsessions around physical deterioration. Under the delusion that her hair was falling out in clumps, one woman refused to leave the house without a hat.

In contradistinction to much of the literature in the field, menopause did not trigger clinical depression in the women in this study. Patients who had had prior depressive episodes or who were chronically depressed might experience a recurrence or exacerbation of depressive symptomatology, but women with different primary ways of reacting to internal and external stressors handled the menopausal situation in the same fashion they had coped with other life experiences and developmental passages. The same trend was noted in regard to fluctuations in self-esteem and in the sense of depletion of narcissistic supplies. Women with previous specific vulnerabilities in this area tended to react with feelings of bodily deterioration and a sense of "falling apart" or losing control, whereas other women experienced a relatively narrow range of fluctuation in self-esteem and were more likely to retain and even enlarge their sense of body narcissism and pride. In fact, although a number of themes are held in common among the majority of women in this study, the most striking impression is that the menopausal experience, the most recent episode in approximately 50 years of life, resonates with even more specific, individual meanings than do earlier psychophysical crises.

PROFILE OF THE MENOPAUSAL WOMAN

The "average" profile of the menopausal woman as derived from this study shows the following progression: a sense of regret and sorrow over lost capacities and opportunities, followed by a reworking of evoked earlier intrapsychic issues, followed by new levels of reintegration in the context of present reality. This profile of the menopausal woman has certain similarities to the formulations of earlier psychoanalysts. The sense of loss and the regressive revival of old conflicts are apparent, at least on a latent level.[3] However, the emphasis of earlier theorists, such as Deutsch and Benedek, on the intensity and pervasiveness of menopausal concerns across all areas of functioning were not found in this sample of patients. Specifically, clinical depressions, delibidinization of genitality, narcissistic ego-centricity, and a depletion of the ego's resources, rather than being characteristic of this group of women, were found only in the most pathological individuals.

A sociocultural climate less favorable than the current one to the ambitions of women in the second half of their lives may have contributed to early theorists' emphasis on pathological symptom formation. However, this point of view is mainly derived from traditional ideas both about adult development and about the specific development of women. From the vantage point of the classical Freudian position that female development is secondary to and compensatory for male development, it is logical to assume that women lose their femininity with the cessation of their reproductive ability. Deutsch (1925), for example, states that menopause initiates the "final disappearance of feminity" (p. 61). A regressive sequence occurs such that the vagina gives up its primacy to the clitoris and in turn there is regression to the "pregenital, that is to say the post-genital" (p. 61) phase. As they must give up their very femaleness, Deutsch considers that women have a more difficult time aging than men do.

If, however, women are recognized as female from birth, it is far less likely that theorists will regard them as capable of losing so primary an attribute. Certainly, the women in the present study did not regard themselves as unfeminine; at times of unhappiness and difficulty they might consider themselves to be old, ill, barren, or undesirable, but never to be other than female.

MENOPAUSE AS DEVELOPMENTAL PASSAGE

Until recently, psychoanalytic literature conceptualized the developmental process as a stepwise progression, which began in infancy and culminated in a psychicly static adult state. From this vantage point the themes and concerns of adult life were viewed as a reflection of past responses to childhood events. Furthermore, midlife and later years were believed to consist of a series of losses of the acquired psychic gains of childhood and youth, which are compensated for in a variety of frequently pathological fashions. Early conceptualizations about menopause shared this deprivational perspective. To Benedek, for example, menopause initiates a regression of the ego's integrative capacity and a reduction of its capacity to love, due to declining hormonal production.

There are, however, notable recent changes in the conceptualization of the second half of life. Adulthood is now seen as a series of stages of development in its own right, with its own unique tasks, rather than as a developmental end station. During the transitions between these stages, there is a change in psychic structure in which inner and outer patterns are reorganized and transformed. Regressions,

---

[3]The reader should keep in mind the fact that latent concerns are not always reflected on a behavioral or even on a conscious level. Many of the women in the present study, viewed by an external observer, would not appear to be going through a developmental crisis.

rather than being seen as pathological, are considered to be a necessary aspect of the generally progressive, integrative process of further development. Within this context, loss is inevitable, as is mourning that loss, whether it is the toddler's realization that she is no longer "mommy's baby," the new mother's awareness that her careless freedom has vanished, or the menopausal woman's acceptance of the fact that she is no longer a nubile young woman. The loss and mourning of one's former self, capacities, and relationship to others, essential at every developmental stage, is normatively transformed into new levels of individuation and freedom and into a new capacity for creativity in work or in relationships. A majority of women in this study were able to work through this developmental task in a positive and creative fashion.

Significance of Menopause as a Treatment Issue

Despite the fact that menopausal themes were clearly portrayed throughout the interview data, most analysts did not link patient associations and dreams with the menopausal experience. Kestenberg (1976) found a similar tendency in the analysts of pregnant patients as she evaluated data from their analyses. Furthermore, when asked directly, all but one analyst claimed that menopause was not an important issue during treatment and that very little time was spent discussing menopause and its intrapsychic ramifications. Yet, the interview material strongly supports both the notion that menopause was a highly significant factor in the lives of the patients in this study and that, in spite of their verbalized perceptions, analysts generally spent time exploring the topic. I suspect that the analysts surveyed operated under the psychoanalytic assumption that treatment deals chiefly with themes from early life and were, therefore, reluctant to recognize that certain themes were indeed menopausal even when, as talented clinicians, they responded appropriately to their patients' concerns. Michels (1980) believes that psychoanalysis has overstressed the effects of infantile phases on the adult while neglecting the specific concerns of adulthood. Rather than disclaiming the significance of menopause as a treatment issue, it might be more fruitful and more accurate to regard it as a highly significant developmental passage which assumes its specific shape under the pressure of earlier childhood and adult experience, fantasies, and adaptations.

Conclusion

To conclude this study of menopausal patients in analysis, I'll comment briefly on one disadvantage and one advantage of using a patient population to study the topic of menopause. The disadvantage is that the treatment process itself contaminates the results. Successful analytic therapy results in a degree of conflict resolution, of stability of self-esteem regulation, and of intrapsychic reorganization at a more mature level.[4] It is difficult to separate the effects of successful treatment from

[4]The high rate of treatment success among the patients in this sample is an addition to the growing number of examples of the benefit of using analytic treatment for patients in the second half of life.

the effects of the successful negotiating of the transition from one adult developmental stage to the next. An in-depth study of a normal, nonpatient population would be required in order to decide whether the intrapsychic processes found in the women in the present study are similar to those found in a nonpatient population. Unfortunately, it is probably impossible to duplicate the insight into the depth and progression of psychic change seen in analytic therapy in any other modality.

One advantage of using the analytic process to study menopause is to reconsider and enhance the findings of sociocultural studies. Valuable as such studies are, they assume that environmental givens are the major determinent of psychological outcome. However, by dint of intrapsychic exploration, such sociocultural assumptions can be modified. For example, one conclusion drawn from the sociocultural literature is that regrets over lost capacity for childbearing are mainly found in women who have never had children. The present study, by contrast, found that 11 out of 13 women were preoccupied with grief and regret at no longer being able to have babies, independent of whether or not they had children. Psychoanalytic contributions to other areas of knowledge are made by assessing and integrating latent material, to which psychoanalysis has privileged access, with the topics and methods of other fields.

Appendix: Checklist of Issues Discussed during Interviews

1. Open-ended question: "Tell me about your menopausal patient."
2. Request for the first dream that comes to mind when thinking of the patient.
3. Question regarding patient's manifest and latent awareness of menopause, e.g., reaction to menopausal symptoms.
4. Revival of psychosexual stages? What sort of derivatives are evidenced?
5. Any manifestation of concerns about babies? Any dreams?
6. Fluctuations in narcissism or self-esteem, e.g., helplessness, powerlessness; reactions of shame?
7. Depressive reactions? Feelings of sadness, loss, or mourning for youthful self?
8. Uneveness or upheaval in psychic functioning?
9. Changes in feelings regarding bodily integrity and bodily functioning? Sexual interest?
10. Changes in ego interests or functioning? In object relations?
11. What sort of identification with the mother is evident now? Any connection of mother and menopause?
12. Changes in energy level?
13. How much have menopausal issues influenced the treatment?

References

Benedek, T. (1950). Climacterium: A developmental phase. *Psychoanalytic Quarterly, 19,* 1–27.
Bibring, G. L., Dwyer, T. F., Huntington, D. S., & Valenstein, A. F. (1961). A study of the

psychological processes in pregnancy and of the earliest mother-child relationship. *The psychoanalytic study of the child*, Vol. 16 (pp. 9–72). New York: International Universities Press.

Blum, H. (Ed.) (1976). Supplement—Female psychology, *Journal of the American Psychoanalytic Association*, 24, 1–350.

Deutsch, H. (1925). The menopause. *International Journal of Psycho-analysis*, 65, 55–62 (1984).

Deutsch, H. (1945). *The psychology of women: A psychoanalytic interpretation*, Vol. II, *Motherhood*. New York: Grune & Stratton.

Erikson, E. H. (1959). *Identity and the life cycle (Psychological Issues*, Vol. 1, No. 1, Monograph 1). New York: International Universities Press.

Freud, S. (1905). On psychotherapy. *Collected papers*. New York: Basic Books (1959).

Greene, J. B. (1984). *The social and psychological origins of the climacteric syndrome*. Brookfield, VT: Gower.

Greenspan, S. I., & Pollack, G. H. (Eds.) (1980). *The course of life: Psychoanalytic contributions toward understanding personality development*, Vol. III, *Adulthood and the aging process*. Washington, D.C.: U.S. Government Printing Office.

Jackel, M. M. (1981). Object loss and the wish for a child. In S. Orgel & B. Fine (Eds.), *Clinical psychoanalysis* (pp. 67–81). New York: Jason Aronson.

Kestenberg, J. (1976). Regression and reintegration in pregnancy. Supplement—Female psychology. *Journal of the American Psychoanalytic Association*, 24, 213–250.

Lampl-de Groot, J. (1980). On the process of mourning. *The psychoanalytic study of the child*, Vol. 35 (pp. 9–13). New Haven: Yale University Press.

Lax, R. (1982). The expectable depressive climacteric reaction. *Bulletin of the Menninger Clinic*, 46, 151–167.

Mendell, D. Ed. (1982). *Early female development: Current psychoanalytic views*. New York: SP Medical & Scientific Books.

Michels, R. (1980). Psychoanalysis and aging. In S. I. Greenspan & G. H. Pollack (Eds.), *The course of life: Psychoanalytic contributions toward understanding personality development*, Vol. III, *Adulthood and the aging process*. Washington, D.C.: U.S. Government Printing Office.

Notman, M. (1979). Midlife concerns of women: Implications of the menopause. *American Journal of Psychiatry*, 136, 1270–1274.

Chapter 13

Menopause
Myth and Reality

RUTH FORMANEK

This chapter charts societal attitudes toward the menopause, highlights the differences between pejorative medical views and the views of women experiencing menopause, and surveys sociocultural influences and the effects of life stress on menopausal symptoms. The sparse research on menopausal symptoms is reviewed, subjective reactions to such symptoms (e.g., hot flashes) are explored and a plea is made for the collection of more information. We begin with definitions.

The word *menopause* derives from *meno*, monthly, and from *pausis*, referring to cessation. A recently invented term, it was preceded by a number of metaphors and the term "change of life." The word *climacteric* derives from the Latin *klimakter*, rung of the ladder, presumably the top rung. The present definitions of the climacteric and menopause derive from the First International Congress on the Menopause (Utian & Serr, 1976):

1. The climacteric is that phase in the aging process of women marking the transition from the reproductive stage of life to the nonreproductive stage.
2. The menopause refers to the final menstrual period and occurs during the climacteric.
3. The climacteric is sometimes, but not necessarily always, associated with symptomatology. When this does occur it may be termed the "climacteric syndrome."

Climacteric symptoms and complaints are regarded as being derived from three main sources:

Miriam Formanek-Brunell's assistance is gratefully acknowledged.

RUTH FORMANEK, PH.D. • Professor of Education, Hofstra University, Hempstead, New York; Chief Psychologist, Jewish Community Services, Rego Park, Long Island; private practice. *Note:* Some portions of this paper are included in "Menopause and Depression: A Socially-Constructed Link." In Ruth Formanek and Anita Gurian (Eds.), *Women and Depression: A Lifespan Perspective* (1987). New York: Springer Publishing Co.

1. Decreased ovarian activity with subsequent hormonal deficiency, resulting in early symptoms (hot flashes, perspiration, and atrophic vaginitis), and late symptoms related to metabolic changes.
2. Sociocultural factors determined by the woman's environment.
3. Psychological factors, dependent on the woman's personality.
4. Combinations of the above.

An understanding of societal attitudes toward the menopause requires an excursion into different historical periods as particular views of the menopause appear to be consistent with prevailing views of women.

HISTORICAL ACCOUNTS

Before 1800

Freind wrote the first book on menstruation, published in English in 1729. He cites the Greek physician Galen (between A.D. 130 and 200), who had a theory about the menopause which became most influential: "The Menses are given to Women, that they may be evacuated for their Healths sake; and yield Nourishment to the Embryo, when suppressed by Conception." It was believed that a plethora existed, an accumulation of blood which was periodically discharged until, at a certain age, "the Fibres of the Vessels grow more rigid and hard; so that a Plethora can neither be accumulated at that Age, nor if it be, can it be discharged, because of the tenacity of the Vessels . . . elderly Women are more dry and abound less with Blood" (p. 59). Freind notes no menopausal symptoms other than ". . . many Women, as soon as they are destitute of their Menses, contract a fuller habit, and grow fat" (p. 62).

This somewhat mechanical view of women's functioning was accepted with minor modifications until the discovery of hormones could explain the phenomena of menstruation and menopause. Although little was known about menopause, its negative effects were widely speculated on and accepted as fact. Beginning in the late 18th century, menopause was viewed as a catastrophe for women.

The exact origin of the alleged association between menopause and symptoms of emotional disturbance is unclear. It is first found in the years following publication of Freind's book. John Leake (1777) believed that,

> At this *critical time of life* [his italics] the female sex are often visited with various diseases of the *chronic* kind. . . . Some are subject to pain and giddiness of the head, hysteric disorders, colic pains, and a female weakness . . . intolerable itching at the neck of the bladder and contiguous parts are often very troublesome to others. . . . Women are sometimes affected with low spirits and melancholy.

Turning Point: From Midwives to Physicians

In colonial America, most medical care for women was provided by women in the home. Women were also prominent as lay practitioners, midwives, and "doctoresses." Until the decline of midwifery around 1800, pregnant women relied on midwives and female relatives and friends, at which time the shift from midwives to male doctors started among urban middle-class women. These well-to-do women had come to accept physicians' claims of superior skill despite some moral opposition to male physicians attending childbirth. Thus, it appears that an interest in the symptoms representing emotional disturbance presumed to arise from women's reproductive crises coincided with the replacement of midwives by male physicians. That male physicians described, and sometimes invented, dangers at such crisis points appears to be related to the demands of the professionalization of medicine, as well as to presumed fears on the part of men of women's elaborate reproductive physiology, in particular, menstruation.

The Victorians

The Victorians used metaphor to describe the menopause (Harland, 1882):

> Before the golden calm of Indian Summer come the long wearying autumnal rains that beat the latest blooming chrysanthemums into the earth and despoil the trees of their liveries of russet and purple. . . . The season is like the passage of the Valley of the Shadow of Death (pp. 314–315).

Florid descriptions of symptoms were the rule. Napheys (1871), a widely read Victorian physician who wrote on women's sexual physiology, speaks of the dangers of the beginning and ending of the period of childbearing, dangers that had not been described by midwives and lay practitioners:

> The green-sickness, chlorosis, is by no means exclusively a disease of girls. It may occur at any period of childbearing life. . . . Hardly any one has watched women closely without having observed the peculiar tint of skin, the debility, the dislike of society, the change of temper, the fitful appetite, the paleness of the eye, and the other traits that show the presence of such a condition of the nervous system in those about renouncing their powers of reproduction (p. 296).

According to Napheys, the "change of life" causes a number of changes in the lives of women: there is a diminution of the sexual passions; soon after this period they quite disappear. Sometimes, however, the reverse takes place, and the sexual sensations increase in intensity, occasionally exceeding what they were before. He suggests that this should be regarded with alarm as it is contrary to the design of nature. He implies that a "deep-seated disease of the uterus or ovaries is likely to be present, or an unnatural nervous excitability is there, which, if indulged, will bring about dangerous consequences. Gratification, therefore, should be temperate, and at rare intervals, or wholly denied" (p. 301). Women are also said to experience "a sense of fulness in the head, a giddiness, and a dulness of the brain, sometimes going so far as to cause an uncertainty in the step, a slowness of comprehension, and a feeling as if one might fall at any moment in some sort of a fit" (p. 297). The menopausal woman develops an "inward nervousness," becomes confused, and imagines that "she is watched with suspicious and unkind eyes . . . every ache and pain is magnified." She becomes a hypochondriac and fears she will die (p. 297).

Napheys noted not only changes in sexual desire, cognitive and psychomotor deficits, but depression as well:

> Vibrating between a distressing excitement and a gloomy depression, her temper gives way. . . . She becomes fretful, and yet full of remorse for yielding to her peevishness; she seeks for sympathy without being able to give reasons for needing it; she annoys those around her by groundless fears; and is angered when they show their annoyance. In *fine*, she is utterly wretched, without any obvious cause of wretchedness.

In contrast to the medical literature, popular magazines omitted references to women's reproductive life, in line with custom: "A women would not complain about any ailment occurring between her neck and her knees" (Kunciov, 1971, p. 152). According to Showalter (1985), Victorians still believed the old notion that madness was a disease of the blood, that menstrual blood predisposed women to insanity, in that an abnormality of the flow might affect the brain. "Suppressed" menstruation was forcefully treated with medicines, purgatives, or leeches applied to the thighs.

The menopausal form of insanity (later named "involutional melancholia") accounted for 196 out of 228 cases in the Royal Edinburgh Asylum, between 1874 and 1882, and the diagnosis seems to have been a convenient label for all older women patients. Treatment was cruel, especially if the woman patient exhibited signs of unconventional erotic behavior. Smith (1848) recommended injections of ice water into the rectum, ice into the vagina and leeching of the labia and the cervix. Clitorectomies were performed for many conditions, including masturbation, disobedience, and digestive troubles. The operation was believed to be the treatment of choice for both nymphomania and insanity. In the United States in particular, the removal of the ovaries—oophorectomy—was used as a treatment for insanity during the latter part of the 19th century, especially on institutionalized women (Showalter, 1985). Thus, it is clear that the medicalization of women's reproductive crises led to crippling operations, in total ignorance of the nature of women's physiology, and without regard for their well-being.

The medicalization and pathologization of puberty and menopause by male physicians was influenced by sociohistorical factors which also influenced the consciousness of the larger society. We must therefore consider changes in the perception of women, specifically the idealization of the maternal role, a 19th century development associated with the rise of the middle class.

The Idealization of Motherhood (1800–1860)

In addition to the replacement of women practitioners and midwives by male physicians, and the professionalization of medicine, a new type of family life emerged with the rise of the middle class. It was characterized as "women's sphere" and linked women together in domesticity and child rearing. Female character was redefined: the home was idealized as "a bastion of feminine values, of piety and morality, affection and self-sacrifice" (Woloch, 1984, p. 116). Concomitant with the increasing importance of the home, the family was becoming smaller.

While the average family in 1800 had seven children, by 1900 the average was between three and four children. And as the size of the family began to shrink, the value of motherhood rose. Child raising became the family's central focus. Nationally distributed magazines (*Ladies Magazine, Godey's Lady's Book*) featured scenes of mothers at home, surrounded by children. Motherhood was celebrated as the "ultimate opportunity for self-sacrifice and as the major role for women" (Woloch, p. 118).

The emphasis on, and the idealization of motherhood and feminine qualities influenced the construction of women's identity. If motherhood was woman's main role and function, it was presumed that the end of her reproductive capacity was cause for unhappiness. But the descriptions of the symptoms accompanying the end of woman's reproductive functioning were written by male doctors, and women were not considered. Since not all menopausal women consult physicians today, we may assume that those without complaints were unknown to physicians during the 19th century. That physicians assumed that all women who had reached the menopause were ill was based on faulty generalizations, misogynist perceptions, the needs of the new professional class of physicians to minister to the ill, and physicians' fears of the as yet unexplained phenomena of menstruation and its cessation. That physicians included prohibitions to women in regard to their pursuit of higher education or suffrage further suggests a political agenda. Thus, it appears that the sufferings of the menopause were socially constructed and projected onto women, many of whom probably innocently cooperated by reporting the symptoms expected by their physicians.

DISCREPANT MEANINGS OF THE MENOPAUSE

There was and still is a discrepancy between the views of physicians and the actual experience of menopausal women. Causes of the discrepancy include limited communication between physician and patient and a hesitancy on the part of the male physician to inquire into the intricacies of women's reproductive experiences. With the advent of women physicians in the late 1800s, one assumes that communication improved. Still in 1913, physicians were advised to be "delicate" in taking a case history: "Having inquired regarding the regularity of the bowels, one may ask if the patient is 'regular in her own health,' or 'regular in her unwell times'." Further questions are directed to facts: length of menstrual period, intervals between periods, whether it has stopped altogether, how much blood is lost, whether pain is present, the age at which menstruation began, and the occurrence or not of intermenstrual leucorrhea ("white discharge") (Hutchison and Rainy)..

Since these questions refer to objective and statistical events only, it is no wonder physicians knew little of either menstrual or menopausal experience. And knowing little probably served to perpetuate earlier myths as well as aiding the construction of pathological conditions which either had no reality (e.g., chlorosis) or which were usually benign (e.g., leucorrhea).

Yet menopause must have had positive meanings for individual women who longed for a limitation of their reproductive powers. "I am forty-four years of age and the mother of fourteen living children," a letter to Margaret Sanger (1928) begins. "My baby is five months old. I am anxious to know what you can tell me. Please send me the information (on birth control) at once for I am still thinking that my age won't interfere with me continuing to become a mother yet awhile . . ." (p. 206). According to Mrs. A. M. Longshore-Potts (1895), one of the new female physicians, "many pass on until ten, twelve, or even fifteen children have been born, with an accumulation of troubles to correspond. . . . But after these years have passed, and the climax of her womanhood has been reached, when there are no more children to be born, no more teeth to come, no more measles or whooping-cough, and no more babies' deaths to break her heart. . . . Now they have leisure to read, think, and talk on subjects congenial to their age and development, now is the time for them to lay aside the more worldly cares, and to let the intellect have opportunity to grasp what may be learned in social life, or from public lectures . . ." (p. 102). Social reformer and suffrage advocate Eliza Farnham believed that menopause could become women's golden age and the postmenopausal years the period of woman's "super-exaltation" (Smith-Rosenberg, 1976).

Thus, by the end of the 19th century, menopause had two different meanings depending on who was consulted: a male physician or a female physician, social reformer, or menopausal woman, especially one with many children. Men tended to view "the changes" as the beginning of a decline of physical, emotional, and cognitive functioning. For most women, however, it was a golden age, a time at which pregnancies were no longer dreaded.

The two meanings of menopause continue to exist today as well. Cowan, Warren, and Young (1985) asked 35 physicians, 43 nurses, and 35 menopausal or postmenopausal women to rate the frequency, severity, and causality of 15 menopausal symptoms. Results suggested that medical persons saw the menopausal symptoms as more pathological than the menopausal women and that physicians adhered to a psychogenic model, in which psychological causality and symptoms are given greater emphasis than menopausal women give them. Posner (1979), on the basis of a content analysis of gynecological textbooks, concluded that the medical model of menopause is a psychological one. Physicians thus are prepared to expect that psychologically well-adjusted women will experience few menopausal problems. In another review, not specifically dealing with the menopause, Fidell (1980) noted that physicians are predisposed to attribute symptoms presented by women in general to psychogenic rather than organic causes.

There has been, however, an increasing awareness within the nursing profession of the discrepancies in views between physicians and women, particularly those concerned with women's health. MacPherson (1981) contrasts the "health and illness" approach, in a paper titled, "Menopause as Disease: The Social Construction of a Metaphor." MacPherson goes beyond a description, however, and calls for the dismantling of the metaphor by the nursing profession.

By the end of the 19th century, little progress had occurred in regard to the understanding of the causes of menopause. With hormones not to be discovered until the 1920s, Galen's theory of a "plethora" and the increasing rigidity of women's vessels continued to be reformulated, albeit in jargon which sounded more sophisticated. For example, statements are found in the medical literature of the 1890s referring to the radiating currents of ganglionic centers, whose reflex action cause the phenomena of the climacteric.

INVOLUTIONAL MELANCHOLIA

Out of earlier collections of emotional symptoms suggestive of insanity and depression, Kraepelin (1909), an influential German psychiatrist, reformulated "involutional[1] psychoses"—depressive episodes of major proportions occurring for the first time in the involutional ages without a prior history of depressive illness. According to Kraepelin, involutional psychoses constituted one-third of all functional psychoses, the other two being dementia praecox and manic-depressive psychosis. Involutional melancholia had a gradual onset during the climacterium, was marked by hypochondriasis, pessimism, and irritability, and led to a full-blown depressive syndrome. The most prominent features, according to Kraepelin, were agitation, restlessness, anxiety and apprehension, occasionally bizarre delusions or paranoid ideation, insomnia, anorexia, and feelings of guilt and worthlessness.

PSYCHOANALYTIC FORMULATIONS: HELENE DEUTSCH

In the presence of taboos and the absence of precise information, old myths rarely fade away. Rather, they are sometimes given new life through reinterpretation. Helene Deutsch (1924) retained 19th-century pejorative medical myths about the menopause but reformulated them in accord with Freud's account of psychosexual development. The myths Deutsch retained include the following:

1. The similarity between the course of puberty and menopause.
2. The correlation between the ending of menstruation and the ending of women's sexuality, together with inappropriate sexual desires.
3. The presence of multiple symptoms, especially depression, ascribed to menopause.
4. Woman's presumed yearning for a continuation of her ability to reproduce.

The menopause, according to Deutsch, "woman's last traumatic experience as a sexual being . . . is under the aegis of an incurable narcissistic wound." Parallel to the physical process, the menopause represents a psychosexual regression toward earlier, infantile libidinal positions, a "dethroning" of libido. At puberty, Deutsch states, "the narcissistic wound of the final renunciation of masculinity is wiped out by the appearance of secondary sexual characteristics and a new feminine physical attractiveness" (p. 56). At menopause, what was granted at puberty is now taken back, at the same time that the woman's attractiveness is lost.

Deutsch speaks of typical behavioral changes during menopause, similar to those attending puberty. "She feels like a young girl, believes herself able to make a fresh start in life . . . feels ready for any passion, etc. She starts keeping a diary as she did when she was a girl, develops enthusiasm for some abstract idea as she did

[1]*Involutional* is used in biology to denote a retrograde or degenerative change (*Webster's New 20th Century Dictionary*, 1970).

then, changes her behavior to her family as she did before, leaves home for the same psychical reasons as girls do at puberty, etc. . . . Many women who were frigid during the reproductive period now become sexually sensitive, and others become frigid for the first time. . . . Others who have hitherto put up well with frigidity now begin to demonstrate all its typical concomitant phenomena; changes of mood, unbalanced behavior and irritability set in and make life a torment for the woman herself and those about her . . ." (p. 58).

Although Deutsch later, in 1945, revised some of her views, she continued to interpret the meaning of the menopause according to the stages of psychosexual development. Yet she differed with Freud who had considered libido as masculine, and she referred to "the unappreciated female libido." Deutsch, despite her overall negative view in regard to the menopausal woman also stressed the need for a psychology of women, one deserving equal importance to that of men.

Psychoanalyst Benedek's (1947) view of the menopausal woman is more benign than that of Deutsch. She criticizes Deutsch's account of the menopausal woman as more descriptive of an infantile personality than of a normal woman. According to Benedek, the climacterium is a "developmental phase, . . . a progressive psychologic adaptation to a regressive biologic process" (p. 322). She suggests that, parallel with declining hormone production, menopause desexualizes emotional needs; thus sublimatory energies are freed which further the integration of the personality. In addition, cultural patterns exert an influence on women's expectations of the menopause.

Analogous to 19th century medical opinion and to Helene Deutsch, Benedek also believed that certain psychological aspects of the menopause represent a repetition of the affect, behavior, and perception of self which was typical of the woman's puberty. Benedek described women who become anxious and overactive instead of, or before the development of depression. Some climacteric women feel that they did not achieve the goal of femininity, and may be seized by fear of aging or of losing their sexual attractiveness.

A more recent psychoanalytic view, one influenced by psychoanalytic object relations and developmental theory, is exemplified by Lax (1982). She has suggested that a woman's climacteric response will be determined by the severity of her physiological symptoms, the nature of her past experiences, her internalized object relations, her psychic structure, her libidinal investments, the width of her conflict-free ego sphere, her ego interests, her healthy narcissism, her current object relations and the nature of her familial and social setting—in other words, both internal and external reality are capable of exerting an influence on a woman's response during this period. Moreover, Lax argues that the changes attending the climacteric "make it more difficult and sometimes even impossible for the menopausal woman to achieve those goals of her wishful self-image which she had previously taken for granted. This whole constellation of factors accounts for the development of the expectable depressive climacteric reaction" (p. 163). However, successful mourning allows a woman to renounce the no longer attainable goals and ideals of her youthful self-image, and to develop an identification with an idealized matriarchal model whose generativity, generosity, and compassion become her own goals.

While empirical studies tend to find primarily vasomotor symptoms among menopausal women, psychoanalytic investigations have focused on depressive reactions. It is therefore of interest that recent life-event studies measuring stress have similarly documented the presence of a vulnerability to depression among menopausal women, but only in certain cultures with particular sensitivities to loss (Greene, 1984).

FLASHBACK TO THE 1920S: THE DISCOVERY AND MARKETING OF ESTROGENS

When Butenandt, a Nobel prize winner in chemistry, isolated a hormone from the urine of pregnant women in 1929, the physiology of the menopause began to be understood. Despite this important discovery, however, the myths and stereotypes of menopausal women remained unchanged. Moreover, the 1960s saw a recurrence of the exaggeration of women's hormonal deficiency, this time motivated by the greed of pharmaceutical manufacturers and members of the medical profession supported by them.

According to writers such as Wilson and Wilson, women were said to show a stiffness of muscles and ligaments, the "dowager's hump," and a "negativistic expression." "Some exhibit signs and symptoms similar to those in the early stages of Parkinson's disease. They exist rather than live." The Wilsons describe "unfortunate women abounding in the streets walking stiffly in twos and threes, seeing little and observing less. The world appears (to them) as through a grey veil, and they live as docile, harmless creatures missing most of life's values . . . in a vapid cowlike negative state." Wilson defined the menopause as an estrogen deficiency disease and, in his book *Feminine Forever* (1966), he offered women estrogen replacement therapy. Although the book was excerpted in *Look* and in *Vogue* and sold 100,000 copies in the first 7 months after publication, Wilson was dismissed as a quack by his more responsible colleagues.

What Wilson had promised was relief from 26 symptoms of estrogen deficiency which included anxiety, hot flashes, joint pains, melancholia, crying spells, headache, loss of memory, indigestion, itching, backache, neurosis, a tendency to take alcohol and sleeping pills, and even to contemplate suicide. The Wilson Research Foundation, headed by Dr. Wilson, received, in 1964, $17,000 from the Searle Foundation, $8700 from Ayerst Laboratories, and $5600 from the Upjohn Company, according to the *Washington Post* (Seaman & Seaman, 1977, p. 289). Ayerst also supported the Information Center on the Mature Woman, a public relations firm that promoted estrogen replacement therapy. Estrogen in the form of Premarin (Ayerst) was prescribed for long-term use for 6 million women and became the fourth or fifth most popular drug in the United States. The drug rapidly lost its popularity when, in 1975, a report was published that indicated a correlation between estrogen replacement therapy and uterine cancer.

The negative effects the campaign advertising Premarin had on menopausal women has not been researched. There can be no doubt, however, that women must have cringed, and perhaps felt depressed when they read that "no woman can be sure of escaping the horror of this living decay" (Wilson, p. 43).

MENOPAUSAL SYMPTOMS

On the basis of empirical findings, Kraepelin's diagnosis of involutional melancholia is now considered untenable as a specific condition which has its first onset during the climacteric. When menopausal or postmenopausal women are depressed, it is usually possible to discover episodes of depression at earlier times in their lives (Greene, 1984; Weissman, 1979). In view of the lack of empirical verification, involutional melancholia was omitted as a diagnostic category in DSM III.

Although menopausal women may not have a first-onset depressive episode, some women experience some symptoms as a result either of natural or surgical menopause. Greene (1984), on the basis of 14 nonclinical population surveys of symptoms among menopausal women, concludes that the only symptoms closely related to the menopause are vasomotor ones. Hot flashes peak during the menopause, are reported by 18% of women before the menopause and 75% during the perimenopause. No other symptoms show such dramatic increases during this time period.

The nonspecific symptoms due to aging need to be separated from the symptoms of estrogen deficiency (e.g., hot flashes, or flushes, and atrophic vaginitis). The ascribing of pathological symptoms, such as memory loss or other cognitive impairment and hypochondriasis, to the menopause has had a generally disparaging effect on women's feelings about themselves (Formanek, 1986). Women have often been fearful of the approach of the menopause since they expected to experience such pathological concomitants. The meaning of symptoms to individual women have to be explored and stereotypical expectations recognized as damaging.

Research on menopausal symptoms has been poor and sparse. Clinical studies find that women report many symptoms, whereas community samples estimate that the majority of women are symptom-free. Sleep disturbance, as other non-vasomotor symptoms, may be a reflection of increasing age rather than be directly related to menopause.

To comprehend women's reactions to the menopause requires attention to societal attitudes and perceptions of the menopause as well as the exploration of self-representations. How do women internally represent reproductive functioning and its cessation? In contrast to men, women are genetically programmed to develop cyclical functioning (Tanner, 1978). Although not observable before puberty, cycles become and remain salient to conscious and unconscious states for several decades until they disappear with menopause. Cycles punctuate and organize women's existence between puberty and menopause. Women's perception of the flux of time as a function of their awareness of ovulation, menstruation, pregnancy, and lactation suggests that cyclicity affects their intrapsychic life, although little research exists beyond the observations of women and their therapists.

In addition to cyclicity and the awareness of time, women may also be more aware of their varying bodily states in the course of their menstrual month. Could one link woman's allegedly greater capacity for empathy or intuition to the awareness of her own ever-changing bodily and psychological states?

In addition to cyclicity, some experiences are also characterized by wave-like phenomena. While physiological functioning in both males and females has a wave-like character (e.g., orgasm, peristalsis), women's physiology includes more such events: menstrual cramps, labor pains, and menopausal hot flashes. From this it follows that the experience of menopause should be accompanied by major changes of awareness now that cyclicity is at an end. Will there be changes in women's sense of time? Interpersonally? In the perception of bodily states?

Yet, menopause does not appear to constitute a major change in awareness in the lives of most women, and longings of menopausal women for their earlier cyclicity are rarely heard. Is it possible that the cyclicity exerts an influence on women's psychical functioning only between puberty and menopause? The absence of a change in awareness as women traverse the road from cyclic to noncyclic functioning is astounding.

The answer to the riddle might be the late beginnings of cyclicity in the lives of women. Since cyclical functioning does not establish itself until puberty, a girl's gender identity has already developed. Thus, the new cyclical functioning exerts less of an effect than one might expect were it to begin at birth. Analogously, most women slip back into noncyclic functioning, without a crisis.

What are women's idiosyncratic reactions to the experience of menopause? While not all women report the presence of symptoms due to estrogen depletion, many are plagued by hot flashes, accompanied by perspiration, as well as by atrophic vaginitis. It is clear that hot flashes are most unpleasant to many menopausal and postmenopausal women although the duration of each flash is brief and painless. Yet flashes vary in their frequency per day or per hour, in the degree of heat they create, and in the number of years they are present. Hot flashes are dramatically eliminated when estrogens are administered, and the same medication, locally applied, relieves atrophic vaginitis. The administration of estrogens, sometimes combined with progesterone, is presently still controversial and only longitudinal studies will determine their safety. While it is assumed that, with increasing age, the frequency and intensity of the hot flash will decrease, it is unknown whether the administration of estrogens and their discontinuation after a few years will lengthen the duration of the hot flash over time.

The nature of the hot flash is presently barely explored. Only five studies are noted in the *Index Medicus* between 1903 and 1973. Molnar (1975) described the hot flash of one woman, ascribing the paucity of information on this symptom to the reluctance of women to step forward and be measured. Other researchers have found women without such hesitations, although samples have remained relatively small. Sturdee (1978) included 8 women, Coope *et al.* (1978) 25, Tataryn *et al.* (1979) and Casper (1979), 6 women each, and Voda (1978) 67 women.

Voda asked women to record each flush, to indicate the bodily sites where they were first experienced and their wave-like travels across portions of their bodies. Although the menopausal experience differs from woman to woman, the flash is perceived in similar ways. Equally little is known about women's subjective experience or symbolic representations of the hot flash. Voda's sample recorded "coping strategies" which permit speculation about women's reactions. Most women in her sample attempted to cope with the hot flash by means of cooling their bodies: by drinking cool liquids, fanning themselves, standing in front of an air conditioner or fan, by swimming, showering, or opening a window. "A few subjects chose to ignore the hot flash and/or to cope with it by recording it, trying to forget it, or actively telling the hot flash to 'go away'" (p. 238). Many women reported doing nothing.

Reactions to the hot flash appear to differ vastly in regard to its subjective meanings, but so far most data are clinical or anecdotal. Several continua may be postulated about the subjective meanings of the flash, in regard to (1) awareness of the flash and its relationship to menopause, (2) sensitivity, and (3) viewpoint. Ms. A., for example, a 50-year-old woman whose family lives in a distant city, who had no close women friends, and who was not knowledgable about women's health issues, reported that she believed she was ill since she had been awakened several times a night by perspiration, suddenly felt hot during the day, and suspected that she might have an infection and a fever. On the other end of the continuum are those women who are well informed, know what to expect and endure hot flashes as they earlier endured menstrual discomfort. Other women differ in sensitivity to their symptoms. Some become sensitive to symptom meanings and to them menopause represents aging, being "over the hill" and, as such, a narcissistic injury. On the other end of the continuum are those women who minimize the meanings and the effects of menopause, who are insensitive to their symptoms, or who lack symptoms altogether. Some view menopause as "the golden age," which provides them with a natural method of birth control. On the other hand, sadness is frequently felt by those women who want children, who now realize they will never bear them. For them, each hot flash is a reminder of the cruelty of their limited years of reproductive ability. Since women have always experienced their menstrual or menopausal functioning as shrouded by taboos, they usually keep their reactions to menopausal symptoms to themselves.

THE INFLUENCE OF LIFE EVENTS ON SYMPTOMS

The climacterium is a developmental phase and, as such, has its specific characteristics. It exerts a particular effect on women, based partly on its meaning to the individual as well as cultural expectations. Epidemiological researchers (e.g., Brown & Harris, 1978; Brown & Prudo, 1981; Cooke & Greene, 1981; Greene, 1984; Paykel *et al.*, 1971) have focused on measuring life events as contributing to stress for the individual. However, researchers don't conceptualize a simple causal link between life event and effect on the individual. Rather, sophisticated models have been proposed which consider "vulnerabilities" in individuals as following "provoking events."

Life stress scores have been calculated and examined in regard to menopausal and climacteric status. Total life stress increases and peaks during the early climacteric period, but being menopausal does not contribute to increased vulnerability to life stress. However, when *types* of life events of urban Scottish women were investigated (Greene & Cooke, 1981), the life event which differentiated older from younger women was "exits." These are defined as departures of others from the social field of the subject, and were more numerous among the climacteric women. The "exits" included children leaving the home, separations, and the deaths of close friends or family members. Greene (1984) concludes that the increase in symptoms among his Scottish sample is associated with the degree of current life stress to which they are exposed. Moreover, different symptoms were influenced by different life events in complex ways. Psychological symptoms seemed to be related to stress arising from financial, legal, work, housing conditions, illness in the family, etc., but such stressful events did not increase among the climacteric women. However, at the time of the climacterium, some women became vulnerable to common difficulties, and this vulnerability manifested itself in the form of psychological complaints. Somatic symptoms, like psychological symptoms, were also reported more frequently by climacteric women who were experiencing high levels of stress, but *only* if the women had also experienced a recent bereavement. Brown and Harris (1978) earlier had found that severe events and major long-term difficulties could bring about depression in a woman, especially if she had more than three children under 14 years of age at home, had lost her mother in childhood, had no confiding relationship with her spouse, and had no job. Brown *et al.* (1979) consider further susceptibility factors to depression, and refer to aging, which involves physiological changes as well as psychosocial ones. A midlife crisis, according to Brown *et al.*, may develop in response to quite minor events.

Brown and Prudo (1981) report that bereavement appeared to provoke psychiatric disorders among 48% of onset depressive cases in the Hebrides, but only in 16% of London women. Chronicity of psychiatric condition showed a similar pattern: the loss of a member of the woman's primary family preceded chronicity of psychiatric condition in 77% of Hebrides women, but in only 16% in London. The authors consider the greater sensitivity of Hebrides women to death—a cultural factor—to add to the women's vulnerability.

The climacteric may act as a "vulnerability" factor in that minor life events may provoke symptoms during this time to a greater degree than at other times of the lifespan. In particular, the death of a close relative may act as a provoking agent to depression in societies with a cultural sensitivity to such deaths. Moreover, deaths, or the illness and symptoms of the recently deceased person may exacerbate somatic symptoms among women already experiencing somatic discomfort for hormonal or other reasons. What makes climacteric women even more vulnerable is that the death of a close person deprives the woman of social support. It is important to note that researchers speak of climacterium rather than of menopause. Thus they differentiate physiological contributions to the vulnerability to depression from those due to aging.

SOCIOCULTURAL DIFFERENCES

Negative attitudes toward the menopause in our society are usually based on stereotypes and are found to be stronger in younger than in older women. Women who are actually experiencing the menopause show a decline in negative attitudes. In addition to younger women, those of lower socioeconomic status, income, and education also show more negative attitudes toward the menopause. In general, as age, years of education, and information about the menopause increase, so do more positive attitudes (see Notman, 1979; Neugarten & Kraines, 1965).

In regard to individual women, the more a woman has valued her reproductive role the more negative her attitude toward menopause is likely to be. However, this appears to be subject to cultural influences, as the social consequences of menopause in a particular society affect a woman's role and status, and thus her attitudes (see Kaufert, 1985).

Datan *et al.* (1985) studied 1148 women from five Israeli subcultures ranging along a continuum from modernity: immigrant Jews from Central Europe, Turkey, Persia, and North Africa; and Israeli-born Muslim Arabs. The researchers conclude that cultural patterns produce greater stress in the modern culture, manifested at the extreme as depression, and that there are different modes of stress expression: Persian and North African women tend to have more psychosomatic complaints, while Europeans voice more psychological distress. The most important finding of the research is that clinical depression is rare but appears in approximately equal rates across cultures. Datan *et al.* conclude that "the response to middle age and to the climacterium is shaped by ethnic origin, that the balance of gains and losses is specific to each subculture, that there is no linear relationship between psychological well-being and the degree of modernity, and finally, that the cessation of fertility is welcomed by women in all cultures" (p. 179).

A more recent study also focused on the cessation of fertility. Kaufert (1985) has reported on the Manitoba project, a questionnaire study of 2500 women between the ages of 40 and 59. Tentative findings include the following:

- When questioned about whether the women had wanted more children after their last child was born, 89% responded no.
- To the question, "Looking back, do you wish you had another child?" 82% said no.
- "Would you like to have a child at some time in the future?" No, was the response of 96%.
- "Do you worry about being too old to have children?" Not at all, was the response of 96% of respondents.

It must be noted that only 8% of the 2500 women were childless.

What both common sense, personal experience, and empirical research agree on is the lack of general statements that can be confirmed for all menopausal women regardless of age, number of children, socioeconomic status, education, culture, and many other factors. The idiosyncratic responses to menopause have in the past been muted, not talked about, considered taboo. As a result, strong statements from medical and psychiatric sources have been accepted as they offered to define the darkness.

This chapter has examined the historical development of pejorative views of the menopause, the meaning of menopause in some societies and time periods, and the effects of such views on the experiences of women. The last 25 years have seen efforts to research women's functioning during the climacteric by means of both clinical and population surveys. Early but firmly held assumptions based on myth rather than reality about the pathology of women's being "unwell," as well as the cessation of their being "unwell," have crumbled or are about to crumble.

More research needs to be done. Stressors due to negative life events must be further examined as they interact with cyclicity, life experience, life style, relationships, culture, etc. The almost total absence of the understanding of the subjective experience of the menopause must be replaced with first-hand accounts, psychoanalytical and other explorations, structured interviews, and information from women's physicians and women physicians.

REFERENCES

Ballinger, C. B. (1976). Subjective sleep disturbance at the menopause. *Journal of Psychosomatic Research, 20,* 599–513.

Benedek, T. (1947). Climacterium: A developmental phase. In *Psychoanalytic investigations. Selected papers.* New York: Quadrangle, 1973.

Brown, J. K., & Kerns, V. (Eds.) (1985). *In her prime. A new view of the middle-aged woman.* South Hadley, MA: Bergin and Garvey.

Brown, G. W., & Harris, T. (1978). *Social origins of depression.* New York: Free Press.

Brown, G. W., Ni Bhrolchain, M., & Harris, T. O. (1984). In J. B. Greene (1984), *The social and psychological origins of the climacteric syndrome.* Brookfield, VT: Gower.

Brown, & Prudo, (1981). In J. B. Greene (1984), *The social and psychological origins of the climacteric syndrome.* Brookfield, Vt.: Gower.

Casper, (1979). In A. M. Voda, M. Dinnerstein, and S. R. O'Donnell (Eds.), *Changing perspectives on menopause.* Austin: University of Texas Press.

Cooke, D. J., & Greene, J. G. (1981). Types of life events in relation to symptoms at the climacterium. *Journal of Psychosomatic Research, 25,* 5–11.

Coope, et al. (1978). In A. M. Voda, M. Dinnerstein, & S. R. O'Donnell (Eds.), *Changing perspectives on menopause.* Austin: University of Texas Press.

Cowan, G., Warren, L. W., & Young, J. L. (1985). Medical perceptions of menopausal symptoms. *Psychology of Women Quarterly, 9,* 3–14.

Datan, N., Antonousky, A., & Maoz, B. (1985). Tradition, modernity and transitions in five Israeli subcultures. In Brown, J., & Kerns, V. (Eds.) (1985). *In her prime. A new view of the middle-aged woman,* South Hadley, MA: Bergin and Garvey.

Deutsch, H. (1924). The Menopause. *International Journal of Psycho-analysis, 65,* 55–62, 1984.

Deutsch, H. (1945). *Psychology of women.* New York: Grune & Stratton.

Fausto-Sterling, A. (1985). *Myths of gender.* New York: Basic Books.

Fidell, L. S. (1980). Frequency and severity of menopausal symptoms. In S. Campbell (Ed.), *The management of the menopause and post-menopausal years.* Baltimore: University Park Press.

Formanek, R. (1986). Learning the lines: Women's aging and self esteem. In J. Alpert (Ed.), *Women and psychoanalysis.* Hillsdale, NJ: Analytic Press.

Freind, J. (1729). *Emmenologia.* London: T. Cox.

Golub, S. (1983). *Lifting the curse of menstruation. A feminist appraisal of the influence of menstruation on women's lives.* New York: Haworth Press.

Goodman, M. (1980). Toward a biology of menopause. *Signs: Journal of Women in Culture and Society, 5,* 739–753.

Greene, J. B. (1984). *The social and psychological origins of the climacteric syndrome.* Brookfield, VT: Gower.

Harland, M. (1882). *Eve's daughters, or common sense for maid, wife and mother.* New York: Anderson and Allen.

Hutchison, R., & Rainy, H. (1913). *Clinical methods.* New York: Funk & Wagnalls.

Kaufert, P. (1985). Midlife in the midwest, Canadian women in Manitoba. In J. K. Brown, V. Kerns (Eds.), *In her prime. A new view of the middle-aged woman.* South Hadley, MA: Bergin and Garvey.

Kraepelin, E. (1909). *Psychiatrie,* 8th Ed. Leipsic: J. A. Barth.

Kunciov, R. (1971). *Mr. Godey's ladies*. Princeton, NJ: Pyne Press.

Lax, R. (1982). The expectable depressive climacteric reaction. *Bulletin of the Menninger Clinic,* 46, 151–167.

Longshore-Potts, A. M. (1895). *Discourses to women on medical subjects*. Published by the author, National City, San Diego County, Calif.

MacPherson, K. I. (1981). Menopause as disease: The social construction of a metaphor. *Advances in Nursing Science, 3,* 95–113.

Molnar (1975). In A. M. Voda, M. Dinnerstein, & S. R. O'Donnell (Eds.), *Changing perspectives on menopause*. Austin: University of Texas Press.

Napheys, G. H. (1871). *The physical life of woman: Advice to the maiden, wife and mother*. Philadelphia: MacLean.

Neugarten, B. & Kraines, R. J. (1965). Menopausal symptoms in women at various ages. *Psychosomatic Medicine, 27,* 266–273.

Notman, M. (1979). Midlife concerns of women: Implications of the menopause. *American Journal of Psychiatry, 1:* 1270–1274.

Paykel, E. S., Prusoff, B. A., & Uhleahuth, E. H. (1971). Scaling of life events. *Archives of General Psychiatry, 25,* 240–347.

Polit, D. F., & LaRocco, S. A. (1980). Social and psychological correlates of menopausal symptoms. *Psychosomatic Medicine, 42,* 335–345.

Posner, J. (1979). It's all in your head: Feminist and medical models of menopause. *Sex Roles, 5,* 179–190.

Sanger, M. (1928). *Motherhood in bondage*. New York: Brentano.

Seaman, B., & Seaman, G. (1977). *Women and the crisis in sex hormones*. New York: Rawson Associates.

Showalter, E. (1981). *Female maladies*. New York: Pantheon.

Smith-Rosenberg, C. (1976). Puberty to menopause: The cycle of femininity in nineteenth-century America. In C. Smith-Rosenberg (Ed.), *Disorderly conduct*. New York: Oxford University Press.

Sturdee (1978). In A. M. Voda, M. Dinnerstein, & S. R. O'Donnell (Eds.), *Changing perspectives on menopause*. Austin: University of Texas Press.

Tanner, J. M. (1978). *Fetus into man*. Cambridge, MA: Harvard University Press.

Tataryn et al. (1979). In A. M. Voda, M. Dinnerstein, & S. R. O'Donnell (Eds.), *Changing perspectives on menopause*. Austin: University of Texas Press.

Utian, W. (1980). *Menopause in modern perspective*. New York: Appleton-Century-Crofts.

Utian, W. H., & Serr, D. (1976). Report on workshop: The climacteric syndrome. In P. A. van Keep, R. B. Greenblatt, & M. Albeaux-Fernet (Eds.), *Consensus on menopause research*. Lancaster: MTP Press.

Voda, A. M. (1982). Menopausal hot flash. In A. M. Voda, M. Dinnerstein, & S. R. O'Donnell (Eds.), *Changing perspectives on menopause*. Austin: University of Texas Press.

Weissman, M. M. (1979). Sex differences and the epidemiology of depression. *Archives of General Psychiatry, 34,* 98–111.

Wilson, R. A. (1966). *Feminine forever*. New York: Mayflower-Dell.

Woloch, N. (1984). *Women and the American experience*. New York: Knopf.

Part V

Twentieth Century Female Issues and Problems

In the last part of this book we enter passages that are characteristic of the 20th century and look ahead. Susan Lichtendorf, author and medical journalist, departing somewhat in tone, holds a mirror up, reflecting on the influence of mass media, health food, "hot topics," and their influence on women's psyches today, with special focus on body image, body damage, and cosmetic surgery. Bonnie Robin Aronowitz offers us an astute researcher's perspective on the psychodynamics of abortion. Using data from interviews of outpatient abortion applicants, she provides a rich data base from which to arrive at some understanding of this prevalent and increasing 20th century phenomenon. She also underscores the idea that abortion, like the other passages in this book, affords the woman a developmental task in which the psychological and physical are combined, and how she, amidst specific psychological endowments and deficits, can reintegrate this experience into a reformulated feminine self-concept.

Melinda Gellman discusses eating disorders in women as a prevalent psychophysical passage occurring in the life of a woman. She reviews theories on anorexia nervosa, bulimia, and compulsive overeating, and traces the ongoing failures in female separation–individuation from their pregenital roots to young adulthood. Sue A. Shapiro discusses with sensitivity and depth the psychological impact of infertility, the subsequent psychological adjustment, and the ways individuals cope with the inevitable despair and desolation. Shapiro's chapter on infertility and her reference to the 10 million infertile Americans living today leads us naturally to look ahead to the new frontier: the intervention of biotechnology and all that this may mean psychologically, sociologically, ethically, legally, and politically.

Chapter 14

Body Image in the 21st Century

Susan S. Lichtendorf

> Men's magazines never say, "Do you weigh 300 pounds and are
> your thighs flabby?" They know a man would never buy a
> magazine that made him feel insecure or unattractive. They
> make men feel like heroes whereas magazines make us feel like
> failures.
> —Judith Krantz (in Dullea, 1986)

> How Do You See Yourself? . . .
> What would it take for you to finally feel good about what you
> see in the mirror?
> —"How Do You See Yourself" (1986)

As we race toward the 21st century, that quote (Dullea, 1986) from Judith Krantz, a women's magazine writer and novelist whose spectacular success demonstrates a keen perception of what sells, and those opening lines from an advertisement (*New York Magazine,* May 1986) hawking the services of a cosmetic surgeon, merit serious attention from those concerned with triggers of the unconscious and the physical and emotional health of women.

From youth to old age, women are the target of powerful, insistent messages from the mass media, provoking self doubt. Some of the messages are subtle, for example, the use of near-perfect models as exemplars for ordinary women, automatic losers by comparison. Some of the messages are as blatant as in Krantz's knowing comments.

Insecurity sells, but so does hope. The other side of the media's negative message is a seemingly positive one: salvation through diets, clever "makeovers," fashion, exercise, and the startling possibility of actual physical change. "The New You Is Waiting . . ." promises a cosmetic surgery advertisement ("The New You," 1986).

Healers of the psyche might be more apt to ask, "What's wrong with the old

---

Susan S. Lichtendorf • Medical Science Writer, Journalist, and Author; Member, National Association of Science Writers; Women in Communications.

you?" Valuable insight might come from reflection on an answer. But outside the "quiet" of the therapy room, reflection is all but drowned out by the constant roar of the media reminding women that indeed something is wrong. The diets, makeovers, and self-improvement plans touted are positive-seeming, but in fact are insidiously negative. After all, salvation wouldn't be necessary if women were acceptable as they are.

In counterpoint to that roar is a siren song. A promise of immediate change in a world that moves quickly. "Trade in Your Beak for a Darling Little Restroussé Nose," is the advice to be found in glossy magazines. Transformation—faces changed, bodies recontoured, wrinkles erased—which would have seemed to be science fiction in the time of Freud is reality today. And there is every reason to believe it will be even more commonplace in the future.

Nonetheless, physical change and the desire for physical change have implications that go beyond the strictly physical. In a 1985 commentary on a study of self-consistency approach to the psychology of cosmetic surgery Edgarton noted, "The *only basic justification for cosmetic surgery is to improve the emotional health of the patient*" (Edgarton's italics.) Unless this is accomplished, the real magic of plastic surgery does not occur." At the brink of the 21st century it would seem that a woman has a choice. She can invest time and money in therapy to understand why she detests part of herself; or, she can spend less time and probably less money and buy a new part. It's not that simple, of course.

Unlike the candidate for traditional plastic surgery seeking rescue from the marks of a gruesome accident or the misery of a congenital defect, the cosmetic surgery patient is normal in appearance. Of the cosmetic surgery patients that I have interviewed from 1979 to 1986, not one was grotesque before surgery. Yet each spoke of being loathsome, unacceptable, and wounded within. Looking at the statistics, it appears that incredible numbers of women feel unacceptable as they are.

Eighty percent of the more than one-half million Americans operated upon each year are women ("New Bodies," 1985). These are women of different social backgrounds and income levels. Whether or not cosmetic surgery improves emotional health (a point to be discussed later), the cosmetic surgery phenomenon is astounding and skyrocketing.

But what does this mean? It must be remembered that while cosmetic surgery is rarely life threatening, it is a drastic decision and experience. Even in a resort-like setting with a caring expert surgeon and well-trained supportive attendents, cosmetic surgery involves risk and demands courage. A candidate for a nose reconstruction may not feel pain during surgery, but she is aware of her bones being cracked and reassembled. A woman who wants her breasts made smaller undergoes the oblivion of anesthesia knowing that whatever the outcome, she will be scarred for the rest of her life.

For all of the flip comments about darling little retroussé noses, to walk into a cosmetic surgeon's waiting room of bruised and bandaged patients is to be struck by a certain resemblance to a war zone. Unlike stray victims on the streets of Lebanon, these are people who have marched willingly to the scalpel. And, the vast majority of them are women. Normal-appearing women. It is important therefore to ask, why?

In search of an answer, it is suggested here that powerful outside forces are bearing down on something inner, essential to human well-being, but too often neglected: body image.

It is further suggested that while the potential for body image disturbance is a given in the ordinary course of women's lives, the media help to create a climate for more severe body image disturbance and distortion that the trend toward cosmetic surgery both exemplifies and exploits.

To examine these ideas, this chapter (1) discusses the concept of body image, (2) relates it to the normal pattern of change in women's lives, (3) notes the potential for disturbance and distortion and the role of the media, and (4) examines the cosmetic surgery phenomenon as a case in point.

The ultimate hope of this presentation is to raise awareness of body image issues among professionals so that we might have more complete answers.

DEFINING BODY IMAGE

Body image is one of those terms commonly used, its meaning taken for granted, but difficult to actually define. Is it the image of the body or of the self or of both? Is it a technicolor picture in the mind's eye? Is it fixed like a statue in a park, eroded perhaps by the passage of time, but enduring?

Henker (1979) noted that it was in the 1920s that the basic concept of body image as a unity in the sensory cortex was described. In the 1930s the concept was expanded beyond the perceptive aspect to a tridimensional image involving interpersonal, environmental, and temporal factors.

More recently, in 1985, aware of the diverse and often esoteric descriptions of body image and aware as well of the importance of body image to personality theories and its relationship to the causations, symptoms, and treatment of such disorders as hysterical paralysis, social phobias, and histrionic, narcissistic, and avoidant personality disorders, van der Velde proposed a new concept of body image. Departing from the traditional view suggesting that human beings have only one body image, van der Velde notes that, "the limitations of our visual perception make it impossible to perceive our body as a whole." He goes on to say that "our bodily perceptions result in a multitude of different independently established body images . . . our notion of our body as an entity represents a conceptual composite of innumerable body images" (p. 527).

Part of that conceptual composite includes association with how others see and react to one's appearance. This is an aspect of body image of particular significance to women whose worth has traditionally been linked to being attractive. According to van der Velde, "because one's own body images are the mental representations of the physical self and inseparably associated with the reflections of the psychological self, they are, in the most comprehensive sense of the term, self-images . . . the foundation for . . . self-concept" (p. 532).

This understanding adds insight to the author's observation from speaking with women that for many, the body equates to the self. It is perhaps additionally significant that the most important and popular book of the women's health movement is entitled *Our Bodies, Ourselves* (The Boston Women's Health Collective, 1971).

Female or male, body image is an integral part of being human. For example, body image, a sense of our physical selves, helps us negotiate a space in a crowded room. For another example, consider how, in our early years, the development of body image contributes to individuation and eventual separation. Throughout life, an intact body image would appear to be crucial. Our pathways are so programmed that when a limb is removed, the well-known phenomenon of a "phantom limb" may remain.

A study of severely ill patients (Viney, 1984–1985) showed that while the threat of death generated feelings of indirectly expressed anger, uncertainty, and many positive feelings, threat of loss of bodily integrity was associated with indirectly and directly expressed anger, hopelessness, and helplessness. Each year hundreds of thousands of women demonstrate the need for an intact body image as they struggle to go on with their lives after the trauma of mastectomy or hysterectomy. Working their way through grief and anger at the loss of a body part, they must repair the damage to their image of themselves and their sense of bodily and self-wholeness.

Mastectomy and hysterectomy, while common, are of course extreme experiences. It does not take professional training to recognize that body image disturbance is present or that it is one of the compelling psychic issues that must be resolved. It does take heightened awareness however to recognize that the potential for body image disturbance is always there as women experience the normal, "garden variety" events of life in a female body across the time span. Such disturbance, a jolting of the body image, can go on to become a body image distortion that a woman accepts as true. When that occurs, it may be a red flag signalling distress.

Body Image Disturbance and Women's Lives

Change is the constant in women's lives. From month to month, cycle to cycle, pregnancy to menopause, from little girl to sexually mature adult, the female body is always changing. The idea of a composite body image would seem elastic, well suited to this kind of continually shifting reality. Nonetheless, as Weinberg (1978) reminds us, "a distortion of customary body image is experienced as a distortion of self." Therefore, even normal, natural, ordinary, events—for example adolescence or pregnancy—can be a source of body image disturbance, a jolt to the inner self.

Adolescence

Body image disturbance is a given in adolescence when tremendous changes occur and, particularly for females, the social pressure to be attractive are forces that can't be ignored. As Freedman (1984) has noted,

> In a sense, puberty transforms a girl into a woman without her consent . . . the hormones that inflate her breasts, also layer her thighs with "unsightly" fat and cover her legs with "superflous" hair (p. 36).

The adolescent female can no easily longer conform to the delicate dainty stereotype operative when she was a little girl. Yet, the need to meet new definitions of being appealing and attractive is imperative. It is a time of great anxiety and dissatisfaction. Citing a study of 20,000 adolescents that showed that girls have more negative feelings about their bodies than boys, Freedman notes that,

> An unattractive changing body translates into a lack of self-esteem. The connection between good looks and worthiness as a female may be so deeply ingrained that it can remain throughout a woman's life, making her insecure and dependent on others for approval of appearance.

The media help stir anxiety by establishing ideal beauty types, helpless innocent "dolls," or "extroverted free spirits packaged in artifice" (Freedman, 1984). Not unexpectedly, the media sells all kinds of artifice, for example, truckloads of makeup.

Despite parental reaction to violet eyelids and scarlet lips on an 11-year-old girl, cosmetics are a way of dealing with body image disturbance of adolescence and the need to be perceived as attractive. A fifth grade teacher commented, "I can almost divide my classes in two, the half still in childhood, the half jumping into adolescence; the marker is an interest in makeup."

As Singer explained in a 1986 article, "The Makeup Mystique," to the adolescent, the use of makeup is a sign of being grown up, of being attractive, of being female, of bonding with other girls and women on shopping expeditions, but of a means of female competition as well.

Describing a 10-year-old trying cosmetics for the first time for a school play, Singer commented, "life would never be the same." Three years later, the girl was an established teen whose greatest thrill was to shop for cosmetics in a department store and be "made over."

As Freedman has pointed out, media exacerbation of adolescent adjustment problems can have emotional and physical consequences evidenced in the increase in eating disorders, the decision to have breast surgery, and the occurrence of certain forms of acne. To illustrate in terms of teen skin problems, while acne is genetic in origin and seriously affects one in four adolescents, adolescent girls set themselves up for two kinds of acne not usually suffered by adolescent boys. The first is acne excoree, caused by compulsive picking at trivial blemishes (behavior that other investigators have linked to self-punishment to confirm feelings of worthlessness), and, second, cosmetic acne caused by makeup routines using potent ingredients. Because cosmetic acne may take time to develop and may therefore be difficult to diagnose, a vicious cycle may ensue in which more cosmetics are used to cover up a condition caused by cosmetics in the first place.

Ironically, the makeup that helps a teen feel "grown up" can make an older woman feel younger. The grandmother of the young makeup shopper in Singer's article had this to say: "I discovered if you smear your face with something red—rub it in—when you wake up in the morning, you can look in the mirror and smile at yourself."

Many women feel "naked" until they paint a "face" on. More than cosmetics are at issue. Body image disturbance stirred in adolescence, the adjustment to change, the need to be seen as attractive and to feel attractive, continue in many guises across the life span.

Pregnancy

Pregnancy is a profound body/mind experience which raises many issues, among them body image disturbance. From any perspective, the pregnant woman—particularly in late pregnancy—is not dwelling in the same body. She is swollen, ungainly, sometimes off balance, occupying a different space.

Gradually, perception of size adjusts to the growing pregnancy to the extent that it takes several weeks after childbirth for a woman to correctly estimate her size. In addition to size adjustment, there is the matter of being attractive. While many pregnant women are considered and consider themselves highly attractive, albeit changed, some women may have to contend with negative perceptions. As a dismayed, newly pregnant woman explained, "I asked my husband, 'Don't you think that's a terrific maternity outfit that woman's wearing?' He didn't even know what woman I was talking about because he never bothered to look at pregnant women!"

Pregnant women can be disparaging in their own comments about their appearance as well. One woman described herself as a "watermelon in sneakers" (Lichtendorf & Gillis, 1981).

Zuckerberg (1980) has pointed out that during pregnancy any of a number of physical and psychological signs may indicate underlying conflict about pregnancy, mothering, and the feminine role function. Such signs may include undue nausea, inappropriate weight gain, blushing, fainting, vague aches and cramps in the genital area, excessive worries, unusual fantasies or thoughts experienced as being out of control, or unusual mood swings without source.

In an investigation of the relationship between extreme incidence of these symptom complexes in pregnant women and relatively unconscious conflict as well as consciously expressed attitudes toward pregnancy, Zuckerberg found body image problems to be one of the sources of distress expressed in symptoms. Commenting on her clinical analysis of fantasy responses to a specially devised Pregnancy Thematic Apperception Test (PTAT), Zuckerberg noted,

> Body image problems were associated with the acceptance of the physical changes involved in pregnancy and were accompanied by fears of body damage and vulnerability. That all women are concerned about their body image changes during pregnancy may be mentioned here. The judged evaluation of the PTAT prints indicated that the card depicting the pregnant woman looking at her reflection is by far the most conflicted.

Despite the potential for body image disturbance in the normal events of women's lives, and what Freedman (1984) calls "a growing awareness among psychologists that physical attractiveness is a highly significant psychosocial variable," there is still a tendency to neglect or downplay body image. Linked as it is with seemingly fluff topics like cosmetics, makeovers, fashion, reminiscent of valuation of woman as decorative object, body image would not seem to be the stuff of serious scientific concern. But as the late Stella Blum, for many years curator of the Costume Institute of the Metropolitan Museum of Art has been quoted (Morris, 1985) as saying of those who discounted fashion, "Fashion is so close to revealing a person's inner feelings . . . people tend to push it away . . . it's really too close to the quick of the soul."

As always, it is the extreme that commands respect and attention.

Body Image Distortion

In recent years, the extreme in body image issues has been anorexia nervosa, a vivid and frightening example of body image distortion. In an anorectic, body image disturbance—a condition experienced by every adolescent girl in the process of change—escalates and takes hold. Body image disturbance is not the only cause of anorexia, but body image distortion is a marker of the illness. Since anorexia is discussed in Chapter 16 of this book, the subject is raised only to make the following points:

- Just as the "phantom limb" phenomenon demonstrates the human insistence on body integrity, the emaciated anorectic, who stares into a mirror and insists that she sees gross fat, demonstrates that body image is an individualized construct.
- We see in the mirror the image within—even if no one else is able to see it.
- If that image is not acceptable, drastic action may be taken to correct it.

For the anorectic, drastic action is starvation.

For many women, drastic action is the cutting, bleeding, pain, swelling, risk of possible complications, uncertainty, and potential disappointment of cosmetic surgery. In the 1880s, pioneering plastic surgeons spoke of the wish to relieve patients of "lifelong marks of disfigurement . . . never ceasing sources of embarrassment and mental distress to themselves, amounting in many cases to a positive torture" (Converse, 1977).

Today, cosmetic surgeons address themselves to disfigurement that is far less visible to others, but often as torturous.

> 'There's no reason for it,' the worried and unhappy father of a teenage girl insisting on nose surgery told the plastic surgeon, 'She's not perfect but she is fine as she is.' 'You are not a sixteen-year-old girl,' the surgeon said in reply.

> A woman who had breast reduction explained, 'you can't image how horrible I was, spilling out of my brassiere. From the time I developed I never put on a bathing suit.' Although she was endowed like a *Playboy* fantasy, she felt repugnant. She undressed in the dark, hurrying her husband's hands over her breasts. She could never understand why he would want to touch her because her breasts seemed so huge, so grotesque.

A woman who had her nose fixed commented, "it was a nice nose. It just wasn't a perfect nose." (Morrisroe, 1986). For the woman suffering the anguish of body image distortion, for the woman unsettled by how she differs from ideals projected by film, television, and other sources of approvals, for the woman adjusting to a major body image disturbance—aging—cosmetic surgery appears to offer an almost magical solution.

Ours is a consumer-oriented society. Demand leads to change and growth of services. Availability in turn makes it necessary to stir excitement in order to keep demand high.

The Cosmetic Surgery Boom

After *Newsweek* ran a cover story, "New Bodies for Sale" (1985), it was not surprising to find the article ripped out of binders at a major library. The demand for cosmetic surgery is such that in an average day, a prominent, urban, plastic surgeon doing nose and breast operations can earn $11,000 a day (Morrisroe, 1986). According to *Newsweek*, plastic surgery was up 61% from 1981 to 1984, and plastic surgery is one of the fastest-growing medical specialties in the United States.

While elective aesthetic or cosmetic surgery is done in hospitals, many procedures can be done in clinics, surgeons' offices, and even in resorts such as the Bahamas. The stigma of being a second-class patient having seemingly frivolous surgery in a place for the seriously ill is, to a large extent, gone.

At Christmas time in Manhattan, Geist (1985) has reported, there is a rush of college students using the holiday to have "nose jobs," vacationers having a few collagen injections to erase wrinkles before heading south, people trying surgical uplift to fight holiday depression, and the fiscally savvy scheduling both surgery and a medical deduction before New Year's Eve when the personal income tax year ends.

Cosmetic surgery has much of the razzle dazzle of the "Star Wars" era: silicone implants, fat suctioning; it is a gesture of defiance at the passage of time itself. Computers can preview what a person will look like after surgery (Kristof, 1986). Using an electronic "pencil," a surgeon can "operate" on one's face projected on a video terminal screen. In the near future, it will be possible to show change in life-like three dimensions. It is even expected that it will be possible to mold a correctly sized implant while the 3-D image is on the screen.

Along with the razzle dazzle of technology, there is a touch of artistry. The offices of cosmetic surgeons tend to be impressively decorated. Some surgeons are sculptors in leisure time. Advertisements tend to emphasize aesthetic sensibility as well as surgical skill and judgment.

And cosmetic surgeons can advertise. A 1979 ruling permitting physicians to advertise has been said to have done more for plastic surgery than any other medical or surgical specialty. Advertising is a paid medium, but print features, television specials, radio interviews are a form of free publicity (although it should be noted that some surgeons and clinics use public relations experts to initiate or "place" stories).

"The Cosmetic Specialists: Who Does What Best," "How to Interview Your Plastic Surgeon," "A Teen's Guide to Cosmetic Surgery," "Forever Young," are some of the headlines promising information and inspiration. Comments like "It's easier than shopping in Bloomingdales," (Morrisroe, 1986) and vivid before-and-after pictures are part of a successful sell.

The baby boom generation has always been considered a prime target. As advertising whiz Jerry Della Femina commented in a published interview (New York Times, 1986), "we'll be chasing baby-boomers until they die; we'll be trying to sell them funerals." Now that the baby-boomers, 77 million strong, are nearing their forties and are seeing the first inevitable signs of aging despite their craze for fitness, a vast new market for cosmetic surgery is opening up.

While there are predictions that more men will be having surgery to keep a youthful appearance, the cosmetic surgery patient is still most likely to be a woman. Given the number of women holding jobs, and the advertising and competition that makes cosmetic surgery economically available, the possibility of insurance coverage and/or tax considerations, cosmetic surgery can be obtained by the woman who wants it.

When finances are a strain, women determined to have surgery can be amazingly resourceful and clever. Surgery might be done at low cost at a teaching hospital under the supervision of an expert. One woman interviewed obtained cosmetic surgery free of charge by agreeing to allow the operation to be videotaped to be shown as part of a mini-documentary on a morning news show at a later date. Rather than have her lover guess that her enlarged breasts were not entirely her own, she set their alarm clock an hour earlier so that he would be long gone to work when the morning news came on!

There is practically no time in a healthy woman's life when cosmetic surgery can't be done. From the "nose jobs" with or without chin augmentation of the teen years, to breast change from the late teens through old age, to surgery for the aging face, which can begin in the late forties, cosmetic surgery is an alluring option.

The question is, what are women actually buying? One woman described it as "a gift I wanted to give myself." Others describe it as rescue, a miracle, a desperate wish fulfilled. But just whose wish is being fulfilled? Reputable surgeons caution against having surgery for anyone else. Yet, it's not unusual to interview a woman who has had breast augmentation to flesh out the fantasies of a particular man.

Reputable cosmetic surgeons are very careful to warn or even reject potential patients who expect surgery to change their lives or transform them into new beings. Yet, surgeons say that following surgery they see new aspects of personality emerge, a new willingness to take part in life.

The hidden promise of cosmetic surgery may not be openly stated but it is there. Ads that are not technically false can be "emotionally deceptive" ("New Bodies," 1985). Even a very carefully done guide to cosmetic surgery in *Seventeen*, (Sabin, 1984), replete with caveats, notes that, "We live in a society that admires attractiveness, and wanting to look attractive is psychologically healthy." In the bestseller *Queenie* (Korda, 1985), a brilliant plastic surgeon tells the heroine, an exquisite movie star," "The purpose of beauty is happiness. It should make you happy. It should make others happy. . . . I wanted to be a psychoanalyst you know. It's more important to repair the mind than the face."

It may be more important to repair the mind than the face, but the nearly 800-page novel pivots on the movie star's beauty, and when it fades, she disappears from public view and dwells in a half-world of flattering pink lights.

Women, the main readers of fiction, do not need to have the message about what's really important spelled out. As a saucy showgirl in the hit musical *A Chorus Line* sings it, "tits and ass" are what count. A woman who wants to change her life has only to make an appointment to see a "wizard" on Park & 73rd. The song always gets an ovation.

THE WOMAN WHO OPTS FOR COSMETIC SURGERY

We have looked at the cosmetic surgery phenomenon in some detail to convey a vivid idea of how enormous, appealing, and available it is. We have noted the pressures on women to conform to beauty standards, to change if they do not, but we have not zeroed in on the woman who decides to change. She is basically normal in appearances; but is she normal, that is, emotionally healthy, within?

While this question has intrigued many, a great deal of conclusive research has not been done. Concerning breast augmentation, for example, in the 1960s when the operation was newer and more of an ordeal, studies indicated that women seeking breast enlargement were unstable. Depression, low self-esteem, and hysterical traits were diagnosed.

In a review of past thinking, Burk, Zelen, and Terino (1985) have noted that, in terms of psychoanalytic orientation, the patient undergoing augmentation may reflect guilt about affection and sexual feelings for the father and consider her small breasts as punishment for these feelings. Unconscious ambivalent identification with the mother and strong identification with the father may be factors in the female seeking to change her nose, a symbol of father and penis. Psychiatric diagnosis of face-lift patients found them to be depressed dependent or overly independent and rigid.

Burk *et al.* point out that the cosmetic surgery patient was first conceptualized

> within the context of unconscious motivations, involving the symbolic meaning of body parts, and second in terms of the illness model of psychological motivation . . . this illness conceptualization of cosmetic plastic surgery fails to take into account the strong, if unspecified, and public norms for feminine beauty prevalent in our culture as well as the social world of the patient.

Setting aside the concept of the cosmetic surgery patient as "peculiar," "abnormal," or reflective of underlying disease, Burk *et al.* applied a self-consistency approach to studying forty cosmetic surgery patients. They concluded that self-consistency theory reflects "a normal woman in terms of general self-esteem who is attempting to remediate a consciously felt inconsistency between general and specific body-part esteem. Cosmetic surgery seems to reduce this inconsistency."

A great deal more remains to be investigated about the cosmetic surgery patient. For example, what is the psychology of the cosmetic surgery junkie who goes from nose job to breast lift to face lift to buttock reshaping in an insatiable quest of change? More, too, needs to be learned about the lasting value of cosmetic surgery as treatment. However, we do know what the ads imply, that physical change has implications beyond the physical. It's not a nose that a woman really seeks to change, but her very self.

CONCLUSION

In conclusion, an observer of trends in women's health has to wonder what the extraordinary rush to cosmetic surgery means. Since for many women, her body is equal to her self, are we speaking of self-love or self-hate? With hundreds of thousands of women each year subjecting themselves to surgical change, what does this say about what women think of themselves? Why must women look at themselves with despair and dislike?

We look to the past and accuse the Chinese of inhumanity and cruelty in practicing foot binding on vulnerable girls. Girls becoming women who smiled at themselves in the mirror, schooled to see themselves as attractive despite crippling and pain. With our skin peelings, silicone implants, truncated noses, and breasts often deadened to sensation and erotic arousal, are women in our society that different?

At the start of the women's movement for better political and economic and social opportunity, plastic surgeons thought they might be doing less cosmetic surgery. Instead, they are doing even more. Why is this happening when women are taking a great leap forward to new accomplishment and pride? Why is it that thousands of operations are performed each year on the timeless symbol of feminity, the female breast?

Earlier it was noted that a cosmetic surgeon's waiting room can resemble a war zone. I am speculating that the war is being waged between the outer world and the inner self.

Earlier it was noted that a body image distortion can be exemplified by an emaciated anorectic looking into a mirror and seeing gross fat. I am speculating that for the hundreds of thousands of women who elect change by surgery, the media is the mirror. A suspect mirror that can reflect back distortion.

REFERENCES

Advertising in post-martini age on Madison Avenue (1986). *New York Times,* p. B3, May 20.
The Boston Women's Health Collective (1971). *Our bodies, ourselves.* New York: Simon and Schuster.
Dullea, G. (1986). At a party for Judith Krantz, life imitates art. *New York Times,* p. A24, May 2.
Burk, J., Zelen, S. L., & Terino, E. O. (1985). More than skin deep: A self-consistency approach to the psychology of cosmetic surgery. *Plastic and Reconstructive Surgery, 76* (2), 270–276.
Converse, J. M. (1977). In *Reconstructive plastic surgery,* 2nd Ed., Vol. 2 (p. 1041). Philadelphia: W. B. Saunders.
Edgarton, M. T. (1985). Discussion of J. Burk, S. L. Zelen, & E. O. Terino, More than skin deep: A self-consistency approach to the psychology of cosmetic surgery. *Plastic and Reconstructive Surgery, 76*(2), 276–277.
Freedman, R. J. (1984). Reflection on beauty as it relates to health in adolescent females. *Women and Health, 9,* 29–45.
Geist, W. (1985). About New York: New hips for the holidays. *New York Times,* Dec. 11, B3.
Henker, F. O. (1979). Symptom substitution after obesity therapy. *Psychosomatics, 29,* 10.
How Do You See Yourself? (1986). *New York Magazine* advertisement, May.
Korda, M. (1985). *Queenie* (p. 548). New York: Warner.
Kristof, N. D. (1986). A video preview of plastic surgery. *New York Times,* A24, Jan. 27.
Lichtendorf, S. S. (1979–86). Comments and quotes from interviews with cosmetic surgery patients and plastic surgeons.
Lichtendorf, S. S., & Gillis, P. L. (1981). *The new pregnancy: The active woman's guide to work, legal rights, health care, travel, sports, dress, sex and emotional well being.* New York: Bantam.
Morris, B. (1985). Stella Blum, 68, former curator of costumes. *New York Times,* A16, Aug. 1.
Morrisroe, P. (1986). Forever young. *New York Magazine, 19*(23), 44–49, June 9.
New Bodies for Sale. (1985) *Newsweek,* pp. 64–72, May.
Sabin, F. (1984). A teen's guide to cosmetic surgery. *Seventeen, 43,* 253–254, March.
Singer, A. (1985). The makeup mystique. *New York Times Magazine, CXXXV* (46736), 72, April 6.
The New You Is Waiting (1986). *New York Post* advertisement.

van der Velde, C. D. Body images of one's self and of others: Developmental and clinical
significance. *American Journal of Psychiatry, 142*(5), 527–537.

Viney, L. L. (1984–1985). Loss of life and loss of bodily integrity: Two different sources of
threat for people who are ill. *Omega Journal of Death & Dying, 15*(3), 207–222.

Weinberg, J. S. (1978). Body image disturbance as a factor in the crisis situation of pregnancy.
Journal of Obstetrics and Gynecology Nursing, pp. 18–20.

Zuckerberg, J. (1980). Psychological and physical warning signals regarding pregnancy, adaptation and early psychotherapeutic intervention. In B. Blum (Ed.), *Psychological aspects of
pregnancy, birthing and bonding* (pp. 151–173). New York: Human Sciences Press, 1980.

Chapter 15

Psychodynamics of Abortion
Regression or Rebirth?

BONNIE ROBIN ARONOWITZ

To date, epidemiological and sociodemographic research characterize much of the literature on abortion. Psychological research is typically of a social-personality nature where psychological factors or attitudes toward abortion are articulated and related as correlates of the abortion experience. Research methodology of this type tends to compromise the multidimensionality and mutual interaction between the social, psychological, and physiological matrix of abortion decision-making and sequelae. Due to the lack of longitudinal studies and other methodological shortcomings in the abortion literature, there is little empirical evidence concerning the psychological aspects of abortion.

Abortion, like politics and religion, is a heated issue, due to the belief system inherent in each. Rational, objective data, devoid of implicit philosophical and moral positions, is difficult, if not impossible, to obtain. Although value judgments are inherent aspects in any research design, it is in the area of abortion, in particular, that these value systems are inextricably intertwined. Thus, the abortion literature is markedly contradictory in its methodology and conclusions about psychological process and outcome.

This chapter attempts to highlight psychodynamic issues for the abortion patient, in light of research findings complemented by my clinical experience with abortion patients. The intent is to delineate the personal subjectivity, sociological, and methodological issues that have contributed to the controversy in the abortion literature. Thus, an attempt is made to resolve the psychopathology model of abortion with the psychological maturation viewpoint. The rationale for a psychodynamic conceptualization of abortion has more general applicability in terms of enhancing the understanding of the psychology of women. Moreover, it provides

BONNIE ROBIN ARONOWITZ • Ph.D. Clinical Psychology Candidate, Ferkauf Graduate School, Yeshiva University-Einstein College of Medicine, Bronx, New York; Neuropsychology Intern, Neurological Institute, Columbia Presbyterian Medical Center, New York City; Psychology Intern, Postgraduate Center for Mental Health, New York City; Psychologist in Training, New York City Police Department, New York City.

the opportunity for examining the psychophysiological integration that typifies the condition of the woman throughout her life cycle.

This chapter does not deal with those topics which are significant subdivisions of abortion in their own right—the effect of the abortion on others, for example, the child of the mother denied abortion or abortion survivors, later term pregnancies, the male partner, or family members. Nor does it focus on ethical issues, abortion legislation, epidemiological studies, medical risks, complications, or abortion innovations. Likewise excluded are special cases such as abortion in battered women, rape, incest, and child abuse victims, and in those women who carry pregnancies with diagnosed fetal abnormalities, or who themselves have physical anomalies. Cases such as these lend less toward a general psychology and instead warrant specific psychodynamic investigation as entities unto themselves, and are thus far beyond the scope of this chapter.

U.S. DEMOGRAPHICS

The Alan Guttmacher Institute and the Centers for Disease Control (Henshaw, Binkin, Blaine, & Smith, 1985) estimated that 1,577,340 abortions were performed in 1981. Of these procedures, 1% were obtained by women under age 15, 11.2% by 15 to 17 year olds, and 16.3% by 18 to 19 year olds. The highest abortion rate, 35.2%, was represented by 20 to 24 year olds. Although adolescents under age 15 had the highest abortion ratio, a greater number carried to term than did abort.

Eighty-one percent of all aborters were never married, 58% were nulliparous, 91% had procedures performed before the 13th week of the last menstrual period, and less than 1% had abortions after the 20th week. Although 70% of the abortions were obtained by white women, the abortion rate was higher for nonwhites than for whites (56 per 1000 vs. 24 per 1000 women), with unmarried nonwhites being more likely to carry to term.

There has been an increase in multiple aborters, those women who repeatedly obtain abortion procedures. However, the authors of these studies contended that the incidence of repeat abortion may be understated due to the problem of selective forgetting in retrospective recall studies (Daily, Nicholas, Nelsen & Paxter, 1973). Additionally, better reporting of Board of Health certificates and more truthful disclosure by women and agencies are needed (Potter and Ford, 1976). Thus, Heinrich and Bobrowsky, 1984 (as cited in *Abortion Research Notes*, 1984) found that of 403 aborters between the years 1975 and 1980, 45% had at least one prior procedure, 17% had two or more, and 15% had a termination within a year of their present abortion.

ADOLESCENT PREGNANCY AND ABORTION

According to national statistics, 55% of all never-married teenagers have had sexual intercourse by age 19. This level of sexual activity has resulted in a rate of 1.1 million adolescents becoming pregnant each year. In addition, teenagers often present for termination after the 15th week of pregnancy (Gisbert & Falk, 1978), which increases medical risks. There are approximately 350,000 abortions performed on adolescents yearly. According to Baldwin (1977) and Zelnick *et al.* (1981), more abortions are opted for by white vs. black women, those of higher vs. lower socioeconomic status, and those who are more vs. less educated. Fischmann (1977) found that over two-thirds of all teenage pregnancies were unintended, unwanted, and were a disruptive and frightening experience for the concerned adolescents.

Teenagers reluctant to seek out medical termination have tried to self-induce abortion by ingesting toxic substances or drugs that are rumored to be effective in terminating a pregnancy. Occasionally, some teenagers may employ intrauterine mechanical manipulation and unsterile instruments, such as knitting needles or button hooks, to dislodge the fetus.

Early research on teenage pregnancy and abortion (Semmens & Lamers, 1968) has been characterized by a symptom-approach to adolescent pregnancy. Although authors of this paradigm acknowledge that the answer to the question of why there are so many teenage pregnancies is not a unidimensional one, the problem is categorized in terms of levels of psychopathology, consultation, planning, diagnosis, and treatment.

Typical of early research on adolescent pregnancy and abortion was an oversimplification of the complex of psychodynamic characteristics for the teenager and the multidimensional factors contributing to teenage pregnancy. Oftentimes, the adolescent girl has been viewed as getting pregnant due to an insufficient knowledge about the physiology of sex, for which the remedy is a school or family sex instruction program. However, the teenager, when provided with the lacking sex education, will not ipso facto comply with instructions due to the simple provision of information. To understand why this is so necessitates an understanding of general adolescent psychology. The rules of formal operational logic often do not apply to the psychology of adolescence and are especially not applicable to young adolescents. Teenagers' cognitive and emotional capacities have not evolved into a stable, integrated personality organization which links cause with effect. Instead, the adolescent developmental framework is comprised of personality and cognitive characteristics unique to that stage. Unfortunately, treatment strategies are often intended to suit a developmentally mature logic system when the recipient is developmentally immature. The adolescent's ability to anticipate, to plan, to project into the future, to abstract, and to behave in a way that replaces magical thinking with causal connections has not reached adult proportion. Unless contraceptive information is accompanied by an appeal to these psychological characteristics, its sole provision is doomed to fail in preventing teenage pregnancy.

Current research in the psychological literature has addressed some variables related to teenage pregnancy and abortion. Studies suggested that the psychodynamics of adolescent pregnancy and abortion may not be radically discrepant in nature from the psychodynamics of other adolescent phenomena such as acting out, suicide, and peer group membership.

Research interest in all aspects of teenage pregnancy and sequelae has intensified. Situational, sociodemographic, and psychological correlates of adolescent pregnancy have been conducted by social scientists of diverse theoretical orientations (Alan Guttmacher Institute, 1976, 1981; Eisen *et al.*, 1983; Fawcett, 1973; Finkel & Finkel, 1975; Forrest *et al.*, 1978; Kinch *et al.*, 1969; Levering, 1983; O'Leary *et al.*, 1984; Tietze, 1977, 1978; and Zelnik *et al.*, 1981).

Denial is characteristic of the younger adolescent brought into the abortion clinic by her mother who is typically punitive, puritanical in her attitudes, and has an investment in keeping her daughter sexually naive. The teenager vehemently insists upon presenting for abortion that she could not possibly have become pregnant because she was not told how to. This denial of responsibility and attribution of blame onto an older caretaker may be observed in those adolescents who are simultaneously angry at a mother who, in general, is not psychologically or emotionally protective of her daughter. The teenager may insist, "I'm having an abortion because my mother never told me to use birth control." Others more benignly assert that they "did not think it could happen" to them.

Psychological characteristics such as denial, idealization, magical, or overromanticized thinking typify the adolescent's affect and cognition. Abstraction ability, which allows one to link cause and effect, is in transition from concretist cognitions to abstract formulations with regard to the adolescent's conceptualization of psychophysical events. For example, the teenager believes that "going all the way" or sexual intercourse, is qualitatively different from "first or second base" or foreplay, despite extremely intimate contact and orgasm. Speaking from a mere concrete physical sense, foreplay is not equal to sexual intercourse. However, the level of physical intimacy is either identical or may be more intimate in the former than the latter. Thus, the meaning of a specific act is not construed. Instead, ramifications of that act and cognitive abstractions derived from the act are interpreted in strictly concrete terms.

Making the broad, abstract, conceptual leap from the egg and sperm in the classroom to intimate sexuality with no concrete physical frame of reference is difficult for the adolescent, if not impossible for the young adolescent. Perhaps this concept is less striking when, in the course of abortion work, one encounters 40-year-old women who express frank ignorance about their anatomical capacities and reproductive functioning. If one considers sexuality as a lifetime psychological unfolding aided by experience, which enhances knowledge and in turn sexual identity, ignorance may likewise be understood if any of the contributing elements are absent.

It is the limited capacity for abstraction, denial, and projection into the future that actually safeguard the teenager from the full realization of the impact of her actions in the case of abortion. While the mature woman may hypothesize about the sex and appearance of the fetus, the teenager's link from the operating table to the ramifications of the abortion are superficial. Concerns center around when she may resume normal activities or about a party she wishes to attend. She asks about when the symptoms of nausea, breast tenderness, and fatigue will subside in order that she may "feel like everyone else again." The focus is with feeling and appearing different from peers.

At the other extreme is the adolescent who, in order to obtain nurturance, intentionally becomes pregnant and who, consequently, is ultimately preoccupied with "the baby" and what it could have provided if it was carried to term. Research has validated the profile of the adolescent who is typically seen in the outpatient abortion setting. These teenagers suffer from low self-esteem and an inadequate sense of self, which is exacerbated by the identity diffusion characteristic of the adolescent stage of development (Blos, 1969; Floyd & Viney, 1974; Raphael, 1974). The pregnancy may thus be viewed as an attempt to establish oneself as a useful human being. The identity of "mother-to-be" may replace the diffuse identity of "uncertain adolescent" (Raphael, 1974).

In general, the literature confirmed the notion that for teenagers who carry to term, fatalistic self-punitive and self-deprecatory attitudes abound. However, this attitude is exaggerated in those adolescents who visit the clinic in the second trimester of pregnancy. It appears that the later the pregnancy is presented for termination, the greater the likelihood that the teenager will be primitive in her needs for nurturance, that her affect will be irritable and angry, and that her general outlook will be one of futility. Term carriers and second trimester adolescent aborters have said, "I can't please my parents any way I do things, so big deal if I get pregnant. Who cares?" In essence, the adolescent is provocatively asking the counselor for nurturance and for hopeful solutions. She is daring the counselor to prove her wrong. This dynamic smacks of the same psychological flavor of the psychotherapy patient who is provocative in her attempts to gain the therapist's caretaking qualities. For example, "I felt so overwhelmed by your interpretation last week that I got into a car accident; I can't afford your fees, so I'll go into prostitution in order to pay for the sessions." These developmentally arrested patients aggress against their physical selves in order to demand the nurturance they felt entitled to, but which did not ensue.

After the pregnancy is confirmed in the self-punitive adolescent, a fatalistic resignation to carry the pregnancy to term and raise the child often occurs, e.g., "If you make your bed, you have to lie in it" (Fischmann, 1975, 1977). Or, "Well, if you don't want to have a baby, you shouldn't have sex in the first place." These adolescents appeared to be reiterating internalized parental prohibitions and were employing them in the service of further self-punishment and deprecation. They felt there to be no alternative but to accept the deserved consequences of their actions, much in the same way that they have been sent to their rooms by parents for punishable behavior. Alongside mature sexual behavior lies immature harsh logic of a less developed, primitive, self-punitive psychological structure. Adolescents' needs and expectations regarding sex, pregnancy, and motherhood in these instances were often based on a temporary or chronically poor disturbed self-image, lack of self-esteem, feelings of emptiness, helplessness, worthlessness, and hopelessness about themselves and the future. The literature suggested that other significant variables in teenage pregnancy involved passivity (Graves & Bradshaw, 1964), impulsivity (Kane & Lachenbruch, 1973), poor reality testing, and inability to plan ahead (Raphael, 1974), primitive defensive structure, low frustration tolerance, and intense dependency needs (Babikian & Goldman, 1971). Indeed, Hilton and Kunkes (1980), in their assessment of defense mechanism organization, found that first trimester and sexually active nonpregnant adolescents utilized higher-order defenses such as denial of affect, intellectualization, and sublimation. Full-term carriers utilized lower-order defenses such as denial of reality, projection, splitting, acting out, avoidance, and undoing.

In my blind interpretations of adolescent and adult repeat aborters' Thematic Apperception Test (TAT) data (Murray et al.), both groups evidenced higher ratios of dependency, need frustration, and need gratification when compared to their age-matched never-aborting and single-aborting counterparts. Responses that reliably discriminated adolescent from adult patients involved the tendency for the former to view the behavior of the heroes in the stimuli as externally controlled, or dependent upon luck and chance factors. When all groups were asked if they thought they could prevent another pregnancy, the controls felt they could if they used contraception. The adult repeaters felt that if they "were extra careful, [they] may be able to," or if not, they "should have [their] tubes tied." Finally, the adolescent repeaters responded, "I don't know. It's like Russian roulette. Sometimes you just come out pregnant. It depends if you really want to be. Maybe I would if I wasn't being good. It's hard to tell what will happen to you. Only God knows."

Amidst the various results obtained in examining sociodemographic versus psychological correlates of teenage pregnancy and abortion, the former variables appeared to be more consistent across the literature in comparison to the latter. This may be attributed to the discrete nature of measurement techniques employed in the assessment of sociodemographic variables, e.g., either subjects are or are not members of a particular sex, age group, ethnic concentration, and socioeconomic status. The issues are less clear in differentiating psychological variables by employing "continuous" vs. "discontinuous" measurement methodology. Projective tests, although yielding valuable information regarding underlying conflicts and motivations, are the least reliable and valid of psychometric instruments. In abortion research, in general, methodological difficulties are abundant, since different measurement techniques assessing the same psychological constructs confound generalizability of findings across studies. This is an inevitable shortcoming in the psychometric status, which initially typifies any research area striving to establish empirical roots. As of yet, there are relatively few standardized reliable and valid abortion instruments with which to assess adjustment, sequelae, and thus, adolescent psychodynamics.

Generally, as is true of adult abortion psychodynamics, a complex set of mutually interacting variables accounted best for the data when compared with more unidimensional conceptualizations of teenage pregnancy and abortion.

Suggestions for further research include the comparison of adolescent pregnant subjects with mature adults and mature adolescents, in order to establish base rates for types of psychological responses to abortion. The design would ascertain, for example, if adult aborting women or repeaters were psychologically and sociodemographically similar to adolescent full-termers, aborters, and their never pregnant counterparts. This would begin to strengthen the nomological net specific to teenage pregnancy and abortion.

REPEAT ABORTION

The literature on those women who undergo multiple or repeat abortion procedures focuses on incidence, demography, prediction, and biosocial characteristics, with scant attention devoted to psychological aspects (Daily et al., 1973; Jacobbsson, von Schoultz, & Solheim, 1976; Tietze, 1974). Some authors have alluded to psychological characteristics of repeat aborters. Carlsson and Hamilton (1970) commented on the poorer general health and less favorable personality structure of habitual abortion applicants when compared to controls in Uppsala. The authors found that in women with "recidivist abortions," there was a greater disposition to depression, psychological immaturity, somatic disorders, and other disabilities. Cullhed (1971) found an accumulation of "ailment and weakness or personality defects" in repeaters. Jacobsson *et al.* (1976) suggested that the problems occurring in the abortion situation may be even more pronounced in the case of repeat abortion. The authors found that repeaters had more pronounced symptoms when compared to the first abortion group. They hypothesized that repeat aborters have personal problems of a different kind and try to compensate for them through sexual activity. Repeaters tended to come from more broken homes, had more alcoholism in their families, and tended to judge their childhood conditions more negatively than did the first abortion group.

There are many reasons for recidivist abortions, such as contraceptive failure, using abortion as an alternative method of birth control (especially in many European countries; Rovinsky, 1972), and failure of the contraceptor. Repeat abortion has been implicated as a neurotic response to unconscious needs (Fischer, 1974).

As in the case of adolescent abortion, even procedures that involved concomitant contraceptive education and motivation attempts have not aided in reducing the recidivism rate (Rovinsky, 1971). Thus, a psychological mechanism is alluded to in the case of repeat aborters. If the issue were simply a lack of knowledge or availability of contraception, the mere provision of information would be effectual. Byrne (1977) maintained that to understand any phenomenon in sexual behavior requires fully understanding an individual's expectations, motivations, evaluative, and affectual responses as well as information and conditioned responses.

Su and Chow (1976) have studied repeaters in Taiwan who relied on abortion as a fertility control method. They viewed repeaters as "hard core" resisters to contraceptive usage on whom abortion had a negative effect. Repeaters were coined by the authors as "repeat abortion seekers."

Gibb and Millard (1981) cited literature providing psychologically based explanations to account for repeat abortions (Abernathy, 1973; Corenblum, 1973; Fischer, 1974; Monsour & Stewart, 1973; Rothman, 1973). Abernathy found that repeat aborters came from homes with unsupportive, traditional, distant, unloving mothers. Denial of sexuality (Monsour & Stewart, 1973; Oswalt, 1974) has been posited as a reason for repeat abortions. Fischer (1974) and Rothman (1973) postulated that abortion is an unconscious wish to dramatize a woman's rage toward her parents, especially the father, if guilt is felt from desiring the father's penis and carrying his child. Fischer characterized repeat abortion as anal expulsive behavior, where patients feel euphoria, relief, and a feeling of being "cleaned out" afterward, as in a purification ritual.

Personality characteristics that typify adolescent aborters, especially in the second trimester, similarly can be observed in the case of repeat abortion seekers. Typically, the woman who presents to the abortion clinic with eight or more previous procedures can be predicted by the staff, reliably, to refuse to stay for postoperative counseling, especially around the issue of contraception. Should she participate, her behavior tends toward passive-aggressive, e.g., she sits, does not contribute to the conversation, sometimes snickers or smiles, but will not verbalize the reason, looks out the window, and asks, "Can I leave now?" In the few cases where these women can be committed to explaining their reactions, they have commented, "I know it already. I heard this a million times. I know what to do." One is reminded of an overintellectualized psychotherapy patient with much in-

sight and little capacity to effect behavioral change. There is an aura of futility and
cynicism in these women's attitudes. They simply do not wish to be reminded of
the fact that they are repeating, in effect, not simply a contraceptive error or abortion, but an entire psychological process.

Multiple abortion, in the sense of a repetition compulsion, serves only as a
partially conscious symbolic physiological marker as to more unconscious feelings
regarding the functions of the pregnancy. These are the repeaters that Su and
Chow (1976) spoke of. There is an emphasis on *not* knowing and seemingly a
perpetuation of the process, a subjective feeling of incapacitation, and a perceived
inability to effect change. Thus, repeaters appear to be satisfying some unconscious
psychological need which necessarily varies according to the meaning that the
pregnancy has for each patient. If the patient remains unchallenged, she is most
comfortable. She is conspicuously uncomfortable and quite angered, however,
when the topic is broached, since she is invested in keeping her motivations
unconscious.

Abortion counselors are often perplexed when they ask the repeater what birth
control method she is using and they are met with the sarcastic retort, "What
makes you think I'm using a birth control method?" At this point, the counselor
may inquire further, "Will you plan on using a method?" to be met with a sharp
"No!" Finally, the question may be asked, "Would you like some information?" to
which again the response is a flat "No." Counselors feel, at this point, that their
obligation to protect the patient ends, since the patient is not only failing to protect
herself, but is actually going out of her way to ensure that she remains unprotected.

Luker (1975) viewed repeaters as "contraceptive risk takers" who failed to
understand the rationality of their options not to use birth control methods. They
were unable to encompass new information, such as previous abortions, into decision making, like adolescents who could not integrate all aspects of the pregnancy.
Luker maintained that repeaters should become aware of the reasons for their risk
taking, e.g., independence, rage, excitement. Other personality correlates of repeaters, such as impulsivity, lessened ability to foresee the consequences of their
actions, and difficulty with accepting limitation, have been isolated (Rovinsky,
1972). Corenblum (1973) found that repeaters felt more externally controlled than
nonaborters on locus of control measures.

Personality correlates may not be specific to repeaters, but have been observed
in adolescents, immature personalities, and other populations such as battered
women. Further research may determine the extent to which these characteristics
overlap or discriminate between groups.

ABORTION AND PSYCHIATRY: THE MYTH OF BEHAVIORAL PREDICTABILITY

In the early years of legalization, the role of the psychiatrist in arguing for
therapeutic abortion required that "there be a substantial risk that continuation of
the pregnancy would gravely impair the mental health of the mother to a degree
that she would be dangerous to herself or the person or property of others, or
would be in need of supervision or restraint." The loose term "substantial risk"
required that the psychiatrist predict a severe or overt psychosis, suicidal state,

major depression, or regression. The situation resembled present-day psychiatric emergency room consultation. In approximately 45 minutes, the interviewer ascertains whether, based upon predictive clinical judgment unamenable to precise investigation, an individual will be a danger to himself or to others. It is no wonder that many psychiatrists prefer to err in the direction of overadmission to the hospital or creating false positives rather than perhaps allowing an ambiguously homocidal psychopath to run free and incur a more costly false negative.

The practical result of early abortion legislation presented psychiatry with a paradoxical situation. Those women who had their pleas for abortion approved were the most psychiatrically disturbed, and whose abortions consequently resulted in more negative sequelae. Conversely, abortion seekers with overall intact adjustment who were denied abortion would have had more positive sequelae. A situation was created by the legislative system that fulfilled its own prophecy of the ill psychological effects of abortion.

Although formal psychiatric consultation for abortion has essentially become obsolete, in special cases it is informally required. The social worker or mental health professional in an outpatient abortion clinic is often in the position of assessing the mental health of an abortion applicant with a special issue—rape, incest, past psychiatric history—patients who present with bizarre behavior. The task becomes similar to the psychiatrist's task, but exists for different reasons. That is, the mental health professional is to determine, usually in less than 20 minutes, the psychological suitability of the patient to undergo a termination in an outpatient setting. With little available evidence at her disposal, a prediction is made as to psychological sequelae. If necessary, the patient's case is cancelled as she is referred to a hospital facility, which has psychiatric backup, should it be necessary.

Again, psychology/psychiatry is introduced into the uncomfortable ethics of behavioral prediction for which it is ill equipped. Admittedly, in present-day abortion clinics, the costs to the patient are less limiting—referral to an alternative facility vs. complete denial of abortion. However, this fact should not be offered as an explanation or as a justification of the means.

Early Abortion Experiences and the Abortion Transference

An insidious psychological side effect created by the necessity of psychiatric consultation in the early days of abortion legislation was the emotional cost to these women who masked or denied their honest motivations for abortion. The abortion applicant was forced into exaggerating her symptoms, her life situation, losing self-esteem and personal dignity by feigning bizarre behavior. She became manipulative through her psychotic and oftentimes suicidal enactments before the committee. The result was that she became increasingly estranged from her emotions, her ambivalence, and from any positive feelings toward the pregnancy.

Instead, alleviation of anxiety and "winning" by obtaining the abortion became the sole motivational force—an end unto itself, which eclipsed psychological conflicts. To be in touch with ambivalence was a danger to winning the case. To feel tenderness toward the fetus was a threat to the counterargument of proabortion to the committee. As one woman has commented, "You twist your mind in weird ways to get what you want. But what you lost—your soul—you can never get back." The entire process is antithetical to psychological growth.

One may observe remnants of the prelegislation and early legalization attitudes in today's abortion clinic patients. This trend is particularly pronounced in those women who either obtained illegal abortions or who stood before an abortion committee for consideration in the early legalization period. Often patients, in a nonsequitur fashion, will blurt out with "I would keep it, but I can't," as they list numerous reasons why a pregnancy would be impossible at this time in their lives in order to make a case for obtaining an abortion. The patient's tone is often defensive in the absence of feedback or counterarguments from the counselor. This is the case even with the counselor's providing support for the patient's decision to abort. It is as if the patient, aside from any guilt feelings, is fighting with an imaginary committee in her head that she projects outward. The result is that the entire exchange takes on an inappropriate flavor, e.g., "I really can't have it now. I'd go insane. What kind of life would it have anyway? I can't even afford to support the ones I got. There's no man in the house. I couldn't take on anything else right now."

An implicit assumption, made especially by those women who obtained illegal abortions, is that abortion personnel are thinking that they are bad people—as has been their past experience—for undergoing the procedure. Statements that serve to rationalize the patients' intent are, in part, exculpations of guilt. However, the process is more profound and can be compared to the transference developed in psychotherapy. In this case, the patient is projecting all of her primary abortion experiences onto the present-day clinic and clinic personnel, as if the situation was recurring in the present. In this sense, one may hypothesize that the abortion transference is a recapitulation of all other abortion experiences. It is predictable from the attitude that the patient brings to the clinic whether she has had positive or negative past abortion experiences. For example, a patient surprised at the clinic's appearance and staff support typically has had negative past experiences or has known someone with such experiences, should she be a first aborter. A hostile patient is often more hostile at herself, despite the therapeutic milieu, and has a history of hostility across clinics.

THE COMMITMENT TO ANONYMITY

A few words are in order regarding the therapeutic milieu of contemporary abortion clinics. There is typically a collusion between clinic and patient to maintain an environment removed from the reality of the situation. The abortion is termed "procedure." The patient often refers to the fetus as "it." Questions regarding the disposal of tissue or sex of the fetus are handled as if they originated from disturbed motivation and are sidetracked or left unanswered. Lovers and husbands are not allowed to be included in the experience. Complications are often not verbally discussed, save the consent form. Little to no psychological intervention is conducted, unless a case is unusual. The patient has virtually no contact with the physician prior to surgery, should she undergo general anesthesia. Thus, a clandestine environment is created. Most of the patients' more realistic curiosities are shunned by the abortion staff. This sugar-coated attitude is soon incorporated by the patient as she learns to ask only appropriate questions such as those regarding aftercare procedures. One is reminded of a parent invested in hiding the details of sexual intercourse from a child so the aura of espionage or the illogical linking of cause to effect is provided in place of reality. The result is that the shameful emotional tone, which is so much more damaging than factual information, is conveyed to the child. Indeed, Allgeier, Allgeier, and Rywick (1981) found that affective messages accompanying the sexual socialization of children and adolescents may be more predictive of orientations toward abortion than the weight of intellectual arguments regarding the rights of the fetus, its point of viability, or a woman's right to control her own body.

It is only until the abortion experience is dealt with in a realistic therapeutic milieu that women can become responsible and mature adults and exhibit reality-oriented behavior in coping with an unwanted pregnancy. Although we have come a long way from guilt-producing legalistic consultation, old abortion attitudes accompanying this consultation are residuals that are slower to extinguish. Moreover, antiabortion personnel, many of whom are anesthetists and nursing staff, often work in inpatient and outpatient clinics. Staff should be carefully screened regarding their attitudes toward abortion when being considered for such positions, since these attitudes may be explicitly or implicitly conveyed to aborting patients.

To exacerbate the situation, picketers from the prolife organization exhibit pictures of mangled fetuses and shout "Murderer!" to incoming patients. More extremely, prolifers offer physical resistance to patients. What is highlighted, however, is the passivity of both abortion patients and their escorts. Even though these women are furious with the harassment and become quite upset and tearful, retaliation is completely absent. When they are questioned as to why they refuse to take the necessary legal steps to appeal the situation, responses invariably include some element of embarrassment. Patients do not wish to be exposed as abortion applicants in a courtroom. They simply desire to remain as anonymous as possible and to forget the procedure as soon as possible.

PSYCHOLOGICAL SEQUELAE

As is characteristic of the psychological research on abortion in general, extreme contradictory findings abound with regard to psychological sequelae of abortion. Psychological sequelae range from benign (Athanasiou, Oppel, Michelson, Unger, & Yager, 1973; Belsey, Greer, Lal, Lewis, & Beard, 1977; David, 1978; Ekblad, 1955; Ewing & Rouse, 1973; Fingerer, 1973; Fleck, 1970; Francke, 1978; Gillis & Marsjalek, 1971; Greer, Lal, Lewis, Beisey, & Beard, 1976; Halmosh, 1975; Illsley & Hall, 1976; Jacobsson & Solheim, 1975; Kummer, 1963; Lask, 1975; Lebonsohn, 1977; Meyerowitz, Satloff, & Romano, 1971; Osofsky & Osofsky, 1977; Pare & Raven, 1970; Patt, Rappaport, & Barglow, 1969; Payne, Kravitz, Norman, & Anderson, 1976; Robbins, 1979; Smith, 1972, 1973; Treggold, 1964; Werman & Raft, 1973) to severe (Cavenar, Maltbie, & Sullivan, 1978; Ebaugh & Hauser, 1947; Ford, Castelnuovo-Tedesco, & Long, 1972; Friedman, Greenspan, & Mittleman, 1977; Kumar & Robson, 1978; Olley, 1970; Pines, 1982; Taussig, 1936; Winnik, 1958). It is noteworthy that the subjectivity of the evaluator is oftentimes a confounding bias in these findings. It is thus not coincidental that authors presenting positive sequelae were proabortionists and those suggesting negative sequelae were antiabortionists.

A number of psychological sequelae of abortion have been investigated, including guilt, anxiety, mental disability, negative adjustment, regret, self-reproach, ambivalence, depression, and general psychopathology. However, contextual effects must be taken into consideration. When the societal context is one of taboo, the psychological expectation would be one of increased conflict. Thus, the higher Minnesota Multiphasic Personality Inventory (MMPI) psychopathology scores obtained in studies of aborting women vs. their nonaborting counterparts should be viewed in light of social factors. This argument is comparable to the psychodynamics of women and alcoholism vs. men and alcoholism. Since there is a greater social stigma attached to female vs. male problem drinkers and alcoholics, females experience more role conflict and are thus at greater risk for psychopathology. Consequently, there is a higher rate and greater severity of psychopathology in female vs. male alcoholics.

The Necessity of Chronological Interpretation

Contradictory evidence may be viewed in light of the following explanations. A chronological view of the abortion sequelae literature may be defended on several accounts. First, earlier literature reported the abortion experience anecdotally. This trend is especially marked in the psychiatric and psychoanalytic literature, where findings were based on uncorroborated clinical lore. Often reflected was the paradigmatic commitment to biological determinism, which ascribed mental illness to a woman desiring termination simply by reason of her desire (Bolter, 1962; Dunbar, 1954; Galdston, 1958). Thus, a woman opting for abortion was said to have psychopathology and was viewed as immature since she denied or rejected her natural female reproductive, maternal, and nurturant sex role (Blumenfield, 1978; Ford et al., 1972; Martin, 1973; Sorrel, 1967; Walbert & Butler, 1973). Consequently, adverse psychological sequelae were said to ensue. Simon, Rothman, Goff, and Senturia (1969), and Ford et al. (1972) suggested that aborters had marked emotional conflict about their feminine identity and reproductive role, and underwent terminations to satisfy sadomasochistic impulses.

Early abortion studies of this sort, however, were often conducted under the woman's psychological duress. That is, the abortion applicant stood before a committee and often gave a plea of psychopathology in order to be granted a procedure (Ford et al., 1972; Levene & Rigney, 1970; Olley, 1970). In addition, conflict, shame, and guilt resulted from the exhibitionistic stance that the woman seeking abortion was forced to undergo in legalistic consultations. Thus, results of this time period indicating negative sequelae must be interpreted with caution. Abortion research assessing psychological outcome cannot be divorced from the political, social, ethical, and religious climate specific to that time period.

This belief in severe sequelae and cultural climate was typified by Iago Gladstone, executive secretary of the New York Academy of Medicine, who stated, "If and when a so-called adult woman, a responsible female, seeks an abortion, unless the warrant for it is overwhelming—say in the case of rape or incest—we are in effect confronted both with a sick person and a sick situation" (in Calderone, 1958,

p. 119). As Fleck (1970) succinctly phrased it, "Until these extrapsychological but psychopathogenic conditions are removed, any assessment of intrapsychic consequences of abortion is not possible." Thus, earlier studies conducted during initial legalization are uncomparable to more recent research from a psychological standpoint. Even relatively recent research may not apply to current psychodynamics of abortion, since attitudes of those performing the procedure, the patient herself, and her social milieu have changed and continue to change quite rapidly. Moreover, cross-cultural abortion research with differing societal, legal, and moral prohibitions is ungeneralizable in terms of psychodynamic formulations. Generally, the greater the social stigma, the greater the probability of negative sequelae, of ambivalence, of guilt, and thus, of psychopathology.

Later research has taken societal stigma regarding abortion into consideration (Fingerer, 1973). The author stated that minor postabortion depression or psychological disturbances may be transient, socially learned situational reactions or societal myths rather than the result of a traumatic event.

Cohen and Roth's (1984) account of psychological sequelae of abortion provided a counterbalance to the either–or controversy in the literature with regard to positive vs. negative outcome. The authors argued that women respond to abortion with a range of different reactions and at least some respond with negative sequelae. Instead of isolating positive from negative responders, their emphasis was on response styles of aborters.

It is most likely that the abortion may act as a nonspecific physiological trigger that precipitates a psychopathological condition which would have occurred in a psychologically vulnerable woman. The task is then to identify those women who are psychologically vulnerable to negative sequelae.

Payne *et al.* (1976) proposed that women most vulnerable to conflict were single, nulliparous, with preexisting emotional difficulties, conflictual relationships to lovers, intense ambivalence regarding abortion, past negative relationships to the mother, or negative religious or cultural attitudes toward abortion. Thus, it is most logical to assume a complex multivariate constellation in accounting for sequelae.

Literature on the psychological sequelae provided confirmatory evidence that psychological adjustment is benign unless there is preexisting or severe psychopathology (Taussig, 1936).

It is intuitive to suppose that one isolated psychophysiological event in an otherwise intact personality structure should not introduce psychopathology de novo. Indeed, studies asserting negative abortion sequelae involved women with preexisting psychopathology. In these instances, the abortion may have served as a precipitation or exacerbation of depression, psychosis, etc. Any surgical procedure may be viewed as an intrusion into a woman's physical and psychological integrity. However, the method by which this intrusion is handled should logically follow the guidelines of each woman's response style in integrating the physical and psychological aspects of her femininity, which has been typical throughout her life. The entire constellation of defenses and of coping mechanisms around a woman's femininity which antedated the abortion continue to be enlisted postabortion.

Psychodynamics of abortion will necessarily include the psychophysical integration of a woman's sexuality, mothering capacities, attitude toward her own mother or caretakers, her family—in short, elements which constitute her femininity. In this sense, the abortion is a personal event involving the most intimate spheres of a woman's life.

Psychological Factors: Public vs. Private Events

The general psychological abortion research literature ranges from isolated psychoanalytic case reports and accounts of severe psychopathology (Lipper & Feigenbaum, 1976; Noble, 1968; Spaulding & Cavenar, 1978; Tollefson & Garvey, 1983) to personality correlates and attitudes of abortion applicants from a social-personality psychological standpoint, with a deemphasis on severe psycho-pathology and severe sequelae (Allgeier et al., 1981; Barnartt & Harris, 1982; Fischer & Farina, 1978; Freeman, 1977; George, 1980; Gibb & Millard, 1982; Rosen & Martin-dale, 1978, 1980; Lackey & Barry, 1973; Ray & Lovejoy, 1982; Wagenaar & Knol, 1977).

Epidemiological, sociodemographic outcome research and personality correla-tional research are complementary in contributing to an understanding of abortion, since abortion is a medical, social, and psychological event, necessitating investiga-tion from various methodological vantage points. Additionally, phenomenological reports enhance factor analytic and correlational research.

Subdivisions exist within the area of psychological aspects of abortion. Ante-cedent variables are psychological variables occurring prior to abortion, such as reasons for contraceptive failure and abortion decision making. Consequent vari-ables are psychological reactions occurring after the fact of abortion, such as psy-chological sequelae or adjustment reactions.

There is a growing preabortion and postabortion psychological literature. However, for obvious reasons, such as inaccessibility or patient privacy, there is a lack of data on psychological aspects during the entire abortion process, i.e., from the waiting room to leaving the clinic and during the actual abortion procedure itself.

The intent is to briefly delineate those events, which may appropriately be termed as private, since they are not amenable to empirical investigation. Accounts of these private events may serve to bridge the "either–or" controversy over positive vs. negative psychological sequelae. In addition, they are illustrative of certain crucial psychodynamics of abortion.

General Anesthesia

The administration of general anesthesia provides the opportunity to observe more unconscious components in the patient's reaction to abortion. It has been said by abortion personnel that "anesthesia pops the lid off the id." The transition into this primary process dream state functions to release, at the time of abortion, underlying psychodynamics. It is striking to observe an intact woman entering and leaving the clinic unremarkably, when her verbalizations and behavior about the procedure before and after anesthesia were markedly emotional, distressed, and conflictual. It is conspicuous that those patients who are most seemingly intact and in affectual control are the ones who respond the most poorly to anesthesia. This response may be likened to individuals committed to denial and rationalization in reality. Their dreams often take on nightmarish proportions or are replete with conflictual material as a counterbalancing emotional release. The same woman who cries, "My baby! My baby!" after emerging from anesthesia may have no recollection of the event or converse freely with other patients about strictly medical details regarding the procedure postabortion. Other patients describe various aspects of previous pregnancies and deliveries prior to the procedure, and assert that in comparison, this experience is "like getting a tooth pulled." However, once the administration of anesthesia has begun, conflicts are readily evidenced, e.g., "I had to do this. I didn't want to kill this baby. My husband didn't want it. My poor baby. I hate him." Religious and superstitious women appear to have the most difficulty in this semiwaking state, apparently due to their guilt and consequent conflict. These women tend to be the most tearful and are virtually impossible to soothe or to awaken.

There are women who awaken from anesthesia almost immediately, handle postoperative cramping with only minor distress, and for whom the entire procedure is a matter of course—even if it is the first one.

In accounting for the vast discrepancy in reaction between patients, it appears that those women with a history of self-soothing and self-tolerance or general ego strength in response to psychophysical events had the best preoperative and postoperative adjustment. These women were more likely to have realistic expectations regarding the procedure and anesthesia. In addition, they conveyed a healthy and trusting attitude about their sexuality and most importantly, have incorporated the nurturant qualities of their own primary caretakers into their self-structure. For these women, the procedure does not take on the same "raw" quality that it does for their less fortunate counterparts.

These women are the ones for whom the procedure may be viewed as a growth-promoting experience. Indeed, Dundar (1973) proposed that the circumstances surrounding the abortion may even be a self-enhancing occasion for the woman. One 28-year-old woman asserted that the abortion allowed her to greatly appreciate her lover's genuineness, acceptance, and coping in the face of a crisis. It enabled her to develop trust for a man, something she was loath to do in the past. Another nulliparous 25-year-old woman expressed gratitude for the support she received at the clinic and said:

> You have to be realistic about this. I will probably get pregnant again. The time is just not right now. Having the abortion has helped me to accept my limitations. I simply cannot be superwoman and accomplish everything. It would put a tremendous strain on myself, on the father, and on the child. Of course, I have to mourn for what could have been, but I feel that under the circumstances this was my best option, and with this thought, I feel confident and resigned. Also, I had a hard time relating to what feelings pregnancy actually stirs up, but I feel that now, having been pregnant, I have a more mature outlook on what I can expect when I finally do opt to have the pregnancy continue full term. It is not just another activity to take on; it's a huge commitment.

Dreams

Dreams about the procedure, at first glance, appear to have psychopathological undertones due to their primitive psychological content. For example, a woman in treatment with me for a year following an abortion recounted repetitive dreams of the fetus climbing up the uterine wall and scratching at her ovaries. The dream took on various forms as she worked through her ambivalence and integrated the abortion into her life, until the same scenario became reparative in content. Instead, she dreamed that the fetus was grateful to her for not yet being brought into the world and assumed a smaller egg shape embedded in the uterine wall, to be born at a later date when both the patient and the fetus were better prepared.

Patients' postabortion dreams have disturbed content, typically characterized by initial vivid physical imagery in response to an event which transpired "behind their backs," that is, out of sight or imagination, due to anesthesia. Dreams of this sort, instead of alluding to severe psychopathology, serve to help the woman process, reorganize herself around the abortion, and ultimately to master this critical psychophysical event.

Seemingly disturbed, unconscious, primitive events that, if interpreted in isolation, would be viewed as pathological exist alongside realistic adjustment with its accompanying defensive structures. In this sense, the abortion experience may be likened to any psychological coping accompanied by its physical concomitant. It is more likely that this gradually diminishing tension state between rationalization and unconscious immersion in the cognitive and affectual processing of abortion is the most natural and characteristic sequelae. Complete denial with consequent repeat abortions in the literal physical sense or lack of mourning for the fetus, although giving the external impression of positive sequelae, in essence is a psychological aberration. One would be more concerned for the latter patients' difficulties with allowing an experience to create a psychological impact, e.g., sociopathic adjustment, overintellectualization and isolation of affect, and spurious flights into mental health.

CONCLUSION

The importance of a multidimensional approach to the study of abortion cannot be overstated. The medical, social, psychological, and political aspects of abortion are mutually interactive in providing the richest context in which to conduct research on abortion. Patients' phenomenological accounts complement correlational and sociodemographic data to elucidate private events inaccessible through group studies alone. In addition, case reports describing "normal" abortion adjustment are conspicuously lacking. Instead, these accounts are most likely to contain psychopathological responses to abortion. What is needed are general psychodynamic assessments characterizing the typical abortion applicant, which encompass a large sample, studied longitudinally, viewed in light of multiple intervening epidemiological, sociodemographic, and physiological variables.

One may expect that with evolving societal norms regarding women's roles and those specifically relating to sexual behavior and thus encompassing abortion, obtaining an abortion will decreasingly be viewed as deviant activity. Instead of being interpreted as a woman's feminine immaturity or incomplete socialization, abortion will be viewed as a viable and respectable option. In turn, shame and guilt over denial of maternal instinct, feelings of moral transgression, and maladaptive reactions based upon these constructs may likewise subside. Extreme negative psychological sequelae are predictable, should the fundamental right to abortion as a legitimate option in attaining control over one's own bodily self be suddenly renounced. Throughout woman's history she has been expected to maintain a calm demeanor while her physical rights were externally regulated and legislated. Consequent ascribed histrionic affect may not be specific to women, but may in fact be the natural response of any human being when his or her fundamental psychophysical birthrights are confiscated. Thus, the right to abortion has far-reaching consequences for the psychological integrity of a population striving for equality in every facet of life.

REFERENCES

Abernathy, V. (1973). The abortion constellation. *Archives of General Psychiatry, 29,* 346–350.
Alan Guttmacher Institute (1976). *11 Million teenagers.* New York: Alan Guttmacher Institute.
Alan Guttmacher Institute (1981). *Teenage pregnancy: The problem that hasn't gone away.* New York: Planned Parenthood Federation of America.
Allgeier, A. R., Allgeier, E. R., & Rywick, T. (1981). Orientations toward abortion: Guilt or knowledge? *Adolescence, 16* (62), 273–285.
Athanasiou, R., Oppel, W., Michelson, L., Unger, T., & Yager, M. (1973). Psychiatric sequelae to term birth and induced early and late abortion: A longitudinal study. *Family Planning Perspectives, 5,* 227–231.
Babikian, A., & Goldman, A. (1971). A study of teenage pregnancy. *American Journal of Psychiatry, 28*(6), 755–760.
Baldwin, W. (1977). Adolescent pregnancy and childbearing—Growing conscious for Americans. *Population Bulletin, 31,* 34.
Barnartt, S. N., & Harris, R. J. (1982). Recent changes in predictors of abortion attitudes. *Sociology and Social Research, 66*(3), 320–334.
Belsey, E. M., Greer, H. S., Lal, S., Lewis, S. C., & Beard, R. W. (1977). Predictive factors in emotional response to abortion. King's termination study IV. *Social Science and Medicine, 2,* 71–82.
Blos, P. (1969). Three typical constellations in female delinquency. In O. Pollak & A. Friedman (Eds.), *Family dynamics and female sexual delinquency* (pp. 99–100). Palo Alto, CA: Science and Behavior Books.
Blumenfeld, M. (1978). Psychological factors involved in request for elective abortion. *Journal of Clinical Psychiatry, 39,* 17–25.
Bolter, S. (1962). The psychiatrist's role in therapeutic abortion: The unwitting accomplice. *American Journal of Psychiatry, 119,* 312–314.
Byrne, D. (1977). Social psychology and the study of sexual behavior. *Personality and Social Psychology Bulletin, 3,* 3030.
Calderone, M. (Ed.) (1958). *Abortion in the United States.* New York: Hoeber-Harper.
Carlsson, M., & Hamilton, G. (1970). 53 "abortrecidiv" 1969. *Stencil. Uppsala läns låndstings familjeradgivnings-byra,* Uppsala.
Cavenar, J. O., Maltbie, A. A., & Sullivan, J. L. (1978). Aftermath of abortion: Anniversary depression and abdominal pain. *Bulletin of the Menninger Clinic, 42*(5), 433–438.
Cohen, L., & Roth, S. (1984). Coping with abortion. *Journal of Human Stress, 10*(3), 140–145.
Cullhed, S. (1971). Abortion in New York City: Preliminary experience with a permissive abortion statute. *Obstetrics and Gynecology, 39,* 649–660.
Corenblum, B. (1973). Locus of control, latitude of acceptance and attitudes towards abortion. *Psychological Reports, 32,* 753–754.

Daily, E., Nicholas, N., Nelson, F., & Paxter, J. (1973). Repeat abortions in New York City 1970–1972. *Family Planning Perspectives, 5,* 89–93.

David, H. (1972). Abortion in psychological perspective. *American Journal of Orthopsychiatry, 42*(1), 61–67.

David, H. (1978). Psychosocial studies of abortion in the United States, In: David, H. P., Friedman, H. L., van der Tak, J., Sevilla, M. J. (Eds.): *Abortion in psychosocial perspective.* New York: Springer-Verlag.

Dunbar, R. (1954). The psychosomatic approach to abortion and the abortion habit. In: Rosen, H. (ed.), *Therapeutic Abortion.* New York: The Julian Press, Inc., 22–31.

Dudar, H. (1973). Abortion for the asking. *Saturday Review of Society,* 30–35.

Ebaugh, F., & Hauser, K. (1947). Psychiatric aspects of therapeutic abortion. *Postgraduate Medicine, 2,* 325–332.

Eisen, M., Zellman, G. L., Leibowitz, A., Chow, W. K., & Evans, J. R. (1983). Factors discriminating pregnancy resolution decisions of unmarried adolescents. *Genetic Psychology Monographs, 108,* 69–93.

Ekblad, M. (1955). Induced abortion on psychiatric grounds. *Acta Psychiatrica et Neurologica Scandinavica, Supplement, 99.*

Ewing, H. A., & Rouse, B. A. (1973). Therapeutic abortion and a prior psychiatric history. *American Journal of Psychiatry, 130*(1), 37–40.

Fawcett, J. (Ed.) (1973). *Psychological perspectives on population.* New York: Basic Books.

Fingerer, M. E. (1973). Psychological sequelae of abortion: Anxiety and depression. *Journal of Community Psychology, 1*(2), 221–225.

Finkel, M., & Finkel, D. (1975). Sexual and contraceptive knowledge, attitudes and behavior of male adolescents. *Family Planning Perspectives, 7,* 256–260.

Fischer, E., & Farina, A. (1978). Attitude toward abortion and attitude-relevant overt behavior. *Social Forces, 57*(2), 585–599.

Fischer, N. (1974). Multiple induced abortions—A psychoanalytic case study. *Journal of the American Psychoanalytic Association, 22,* 394–407.

Fischmann, S. (1975). The pregnancy resolution decisions of unwed adolescents. *Nursing Clinics of North America, 10,* 217–227.

Fischmann, S. (1977). Delivery of abortion in inner-city adolescents. *American Journal of Orthopsychiatry, 47,* 127–133.

Fleck, S. (1970). Some psychiatric aspects of abortion. *The Journal of Nervous and Mental Disease, 151,* 42–50.

Floyd, J., & Viney, L. (1974). Ego identity and ego ideal in the unwed mother. *British Journal of Medical Psychology, 47,* 273–281.

Ford, C. V., Castelnuovo-Tedesco, P., & Long, K. D. (1972). Women who seek therapeutic abortion compared with women completing pregnancy. *American Journal of Psychiatry, 129,* 546–552.

Forrest, J., Tietze, C., & Sullivan, E. (1978). Abortion in the United States, 1976–1977. *Family Planning Perspectives, 10*(5), 271–279.

Franke, L. B. (1978). *The ambivalence of abortion.* New York: Random House.

Freeman, E. W. (1977). Influence of personality attributes on abortion experiences. *American Journal of Orthopsychiatry, 47*(3), 503–512.

Friedman, C. M., Greenspan, R., & Mittleman, F. (1977). The decision-making process and the outcome of therapeutic abortion. In R. Kalman (Ed.), *Abortion.* Dubuque, IA: Kendall/Hunt.

Galdston, I. (1958). Other aspects of the abortion problem. In M. Calderone (Ed.), *Abortion in the United States* (pp. 117–121). New York: Hoeber and Harper.

George, E. I. (1980). An empirical study of medical termination of pregnancy. *Psychological Studies, 25*(2), 118–121.

Gibb, G. D., & Millard, R. J. (1981). Research on repeated abortion: State of the field: 1973–1979. *Psychological Reports, 48,* 415–424.

Gibb, G. D., & Millard, R. J. (1982). Divergent perspectives in abortion counseling. *Psychological Reports, 50*(3, Pt. 1), 819–822.

Gillis, A., & Marsjalek, M. (1971). Unwanted pregnancies. *Newcastle Medical Journal, 31,* 196–199.

Gisbert, M., & Falk, R. (1978). Adolescent sexual activity: Contraception and abortion. *American Journal of Obstetrics and Gynecology, 132,* 620–628.

Graves, W., & Bradshaw, B. (1964). Some social and attitudinal factors associated with contraceptive choice among low income black teenagers after an illegitimate birth. *Advances in Planned Parenthood, 9,* 28–33.

Greer, H. S., Lal, S., Lewis, S. C., Belsey, E. M., & Beard, R. W. (1976). Psychosocial consequences of therapeutic abortion. King's termination study III. *British Journal of Psychiatry, 128,* 74–79.

Halmosh, E. (1975). Postpartum emotional trouble (In Hebrew). *Harefuah, 52,* 142–144.

Heinrich, R. F., & Bobrowsky, R. P. (1984). In *Transitional Family Research Institute, Abortion Research Notes, 14,* 1–2.

Henshaw, S. K., Binkin, N. J., Blaine, E., & Smith, J. C. (1985). A portrait of American women who obtain abortions. *Family Planning Perspectives, 17,* 90–95.

Hilton, I., & Kunkes, C. (1980). *Adolescent pregnancy: Causes, risks and social implications.* Paper presented at grand rounds in adolescent psychiatry, Mount Sinai Hospital, New York.

Illsley, R., & Hall, M. H. (1976). Psychosocial aspects of abortion. *Bulletin, World Health Organization, 52,* 83–106.

Jacobsson, L., & Solheim, F. (1975). Women's experience of the abortion procedure. *Social Psychiatry, 10,* 155–160.

Jacobsson, L., von Schoultz, B., & Solheim, F. (1976). Repeat aborters-first aborters, a social-psychiatric comparison. *Social Psychiatry, 11,* 75–86.

Kane, F., & Lachenbruch, P. A. (1973). Motivational factors in abortion patients. *American Journal of Psychiatry, 130,* 290–293.

Kinch, R., Wearing, M. P., Love, E. J., & McMahon, D. (1969). Some aspects of pediatric illegitimacy. *American Journal of Obstetrics and Gynecology, 105,* 20.

Kumar, R., & Robson, K. (1978). Previous induced abortion and ante-natal depression in primiparae: Preliminary report of a survey of mental health of pregnancy. *Psychological Medicine, 8,* 711–715.

Kummer, J. (1963). Post-abortion psychiatric illness—A myth? *American Journal of Psychiatry, 119,* 980–983.

Lackey, H. S., & Barry, J. R. (1973). A measure of attitudes toward abortion. *Journal of Community Psychology, 1*(1), 31–33.

Lask, B. (1975). Short-term psychiatric sequelae of therapeutic termination of pregnancy. *British Journal of Psychiatry, 126,* 173–177.

Lebonsohn, M. (1977). Legal abortion as a positive mental health measure in family planning, In R. Kalman (Ed.), *Abortion.* Dubuque, IA: Kendall/Hunt.

Levene, H. I., & Rigney, F. J. (1970). Law, preventive psychiatry and therapeutic abortion. *Journal of Nervous and Mental Disease, 150*(1), 51–59.

Levering, C. S. (1983). Teenage pregnancy and parenthood. *Childhood Education, 59*(3), 182–185.

Lipper, S., & Feigenbaum, W. M. (1976). Obsessive-compulsive neurosis after viewing the fetus during therapeutic abortion. *American Journal of Psychotherapy, 30*(4), 666–674.

Luker, K. (1975). *Taking chances: Abortion and the decision not to contracept.* Berkeley: University of California Press.

Martin, C. (1973). Psychological problems of abortion for the unwed teenage girl. *Genetic Psychology Monographs, 88*, 23–110.

Meyerowitz, S., Satloff, A., & Romano, J. (1971). Induced abortion for psychiatric indication. *American Journal of Psychiatry, 127*(9), 1153–1160.

Monsour, K., & Stewart, B. (1973). Abortion and sexual behavior in college women. *American Journal of Orthopsychiatry, 43*, 804–814.

Murray, H. A. (1943). *Thematic Apperception Test* (TAT). Cambridge, MA: Harvard University Press.

Noble, D. (1968). Psychiatric problems in therapeutic abortion. In R. C. Allen, E. Z. Ferster, & J. G. Rubin (Eds.), *Reading in law and psychiatry*. Baltimore: Johns Hopkins University Press.

O'Leary, K. M., Shore, M. F., & Wieder, S. (1984). Contracting pregnant adolescents. Are we missing cues? *Social Casework, 65*(5), 297–306.

Olley, P. C. (1970). Age, marriage, personality and distress. A study of personality factors in women referred for therapeutic abortion. *Seminars in Psychiatry, 2*, 341–351.

Osofsky, J., & Osofsky, H. (1977). The psychological reaction of patients to legalized abortion. *American Journal of Orthopsychiatry, 42*, 48–60.

Oswalt, R. (1974). Sexual and contraceptive behavior of college females. *Journal of the American College Health Association, 22*, 392–394.

Pare, C. M. B., & Raven, H. (1970). Follow-up of patients referred for termination. *Lancet, I*, 653–658.

Patt, S. L., Rappaport, R. G., & Barglow, P. (1969). Follow-up of therapeutic interruption of pregnancy. *Archives of General Psychiatry, 20*, 408–414.

Payne, E. C., Kravitz, A. R., Norman, M. T., & Anderson, J. V. (1976). Outcome following therapeutic abortion. *Archives of General Psychiatry, 33*, 725–733.

Pines, D. (1982). The relevance of early psychic development to pregnancy and abortion. *International Journal of Psychoanalysis, 63*, 311–319.

Potter, R., & Ford, K. (1976). Repeat abortion. *Demography, 13*, 65–82.

Raphael, B. (1974). Youth in a world of change. *Australian and New Zealand Journal of Psychiatry, 8*(2), 131–137.

Ray, J. J., & Lovejoy, F. H. (1982). Conservatism, attitude to abortion, and Maccoby's biophilia. *The Journal of Social Psychology, 118*, 143–144.

Robbins, J. M. (1979). Objective versus subjective responses to abortion. *Journal of Consulting and Clinical Psychology, 47*(5), 994–995.

Rosen, R. H., & Martindale, L. J. (1978). Sex role perceptions and the abortion decision. *The Journal of Sex Research, 14*(4), 231–245.

Rosen, R. H., & Martindale, L. J. (1980). Abortion as "deviance"—traditional female roles vs. the feminist perspective. *Social Psychiatry, 15*, 103–108.

Rothman, D. (1973). Habitual abortion and sexual conflict. *Medical Aspects of Human Sexuality, 7*, 56–67.

Rovinsky, J. (1971). Abortion in New York City: Preliminary experience with a permissive abortion statute. *Obstetrics and Gynecology, 39*, 649–660.

Rovinsky, J. (1972). Abortion recidivism: A problem in preventive medicine. *Journal of Obstetrics and Gynecology, 39*, 649–660.

Semmens, J. P., & Lamers, W. M. (1968). *Teenage pregnancy: Including management of emotional and constitutional problems*. Springfield, IL: Bannerstone House.

Tietze, C. (1978). Teenage pregnancies: Looking ahead to 1984. *Family Planning Perspectives, 10*(4), 205–207.

Tollefson, G. D., & Garvey, M. J. (1983). Conversion disorder following termination of pregnancy. *Journal of Family Medicine, 16*(1), 73–77.

Tredgold, R. F. (1964). Psychiatric indications for termination of pregnancy. *Lancet, 2*, 1251–1254.

Wagenaar, T. C., & Knol, I. W. (1977). Attitudes toward abortion: A comparative analysis of correlates for 1973 and 1975. *Journal of Sociology and Social Welfare, IV*(6).

Walbert, D., & Butler, D. (1973). *Abortion, society and the law*. Cleveland: Case Western Reserve University Press.

Werman, D. S., & Raft, D. (1973). Some psychiatric problems related to therapeutic abortion. *N.C. Medical Journal, 34*(4), 274–275.

Winnik, H. Z. (1958). Therapeutic abortion (In Hebrew). *Harefuah, 55*, 8.

Zelnick, M., Kantner, J., & Ford, K. (1981). *Sex and pregnancy in adolescence*. Beverly Hills, CA: Sage.

Chapter 16

Women and Eating Disorders

MELINDA GELLMAN

It is unfortunate that a contemporary volume on female psychology is incomplete without addressing eating disorders. In recent decades, the incidence of anorexia nervosa and bulimia has increased disproportionately among women in Western cultures. Estimates of prevalence range from 2% of young women at a family planning clinic (Cooper & Fairburn, 1983) to 7.8% (Pyle, Mitchell, Eckert, Halvorson, Neuman, & Goff, 1983) and 19% (Halmi, Falk, & Schwartz, 1981) of normal female college populations. It has been repeatedly observed that eating disorders predominantly affect Caucasian women from upper socioeconomic classes (Bemis, 1978; Bruch, 1973; Crisp, Palmer, & Kalucy, 1976). There is evidence suggesting, however, that eating disorders are not limited to this racial and social sector (Garfinkel & Garner, 1982). This chapter discusses eating disorders, the context of their rising incidence, and issues in female development pertinent to eating disorders in women.

Eating disorders are clinical syndromes involving disturbances in behavior, feelings, perceptions, cognitions, and attitudes about food, eating, and body shape. Beneath the overt symptoms are profound deficits in ego functions and disturbances in identity. Though the relationship remains unclear, instability of affect and depression often coincide with eating disorders (Halmi, 1985; Swift, Andrews, & Barklage, 1986). These features become masked by obsessive preoccupations with seemingly superficial and distorted concerns about food. Eating, and food itself, acquire psychic functions and symbolic meanings that ultimately fail to contain anxiety and conflict. It is often at this point of failure, with an entrenched sense of isolation, shame, despair, and hopelessness, that women first seek professional help. Their conscious fears of losing control over food are soon translated into dread of feeling out of control over their inner lives and interpersonal worlds.

In addition to psychologically disturbing factors in eating disorders, their physically harmful consequences beckon serious alarm. They resemble psychosomatic disorders in their maladaptive use of the body to channel emotional distress. Phys-

MELINDA GELLMAN, PH.D. • Director, Division of Eating Disorders, Fifth Avenue Center for Counseling and Psychotherapy, New York City; private practice.

ical health and vital bodily needs often become jeopardized. The harm may include, among other physical problems, temporary swelling of salivary glands, characteristic deterioration of the teeth, electrolyte disturbances, or cardiac irregularities that can result in death (Garner & Garfinkel, 1984). Psychological and physiological features secondary to the initial symptoms, such as the clinical effects of starvation (Garfinkel & Garner, 1982; Garfinkel & Kaplan, 1985; Keys, Brozek, Henschel, Mickelson, & Taylor, 1950), compound the damage done. Once established, anorexia nervosa and bulimia acquire an addictive, self-perpetuating nature that renders their victims highly resistant to change. Responsibility thus lies with therapists, educators, physicians, dentists, and parents to recognize manifestations of eating disorders and to appropriately intervene.

ANOREXIA NERVOSA, BULIMIA, AND RELATED DISORDERS

References to the symptoms of anorexia nervosa, albeit with misconceived interpretations, can be traced back through history. Anorexic girls in medieval times were at times elevated to saintliness on the basis of their asceticism (Lacey, 1982), and at other times persecuted for witchcraft (MacLeod, 1981). Few early physicians speculated about pathological processes in the symptoms they observed (Morton, 1694). Anorexia nervosa was first labeled a disease in the 1870s (Gull, 1874; Lasegue, 1873). Scientific study was sidetracked by a common diagnostic error made after the identification of Simmonds' disease in 1914. This dysfunction of the anterior lobe of the pituitary gland shares with anorexia nervosa the symptom of emaciation. For approximately 30 years, physicians failed to differentiate psychogenic anorexia from Simmonds' disease. Thus, despite detection as a psychological disorder more than 100 years ago, our inquiry and understanding of anorexia nervosa is relatively new.

Anorexia nervosa is marked by a driven need to be thin and a dreaded fear of weight gain that results in a refusal to eat. The anorexic organizes her life around controlling her weight and literally becomes emaciated. Her personality grows rigid, narrow, and perfectionistic. Hyperactivity is common and frequently channeled into hours of rigorous daily exercise. Thoughts become preoccupied with calories and food. Compulsive behavior evolves in idiosyncratic rituals regarding the regulation of food intake. There is often exaggerated involvement in preparing meals and feeding others. Coinciding with major weight loss, the anorexic suffers from profound body image distortions that prevent her from perceiving the deteriorated state of her body. Denial of her abnormal appearance often reaches delusional proportions and is uneffected by the onset of starvation-based symptoms, such as amenorrhea, sleep disturbances, or growth of a thin layer of body hair.

The denial of hunger, fatigue, and misperception of reality reflected in characteristic anorexic behavior is frightening to observers. Low weight and bizarre behaviors, rather than emotional needs, often pull for intervention from the family. The focus on food, calories, and body size, however, distract both the anorexic and her family from the true feelings and interpersonal difficulties that underlie her disorder. Typically, these include maladaptive patterns of family functioning. Families of anorexics are characterized by apparent togetherness and closeness at the cost of intrusiveness, rigidity, and failure to effectively confront and resolve conflict (Minuchin, Rosman, & Baker, 1978). Fearful of disrupting the family's harmony, the anorexic unconsciously denies developmental struggles around independence and adulthood. She symbolically attempts to control them by controlling her diet and body. The response of others to her relentless pursuit of thinness is experienced as intrusive, unwarranted, and controlling. By the time the family does intervene, a true struggle is set up on the overt level of the symptoms. Authority provides the anorexic with external forces to struggle against. The struggle itself keeps her emotionally attached to the family, avoiding frightening but imminent separation and autonomy, and keeps all family conflict focused on the anorexic child.

Bulimia has been identified as a psychological disorder more recently than anorexia nervosa, and controversy lingers regarding the most appropriate diagnostic criteria and terminology (Russell, 1985). According to the experiences reported by patients, bulimia refers to a self-perpetuating cycle of binge eating followed by self-induced purging. The combination of the binge and the purge, and their addictive functions, leaves a growing number of young women feeling depressed, worthless, and hopelessly out of control. In addition, they feel ashamed of their uncontrollable, socially undesirable behaviors and devote much energy to keeping them secret.

Binge eating entails the quick consumption of large amounts of food over a short period of time. Some bulimics participate in series of binges over a longer predesignated period, such as a weekend. The foods selected typically have high caloric and high carbohydrate content. Critical features include being alone and feeling unable to stop. Phenomenologically, patients assign different meanings to the experience of binging. For most bulimics, gorging on forbidden foods provides an escape from all feelings, concerns, and people into a dissociative state. It becomes a maladaptive self-soothing and self-medicating process. Many are puzzled by the sensual feelings the act of binging evokes. Some liken the sense of abandon of binging with sexual indulgence. Common to all bulimics are feelings of guilt, despair, and hopelessness following episodes of binge eating.

Binge eating ends by exhaustion, sleep, physical limitations, or purging. Like anorexics, bulimics dread getting fat. In contrast to anorexics' harsh restriction of food intake to prevent weight gain, bulimics alternate uncontrolled binges with a variety of ritualized efforts to regain control. Purging serves as a means to undo lapses of self-control and is rationalized as a means of weight control. Some methods of purging are obvious, such as self-induced vomiting or laxative abuse. Other forms are more elusive to both the observer and the bulimic. She may be using exercise, fasting, diuretics, diet pills or cocaine to purge her system of unwanted calories and undo her loss of control over eating.

The origin of the word "bulimia" is from the Greek word for "ox hunger." As such it captures poetically the bulimic's binge eating. It is perhaps a more apt title for conditions defined by similar episodes of lost control over eating that are not followed by purging. Diagnosis of such eating disorders is not as clear as anorexia nervosa or bulimia because the clinical significance of binge eating may be a matter of degree (Wardle & Beinart, 1981). Compulsive overeating can achieve the same frequency and psychic functions as the bulimic's binge–purge cycle thus leaving the overeater feeling terribly out of control. If chronic, driven eating results in obvious increases in weight. Obesity itself cannot be considered an eating disorder, but it can be the result of an eating disorder. With perhaps less intensity of focus and dissociation while eating, food is relied upon to soothe, self-medicate, contain feelings, and keep an emotional and social distance from the outside world. When the overweight person's behaviors develop such a functional dependence on food and eating, the label of obesity nervosa may be in order.

For purposes of discussion, this chapter uses a developmental perspective to distinguish two groups of female eating-disordered patients. The first, early onset group tends to be younger, brought to treatment at the insistence of family and physicians, and appears stuck in restrictive, overcontrolled anorexic symptoms. The second group expresses symptoms later along the developmental pathway than the first. These women tend to seek treatment voluntarily during their late teens through 20s and struggle with inconsistent, uncontrollable bulimic symptoms. The level of psychological development and symptoms, not chronological age, determines group assignment. There is a great deal of overlap in personality features. Both groups present ego deficits reflective of pre-Oedipal failure. The restricting group fixates early in order to ward off development. Outside of their anorexic symptoms, these young women behave like perfectionistic, compliant, good little girls who never reached adolescence. Patients from the bulimic group seem to move more receptively through the developmental sequence. Their journeys, however, are marred by conflict from cumulative developmental failures. They often appear like capable young women with enough autonomy to take on the appropriate tasks of social, academic, and career life. They are often successful by societal standards and demonstrate adequate coping skills in certain areas. It has been postulated that deficient impulse control suggests greater psychopathology among this group (Bruch, 1973). It may be that the restrictors are not less disturbed, just less messy. Binging and purging is a messy but ritualized defense against the impulses and feelings that developmentally arrested anorexics never experience. Controlling impulses by complete denial looks cleaner but is very primitive. The older, more ambivalent patient may experience her impulses and loss of control, but often has taken some steps away from her family and begun to participate in life and its struggles.

A developmental framework helps to clarify the observed overlap in the symptoms of eating disorders. Despite their rigid refusal of food, many anorexics report episodes of binging and purging (Casper, Eckert, Halmi, Goldberg, & Davis, 1980; Russell, 1979). Conversely, it is not uncommon for bulimic women to report periods of anorexia nervosa in their histories (Russell, 1979), or periodic spells of "fasting" in the present. Early developmental failures underlie the symptoms for all women. While often motivated by the state of starvation (Garner & Garfinkel, 1984), the anorexic's occasional lapses in control can be seen to represent flirtation with advancing development. Growth demands that she risk relinquishing familiar restricting defenses in order to experience and learn to deal with her feelings. The bulimic who restricts, such as in response to disappointment, rejection, or increased stress, may be said to periodically regress in this area of self-regulation. Psychotherapy must help eating-disordered women to explore, develop, and internalize mechanisms necessary for coping with both inner life and outer reality.

THE SOCIOCULTURAL BACKDROP

Discussion of overeating, dieting, body weight, and appearance evokes strong feelings among most persons today, not only among eating-disordered women. Values of contemporary Western culture place the condition of one's body at a premium. These values in turn set the aesthetic ideal, influence personal preferences, and provide guidelines for conformity. A purusal of the styles of this century demonstrates that the ideal female body form is a changing phenomenon rather than a constant fact. The current aesthetic dictates that women be thin. Models presented by the media, fashion, advertising, and entertainment industries uniformly endorse the worship of thinness. Most women's bodies are not naturally as thin as is currently considered attractive. Individuals appear to have internal homeostatic mechanisms that regulate body weight (Bennett & Gurin, 1982). The struggle to maintain a weight below one's optimal range is extremely difficult. Millions of women voluntarily engage in this struggle and millions of dollars have been spent to devise, promote, and purchase a growing variety of diet aids (Kleinfield, 1986). A host of feelings and expectations are culturally associated with slenderness. Being thin, perhaps only 5 to 10 pounds below the body's natural equilibrium, has become equated with beauty, happiness, increased self-esteem, good living, and the expectation of social success. The inability to maintain a low weight is alternately associated with poor self-image, failure, and the expectation of social rejection.

Ironically, the same media sources that endorse often unnatural thinness also lead campaigns promoting physical fitness and health. The public is increasingly educated about the value of proper diet as well as about the dangers of artificial additives, excessive use of familiar foodstuffs, and substance abuse. Information about medical conditions, previously kept within the physician's domain, is continually disseminated through television, radio, and popular magazine articles. Regular exercise has become a mainstay of Western culture for many persons of all ages. The effect of these contemporary values results in a definition of being overweight as more than simply unfashionable and unattractive. It is deadly. Uncontrolled body weight suggests disregard for one's health and life. It is a bitter irony that patients with eating disorders are often astonishingly knowledgeable about nutrition. Unfortunately, their study of nutrition tends to be motivated by preoccupation with controlling food and their bodies rather than by practical and healthy curiosity. The knowledge they boast typically remains split off from the damage inflicted upon their bodies and is used to reinforce self-punitive attitudes. Frustration and self-blame when losing control become intensified by their heightened awareness of how they violate themselves.

In addition to the aesthetic and nutritional value placed upon thinness, conflicts and stress unique to women of today's culture contribute to the rising incidence of eating disorders. Positive outcomes of the social and sexual revolutions of the 1960s and 1970s include the deterioration of rigid traditional role definitions for women. The field of choices regarding dating, marriage, career, family, and essentially, identity, has been greatly expanded within a brief period of time. While our culture is in the process of assimilating these social changes, young women find themselves in unchartered territory. The more traditional model for women, while often oppressive to the individual, provided clear criteria for direction and self-esteem. Internalization of traditional values assured a high correspondance between societal and self-expectations and approval. Today, internalized ego ideals based solely on traditional values leave women unprepared for the broader social reality. Peer pressure directs toward participating in an expanded vocational, leisure, and social world. Those who devote their energies to personal development, however, struggle with integrating family life and motherhood. Despite an outer appearance of successful coping, many are deeply confused and unsure of themselves. Changing standards provide little certainty about what makes women feel good about themselves. Young women today are in the fortunate but difficult position to make critical choices about the shape of their lives. Overwhelmed by this task, many falsely displace their energies toward choosing the shape of their bodies.

Young women from adolescence through early adulthood comprise the population at risk for eating disorders. It requires little imagination to understand how our cultural climate predisposes women at these critical passages to experience stress about their appearance and identity. The symptom choice of preoccupation with control of food, calories, and body weight, however, is multidetermined. Certainly, the cultural drive for thinness and fitness makes these symptoms likely choices. Furthermore, in a world of unprecedented conflict in roles and competition to achieve, regulation of food intake and weight deceptively appears to be one accessible goal. Undeniable influence from the sociocultural context, however, in no way suggests that eating disorders are attributable to external causes. Developmental and psychodynamic issues that predispose women to select this avenue for expressing psychopathology are discussed in the following section.

FEEDING AND EATING AS PRIMARY HUMAN EXPERIENCE

As recognition of deviancy often prompts examination of normalcy, disorders of eating suggest the existence of normative development of the eating process. This section outlines Anna Freud's (1965) description of a developmental line for the feeding process. Developmental lines are maturational sequences of expectable behaviors that reflect the child's level of psychological growth, socialization, and behavioral independence. Freud's (1965) keen observations of children and subsequent developmental framework emphasize a critical feature of eating disorders, namely, their expression of the struggle to establish autonomy and self-control in the process of adapting to external reality. Freud (1964) identified the emergent roots of autonomy in eating behaviors during the oral and anal phases. Prior to the establishment of autonomy, eating assumes the merger of ego, mother, and food. As the infant suckles at the breast or bottle, feeding and eating are experienced as a single process. In time, the infant is weaned. With physical and psychological maturation there is a transition from being fed by others to feeding oneself. Finally, the successful use of implements for self-feeding establishes the toddler's sense of autonomy in the area of eating. At this point, the child is no longer merged with food and mother. It is likely that vulnerability to eating disorders originates during these initial steps of Freud's developmental line.

According to Freud (1965), disturbances in eating during the Oedipal period reflect internal structural conflicts appropriate to this phase. It is here, for instance, that the refusal of the Oedipally fixated girl to eat may symbolize unconscious fears of sexual impulses and impregnation (Waller, Kaufman, & Deutsch, 1940). This stage-specific interpretation formed the basis of earliest psychoanalytic understanding of anorexia nervosa, and is described later.

The final step in Freud's (1965) developmental line coincides with latency and is characterized by an appropriate desexualization of feeding and eating. The consolidation of self-determination, rational attitudes, and pleasure in eating that occurs here provides the foundation for the mature individual's relationship to food. Women with eating disorders lack this foundation. They harbor irrational attitudes about food and experience it as a controlling force in their lives. As maturity in this area has been stunted prior to latency, feeding and eating become a likely battleground for the enactment of unresolved Oedipal and pre-Oedipal conflicts.

Pre-Oedipal Development

The pathology underlying eating disorders is commonly traced to pre-Oedipal failures. While Anna Freud's (1965) descriptions of behavioral sequences are useful for monitoring normal expectable growth, the theoretical foundation of Margaret Mahler and her colleagues (Mahler, Pine, & Bergmann, 1975) is useful for understanding the meaning and treatment of eating disorders. According to their theory of pre-Oedipal development, psychological life begins in a state of normal autism. For the first 2 months, the infant's experience of the world is undifferentiated and impressionistic. Suckling, the earliest eating behavior discussed by Freud (1965), is an innate reflexive means to obtain nutrients necessary for growth and survival. From autism, the infant enters the stage of normal symbiosis where the mother's body, feelings, and ministrations provide definition of self and the world. The earliest differentiation of inner experience occurs within the context of symbiosis with mother. Feeding and eating are critical to the infant's ability to discriminate two global states. When hungry, the infant feels uncomfortable, anxious, and bad. When sated, the infant feels comfortable, gratified, and good. It is here that the universal association of food with satisfaction, soothing, safety, and wholeness is made.

The regulation of the infant's two global states is completely dependent upon the quality and timeliness of the mother's care, which establishes the basis for later tension regulation. If needs are infrequently or erratically met, the infant will develop little trust in the world, and thus within the self, to regulate inner states. As such, bad feelings remain global and overwhelming. Coordination of feeding with the infant's needs instills a more reliable pattern of mounting tension followed by tension reduction that forms a prototype for effective self-regulation of inner states. Eating-disordered women lack internal mechanisms necessary for tension regulation and self-soothing (Brisman & Siegel, 1984; Goodsit, 1983). They do not trust their ability to tolerate and modulate their own feelings, whether hunger or more complex affects. The anticipation of uncomfortable feelings is overwhelming. Some prevent the experience of badness by restricting and denying hunger and other sensations. This strategy precludes the inevitable flood of affect feared to shatter the fragile self. Others unconsciously take a more ambivalent approach. They alternately experience impulses and feelings without advantages of internalized self-regulation, and then undo such experience by purging or deprivation. This process acquires a harsh punitive nature that generates greater stress and frustration. In turn, binging is relied upon to soothe these bad feelings. In this way the binge–purge cycle becomes addictive. The consistency of the therapist and predictable rhythmic structure of the psychotherapy relationship help to correct developmental deficits resulting in defective self-regulation and self-care.

In the course of physical and psychological maturation, the infant emerges from symbiosis and begins the normal separation–individuation process. Literal separation from the breast or bottle, as described by Anna Freud (1965), is one marker signifying the onset of this process. The infant begins to distinguish food from mother as the source of food, and internal states from conditions imposed and regulated by the outside world. Quite concretely, the infants' physical body may serve as a transitional object in facilitating separation (Sugarman & Kurash, 1982). The body itself provides comfort and reduces anxiety by representing a state of merger with mother. This eases the infants' task of learning that her hunger is her own, and that it is distinct from other uncomfortable sensations.

Subphases of separation–individuation entail experimentation with newly developing physical and emotional skills. Development of autonomous ego functions, such as locomotion, allows the healthy toddler to gloat in her ability to master the environment. Learning to manipulate food and utensils, as Freud (1965) describes, provides one arena for expressing assertion, control, and mastery, and crystallizing the emerging differentiation from mother and the external world. Self-feeding is inherently reinforcing to the emergence of identity, will, and independence. Once achieved, feeding and eating no longer represent merger with mother, complete dependence, and identity. However, universally and unconsciously, food and eating do retain the capacity for such symbolism. Boundary confusion and primitive meanings attached to food, body, and eating among women with eating disorders strongly suggest developmental failures in the separation–individuation process.

Hilda Bruch's (1973, 1978) seminal contributions emphasize the importance of early object relationships in the prediposition to eating disorders. The foundation for ego functions and later object relations, which are impaired among anorexics and bulimics, lies in the mother–child matrix. Feeding determines the pace of this relationship. Optimally, consistent and appropriate responsiveness to the infant's behavior teaches the child to discriminate inner feeling states. Under less than optimal circumstances, pathogenic transactional patterns around the feeding situation occur. The mother's poor timing, oversolicitousness, permissiveness, inhibitory or controlling behavior, for instance, interferes with the development of awareness and differentiation of body states. In addition to personality characteristics of the mother that taint early interactions, the inaccurate use of food fosters later confusion. Failures may result from the use of food as a panacea for any discomfort, or the withdrawal of food as a form of punishment. This interferes with the gradual learning about how body sensations and functions are organized and controlled. In sum, a mother's failure to respond appropriately to her infant's self-intiated behaviors around the feeding situation interferes with the child's developing sense of ownership and identification with her own body.

Women with eating disorders typically describe overcontrolling, intrusive, emotionally demanding, and narcissistic qualities of their mothers. Younger patients often remain too enmeshed in their families to perceive the nature of the relationships. The mother's inappropriateness is often apparent, however, in reported interactions at home and in psychotherapy sessions with family members. The mother of a 29-year-old, 81-pound woman refused to upset herself by reading about anorexia or listening to the radio any time eating disorders were discussed over the last 8 years of her daughter's illness. She expressed gratitude toward the therapist who would assume responsibility for her daughter's starvation, but refused to stop her daughter from preparing her evening meal. More highly developed patients demonstrate varying degrees of observing ego and ability to evaluate family relationships. Goals of psychotherapy include helping these women understand how family interactions, roles, and relationships have left them feeling frightened to trust, out of control, and unequipped to function independently. This understanding encourages separation and individuation. As such, psychotherapy gradually grants permission for ownership and development of the body and the self.

Derivatives of early developmental failures are observed in the three cardinal features of eating disorders identified by Bruch (1973). Anorexics and bulimics suffer from defective self-awareness of body states, misperceptions and misconceptions of body image, and a pervasive sense of personal ineffectiveness. Deprived of the chance to develop and refine the skills necessary to trust themselves, these women feel inadequate and unprepared to cope. According to Bruch, effects of their developmental deficits are experienced when confronting new situations. Rather than taking initiative, negotiating, or asserting herself, the eating-disordered woman repeats early patterns of relying on other persons or external circumstances to guide her behavior. If external structure is available, she conforms and proceeds. As situations grow more complex with advancing life passages, she experiences the terror of inner emptiness, lack of self-confidence, and fear of being overwhelmed by strong influences and affects.

Pre-Oedipal growth from complete dependency to the establishment of self and autonomy is applicable to children of both sexes. Even at this early stage, however, there are important differences between boys and girls. They are not attributable to innate gender differences, per se, but to qualitative aspects of the mother–child matrix that vary as a function of the child's gender. For instance, the encouragement of physical prowess in boys results in boys' greater confidence and ability to function on their own. Differential treatment leads to differential ability, which in turn reinforces differential treatment. A more subtle effect of the role of gender in pre-Oedipal development lies in qualities specific to the mother's emotional relationship with her female child. The daughter is most likely to be treated by the mother as an extension of herself, as she is created in her image. The daughter, more than the son, provides the mother with a projective screen for her own feelings and conflicts about being female (see Chapter 3). The daughter's embryonic self is burdened with the task of serving this complex role for her mother and meeting her various unconscious demands. The opportunity for primitive identity confusion between mother and self is thus heightened for the female. Difficulty with boundaries between mother and self, and with later consolidation of feminine identity, are salient among eating-disordered women.

Oedipal Issues in Eating Disorders

Consistent with dominant theoretical thinking, the earliest psychological literature on eating disorders focused on psychosexual dynamics (Moulton, 1942; Thoma, 1967; Waller *et al.*, 1940). As theoretical and treatment approaches grounded in ego, self, and cognitive psychology proved more promising than classical psychoanalysis, Oedipal issues have been deemphasized. As the same concrete symptoms in eating disorders, however, have different meanings for different individuals, it is necessary to understand general levels of emotional growth. Some women struggle mainly with Oedipal-phase conflicts. For perhaps the majority of patients, early adaptation was so stunted that pre-Oedipal issues dominate daily functioning and personality. When the developmental sequence was highly tinged by early pathology, ego functions, and interpersonal relations, the mother–child relationship assumes immediacy in psychotherapy. As symptoms subside, and trust and personal validation evolve in treatment, Oedipal issues emerge even for these patients. This section discusses some of these issues in the meaning of eating disorders.

The etiology of anorexia nervosa was believed to lie in unconscious fantasies of oral impregnation (Waller *et al.*, 1940). The normal awakening of Oedipal sexual feelings stirs unconsciously anticipated, desired, and feared fantasies of impregnation. Too threatening to the psychic structure, these fantasies remain repressed and displaced onto nonsexual body concerns. Activity centering around the mouth acquires symbolic sexual significance, and the sexual function of genitalia are denied. The body becomes the arena for expression of sexual conflict and the battleground for the struggle to control sexual impulses. The anorexic who develops an inordinate fear of taking in oral supplies is symbolically attempting to prevent impregnation and repudiate her sexuality. This solution fails, however, as food and eating remain highly sexualized. Jennifer, for instance, is puzzled about why she only binged secretively and at night, and felt guilty when her father "caught" her in the kitchen. Guilty feelings inappropriate to the situation are often reported by women with eating disorders. Confusion over the source and inability to control them creates further distress. Eating disorders may defend women from the content of their Oedipal conflicts, but ultimately fail to contain displaced guilt and anxiety induced by their Oedipal fantasies.

Among higher-functioning women with eating disorders, Oedipal dynamics are often more complex than equating the desire for food and fear of fat with oral impregnation fantasies. A critical task of the Oedipal phase is establishing gender identity, and gender differences here have later implications in women's struggles with eating disorders. Attachment to the father facilitates the emergence from the exclusive bond with the mother for children of both sexes. Oedipal dynamics allow self-definition to expand within the context of the mother–father–child matrix. For boys, attachment to father provides a clear direction for identity formation. Psychological development, physical similarities, and socialization strengthen the male's identification and reinforce his boundary between mother and self. The situation for girls is more ambiguous. While maturation impels her toward father, she confronts anxiety from sexual feelings and from the reality that she will never physically resemble him. For some girls, failures in the pre-Oedipal quality of symbosis and thwarted separation prevent healthy attachment to father. For others, the father's passivity or minor role in the family fails to facilitate the attachment she needs. Successful Oedipal resolution requires the girl to simultaneously distinguish herself from and identify with her mother. She must minimize anxiety and guilt from strivings toward father and boundary confusion from the process of identifying with mother. This set of complex dynamics in the formation of gender identity during the Oedipal phase is highly charged with conflict unique to females. Later confusion over boundaries and sexuality are themes that emerge in psychotherapy with eating-disordered women.

Superimposed over earlier pathological adaptation, other salient Oedipal dynamics may be displaced onto eating disorders. For instance, competition is keen among women with eating disorders. In our times, competition is not limited to persons, or parents, of the same sex. Susan is a medical intern whose father took ownership of her diploma immediately after her medical school commencement ceremony. The unspoken contract in her family was based on pleasing and idealizing Daddy. He made all family decisions, and commanded particularly great respect for his ability to conservatively budget and invest money. Threatened by Susan's career and financial self-sufficiency, he continually devised new means to allocate her earnings in order to limit her lifestyle. He carefully calculated her rent and repayment for medical school expenses based upon her take-home income. In accordance with family custom, the resulting figures and miserliness were never questioned. As Susan realized that her parents were wealthy and continued to earn substantial income while she continued to live like a poor student, she felt she was being controlled and punished for her achievement. She is an extremely bright and capable young woman who feels conflicted and guilty for harboring ambitious goals. She struggles over adopting or rejecting the mediocre goals that her father sets for her, such as working in a clinic in her parent's neighborhood where they can help her with office management. In the hospital, Susan is excited but sad when her skill is acknowledged by colleagues and senior staff. She now recognizes that her sadness represents feelings about exceeding her family's expectations and her father's level of competence. Susan's bulimia is not surprising in light of her controlled, restricted, frugal childhood and the later competitive, threatened response of her father to her individuation. Her binging and purging assumes a short adaptable cycle of eating forbidden food and spitting it out into a cup, even while walking through hospital corridors while taking care of patients. Bulimia soothes Susan's anxieties from self-imposed perfectionistic strivings, longing for family acceptance and approval, and fear of arousing her father's jealousy, fragility, and inadequacy. Over the course of psychotherapy, Susan has moved out of the family's home, begun to partake in entertaining activities, and devoted attention to enhancing her feminine appearance. She sheds many tears over dethroning her father and upsetting the family homeostasis, but only rarely spits up her food.

EARLY ADOLESCENCE

It is no accident that adolescence is the time in a woman's life that eating disorders begin to emerge in vulnerable females. In this normally unsettling phase, physiological and hormonal changes herald the onset of puberty. The pubescent girl experiences rather sudden, publicly obvious, and uncontrollable body changes. Budding breasts, curvaciousness, and the onset of menses evoke tremendous self-consciousness and require profound alteration of body image. Many girls initially misinterpret changing body form as fat. Dieting among teenage girls is common. It likely represents an effort to control one's body while emotionally adjusting to its changes. Anorexia nervosa typically begins with such a popular decision to diet. What distinguishes the anorexic from her peers is her fixation at the point of attempting to control body changes. Rather than indicating an unsettling though normal transition, the anorexic's dieting is the beginning of a maladaptive struggle to ward off further development, autonomy, sexuality, and adulthood. The body itself becomes a symbolic object to control for those girls who desperately want to remain girls.

Excessive preoccupation with controlling her body defends the vulnerable female against experiencing the normal emotional turbulence of adolescence. Contributing to the characteristic turmoil is the second separation–individuation process (Blos, 1962) motivated by psychological and societal demand. Rather than separating from mother, the task now is separation from parents and family unit. Rebelliousness against the family's values and regulation of behavior is a difficult but healthy aspect of growth. Again, differences between males and females contribute to the predisposition among females to develop eating disorders. Firstly, the social mores of Western culture are more ambiguous and restrictive for girls than for boys. Girls are more likely to experience less tolerance for their autonomy and a greater sense of being controlled. On deeper levels, boundary confusion in early adolescence is again heightened for females. Secondary sex characteristics scream out a shared identity between a girl and her mother. Earlier pre-Oedipal conflicts reemerge with an overlay of later developmental issues. Unconscious fears of engulfment, wishes for protective merger with mother's identity, and healthy strivings to individuate are reactivated. Inhibiting the adolescent's potential to become an autonomous, sexual, adult female results in confusion and inadequacy about feminine identity. This can occur in a variety of blatant or subtle ways. The mother who earlier failed to nurture her daughter's emergent self may continue to act in an overly intrusive or self-centered manner. As the daughter continues to provide a projective screen (see Chapter 3), the mother's own conflicts regarding adulthood and sexuality may unconsciously confuse her daughter's adolescent development.

The father's response during early adolescence is critical to his daughter's feelings about herself. A teenage girl is highly sensitive to her father's reaction to her emerging adult female identity. She is likely to be affected by his conflictual feelings about her sexual development. Pamela, for example, is an attractive 25-year-old bulimic woman emotionally fixed in the pain, shame, guilt, and disappointment at her father's withdrawal of physical affection that began when her breasts began to develop. Motivated to maintain their physical relationship, she devoted herself to the sports he liked to play. Being the captain of the girl's basketball team, however, did not recapture her father's earlier affections. Pamela continues to experience disgust for her rather trim and shapely body, and to attribute the failures of her disappointing and ambivalent relationships to its form.

The healthy teen in transition is able to utilize an expanded interpersonal world to work out struggles with separation from parents. Peers and hero figures enter the adolescent's drama and provide the opportunities to experiment with social skills and self-regulation outside of the family. The younger, early-onset eating-disordered patient is unprepared to shift her focus from family to the broader social world. She regresses from appropriate sexual and interpersonal concerns into the tasks of latency, where being a good girl in school and the feedback it brings are most important. As if she harbors the awareness that she cannot weather the storms of adolescence, she avoids them at all costs. The struggle between natural progression and pathological denial of growth is reflected in the struggle to regulate food and her body. The harsh restriction of food reflects condemnation of her own maturity. In this process, body image is distorted by the displaced hatred and fear of adulthood and sexuality that the body receives.

Adolescence is a particularly overwhelming phase for the girl who lacks trust in her feelings and a sense of self. Beneath her facade of obedience and compliance, depression and intense anxiety flourish. Julie is a 26-year-old, 72-pound anorexic who first became ill when her parents separated when she was 16. As she slowly gains insight in therapy she painfully recognized that her anorexia expresses a longing for childhood when the family felt securely intact. Without the family unit to define structure, roles, and self, Julie regressed to a prepubescent girl. Her independent world collapsed as she waited for her parents to reunite. She became homebound after leaving nursing school, leaving her neighborhood job, and refusing to go out with friends. For frightened Julie, the loss of childhood transcends normally expectable mourning and sadness. With terror, she anticipates it will be shattering and overwhelming. Letting go of her preadolescent definition, she can imagine nothing to fill its place. A poignant sense of inner emptiness, hopelessness, and depression in response to the loss of childhood commonly lurks beneath the symptoms of eating disorders.

LATE ADOLESCENCE AND EARLY ADULTHOOD

The majority of women seeking psychotherapy for eating disorders range from college age through their 20s. While early adolescence marks the physiological interface between childhood and adulthood, the next life passages entail confronting and adapting to the sociocultural realities of adulthood. In the context of pressures to reconcile conflicts and achieve, young women must integrate roles, develop intimate relationships, and consolidate adult female identity. Younger anorexics have not progressed far enough to confront these complicated tasks. They remain stuck within the family and shielded by the limitations of childhood. Later-onset bulimics and food abusers have typically established enough autonomy to engage in the tasks of young adulthood, but nevertheless feel inadequately prepared, ineffective, and thus out of control. Accumulated developmental deficits and self-doubts that prevent consolidation of a reliable identity are seen in their relationship with food and eating.

The older, less isolated woman with eating disorders does get involved with persons outside her family. She is capable of struggling with relationships with friends, boyfriends, and acquaintances from school and work. Relationships, however, are experienced with tremendous ambivalence. Analogous to experiences with food and mother, relationships leave the bulimic feeling either too empty or too full. The emptiness brings on feelings of desperation, abandonment, and terror, which are temporarily abated by binging. Filling up the void with food feels soothing until fears of merger, being controlled by others, and obliteration of self are reactivated. At this point, the only relief lies in purging out the symbolic smotherer.

Underlying the bulimic's swings from feeling too empty or too full is profound confusion about adequacy and identity. Accumulated failures to experience consistent predictable care and positive validation of self ultimately result in stunted development of valuable ego functions. These include the ability to recognize and modulate feelings, to soothe oneself in nondestructive ways, and to perceptually discriminate reality, such as the size of one's body, from distortions. What has often developed instead for young women with eating disorders is a strong false sense of self based on accommodating others and fitting in with the demands of the situation. According to Bruch (1973), in new situations they are at a loss for how to act, think, and feel. Experiencing the void inside, they learn that lack of self-awareness is not limited to hunger and satiety. It has generalized to an inability to discriminate most inner feelings, such as appropriate anger and anxiety. Finding themselves out of touch with and out of control over emotional and bodily sensations evokes further anxiety. Unable to effectively tolerate and regulate anxiety, however, binging and purging increases. Over time, this becomes the only available coping strategy.

Confusion about identity in young adulthood surfaces in tasks of forming love relationships outside of the family. It is often in the context of being socially and sexually active, and away from the protection of home, that the bulimic first discovers that she is unprepared to cope. Lacking confidence in her ability to regulate her own impulses and behavior, attitudes toward sex and men are confused and ambivalent. Encounters evoke intense anxiety and fears of losing control. The eating-disordered woman handles her anxiety by becoming controlling within relationships, just as with food. Relationships are too empty or too full, and negotiating a comfortable and safe amount of intimacy is difficult. Higher-functioning women with eating disorders typically report an interest in men and sex, but recreate struggles to retain or relinquish control that prevent them from forming enduring intimate relationships. Many work hard to appear socially competent and confident. This image itself results from overcontrolled efforts to conceal the empty self and keep others too far to detect it.

An expanded interpersonal world is only one tool that helps the normal adolescent evolve into adulthood. A second tool, emerging during middle to late adolescence, is the capacity for abstract thinking. Expanded conceptual abilities enable cognitive analysis, manipulation, and mastery of the world. The sense of mastery achieved with the development of abstract reasoning resembles the toddler's sense of mastery resulting from newly developed motor skills. Both equip the individual with tools to cope, whether by locomotion or thought, autonomously. Without these tools, dependence on others is maintained.

The capacity for abstract thought is disturbed among women with eating disorders. Bruch (1973) discusses anorexics' arrest at a level of cognitive development where concrete thinking dominates their understanding of food, their bodies, and worldview. In staving off psychological and physical maturity, cognitive development as well is inhibited. Among higher-functioning women, cognitive development has proceeded, leaving peculiar lacunae of primitive concrete thinking behind. Concrete distortions about food, fat, and body weight are harbored by women whose accomplishments and verbal skills demonstrate superior conceptual abilities. Emily, for example, is a 25-year-old bulimic who graduated phi beta kappa and began her first job as a stockbroker for a prestigious brokerage firm. She articulately insists that all the food she eats gets deposited, pound for pound, in a specific area of her stomach. Laura, a recovering anorexic, is a high school teacher and graduate student. An ongoing focus of psychotherapy has been confronting the concrete thinking that limits her ability to understand and refrain from repeating self-damaging interactions with her parents that maintain the helplessness and dependence she resents.

Arrested cognitive development affects the way that women with eating disorders think about themselves and about being female. Their inability to entertain hypothetical ideas and plan for anticipated events clearly discourages confidence to handle new situations. Concrete thinking precludes their ability to comfortably integrate different roles and aspects of self. They often feel fragmented and feel bad about unacceptable parts of themselves, such as their eating habits, sexuality, anger, or willful desires. Many approach therapy with a desire to remove, rather than integrate, these split off parts. Their tendency to rationalize cognitive distortions helps to maintain the isolation of feelings and sense of fragmentation. Women with eating disorders often demonstrate conceptually advanced abilities in certain areas, but remain cognitively primitive in others. Behaviors and thoughts about food and eating certainly lag behind. Binging, fasting, and purging are concrete, predictable rigid behaviors that are assigned personalized magical meanings. The ritualized pattern of the binge–purge cycle is concretely symbolic of incorporating followed by rejecting, of continued defective self-care, and of extreme denial of feeling that even the brightest eating-disordered women fail to grasp. Their intellectual abilities have been impaired by developmental deficits and scarred by emotionally generated blind spots.

TIMELESSNESS OF DEVELOPMENTAL ISSUES IN EATING DISORDERS

The final case example in this chapter illustrates the tenacity of developmental failures in women with eating disorders. In response to an advertisement, Jane first sought psychotherapy for bulimia at age 62. She had suffered, off and on, for almost 40 years. Recently, her bulimia consisted of nightly binges on cottage cheese and cake followed by self-induced vomiting. By day, she works as an assistant comptroller for a chain of retail stores. She is a thin, attractive, single woman who is meticulously, though in a somewhat outdated style, well-groomed. She always dressed up and went to the hairdresser for her therapist, as if she was on display for her mother.

Jane had tremendous respect and admiration for her mother. She described her as beautiful, talented, cultured, and an excellent homemaker. She was in awe of her mother's ability to return to school and obtain a Ph.D. in musicology after her children were grown. Jane proudly reported that she never disobeyed her mother.

One source of discomfort about seeking psychotherapy was her mother's admonition against discussing personal problems with strangers. Jane took this quite literally, and still has no friends. She discussed her bulimia for the first time with her therapist, speaking like a little girl confessing to her mother. As if development provided no opportunity to modify original superego rules, she began sessions with, "I've been a bad girl," and recounted her bulimic behaviors of the prior week. Statements about other issues were insistently qualified with apologies like, "I shouldn't say this, but . . ." , or, "I shouldn't feel this way, but . . . ."

The second guiding principle handed down from her mother was that Jane never allow a man to touch her before marriage. Tearfully, she reports that she has never disobeyed. Jane has never had any sexual experience with a man. She continues to be anxious about any encounters with men besides relatives, including being helped by a male salesman in a shop. She discusses a rare dinner with a male family friend with a girlish embarrassment inappropriate to the situation or to a 62-year-old woman.

Jane remains merged with the all-good memory of her mother, who died when she was 21 years old. For the next 6 years, Jane lived at home to care for her invalid father. Her father, however, seemed to have little presence in her psychic development. He failed to facilitate her emerging self during her primary or adolescent separation–individuation. It appears that Jane's mother reinforced her symbiotic attachment, and that her father offered little help. Tragically, her development has been sacrificed in order to maintain her symbiosis with the idealized image of her mother. Jane's absence of motivation to separate is striking.

Jane's overly intrusive, narcissistic mother did encourage one aspect of her daughter's individuation. During adolescence, Jane was a promising dancer. She often performed and went on tour with a dance company. Her mother's encouragement, however, was laden with ambivalent messages. She valued Jane's skill and artistic development of her body, but sent her off with warnings to keep her body hidden and distant from others. She could display her self in the name of fine art, but was forbidden to feel any sensations from within or from being touched. Jane remains stuck in the exhibitionism of a little girl, with a body image from a presexual level of development.

Given the restrictive and overcontrolled guidelines internalized from her mother, Jane must have experienced unconscious anxiety from participating in the sensuality of dance and later physical contact required to care for her ill father. In response she learned to repress any impulses or sensations arising from her body. Her physical and sexual self remains denied and split off from her awareness and personality. The severity of her denial deprived Jane of opportunity to experience and learn to modulate her impulses. Her only outlet appears to lie in bulimia. Symbolically, binging provides a channel for displaced floods of impulses and affect. Purging provides relief that her expressiveness and assertion can be contained and controlled. After years of such denial and acting out, Jane is strikingly unaware of her feelings and bulimia serves to regulate all daily tensions.

Jane has globally repressed any self-initiated emotions, strivings, or desires. Throughout adult life she has submitted her own will and remained compliant and obedient. She swallowed completely any advice given by the few family members she speaks with. This included stopping the one activity she recalls with pleasure, ballroom dance lessons. She discontinued her classes when "they" told her they were not practical. Throughout the passages of her life, Jane's self has received little encouragement or validation. She has been trained, and has learned, to totally disregard herself.

The years of denial and repression leave Jane unaware of her apparent depression, deprivation, isolation, and loneliness. Stunted cognitive development leaves her at a loss to conceptualize or describe her inner experience. She speaks concretely of actions without any accompanying feelings. Her eating disorder has clearly served to fill her emotional and interpersonal void, in addition to regulating and numbing her feelings. Jane has endured a painfully empty and lonely life. Every night she sleeps with a transistor radio on her pillow, tuned to a talk show that is broadcast throughout the night. "I like hearing the voice, I guess."

Jane's eating disorder is atypical given her age, but typical in the developmental delays and dynamics expressed. Jane lacks inner awareness, has no trust in her opinions or feelings, and has little reliable self. She lacks ego functions that would enable her to experience feelings, relationships, and life without being overwhelmed and out of control. Locked into a primitive attachment to the memory of her mother, at 62 years old she remains unable to separate and form relationships. Her sense of personal ineffectiveness has been deepened by years of depriving herself of opportunities to grow. Jane's life dramatically and tragically illustrates how disturbed psychological separation, individuation, and identity formation, with concomitant painful feelings and deficits in necessary ego functions, underlie the struggles enacted by women consciously struggling with eating disorders.

REFERENCES

Bemis, K. M. (1978). Current approaches to the etiology and treatment of anorexia nervosa. *Psychological Bulletin, 85*, 593–617.
Bennet, W., & Gurin, J. (1982). *The dieter's dilemma.* New York: Basic Books.
Blos, P. (1962). *On adolescence.* New York: The Free Press.
Brisman, J., & Siegel, M. (1984). Bulimia and alcoholism: Two sides of the same coin? *Journal of Substance Abuse Treatment, 1*(2), 113–118.
Bruch, H. (1973). *Eating disorders.* New York: Basic Books.
Bruch, H. (1978). *The golden cage: The enigma of anorexia nervosa.* Cambridge, MA: Harvard University Press.
Casper, R. C., Eckert, E. D., Halmi, K. A., Goldberg, S. C., & Davis, J. M. (1980). Bulimia: Its incidence and clinical importance in patients with anorexia nervosa. *Archives of General Psychiatry, 37*, 1030–1035.
Cooper, P. J., & Fairburn, C. G. (1983). Binge-eating and self-induced vomitting in the community: A preliminary study. *British Journal of Psychiatry, 142*, 139–144.
Crisp, A. H., Palmer, R. L., & Kalucy, R. S. (1976). How common is anorexia nervosa? A prevalence study. *British Journal of Psychiatry, 218*, 549–554.
Freud, A. (1965). *Normality and pathology in childhood.* New York: International Universities Press.
Garfinkel, P. E., & Garner, D. M. (1982). *Anorexia nervosa: A multidimensional perspective.* New York: Brunner/Mazel.
Garfinkel, P., & Kaplan, A. S. (1985). Starvation based perpetuating mechanisms in anorexia nervosa and bulimia. *International Journal of Eating Disorders, 4*(4), 651–665.
Garner, D. M., & Garfinkel, P. E. (Eds.) (1984). *Handbook of psychotherapy for anorexia nervosa and bulimia,* New York: The Guilford Press.

Goodsit, A. (1983). Self-regulatory disturbances in eating disorders. *International Journal of Eating Disorders, 2*, 51–60.

Gull, W. W. (1874). Anorexia nervosa (apepsia hysterica, anorexia hysterica). *Transactions of the Clinical Society of London, 7*, 22–28.

Halmi, K. A. (1985). Relationship of eating disorders to depression: Biological similarities and differences. *International Journal of Eating Disorders, 4*(4), 667–680.

Halmi, K. A., Falk, J. R., & Schwartz, E. (1981). Binge-eating and vomiting: A survey of a college population. *Psychological Medicine, 11*, 697–706.

Keys, A., Brozek, J., Henschel, A., Mickelsen, O., & Taylor, H. L. (1950). *The biology of human starvation.* Minneapolis: University of Minnesota Press.

Kleinfield, N. R. (1986). The ever-fatter business of thinness. *The New York Times*, pp. 1, 28, Sept. 7.

Lacey, J. H. (1982). Anorexia nervosa and a bearded female saint. *British Medical Journal, 285*, 1816–1817.

Laseque, E. D. (1873). On hysterical anorexia. In M. R. Kaufman & M. Haiman (Eds.), *Evolution of Psychosomatic Concepts* (pp. 141–155). New York: International Universities Press, 1964.

MacLeod, S. (1981). *The art of starvation.* New York: Schocken Books.

Mahler, M. S., Pine, F., & Bergmann, A. (1975). *The psychological birth of the human infant.* New York: Basic Books.

Minuchin, S., Rosman, B., & Baker, L. (1978). *Psychosomatic families: Anorexia nervosa in context.* Cambridge, MA: Harvard University Press.

Morton, R. (1694). *Phthisiologia: Or a treatise of consumptions.* London: S. Smith and B. Walford.

Moulton, R. (1942). Psychosomatic study of anorexia nervosa including the use of vaginal smears. *Psychosomatic Medicine, 4*, 62–72.

Pyle, R. L., Mitchell, J. E., Eckert, E. D., Halvorson, P. A., Neuman, P. A., & Goff, G. M. (1983). The incidence of bulimia in freshman college students. *International Journal of Eating Disorders, 2*(3), 75–85.

Russell, G. (1979). Bulimia nervosa: An ominous variant of anorexia nervosa. *Psychological Medicine, 9*, 429–448.

Russell, G. (1985). Bulimia revisited. *International Journal of Eating Disorders, 4*(4), 681–692.

Sugarman, A., & Kurash, C. (1982). The body as a transitional object in bulimia. *International Journal of Eating Disorders, 1*(4), 57–67.

Swift, W. J., Andrews, D., & Barklage, N. E. (1986). The relationship between affective disorder and eating disorders: A review of the literature. *American Journal of Psychiatry, 143*, 290–299.

Thoma, H. (1967). *Anorexia nervosa.* New York: International Universities Press.

Waller, J. V., Kaufman, M. R., & Deutsch, F. (1940). Anorexia nervosa: A psychosomatic entity. *Psychosomatic Medicine, 2*, 3–16.

Wardle, J., & Beinhart, H. (1981). Binge eating: A theoretical review. *British Journal of Clinical Psychology, 20*, 97–109.

Zuckerberg, J. (Ed.). (1988). *Critical psychophysical passages in the life of a woman.* New York: Plenum.

Chapter 17

Psychological Consequences of Infertility

SUE A. SHAPIRO

Infertility, the failure to conceive after 1 year of trying, is not statistically normal, yet this chapter is included here because infertility does affect a significant (15%) proportion of the reproductive population, and its prevalence is increasing. There are now an estimated 10 million infertile Americans, whose inability to have children is a major life crisis both for themselves, their spouses, and their families (Menning, 1977, 1979). The focus in this chapter is on primary infertility as opposed to secondary infertility that couples may experience after successfully having one or more children.

This chapter begins with a discussion of the initial psychological impact of infertility. It then describes the typical infertility workup for both men and women and its frequent psychological concomitants. Subsequent issues of discussion include the process of psychological adjustment to infertility, the special variants to be expected with different forms of infertility, individual reactions to various solutions to the problem, and the transference/countertransference implications of fertile/infertile patients with fertile/infertile therapists.

The despair and desolation of infertile couples, especially the female partner, has been noted since biblical times. In the past, the expectation that rearing children would be a central part of adult life was almost universally shared. Raising children had such important economic, social, and emotional implications that sterility was long considered grounds for annulment of a marriage. Historically, the "blame" for barrenness in a couple was almost always laid at the feet of the woman. Only recently has the decision to forego parenthood become a socially acceptable option, although women who choose not to mother are still sometimes looked at askance. Ironically, infertile women, who have spent considerable time, money, and emotional heartache trying to achieve a pregnancy, are frequently seen as women who choose not to mother.

Even though we still lack a complete understanding of fertilization and conception, our knowledge has increased considerably since the beginning of the 19th

SUE A. SHAPIRO, PH.D. • Clinical Supervisor, New York University, Doctoral Program in Clinical Psychology; Clinical Instructor of Psychiatry, New York University Medical School; Faculty, Manhattan Institute for Psychoanalysis; private practice.

century. Before the scientific revolution, myths and rituals surrounded conception (Lederer, 1968; Mazor, 1984). These myths have still not been completely put to rest and, even today, infertile women are subject to many well-intentioned, but embarrassing and futile "helpful" suggestions. Even after the general process of conception was understood, many years passed before the male role in infertility could be accepted and explored. We are still paying the price for this delay. For example, contemporary women still generally initiate an infertility workup, frequently accept the public blame for fertility problems to spare their husbands embarrassment, and often go alone to support groups (such as Resolve) and/or psychotherapy.

Even more significantly, male infertility has been less thoroughly researched and is consequently far less treatable than is female infertility. For years, researchers noted this deficiency while continuing to concentrate their research and theorizing on women (Drake & Grunert, 1979; Menning, 1977; Mazor, 1984; Newton, 1984; Walker, 1978; White, 1981). Even though men are the primary infertile partners 40% of the time (Menning, 1980), responsibility for pursuing a solution to the infertility and most treatments involve primarily women. Thus, even when efforts are made to increase sperm count, morphology, and motility, wives of the subfertile men almost always need to monitor their cycles, take medication to increase the likelihood of ovulation and successful impregnation, and when all else fails have husband or donor inseminations.

During those parts of the infertility workup that primarily treat the husband, as well as those instances when the husband receives the entire treatment, women often take charge of the process. There is notably little literature, both technical and otherwise, on male despair and shame over childlessness on the one hand, and male conflicts regarding parenting that may lead to psychogenic infertility on the other. Nor are there studies on the effect of a wife's infertility on her husband, or of male infertility on a man's sense of himself. What literature there is on male infertility places considerable emphasis on the effect of infertility on men's sexual functioning or on the impact of psychological conflicts on sexual dysfunctions rather than on fertility per se (Drake & Grunert, 1979).

For many years most infertility was assumed to be psychogenic and dynamic formulations explaining and blaming the childless woman flourished (Benedek, 1952; De Watteville, 1957; Deutsch, 1945; Ford, Forman, Wilson, Char, Mixson, & Scholz, 1953; Mai, 1969; Mai, Munday, & Rump, 1972; Noyes & Chapnick, 1965; Rubenstein, 1951; Sandler, 1961). Beyond an occasional reference to the effect of extreme stress on lowering sperm count (Walker, 1978), the literature rarely suggested that male infertility, other than sexual dysfunction, which may account for as much as 10% of male infertility, is psychogenic. As research and technology have grown more sophisticated, the rate of reported instances of psychogenic infertility has dropped from 40 to 5%. Myths die hard, however, and many people still expect an infertile couple to conceive after adopting a child despite considerable data that only 5% of adoptive couples do so, about the same number that could expect to conceive after years of infertility without adopting (Hanson & Rock, 1950; Humphrey & MacKenzie, 1967; Orr, 1941; Rock, Tietze, & McLaughlin, 1965; Sandler, 1965).

This is not to suggest that in some cases of infertility, psychological factors do not play a part, at times even a primary one. However, the role of these factors should not be exaggerated while precious time is lost in getting physiological help.

Nor should iatrogenic psychological problems be mistakenly granted causal significance. Debrovner and Shubin-Stein (1975), in an extremely sensitive article, note
the difficulty of determining the role, if any, of psychogenic factors in the etiology
of all but extremely unusual cases of infertility. They go on to say that, "However,
if a couple does not have a psychologic problem as the cause of their infertility, they
will almost invariably develop one as a result" (p. 140). Some infertility does indeed
result from psychosomatic disorders that are physiological and deeply influenced
by stress. Hormone levels and muscular spasms, both of which are affected by
stress, can influence fertility. It is also possible for hormone levels to be pathological
for nonpsychological reasons and affect psychological state. We now know that
most infertility in women is caused by structural difficulties (Menning, 1977; Silber,
1980; Thompson, 1984; White, 1981) that to the best of medical knowledge are not
mediated by stress, although stress can subsequently add other hormonal lia-
bilities. Similarly, the most serious forms of male infertility are caused by either
structural, genetic, bacterial, or viral problems.

The infertility workup itself, as well as the prospect of starting a family, can
place considerable psychological stress on many couples. This stress can decrease
the likelihood of conception directly when, for instance, it leads couples to argue at
midcycle and fail to have intercourse at optimal times, or to midcycle impotence
(Drake & Grunert, 1979). Stress can also decrease the likelihood of conception
indirectly, via the hypothalamic pituitary axis which lowers sperm count in the
man, alters hormone production and delays ovulation in the woman, or via the
autonomic nervous system causing tubal spasms, etc. Emotional stress can lead to
the release of adrenaline which, in turn, affects the production of other hormones.
The primary link between psychological and physiological factors for women appears to be the hypothalamus. It can be activated by physical and psychic stimulation, whether conscious or unconscious, and result in hormonal imbalances (Denber, 1978; Heiman, 1959; Silber, 1980; White, 1981).

Our understanding of the ways in which psyche and soma interact has become
increasingly sophisticated. This encouraging progression is apparent in a comparison of articles from the 1950s (e.g., Benedek, 1952; Rubenstein, 1951) with those
written in the 1980s (Seibel & Taymor, 1982; Moghissi & Wallach, 1983). However,
as suggested in Chapter 5, our acceptance of the possibility of psychologically
regulated hormonal output should lead us to consider the reverse situation in
which constitutionally unusual hormonal regulation may interfere with "normal"
psychological development. For example, what might be the developmental and
psychological impact of biologically determined deficits and abnormalities in hormone production in men and women? How might a woman's development be
affected by continuous anovulatory cycles? What is the psychological effect of the
hormonal conditions causing azoospermia?

The literature on the psychological aspects of infertility has changed its focus
over time. The etiological significance of psychological factors for female infertility
was emphasized in early work such as that of Deutsch (1945) and Benedek (1952)
and continued as a focus through the mid-1970s. This early literature often equated
psychogenic sterility with functional sterility, which encompasses any infertility of
unknown organic basis. Frequently this diagnosis was made by exclusion and by
retrospective analysis of research populations. The percentage of infertility that is
diagnosed as of unknown organic origin in this category has fallen from 40 to 5% in

the last 30 years. Although 15% of today's infertile population has infertility of supposedly unknown origin, sophisticated investigation of these patients indicates that 10% actually have obscure organic problems (Moghissi & Wallach, 1983). Thus, many cases of previously diagnosed psychogenic sterility can now be understood in terms of organic problems.

Psychoanalytic papers have focused almost exclusively on psychogenic factors affecting fertility in the female. These factors include the woman's resentment of the feminine role, overdependency, a hostile dependent relationship with her mother, high manifest anxiety, hatred of her mother, fear that she would kill a child if she had one, or extreme masculine identification (Benedek, 1952; Blum, 1959; Deutsch, 1945; Eisner, 1963; Ford et al., 1953; Karahasanoglu, Barglow, & Growe 1972; Rubenstein, 1951). Theorists seem to attribute the entire process of conception to the woman's will or psyche and to ignore the physiological role of women and the psychological role of men in this process. The few papers that do discuss male psychology primarily emphasize male sexual dysfunction for which they often consider the wive's psychological conflicts responsible (Walker, 1978).

Much early psychoanalytic research had serious design problems. For example, Eisner's study (1963) compared fertile with infertile women and found greater psychological problems among the infertile women. Eisner concluded that the psychopathology was so severe that it must have been causative rather than simply reactive. However, she gives no data to support this statement. These early works should be read with skepticism in light of the fact that women do become pregnant after rapes and incestuous assaults. These pregnancies would be highly unlikely if stress, for instance, actually caused women to be anovulatory or otherwise hostile to conception. Without psychological profiles of women and men before they decide to have children, we cannot conclude that the causes of infertility are psychological. Because of this difficulty as well as the decreased percentage of infertility of unknown physiological origin, current psychiatric and psychological research focuses instead on the psychological concomitants of infertility (Seibel & Taymor, 1982; Mazor, 1984; Mazor & Simons, 1984; Menning, 1977, 1979, 1981, 1984). A prime mover in this shift of emphasis has been Barbara Eck Menning who has written widely on the psychological consequences of infertility and has founded Resolve, the national organization for infertile couples.

Infertility is a chronic disease. Its possible solution requires continuous medical intervention at great cost in time, money, and stress. The often remarkable degree of perseverence and medical sophistication shown by infertility patients has been likened to that of patients with cancer. In our culture, infertility patients tend to be middle or upper class although, in fact, the rate of infertility is higher among the lower class. As infertile patients search for the proper specialist or the doctor who still holds out some hope, they often become experts in their disorders. Infertility often strikes people when they feel at their physical and emotional best. In contemporary society, a couple often decides to have children and cease birth control when they have arrived at a place of relative emotional and financial security. Although many couples have children without such security, these offspring may be considered "accidents" (Lidz, 1978). Infertile couples, by definition, do not have "accidents." For them, childbearing is a conscious decision, usually made with the assumption that conception will be simple to achieve. Often such couples pride themselves on having been responsible and careful (for being in control) until the proper moment for parenthood arrived. For fertile couples mild ambivalence, which is a normal part of the decision to start a family, will not prevent conception. Infertile couples, however, will need to overcome ambivalent feelings in order to make and sustain a determined effort to have a child.

The decision to begin a family may come during a time of deepening closeness and security in a marriage. For some, the decision to have children represents the unfolding of their life script which has always centered on homemaking. For others, the decision has been postponed for many years until both partners are firmly established in their careers. Although the diagnosis of infertility obviously has different meanings to each individual, those who have expected early parenting to be the cornerstone of their lives, and those who are expecting to mix career and family, perhaps, therefore, postponing efforts at conception, are likely to have different reactions. The diagnosis of infertility creates a crisis for all couples, frequently the first serious crisis of their life together. The diagnosis is immediately felt as a serious narcissistic injury. How can this be happening to me? How can I not be able to choose whether or not to have children? For many people the diagnosis will trigger old fears concerning their sexual identity and self-esteem. Fears about reproductive capability are not uncommon in young women. Nevertheless, fears of punishment for sex and concerns about adequacy as a woman can remain relatively quiet unless the woman finds herself part of an infertile couple. Many men and women feel that they are not really full men and women if they are infertile. Consider the frequent statement by sterile men that, "I only shoot blanks" or by infertile women that they are hollow or empty. Frequently the infertile partner will fear that their spouse will no longer wish to stay married and will desert them.

The medical literature is quick to point out the link between fertility and virility and the subsequent need for extreme sensitivity in working with male patients. However, little attention is paid to the impact on a woman's sexual self-esteem, despite the common finding that even women who had frequent orgasmic sex before the infertility workup complain of lack of sexual desire, difficulty achieving orgasm, and even occasional vaginismus during the fertility workup (Walker, 1978; Debrovner & Shubin-Stein, 1975). In part, this differential treatment can be explained by the fact that men must be orgasmic for conception to occur (without high-tech intervention). They must experience sufficient sexual excitement to maintain an erection and ejaculate. There is no such need for women to have sexual pleasure in order for them to conceive. Thus, women frequently report initiating sex more frequently while enjoying it less when trying to conceive during the infertility workup. During the 1940s and 1950s, frigidity was often associated in a causal way with female infertility by various psychoanalytic theorists. However, subsequent research has found that what causal relationship exists is in the opposite direction: orgasm does not increase the likelihood of conception in women, but the infertility workup often does decrease sexual desire and orgasmic potential in men and women. When working with infertile patients, one should remain alert to the acute and more chronic implications of infertility for both partners' sexual and psychological functioning.

Before the cause of infertility is established, both partners may worry that they are at fault and fear rejection as a result. Even before medical intervention, the couple's sex life may become strained as each partner fears their own inadequacy and subsequent rejection. As soon as a couple begins to be concerned about conception, the reason for and timing of intercourse begins to change. Sexual contact is no longer a spontaneous expression of emotion but quickly becomes a means to the goal of making a child. Sexual activity becomes timed to certain days of the month and is often discouraged on certain other days. Couples also anticipate that they will have to discuss their sexual practices in front of a third person, a stressful and undesirable experience often feared sufficiently to disrupt sex. The degree of disruption of a couple's sex life will vary from couple to couple partly in relation to the specific nature of their infertility and the types of interventions used. But most couples will experience some disturbance in this area and may need help in viewing this disruption as both normal and short lived. Interventions that suggest the temporary nature of this disturbance can help limit the secondary damage of infertility.

The investigation and treatment of infertility can take more than 5 years. The need for vast emotional, financial, and intellectual resources to go the course at times brings couples together and often pulls them apart. Couples will frequently need to take charge of their treatment, conveying information from one specialist to another, deciding when to move on to a new specialist, etc. Like any other stressful situation facing the couple, this one will elicit different coping strategies from the partners which may either complement each other or eventually typify differences and discord. Differences in intensity of desire for a child, in attitudes toward medicine, in the expression of grief and anger, and in need for privacy will all be exposed. Increasingly, the more sophisticated infertility specialists, alert to the psychological dangers that infertility poses to couples, will include support groups, counseling and referrals to support groups like Resolve in their battery of treatments.

Causes of Infertility

The reported rate of infertility has increased from 10 to 15% in the last 20 years (see Menning, 1980, Mazor, 1984; Mazor & Simons, 1984). There are several possible reasons for this rise. Delayed childbearing is one of them because both men and women are most fertile in their early twenties. Other factors include certain contraceptive methods, such as the IUD, which can cause infection and subsequent infertility problems; increased sexual freedom and with it the subsequent greater prevalence of veneral diseases, some of which can cause infertility if untreated. Increased exposure to certain toxins either in utero, as in the case of DES, or in the environment can also cause fertility problems. Agent Orange has been implicated in the reduction of fertility in Vietnam veterans, as have many other pesticides and industrial compounds. The landmark case involving American Cyanamide pointed out the feared effect of industrial chemicals on pregnant women and how this fear led to discrimination against hiring women. In fact, chemicals have been shown to pose even graver danger to men (Stellman, 1977; Stellman & Daum, 1973).

The alarming drop in the modal sperm counts in college-age men has also contributed to the increasing rate of infertility. A 1929 study reported modal sperm counts of 100 million/ml, a 1974 study reported modal counts of 60 million/ml, and a 1979 study of student volunteers found modal counts of 20 million/ml. In addition, the 1979 study by Dougherty found alarmingly high levels of four toxic chemicals, three of which are known or suspected carcinogens and teratogens. Drugs, alcohol, and stress can also be held accountable for the decline. ("Sperm Count," 1978; Castleman, 1982; WOHRC, 1981). While a moderately reduced sperm count may not in and of itself explain infertility, it can be a significant factor when combined with mildly reduced fertility in the over-thirty woman.

For the typical couple that is trying to conceive, the following steps are required for conception to occur (White, 1981, p. 12):

1. The male must produce adequate numbers of healthy, mobile sperm.
2. The male must be able to ejaculate into the vagina.
3. The sperm must reach and penetrate the cervical mucus and ascend the uterus to the fallopian tubes.
4. The sperm must be capable of penetrating and fertilizing the egg.
5. The female must produce and release an egg that can reach a tube.
6. The egg must be capable of being impregnated; the tubes must be open and permit the fertilized egg to travel to the uterus.
7. The fertilized egg must meet a properly prepared uterus, successfully implant, and develop.

While investigators differ in their reports on frequency of various etiologies of infertility, the following breakdown of causes of infertility offers some general guidelines:

1. Male factor, 40%
2. Ovulatory factor, 15%
3. Tubal factor, 20%
4. Cervical and uterine factor, 10%
5. Vaginal factor, 5%
6. Immune reaction, 2.5%
7. Infection, 2.5%
8. Unknown, 5%

Although this breakdown outlines the basic difficulties, it must nevertheless be taken with a grain of salt. One of the most frustrating aspects of infertility workups is the degree to which the specialty of the reporter may bias the findings. Infertility specialists seem to develop specific areas of expertise and may overdiagnose that particular dysfunction. For example, a higher percentage of men seen by doctors who specialize in varicoceles will be diagnosed with varicoceles than if these same men were seen by a specialist in infectious agents that cause infertility.

MALE INFERTILITY WORKUP

A couple that is concerned about its failure to conceive will usually turn first to the wife's gynecologist. Gynecologists increasingly ask for a semen analysis or a Huhner postcoital test at the same time that they instruct a woman in temperature charting of ovulation. The postcoital test actually yields somewhat different information from the simple semen analysis. However, this test is often the first because it is somewhat less disturbing for most men than a straightforward semen analysis. If results are not good, a separate semen analysis is necessary. Semen may be deficient in several ways, including quantity of sperm, and its motility, morphology, and longevity. Some of these deficiencies can be relatively easily corrected. For example, an extremely high volume of semen will affect observed sperm count while unusually low volume of seminal fluid may, in a different way, lessen the likelihood of impregnation. Both of these conditions can now be corrected for by various techniques. The split ejaculate method of intercourse can rectify the former and artificial insemination with the husband's sperm suspended in a different medium can compensate for the latter. These techniques can also correct some cases of moderately low sperm count. However, both techniques seriously interfere with spontaneous sex.

Many men find the prospect of sex on command or masturbation in the bathroom of a doctor's office to be threatening and humiliating—a humiliation that is compounded by the fear that they cannot "perform." Thus, while women may also be threatened by procedures in the workup, their sexual performance is less on display and less germane to the ultimate goals of treatment. Men with no previous history of impotence, premature ejaculation, or inhibited ejaculation may suddenly develop these difficulties, especially before postcoital tests (Drake & Grunert, 1979) and other medical intrusions into the bedroom. While doctors often write sensitively about the effect of these procedures on men, in their offices they are all too frequently insensitive to people's needs for privacy. For example, many doctors call patients by name and procedure for everyone in the waiting room to hear.

Sperm count is affected by many factors, including such temporary and easily remediable ones as overexposure to heat (as caused by frequent saunas, tight underwear, or working in a pizza parlor), certain drugs, and frequent ejaculation. However, other factors affecting sperm count are chronic and often difficult to treat. These grave problems include hormone imbalance, infection, varicoceles, and sperm antibodies. In fact, it is in efforts to understand and treat chronic causes of low sperm count that one finds the most disagreement among specialists. Some of the tests and treatments for low sperm count, including testicular biopsy and varicocelectomy, involve minor surgery. The possibility of surgery can be exceedingly threatening and disturbing to men, who at times may refuse this step in a workup. In general, men are less accustomed to the personal and/or intrusive procedures of infertility doctors than are women, who have had frequent internal examinations and grew up with stories of D & C's and hysterectomies. Both men and women need to question the need for invasive procedures during the infertility workup in order to determine whether the additional information gained will in fact lead to a different treatment. Often, the member of the couple who is not being treated can be especially helpful at these times since the designated infertile patient may fear that refusing a treatment might lead to rejection by the fertile spouse.

While treatment for low sperm count and poor sperm quality can be quite frustrating and may ultimately fail, at least the usual procedures employed give the infertile couple time to adjust to the idea of infertility. The most devastating form of male infertility is azoospermia, the total absence of sperm. Occasionally this has an acute, treatable origin. All too frequently, however, azoospermia, whether stemming from a known etiology, such as mumps, chromosomal anomalies like Kline felter's syndrome, or an unknown etiology, is untreatable. Thus, for some infertile couples, the very first test in their workup is the only one needed to know that their union will never create a biological child. The shock and despair of this sudden loss of all hope for a biological child cannot be overstated. These couples have not had time to work through even the first stage of surprise and disappointment over fertility problems, but are instead confronted with their genetic mortality within the first month of investigation. More quickly than others, they must face the ultimate fear of all couples engaged in the infertility workup—that they will never be able to have a biological child together. These couples are comparable to people who experience a sudden death of a loved one with no preparatory mourning. In contrast, most infertile couples may never know absolutely that they cannot conceive (more analogous to adjusting to the loss of a loved one who is missing in action). Still other infertile couples may not be aware until several months into their workup that one of the partners conditions will definitely not respond to treatment. Because of the starkness of their situation, I will use the couple in which the male is found to have azoospermia to describe the psychological impact of a sudden, definitive "coming to the end of the road" in the infertility workup.

Many researchers have compared the psychological adjustment to infertility with Kubler-Ross's (1969) stages of coping with a terminal illness. Sterility is indeed a death. It is a death of one's genetic line. It is a death with no funeral, no ritual, and no circumscribed or permitted mourning period. Furthermore, it is a death that is often mourned in secrecy, while friends, relatives, and acquaintances treat the sterile couple as though they are selfishly choosing child-free living. It is critical that couples work through their grief for their unborn children before deciding on a course of action involving either AID (artificial insemination by a donor), a surrogate mother, adoption, or child-free living. Well-intentioned doctors are often uncomfortable bearing the bad tidings of definitive sterility and consequently engage couples too quickly in plans for AID or other solutions. A couple who reach the conclusion that they will not be able to bear a biological child after 2 to 5 years of trying has, in all likelihood worked through some of the surprise, rage, denial, and bargaining preparatory to accepting this fact. But couples, like the one described above, who are forced to face the biological sterility of their union within the first month of consulting a specialist have had no preparatory mourning. Doctors should encourage them to take the time to grieve and adjust to their new situation. Clamar (1980, 1984) and Menning (1981) both emphasize the importance of taking the time to grieve before commencing AID.

Male infertility problems and their treatment are generally experienced as humiliations, intrusions, and a challenge to a man's virility. Men may feel like failures, worry that their wives will leave them, experience potency problems, and become depressed. Frequently their wives both struggle to console and help them through this period and also feel extreme disappointment and rage which is often covertly expressed. All too often the fertile partner's negative reactions are temporarily covered over. The couple faced with a sudden diagnosis of definite sterility often needs professional help to enable both partners to express their feelings and to come to terms with their problem.

The Female Infertility Workup

Most women expect at some time in their life to mother. They long for this day with varying degrees of intensity, fear, and ambivalence. For many women the decision to have a baby represents the fulfillment of years of fantasy. Although the decision might be frought with ambivalence for a variety of reasons, such as regarding timing, the actual thought of mothering still represents for many the fulfillment of their womanhood. Mothering is historically one of the few legitimate arenas for women's power and authority (Benjamin, 1986). The awesome power of mother may seem too tall an order to fill but it is nonetheless longed for (Dinnerstein, 1976). Girls in our culture are brought up to nurture, to anticipate needs, to take care of those who need care, and so on. The ability to conceive and the fear of conceiving have been central to woman's experience and developing sense of gender and sexual identity. As children they play house and play mommy to their doll babies. Although the majority of women now work whether or not they have children, most still do choose to have children and expect motherhood to be a major part of their lives (Chodorow, 1978).

Thus, on a deep level, the desire to mother may have many meanings to a woman, including the movement from one generation to the next, a way of growing up, of correcting the wrongs of her parents, and of becoming a woman. Psychoanalytic theorists often talk about motherhood as the final stage of maturity for women. After years of trying not to get pregnant, of being responsible, the moment finally arises to "go for it." For 15% of women of child-rearing age, "going for it" will not be so simple. These women may need to spend many years and considerable expense to determine whether or not they can conceive. In 25 to 50% of these cases, no definitive solutions will be found, and the woman and her mate may have to resign themselves to being childless or adopting (Menning, 1977; Silber, 1980; White, 1981).

For a woman to become pregnant, she must be producing eggs and releasing them into the fallopian tubes. These tubes must be open and the egg must be capable of impregnation. Assuming fertilization, the fertilized egg must then travel through the tube to the uterus, which should be structurally and hormonally prepared to receive it, and implantation will occur. Congenital or acquired anomalies of hormone production and timing can impair ovulation. Hormonal irregularities and insufficiencies may be stress related. For the sperm to fertilize the ovum, assuming no male infertility, the woman's cervical mucus must permit entry; various infections, immune responses, and reactions to fertility drugs may cause the cervical mucus to be impenetrable or lethal to the sperm at this point. Structural difficulties in the fallopian tubes and/or uterus may exist because of prior infections, endometriosis, fibroid tumors, or congenital anomalies. Structural tubal occlusion can be mimicked by tubal spasms that may be psychogenic.

A woman's infertility workup generally begins with the least invasive test. She is instructed on keeping a basal body temperature chart to monitor ovulation. A woman's temperature, taken directly upon awakening after the same number of hours sleep the night before, will generally be about 1° lower during the follicular phase of the cycle than during the luteal phase (the second half) of the cycle. By monitoring her morning temperature, a woman can know approximately when and if she is ovulating. This procedure has been used for many years and symbolizes for many couples the years they have spent trying to have children. Recently it has become possible to either eliminate or greatly reduce the number of months during which a woman needs to chart her temperature. Now she may be spared this procedure and rely instead on an over-the-counter chemical kit for monitoring the luteinizing hormone (LH) surge which signals impending ovulation.

No matter which technique she employs, the infertile woman has now been introduced to a primary facet of the infertility experience: the need to monitor her monthly functioning more closely than ever before. If she uses the temperature method, she must wake up every morning; if she uses the home monitoring kit, she must wake up 1 week of every month with her time in the reproductive cycle foremost on her mind. Forgetting to take her temperature before getting up from bed, or forgetting to test her first urination, can be regarded as signs of ambivalence toward pregnancy. (Again it is worth noting that the normally fertile couple need not go to such thoughtful effort to conceive.)

Both procedures for monitoring ovulation give only partially accurate information and may need to be supplemented by high-resolution sonograms, blood and urine tests, and endometrial biopsies to fully determine ovulation and hormonal conditions during the cycle. The temperature change which has been used to indicate the LH surge prior to ovulation, and measurements of the LH surge itself, are still indirect suggestions of ovulation. Some infertility specialists suggest that many women show normal temperature charts because of summation of hormones although they, in fact, are not releasing any eggs (Melnick, 1984). High-resolution sonograms give more direct evidence of ovulation but they are costly and time consuming.

Failure to ovulate, as indicated by a flat temperature chart, lack of LH surge, or on sonogram, often indicates a hormonal failure and is quite amenable to treatment. The first treatment approach is generally to use Clomid (clomiphene), which stimulates the pituitary's production of follicle-stimulating hormone (FSH) early in the cycle. It is taken orally during part of the first week of the menstrual cycle. Usually the increased levels of FSH lead to a sufficient LH surge for ovulation to occur. The LH surge can also be enhanced or mimicked by an injection of human chorionic gonadotropin (HCG). Some doctors object that these hormones may lead older women to ovulate a bad egg, but most specialists feel confident that these measures can be used with no harm. Clomid does slightly increase the likelihood of multiple births. Some women report weight gain, anxiety attacks, depression, drying of mucous membranes, and other side effects from this drug. In addition, as mentioned above, women with previously healthy cervical mucus may develop hostile mucus because of the alteration in estrogen levels. Seventy percent of women who aren't ovulating will ovulate with Clomid. Often Clomid is used for women requiring artificial insemination or in vitro fertilization in order to improve the regularity of ovulation. When Clomid fails to achieve regular ovulation, a stronger drug, Pergonal (human menopausal gonadotropin), a form of FSH plus LH, is given directly. This drug is very expensive and very potent. Blood levels must be monitored daily lest there be multiple births or severe overstimulation of the ovaries which can at times be fatal (Silber, 1980). HCG is necessary with Pergonal to stimulate ovulation.

Thus far, I have described problems in the follicular phase of the cycle and tests to determine the overall condition of the woman's cycle, including the timing of the follicular phase, LH surge, ovulation, and the luteal phase. This last phase, the most stable in a woman's cycle, normally lasts for 14 days. It is marked by increased levels of progesterone which is secreted by the corpus luteum, the temporary organ formed by the follicle after it releases its egg. For a fertilized ovum to implant in the uterus, progesterone levels must be sufficiently high. Brief, undetected pregnancies may occur and spontaneously abort because of inadequate progesterone levels. The most direct way of assessing the state of the uterine lining is through endometrial biopsies. This procedure, although brief, is quite painful for some and may need to be repeated at various stages of hormonal therapy. Often a noninvasive measurement of hormone levels through blood and urine tests at various stages of a woman's cycle may adequately monitor hormone levels and the effect of any medications that are used to improve ovulation.

Several tests are available for assessing the patency of fallopian tubes. These tubes are muscular bodies with a very thin, inner pathway which must be clear so that the sperm can pass through and fertilize the egg at the end near the ovary, and subsequently, the fertilized egg can travel down to the uterus. All of the tests involve some discomfort or pain for the woman patient. The most commonly used test at present is the hystosalpingogram in which radioactive dye is injected into the uterus and x-rays are taken a few moments later to see if the dye has been able to pass through into the abdominal cavity. Some obstructions are not evidenced by this test which often does not fully clarify the nature of the obstruction. The most informative and conclusive test of structural impairment is the diagnostic laporoscopy. This minor surgical procedure, which usually requires general anesthesia, permits the physician to directly observe the reproductive organs and make minor surgical corrections.

Physicians differ on sequencing of tests and treatments for infertility. Some may begin treatment for ovulatory difficulties before testing for tubal patency while others will conduct a preliminary evaluation of both the hormonal and structural dimensions of a woman's reproductive system before initiating treatment. At a later date, physicians who take both approaches may need to do more invasive testing to detect previously unnoticed difficulties. If no pregnancy occurs, many tests will be repeated at various stages of the treatments in order to assess progress and reaction to treatments. Treatments and testing frequently proceed until pregnancy occurs; there is often no definitive answer, only a chance of achieving pregnancy or news that one of the difficulties contributing to infertility has been resolved. I know one couple who tried for 15 years to conceive; the wife had several operations on her fallopian tubes, was told by doctors that it was impossible to conceive and that it was time to move on with their lives, only to have twins at the last moment, without fertility drugs. Some couples, in which both partners are subfertile, have their 1 in 10,000 chance and do conceive. Many more of course, do not. For many couples involved in the fertility workup, the question of how much to do, how long to continue trying, looms in the background.

Once the infertility workup is initiated, women can expect to have various tests performed over a considerable length of time. Patients approach this drawn out process with varying degrees of perseverance and determination. Many women who seek out infertility specialists quickly become immersed in the infertility procedure and struggle to make sense out of and overcome this unforeseen obstacle to their life plans. The cost of infertility treatment and the increased rate of infertility among older couples skews the patient population toward middle-class women. Often these women are not used to wanting something they cannot get or cannot control.

Even women who don't want children believe that they could have them if they chose. The women entering an infertility workup is suddenly facing the possibility that biological motherhood is in doubt. For some women it might quickly become clear that biological motherhood is out of the question. Damage from pelvic inflammatory disease often secondary to IUD usage or sexually transmitted diseases, structural problems from endometriosis or DES exposure might be so extensive that pregnancy is highly unlikely. For most women however, there will be no such definitive answer, no clear moment of loss. For these women a series of slight, correctible problems may cumulatively greatly reduce their chances of conception. Women who are taking medication to improve ovulation may impair the quality of their cervical mucus and run a greater than normal risk of miscarriage and ectopic or tubal pregnancies, which may in turn increase their subsequent infertility problem.

Psychologically, the infertility workup extracts a great toll on the individual woman and on the couple. Throughout the infertility workup, and the years of trying to conceive, the start of each menstruation will be an ongoing reminder and proof of infertility to the woman. Frequently, the physical changes of the premenstruum, the swelling tender breasts, the bloating, may be wishfully interpreted as early signs of pregnancy. Each month these hopes are dashed by the first drops of menstrual blood. In the acute stages of the infertility workup, women are likely to be emotionally quite labile, intermittently depressed and/or raging. At times their husbands are surprised and distressed by their emotionality and "irrationality." Some men will minimize both the physical component of infertility problems and their wives' distress. Often husbands and relatives will tell the woman that she is too stressed and should just relax. Other relatives and friends who do not know of the problem may simultaneously be pressuring the couple to have children. Women's rage about this interference as well as their rage that this infertility is happening to them may cause them to become angry at people who are not infertile and cannot understand their pain. If such women are in psychoanalysis they may rage at their analyst who is assumed fertile and who is impotent in the face of their problem. Frequently, friends' pregnancies and births become quite painful reminders to their infertility and they may find themselves delaying baby gifts, finding excuses not to go to showers, etc. Holiday times become especially painful for an infertile woman who sees most of her cousins and siblings begin to shift their focus to the next generation, a generation to which she cannot contribute. At times, a husband, confused and frightened by his wife's depression and anger, may become withdrawn, consequently isolating the infertile wife all the more and putting great stress on the marriage. In contrast, some couples find that the experience of infertility brings them closer together, feeling that only they know and understand the other's pain. At times, husbands are much more eager to have children than their wives. This can be exceedingly difficult for the infertile wife who must undergo considerable discomfort and inconvenience in her effort to conceive. She may be plagued by concerns that she is unconsciously responsible for her infertility because of her ambivalent attitude toward mothering. This can lead to considerable marital tension.

As mentioned above, infertility in women at times requires years of treatment and testing without definitive results, no clear moment of loss, no clear end to the process. For the women who are not helped by modern medicine, the question arises when enough is enough. At what point should these couples stop trying; how much do they need to try before they can feel resolved? For some women the quest for a biological child becomes the focus of their lives for many years as they go from one infertility clinic to the next, until either their money runs out or they reach menopause. Hoping to hit the jackpot, they participate in experimental or costly procedures with low success rates. The longer women participate in this process, the more difficult it is for them to stop and become resolved to biological child-lessness. The process gathers increasing momentum because of both the amount of energy invested in a given procedure and because of the simultaneous impoverishment of the rest of their lives. The time, money, and devotion that is consumed by the infertility process may leave some women with a great gap in their lives when they finally resign themselves to no baby and no more trying.

At the other extreme are women and couples who don't appreciate that an adequate evaluation of infertility and an adequate trial on medications requires a considerable amount of time. These people may prematurely interrupt treatment or, worse yet, may not consult a specialist in time. It is very difficult for couples to adapt to the ambiguity surrounding many instances of infertility. Sometimes they gradually fade out of treatment as they begin unconsciously to adjust to the idea of being biologically childless. Thus, in some instances resisting treatment may represent a beginning adaptation and resolution. In other instances, resisting treatment may be a way of unconsciously warding off further pain of trying and failing to conceive.

For most infertile couples, there is no clear moment at which the loss of reproductive potential becomes apparent. Often infertility is caused by a number of mild problems which may affect both male and female fertility and additively leave the couple unlikely to conceive without medical intervention. After 5 years of numerous tests and treatments, a childless couple in this category may be told that there is no definitive answer to their fertility problem. Nothing specific makes it impossible for them to conceive and yet no further new treatment may be indicated. Alternatively, the only possible treatment that has not yet been tried may be very costly and have a low success rate. The couple may need a doctor's help in deciding when to stop intervening even though a chance still remains for successful conception. Each infertile couple will need to discover their own limits—how great a personal, professional, and financial sacrifice they are willing to make for a chance of becoming pregnant. Often the two members of the couple will differ on this issue and professional help may be useful to assist the couple to resolve their individual differences regarding the sacrifices they are willing to make.

Menning (1980) describes the emotional stages most infertile couples go through. First there is surprise that there is any difficulty at all. Then there is a stage of denial, of varying intensity, indicating the amount of pain a person is willing to endure at a given time. This is generally followed by anger often directed at doctors, fertile couples, etc. Anger stems in large part from the sense of frustration and helplessness engendered by infertility. Grieving follows anger, and it is this stage that is most important and is most often truncated. It is only by allowing sufficient time for grieving that true resolution can occur. With this process in mind it is easy to see how difficult it can be for people to work through the discovery of untreatable infertility at the start of their workup.

The patients in an infertility specialist's waiting room vividly illustrate the different responses couples have to infertility. Frequently, the waiting room contains a woman who has devoted the last 10 years of her life to getting pregnant while giving up other interests and possibly weakening her marriage. Such a person might need help recognizing the other dimensions of her life and how they might now need renewal, having been neglected over the course of the infertility workup. In contrast, some men or women in the waiting room may be quite restless and uncomfortable, thinking this is much unnecessary ado and preferring to go home and just relax or give up the process altogether. Some patients, consciously or unconsciously, recognize early in the workup that they cannot bear the frustration and despair of trying for what may be unattainable. Some patients may actually feel or convince themselves that childbearing is not that important to them. Very early on these patients become more focused than ever on their careers—an area over which they have greater personal control—and perhaps prematurely lose hope for a child. For every patient who shops around from one specialist to the next, there are others who continue to work with their regular gynecologist who may not be an infertility specialist. Both types of patient, who represent extremes on the continuum, could benefit from attention to the psychological dimensions of the infertility experience and the ways in which it dovetails with attitudes about growing up and parenting, losing control over one's body, the narcissistic injury of being unable to do what one always assumed one could do, the sense of guilt and inadequacy stirred up by infertility, which may lead people to punish themselves by not pursuing parenthood further, etc.

DIFFICULT SOLUTIONS

For many years, infertile couples have had the option of artificial insemination by the husband or a donor. Today there is also the possibility of surrogate mothers. Very little is known of the psychological consequences of using a surrogate mother for husband, wife, and future offspring. But there has been an opportunity to study to some extent the impact of AIH (artificial insemination with the husband's sperm) and AID (artificial insemination with an anonymous donor's sperm) on a couple. While most studies have focused on AID, some of the psychological concerns seem relevant to AIH as well.

When the husband's sperm is deposited for processing prior to insemination, couples often become concerned that a mix-up could occur in the dotor's office and that the child will not really be from the husband's sperm. They may feel cheated of the possibility of romantic conception and will react to the triangulation of the process by the addition of the doctor and/or donor. Husbands may have an increase in sexual difficulties, and women may be surprised by negative feelings toward their husbands and intense positive transferences to their inseminating doctors accompanied by intense fantasies regarding the identity of the donor.

The decision to use donor insemination raises a host of unresolved legal, ethical, and religious questions. Some religions forbid the use of donor insemination because they see it as a form of adultery. Many nonreligious couples may unconsciously have the same opinion and might consequently subvert the process either physically (by becoming anovulatory) or behaviorally, for example, by missing appointments.

Couples need considerable time to adjust to their infertility and then to consider the available options: AID, adoption, or childless living. Couples and single women who opt for AID are entering somewhat uncertain territory. Most states have laws protecting the anonymous donor from any legal obligations toward the child and require strict confidentiality to preserve the donor's anonymity. While genetic screening has become more sophisticated, the donor's honesty still remains a crucial factor. Many couples experience considerable anxiety regarding the unknown donor. They ask themselves, what will the child look like?, Who will it look like?, How will we explain any strong deviations in appearance and personality?, What if they made a mistake and gave us the wrong sperm?, What should we tell the child?

Doctors often make an effort to match the donor to the husband's physical characteristics. Some doctors recommend that couples having AID should have intercourse on the same day so that they will not be certain or can fantasize that it is their biological child. Other doctors feel that this represents a way of remaining unresolved to the reality of infertility. Many doctors recommend that couples using AID should not tell anyone of their decision, lest the information inadvertently leak out to their children. One cannot help but notice how similar this view is to the attitude toward adoption 40 years ago. Sometimes one wonders about the real purpose of the secret. Is it to protect the parents from discussing their painful experiences or to protect the child? As an analyst who is frequently exposed to the corrosive effect of family secrets, I do not believe that knowledge of AID should ultimately be kept from the child. However, I can easily appreciate the difficulty that parents face in deciding how and when to broach this topic with their children.

Women who become pregnant with AID often have psychologically more difficult pregnancies, filled with fantasies about the unknown father and fears regarding the unseen baby. In fact, greater anxiety and disturbing fantasies are normal during AID pregnancies. Women who have already had a child through AID are much less anxious the second time around. Anxiety and fantasies are normal during this experience (Clamar, 1980, 1984; Menning, 1981). The legal status of AID children has been clarified in some, but not all, states; the legal status of surrogate mothered children is currently being decided in the courts.

MISCARRIAGE

Sadly, miscarriage is an all too common experience. On average, one in six pregnancies end in miscarriage. The rate is much higher among those with infertility problems. Of these miscarriages, 75% are in the first trimester. Repeated miscarriages may be due to a structural or hormonal problem and constitute a form of infertility. For most women, a single miscarriage probably represents a failure of a particular egg rather than a repeating problem. In general, miscarriages in the first trimester are not as physically or emotionally devastating as those occurring later in the pregnancy especially after quickening.

Many women are surprised by the depth of their depression after a miscarriage, even a very early one. In addition to mourning the death of a baby they had begun to fantasize about, they must contend with the unsynchronized hormonal shift out of the pregnant state. Thus their bodies may continue to act and feel pregnant after they know the fetus is dead. They will also have an abrupt hormonal shift similar to the postpartum period but without the prize of the live baby.

When a miscarriage occurs in the first pregnancy achieved after an infertile period, the depression is compounded by the sense that one's hopes are dashed and the fear that another pregnancy will not be achieved. Equally painful can be a miscarriage late in one's reproductive life in a pregnancy that represented the last chance for a new baby. As in the case with infertility, we have no rituals to mark the death of a fetus and to sustain the grieving parents of miscarriage. The blow often seems greater for the woman not only because of the hormonal changes she must endure but also because she may fear that it was her fault, that she did something wrong to have caused it. Her fears of being unfit to mother, fears of sadistic impulses, etc., will surface. Also the pregnant woman's attachment (literally) to the fetus leads her to be generally more involved with the fetus early on. Frequently she has had to alter her food and drug habits and may be concerned that early slip-ups were causal in the miscarriage.

Less is known about the impact of miscarriages on men, perhaps because of the greater inhibition against talking about this subject. Fathers of miscarriages may find themselves even more alone with their experience, with fewer social supports than their wives.

INFERTILITY IN SINGLE AND LESBIAN WOMEN

An increasing number of single women in their thirties are choosing to become single parents. Often these women feel their biological clock ticking, sense that time is running out and do not want to lose out on this experience just because they are not involved with a man. Single and lesbian women can choose to become pregnant by a known man either through intercourse, insemination, or by anonymous donor insemination. If all goes well, no more than six inseminations should be required for them to become pregnant.

However, these women might have their own infertility problems, in which case, if they are single, they will have to sustain the psychological and financial drain of an infertility workup largely on their own. Unlike their coupled counterparts, there will be no one to cheer them on and express the other side of their ambivalence when the going gets tough, no one to act as an ombudsman with their doctors, and all the while they may be subject to continuing familial pressure not to have a child in the first place. Like all other infertile persons, they might need supportive therapy to help them maintain a realistic sense of their ambivalence and to help them sustain the energy and interest this process requires.

Some single women's infertility may contribute to their continued single state as they unconsciously avoid confronting both the reality of their infertility and their desires for children. In addition, like other infertile women, single women's self-esteem and sense of being desirable suffer and may undermine their dating behavior. Men and women who either know definitively or fear that they are sterile may consolidate a conviction that they do not want children in order not to experience their sense of loss or fear of disappointment. They may develop life-styles that effectively preclude the possibility of permanent attachments fearing either that no one could possibly want them if they are sterile, or fearing being in a context in which they might want a child and would then find out that they can never have a child. Unconsciously they can continue to believe it possible to conceive if they never have to test it out.

Implications in Psychoanalytic Work

Analytic work with infertile patients is likely to reveal heightened concern about gender and sexual identity and about a spouse's fidelity, along with an increase in their own fantasies about extramarital sex. Infertile patients also frequently experience guilty preoccupations with past misdeeds which they believe are currently being punished by infertility. Diminished interest in sex, depression, rage, and increased marital tension are all common experiences for infertile people. At times, a patient's psychological symptoms will be directly exacerbated by infertility medication leading to panic attacks and depression. Patients undergoing infertility workups may need some direct educational and supportive interventions from their analysts.

Frequently, fertile analysts may not only be the target of considerable rage and envy but may also find themselves feeling guilty that they have something their infertile patient so desperately wants. Infertile analysts may have considerable difficulty accepting their patients fantasies that they selfishly choose to remain childless, or patients' competitive wishes to have children before they do, or their infertile patients' rage at them for being whole and fertile. Pregnant analysts who suffer second trimester miscarriages have to work through a very painful life event while treating patients who had their own fantasies and concerns about this pregnancy. At times these analysts may have to depart from their usual analytic stance since their own emotional state may be overwhelmingly obvious to their patients.

Conclusion

Despite the existing body of literature, the effects on both men and women of the inability to bear children require further study. Many early analysts considered motherhood the end point or goal of female psychological development. If this were in fact true, or to the extent that it is true for any given woman, what deep meaning does it have for a woman when she cannot conceive, or at best can only conceive after considerable biochemical and technological intervention? If on testing, infertile women appear overly dependent or immature, might this be secondary rather than causal of their not mothering. Dinnerstein's (1976) work on the awesome nature of motherhood suggests how difficult it is for the young woman to feel equal to her mother until she herself has become one. Her hypothesis has ramifications for the successful working through of infertility. Thus more attention needs to be paid to the impact of infertility, no matter the cause, on a woman's sense of herself as a woman.

Those working in the area of infertility have been sensitive to the impact of sterility on the male's sense of virility, primarily in sexual terms. There has also been concern that a child conceived by AID might serve as a continuous reminder to the man of his inadequacy. But as is the case with women, little attention has been paid to the deep psychological consequences for a man of being unable to bear a biological child either due to his own infertility or to his wife's. These gaps in our understanding need to be addressed as we strive to understand the meaning of parenting and infertility in both our male and female patients.

References

Benedek, T. (1952). Infertility as a psychosomatic defense. *Fertility and Sterility, 3,* 527–541.

Benjamin, J. (1986). A desire of one's own. Paper presented at the Seminar on Sexual Difference and Psychoanalysis, New York Institute for the Humanities.

Berger, D. M. (1977). The role of the psychiatrist in a reproductive biology clinic. *Fertility and Sterility, 28,* 141–145.

Berger, D. M. (1980). Couples' reactions to male infertility and donor insemination. *American Journal of Psychiatry, 137,* 1047–1049.

Blum, L. H. (1959). Sterility and the magic power of the maternal figure. *Journal of Nervous and Mental Disease, 128,* 401–408.

Bos, C., & Cleghorn, R. A. (1956). Psychogenic sterility. *Fertility and Sterility, 9,* 84–98.

Bresnick, E. K. (1984). A holistic approach to the treatment of infertility. In M. D. Mazor & H. F. Simons (Eds.), *Infertility.* New York: Human Sciences Press.

Bresnick, E., & Taymor, M. L. (1979). The role of counseling in infertility. *Fertility and Sterility, 32,* 154–156.

Castleman, M. (1982). Why Johnny can't have kids. *Mother Jones,* April.

Chodorow, N. (1978). *The reproduction of mothering.* Berkeley: University of California Press.

Clamar, A. (1980). Psychological implications of donor insemination. *American Journal of Psychoanalysis, 40,* 173–177.

Clamar, A. (1984). Artificial insemination by donor: The anonymous pregnancy. *American Journal of Forensic Psychology, 2,* 27–37.

Collotta, S. G. (1984). The role of the nurse in AID. In M. D. Mazor & H. F. Simons (Eds.), *Infertility.* New York: Human Sciences Press.

Debrovner, C. H., & Shubin-Stein, R. (1975). Sexual problems in the infertile couple. *Medical Aspects of Human Sexuality.* January, pp. 140–150.

Denber, H. C. B. (1978). Psychiatric aspects of infertility. *The Journal of Reproductive Medicine, 20,* 23–29.

Deutsch, H. (1945). *The psychology of women,* Vol. II. New York: Grune & Stratton.

De Watteville, H. (1957). Psychologic factors in the treatment of sterility. *Fertility and Sterility, 8,* 12–24.

Dinnerstein, D. (1976). *The mermaid and the minotaur. Sexual arrangements and human malaise.* New York: Harper & Row.

Drake, T. S., & Grunert, G. M. (1979). A cyclic pattern of sexual dysfunction in the infertility investigation. *Fertility and Sterility, 32,* 542–545.

Eisner, B. B. (1963). Some psychological differences between fertile and infertile women. *Journal of Clinical Psychology, 19,* 391–395.

Ford, E. S. C., Forman, I., Wilson, R., Char, W., Mixson, W. T., & Scholz, C. (1953). A psychodynamic approach to the study of infertility. *Fertility and Sterility, 4,* 456–465.

Freishtat, H. W. (1984). Legal implications of AID. In M. D. Mazor & H. F. Simons (Eds.), *Infertility.* New York: Human Sciences Press.

Hanson, F. M., & Rock, J. (1950). The effect of adoption on fertility and other reproductive functions. *American Journal of Obstetrics and Gynecology, 59,* 311–320.

Heiman, M. (1959). Reproduction: Emotions and the hypothalamic-pituitary function. *Fertility and Sterility, 10,* 162–176.

Hendricks, M. C. (1985). Feminist therapy with women and couples who are infertile. In L. B. Rosewater & L. E. A. Walker (Eds.), *Handbook of feminist therapy: Women's issues in psychotherapy.* New York: Springer.

Humphrey, M. (1984). Infertility and alternative parenting. In A. Broome & L. Wallace (Eds.), *Psychology and gynaecological problems.* London: Tavistock Press.

Humphrey, M., & MacKenzie, K. M. (1967). Infertility and adoption follow up of 216 couples attending a hospital clinic. *British Journal of Preventive and Social Medicine, 21,* 90–97.

Karahasanoglu, A., Barglow, P., & Growe, G. (1972). Psychological aspects of infertility. *The Journal of Reproductive Medicine, 9,* 241–247.

Kubler-Ross, E. (1969). *On death and dying.* New York: Macmillan.

Lederer, W. (1968). *The fear of women.* New York: Grune & Stratton.

Lidz, R. (1978). Conflicts between fertility and infertility. In M. T. Notman & C. C. Nadelson (Eds.), *The woman patient,* Vol. 1, *Sexual and reproductive aspects of women's health care.* New York: Plenum.

Mai, F. M. M. (1969). Psychiatric and interpersonal factors in infertility. *Australian and New Zealand Journal of Psychiatry, 3,* 31–36.

Mai, F. M. M., Munday, R. N., & Rump, E. E. (1972). Psychosomatic and behavioral mechanisms in psychogenic infertility. *British Journal of Psychiatry, 120,* 199–204.

Mazor, M. D. (1978). The problem of infertility. In M. T. Notman & C. C. Nadelson (Eds.), *The woman patient,* Vol. 1, *Sexual and reproductive aspects of women's health care.* New York: Plenum.

Mazor, M. D. (1984). Emotional reactions to infertility. In M. D. Mazor & H. F. Simons (Eds.), *Infertility.* New York: Human Sciences Press.

Mazor, M. D., & Simons, H. F. (Eds.) (1984). *Infertility.* New York: Human Sciences Press.

Melnick, H. D. (1984). Clinical aspects of in-vitro fertilization. *The Female Patient, 9,* 115–127.

Menning, B. E. (1977). *Infertility: A guide for the childless couple.* Englewood Cliffs, NJ: Prentice-Hall.

Menning, B. E. (1979). Counseling infertile couples. *Contemporary Obstetrics/Gynecology, 13,* 101–108.

Menning, B. E. (1981). Donor insemination: The psychosocial issues. *Contemporary Obstetrics/Gynecology, 17,* 3–12.

Menning, B. E. (1984). Resolve. In M. D. Mazor & H. F. Simons (Eds.), *Infertility.* New York: Human Sciences Press.

Moghissi, K. S., & Wallach, E. E. (1983). Unexplained infertility. *Fertility and Sterility, 39,* 5–21.

Newton, R. A. (1984). The medical workup: Male problems. In M. D. Mazor & H. F. Simons (Eds.) *Infertility.* New York: Human Sciences Press.

Noyes, R. W., & Chapnick, E. M. (1965). Literature on psychology and infertility. A critical analysis. *Fertility and Sterility, 15,* 543–558.

Orr, D. W. (1941). Pregnancy following the decision to adopt. *Psychosomatic Medicine, 3.*

Resolve. (1985). *Bibliography on infertility.* Belmont, MA.

Rock, J., Tietze, C., & McLaughlin, H. B. (1965). Effect of adoption on infertility. *Fertility and Sterility, 16,* 305–312.

Rosenfeld, D. L., & Mitchell, E. (1979). Treating the emotional aspects of infertility: Counseling services in an infertility clinic. *American Journal of Obstetrics and Gynecology, 135,* 177–180.

Rubenstein, B. B. (1951). An emotional factor in infertility. *Fertility and Sterility, 2,* 80–86.

Sandler, B. (1961). Infertility of emotional origin. *Journal of Obstetrics and Gynaecology of the British Empire, 68,* 809–815.

Sandler, B. (1965). Conception after adoption: A comparison of conception rates. *Fertility and Sterility, 16,* 313–322.

Sarrel, P. M., & DeCherney, A. H. (1985). Psychotherapeutic intervention for treatment of couples with secondary infertility. *Fertility and Sterility, 43,* 897–900.

Seibel, M. M., & Taymor, M. L. (1982). Emotional aspects of infertility. *Fertility and Sterility, 37,* 137–145.

Seward, G. H., Wagner, P. S., Heinrich, J. F., Bloch, S. K., & Myerhoff, H. L. (1965). The question of psychophysiologic infertility: Some negative answers. *Psychosomatic Medicine, 27,* 533–543.

Seward, G. H., Bloch, S. K., & Heinrich, J. F. (1966). The question of psychophysiologic infertility: Some negative answers. A postscript. *Psychosomatic Medicine, 28,* 151–152.

Silber, S. J. (1980). *How to get pregnant.* New York: Warner Books.

Sperm count down. (1978). In frontlines. *Mother Jones.* January.

Stallworthy, J. (1948). Facts and fanatasy in the study of female infertility. *Journal of Obstetrics and Gynecology, 53,* 171–180.

Stellman, J. M. (1977). *Women's work, women's health.* New York: Pantheon.

Stellman, J. M., & Daum, S. M. (1973). *Work is dangerous to your health.* New York: Vintage Books.

Thompson, I. E. (1984). The medical workup: Female and combined problems. In M. D. Mazor & H. F. Simons (Eds.), *Infertility.* New York: Human Sciences Press.

Vanden Bergh, R. L., Taylor, S., & Drose, V. (1966). Emotional illness in habitual aborters following suturing of the incompetent cervical os. *Psychosomatic Medicine, 28,* 257–263.

Walker, H. E. (1978). Sexual problems and infertility. *Psychosomatics, 19,* 477–484.

White, K. (1981). *What to do when you think you can't have a baby.* New York: Holt, Rinehart & Winston.

WOHRC (Women's occupational health resource center) (1981). *WOHRC News.*

Overview
Biotechnology and the 21st Century

JOAN OFFERMAN-ZUCKERBERG

As we concluded working on this volume, history was in the making; literally, "new conceptions" were emerging. The future is here. Themes that recurred throughout this collection of papers included: (1) the inescapable physicality of female core-gender development; (2) the permeable, diffuse body–self boundary delinations between mothers and daughters; (3) the ongoing task that women engage of attaching, identifying, and merging with mother, then child, and the necessity to separate, differentiate, and individuate from mother, then child; (4) the ongoing scenarios: separation brings loss; loss brings mourning for lost youth, lost symbiosis, lost fecundity; and mourning facilitates greater ego strength, creative development, emotional maturity, and empathy; (5) as women, we are given many opportunities to work through and grow, in emotional depth and empathic differentiation. Required is the acceptance to take this journey through these normally occurring psychophysical passages. Now, in 1988, core issues remain the same but the psychic territory is changing—there are new challenges, new questions, a both brave and tentative new world.

On July 25, 1978, in Kershow's Cottage Hospital in Oldham, Lancashire, Louise Brown was born. Prior to this event, every human being had begun his or her existence deep inside a female body. Louise's birth marked the beginning of a new era, an era here and to become, one characterized by artificial insemination, *in vitro* fertilization, surrogate mothers, embryo transplants, gender preselection, test tube babies, amniocentesis, eventuating in the injection of new genetic material into frozen embryos. What had been, since Eve, an exclusive female prerogative has now been invaded by 20th century technology. The woman's womb has been replaced.

Simultaneously has come the dissolution of traditional models of femininity and masculinity. The familiar molds of gender identity are in flux, along with societal institutions, church, and state. Gender enters an androgynous zone as we see reflected in the media. Cultural heroes are changing as well as our ego ideals. As new horizons open up, so do choices—and choices can be experienced as both an existential gift and burden.

As psychoanalytic psychologists, we are aware of the discrepancy between passages, conscious and unconscious. It is an era marked by much conscious choice and with the aid of technology, much conscious manipulation. But we are also humans/unconscious and the unconscious is timeless. "The processes of the system are not altered temporally, are not altered by the passage of time. . . . In fact, they have no reference to time at all."[1] So, as we speed through the 20th to the 21st century, our unconscious will lag behind. Lip service will be given to gender autonomy, gender choice, gender selection: The working through of deeper issues regarding conflicts of emotion, conscience, identification, thought, impulse, and self will be required, and this takes time.

The interface of this new gender psychology and physiology and the psychodynamic repercussions will be the substance of our future research and exploration. As we leave behind the traditional modes and molds of psychophysical events, we enter an unknown entity—the future. For the next generation, as parents, as women, and as men, it is our responsibility to provide safe entry. It is up to our children to make it better.

---

[1] S. Freud, (1915). The unconscious: Collected papers. *Standard Edition, 14,* 186.

INDEX